The Lawless of the Land

The rich widow in the freezer, the thieving funeral director, and a town ready to forgive . . .

The "polo shirt" bandit, the most prolific holdup man in U.S. history . . .

The righteous but bedeviled minister who, they say, tried to murder his wife . . .

The master document forgers of Texas's historical legacy . . .

The honor student who fed his gambling habit with a bank robber's gun . . .

The kids who claimed a nonhuman victim—and outraged the world . . .

TEXAS CRIME CHRONICLES

TEXAS

CRIME

CHRONICLES

FROM THE EDITORS OF

TexasMonthly

WARNER BOOKS

A Time Warner Company

WARNER BOOKS EDITION

Copyright © 2000 by Texas Monthly, Inc.
All rights reserved. No part of this book may be reproduced in any form or by any electronic or mechanical means, including information storage and retrieval systems, without permission in writing from the publisher, except by a reviewer who may quote brief passages in a review.

Cover design by Anthony Russo
Book design and text composition by Stan Drate / Folio Graphics

Warner Brooks, Inc.
1271 Avenue of the Americas
New York, NY 10020

Visit our Web site at
www.twbookmark.com

 A Time Warner Company

Printed in the United States of America

First Printing: September 2000

10 9 8 7 6 5 4 3 2 1

Contents

Introduction

GREGORY CURTIS
Editor, Texas Monthly

There is a story behind every crime, but not every crime makes a good story. A thief breaks into a house and takes the silver and the jewelry; a convenience-store robbery turns fatal; an argument in a bar becomes bloody. These are ugly events. They're sad, and sadly, they're common. They show mankind at its worst. And there's not much else to say about them.

But some crimes seem to open a door into the soul that would otherwise remain closed. These crimes are not as a rule sudden crimes of passion. They have been thought through, brooded over, planned by the perpetrator. That means they have a plot, an essential conflict, and—most important of all—characters of interest. In other words, these crimes have all the elements a good story needs. You will find these kinds of crimes in the stories in this book.

One more thing: All of these crimes were committed, or at least planned, in Texas. The state and its history are evident between the lines in each story. And the stories take place in the cities and towns that have grown up in what was once a frontier area. But these are crimes of modern Texas. Poison and blunt instruments are the murder weapons, not six-shooters, and the only horse here is a victim.

TEXAS
CRIME
CHRONICLES

Leroy's Revenge

GARY CARTWRIGHT

O tis Crater was late for the fanciers' organizational meeting at the Cherokee Lounge for good reason. He had just stabbed a U-Totem attendant following a discussion of the economic impact of a five-cent price increase on a six-pack of beer.

Crater kicked open the lounge door and bounced off the wall, scattering a table of Arabs who had made the mistake of thinking the Cherokee was a hangout for University of Texas exchange students. Crater carried the remnants of a six-pack under one arm and cradled his baby pit bulldog, Princess, under the other. He looked like a crazed, bloody scarecrow.

"That sorry bastard started it," Crater told those already gathered for the meeting. "I had turned my back to leave when he came at me with a butcher knife. He tore open my right side. Daddy was out in the truck with Princess and a load of cedar. I said: 'Don't ask me why right now, just give me your knife.' "

"Did you kill the sorry bastard?" Stout asked.

"I don't know," Crater said, as though he hadn't considered the question until now. "I 'spect I made him a Christian. Daddy told me, 'You're a goddamn fool springing a knife on a man when you can't even see straight. You're liable to cut yourself as him.' I think I got myself in the thigh."

Crater and his family are cedar choppers, a profession they have followed for a hundred years or longer. *Cedar chopper* has become a generic term, like *redneck,* almost without precise meaning. But there are still real people out among the evergreen hills, spring-fed creeks, and wild backroads west of Austin who earn their keep by clearing stands of scrub cedar for land developers. Their wages are the wood they cut in a day. They drive broken-down pickup trucks, deal in cash, preach self-reliance, and maintain a fundamental faith in the use of physical force.

Thus, an increase in the price of a six-pack is of genuine concern. One could well imagine Crater's old daddy embellishing the story for the domino players, who would nod approval and observe that Otis was a good boy, if inclined to be a little hot-headed on occasion. "Heh, heh," his daddy would say, "I taught him better. First slash, he missed by eight inches and cut his ownself in the leg."

Stout, a telephone company lineman, had summoned the fanciers to call to their attention an ad in *Pit Dog Report,* an earthy, nearly illiterate "Mag. of reading and not to many picturs" published in Mesquite and circulated nationally.

The ad read:

> OPEN TO MATCH
> any time . . . any where
> BULLY, male, 54 lb.
> A DEAD GAME DOG!

Parties interested could contact Mr. Maynard at a post office box in Phoenix, Arizona. It wasn't necessary to mention that challengers lacking the proper securities need not respond. They had all heard of Mr. Maynard and his legendary beast, Bully. Mr. Maynard was the Max Hirsch of pit bulldog breeding, and Bully was Man O' War. Bully had every quality a fighting dog can have—gameness, biting power, talent, stamina, bloodline. As the saying goes, a dead game dog.

"We're gonna get it *on*!" Stout declared, cackling and slamming the magazine on the table.

"He's crazy as a mudsucking hen," Crater said, addressing the table. J.K., a professional breeder who works with his daddy, ran the tip of a frog sticker under his walnut fingernails and said nothing. Annabelle, a girl with an Oklahoma Dust Bowl face who lives with J.K., was practically sitting in J.K.'s lap, which was as far away as she could get from Stout.

"I got fifteen hundred bucks," Stout said. "That leaves fifteen hundred for the rest of you."

Crater looked down at Princess, who was chewing on his foot. "What are we gonna use for a dog?" he inquired. "I'm afraid Princess here is a shade might young. Boudreaux's dead . . . Tombstone's dead . . . and that dark brindle of J.K.'s wouldn't make a good lunch for a beast like Bully."

"Tell him," Stout said. Then J.K. related what fate had brought their way.

It seemed that J.K.'s daddy knew a driver who knew a dispatcher who had a brother in El Paso who had a dog named Leroy. Leroy was so god-awful bad nobody in El Paso would speak his name, but for a price his owner was willing to loan him out. J.K. and his daddy had taken a pretty game dog named Romeo out to El Paso where Leroy had had him for high tea.

But that wasn't all. J.K.'s daddy noticed that one of Leroy's toes had been cut off—cut clean, not like in a fight, but like a man had taken a chisel and cleaved the toe with a blow from a mallet.

Crater looked around the Cherokee and whistled. Stout yelled for some beer. They had all heard the story, how you never saw a genuine *Maynard* dog with a full set of toes. This was the result of a legendary training technique peculiar to the Maynard kennel. On a pup's first birthday, Mr. Maynard drops him in the pit with an older, experienced dog. As soon as the animals hit in the center of the pit and get a good hold, Mr. Maynard cleaves off one of the pup's toes. If the pup lets go his hold, if he loses heart and whines and slobbers, Maynard cleaves open his head and goes about his business. But if the pup holds on, if he keeps on fighting, Maynard has found a new beast to ward off the wolves of his trade. Any time you see a three-toed dog, move over.

"You trying to tell us Leroy is one of old man Maynard's stock?" Crater asked.

"I'm trying to tell you Leroy is the son of Bully!" Stout cackled, banging his giant fist on the table. "Only the sainted Doctor Maynard don't know it. He thinks Leroy is dead somewhere out in California."

"He won't for long," Crater said. "Don't you think old man Maynard won't recognize his own work?"

"Me and daddy cut off a toe on his other foot," J.K. admitted. "Then I dyed him brindle."

"Hell," Stout said. "You seen a thousand pit bulls. After a few fights, who knows the difference?"

Crater had to laugh. Leroy, son of Bully. Even his own daddy wouldn't know him.

"That's still a lot of money," he said, tumbling Princess with his other boot. "How do we know he can take him?"

"That's just a chance we have to take," Annabelle said, flinching as Stout grabbed her knee. Stout was leaning forward, grinning like a berserk grizzly bear. His shirttail was out, and you could see the bulge of a .38-Super pushed down into his jeans.

Pit bulldogs. Killers, yes. For two thousand years or longer, pit bulldogs have been bred for a single purpose—to fight. To fight to the death, if necessary. To attack anything with four legs. They do not defend, understand. They are worthless as watchdogs unless the intruder happens to be another dog, or a lion or an elephant. No, they attack. That's their only number. They were bred that way—short neck, tremendously powerful body and legs, an undershot jaw capable of applying 740 pounds of pressure per square inch (compared to a German shepherd's 45 or 50), a nose set back so they can hang on and breathe at the same time. The symbol of Winston Churchill and the English-speaking race.

The American Kennel Club refuses to register the breed. In its well-stocked library in New York, which includes such titles as *The Dog in Action, Spine of the Dog,* and *Canine Madness,* there are few references to the pit bulldog, or *American* pit bull terrier as they call it, careful to distinguish this non-dog from such registered breeds as the ordinary bull terrier, or the Staffordshire bull terrier.

Pure pit bulldogs are descendants of the old English mastiff, which Caesar greatly admired and brought back to Rome after his invasion of England in 55 B.C. Years before the Roman invasion, peasants kept mastiffs, or *tiedogs* as they were called—after the Anglo-Saxon practice of keeping mastiffs tied by day and letting them run loose at night. It was a practical method of regulating populations of wolves and other predators. Nobility, clergy, and other public-spirited citizens enjoyed dog fights and bequeathed legacies so that the common folk might be entertained on holidays.

Common folk are still entertained by the sport, especially throughout the South, the Southwest, and Southern and Central California, but also in Rhode Island, Massachusetts, Ohio, Illinois, Wisconsin, and most likely everywhere else. *Fanciers*, as they call themselves after the old English tradition, gather on Sunday mornings, in the thickets or bayous, along river bottoms or arroyos, in grape arbors, in junk yards, under railroad trestles. They bring their dogs and their wages and plenty of wine and beer and knives and guns, and they have one hell of a time.

Until recently, the fanciers bothered no one except each other, which was by free choice. Then, in the post-Watergate doldrums, newspapers in Dallas, Fort Worth, San Diego, and Chicago joined forces with the *New York Times* in exposing and deploring the sport, which they customarily refer to as a "practice." Boxing and auto racing are sport.

"This metropolitan area has more active dog fighting than any other region nationally," an investigative reporter wrote in the *Dallas Morning News.* Not only that, the story continued, but prostitutes and gamblers are rumored to congregate around the pits.

Almost every state has a law against dog fighting, but the sport is so clandestine that enforcement is nearly impossible. A vice squad detective for the Los Angeles sheriff's department told the *New York Times* that his department knew when and where the fights were being held, but they couldn't get on the property to obtain evidence. Dog fighting is a Class A misdemeanor in Texas and can cost you $2000 and a year in jail; the catch is you can't prosecute without a witness. There is not a pit bulldog breeder alive willing to testify against a fellow fancier.

But now that pit bulldog fighting has become an *issue,* all that may change. The *Dallas Morning News* (which supports the death penalty and Manifest Destiny and longs to invade Indo-China) published an editorial titled "Despicable 'Game,' " the final paragraph of which I quote:

"Every effort should be made to stop these fights. Quite simply, they are inhumane and appalling to any thinking citizen. Such senseless mayhem should not be tolerated in our midst."

Notable sentiments, but if history has taught us anything, it's that one man's mayhem, senseless or otherwise, is certain to be another's calling. Fanciers—like other individualists or subcultures—consider themselves to be a special breed, a class apart from what, to their point of view, are the drones of mainstream society. Fanciers care for their animals fanatically, certainly as conscientiously as most football coaches or generals treat their charges. Preservation of the bloodline is every fancier's solemn duty and privilege. When an insurance man advertised "White Cavalier (Pit) Bull Terriers" in the *Austin American-Statesman,* Crater and Stout called on the gentleman, pointing out that he was attempting to pass off lemons as oranges, and promising to break his spinal column if the ad ever reappeared, which it did not. The American Kennel Club should take note, if not of the method, at least of the diligence.

O tis Crater's jaded old daddy had reached an age where he'd lost interest in most dog fights, but he couldn't resist this one; there he was in Stout's house trailer, spitting Garrett's snuff juice into a paper cup and recalling the morning in Dripping Springs when the legendary Black Jack Jr. went nearly two hours before turning Marvin Tilford's Big Red.

The match ended when Marvin Tilford's dog *turned,* or gave up. Big Red knew when he'd had enough, but Marvin was so humiliated (and broke) that he didn't show up for a year. Big Red was later drowned by a boar coon who got him by the back of the neck in the South San Gabriel River.

"He should of never gone in water," Crater's old daddy pontificated as he rocked slowly and watched Princess chew on his boot. "Men and dogs belong on ground. Birds belong in air. Fish belong in water. When a creation starts believing they invented how things are, they forgot how things are."

"Hey, daddy," Crater interrupted. "Tell 'em about the deputy sheriff."

"That's another story," the old man snorted, dabbing his gums with a frayed matchstick. "We was going pretty good when the deputy called and asked me how things was going. 'Pretty good,' I said. 'The dogs been fighting twenty minutes and the people seventeen.' "

Watching Princess tumble around the floor of Stout's trailer, you wouldn't take her for a killer. She's no larger than a football, this furry little alligator with sad eyes and a wrinkled face, chewing mindlessly, somehow reminiscent of J. Edgar Hoover. According to procedure, Crater had already clipped her ears, which now looked like two raw navels. They were adequate for hearing, but impossible to bite down on.

Princess was fun to play with—the trouble was she didn't like to stop. She was playing with a big black poodle one afternoon when someone noticed that the poodle was no longer playing, or moving: the illusion of movement was caused by the steady jerking motion of Princess' head. Shortly following life's final measure of response, Princess dropped the black curly mess on the lawn and trotted over to examine a rose bush.

Before he got Princess, Crater traveled with a big brindle pit bulldog named Boudreaux. Crater was managing an Austin tavern when Boudreaux tore into a German shepherd three times his size. In the ten seconds or so it took Crater to separate them with his hickory wedge, Boudreaux ripped out the shepherd's chest.

You could already hear the yelps and groans of men and animals down at the creek bottom when Stout arrived, carrying a package wrapped in brown paper.

"I guess you heard Claxon got stabbed," Stout said.

"I heard he got some new marks," Crater said, "What happened?"

"In the bathroom at the Cherokee. Claxon called this

dude a Meskin. The dude was a Indian. Hell, I could tell right away he wasn't no Meskin."

"How's he doing?"

"He's about half dead and half proud," Stout said, and his laugh sounded over-oiled, hollow, and obligatory. He tore away the brown paper and held up a framed, hand-lettered scroll. There were tears in his eyes. The scroll was a poem, written by his mama, Toots; her first poem since Stout's daddy was shot to death by three blacks who hijacked his tiny grocery and market. Toots watched her husband die as she fired off several rounds at the fleeing killers. Austin police captured two of the hijackers, and the third, so it's said, was captured by Stout's vigilantes and is now fertilizing a worthy crop in a cedar chopper's garden. Who knows?

Stout turned his head so that the others wouldn't see the tears, and he looked for a place to hang the scroll. He selected a spot on the wall next to a poster of Pancho Villa enjoying a smoke under a mesquite tree.

Toots' poem went like this:

> *The clock of life is*
> *wound but once*
> *And no man has the power*
> *to tell just when the hands*
> *will stop.*
> *At late or early hour.*
> *Now is the only time we own,*
> *live, love, toil with a mill;*
> *Place no faith*
> *in tomorrow for*
> *The clock may then*
> *be still.*

There was silence throughout the trailer as Otis Crater read the words of Toots' poem aloud, but Stout excused himself and slipped outside. He kept his back to the trailer and his head down, following the fossilized debris of an ancient riverbed. He stopped in front of an oak almost as wide as himself and took something from a homemade cabinet nailed to the tree trunk. It was a package of sunflower seeds. His short knotted arms stretched for a low-hanging branch, and he filled a bird feeder with sunflower seeds.

Judging from the license plates of the campers and trucks scattered throughout the woods, the fanciers had come from as far away as California, Mexico, Florida, and even Canada. It was a young crowd, mostly in their twenties and thirties, a mixed bag of longhairs, cedar choppers, and high-risk investors, with a few blacks and chicanos and some transients from a Houston motorcycle gang thrown in.

There were some women and enough children to make it look like a club picnic. A skinny kid named Tarlton, who stole ten-speed bikes for a living, passed out beer in paper cups. Tarlton wore a homemade T-shirt with a picture of Snoopy dragging a dead cat by the tail. There was no mistaking Mr. Maynard. He was the tall, lean, silver-haired man in a blue jumpsuit and wraparound shades standing by his Winnebago talking to J.K.'s daddy. You'd figure him for a bomber pilot in World War II, but he was just another dog soldier a long way from home. The cold scars in Maynard's eyes reached back to quarrels too horrible to translate: it had been a long time since he found it necessary to look tough or talk big.

There were a dozen bulldogs chained to heavy iron stakes around the perimeter of the clearing, but there was also no mistaking which one was Bully. While the other beasts were whimpering and sniffing blood and straining at their chains for some action, Bully relaxed on his haunches, observing the scene with sad, patient eyes.

Mr. Maynard and J.K.'s daddy talked and shared a drink, not at all interested in the fight in progress or the other fanciers clumped around the hay bales that formed the pit walls. A spotted cur owned by two black kids was trying to survive the jaws of one of Marvin Tilford's pups. The match was hopelessly one-sided, which meant there was hardly any betting, and the crowd was restless.

"Why don't you do the fair thing and give that leopard of yours a rest." Marvin told the black kids. They conferred in whispers, then picked up their pet and paid off. The bet was $50.

That's how most dog fights end, with a humiliated owner "doing the fair thing," picking up and paying off. Dogs are frequently wounded and occasionally killed, but only in serious challenges where the stakes are high and the owners' reputations well traveled. Even then an owner will usually do the fair thing when his beast is clearly outclassed, greatly preferring a healthy animal to an over-exercised ego.

"Dogs that are the best performers aren't necessarily the best dogs," Mr. Maynard told me as we drank Scotch in his Winnebago. He knew that I was a writer. He even helped me with my notes, spelling out names, and carefully considering dates. He was only anxious that the sport not get a bad name.

"People talk about pure Maynards as they do about Picassos," I observed.

"It's an art," he said.

"How do you do it?" What's your secret?"

"No secret," he smiled. "I just breed best to best. Now, knowing what *is* best, that's a gift. I can't tell you about that any more than Sugar Ray could tell you how he boxed. The best performers aren't necessarily the best dogs, that's just one quality. You look for everything from performance to pedigree to conformation to the way a dog holds his head when he pees. 'Course, gameness is everything in a fighting dog, and you're not gonna know that until you see him scratch for the first time. I've heard it said that if fanciers had millions of dollars like horse people we could come up with the perfect fighting dog, but I haven't heard anyone claim they've come up with the perfect race horse yet."

I asked him about he familiar story, how he tested a pup by cleaving off one of its toes, then cleaved its head if the dog wasn't game enough to suit Maynard standards.

"Naw," he said, pouring two more drinks. "That's an old story. I did it once or twice when I was getting started. I'm a businessman. A man growing corn doesn't burn his fields because a few ears aren't sweet. I raise dogs, I don't kill them. *Best to best*, that's the secret of a Maynard dog."

"Some people think this is a cruel sport," I said, understating the position as much as I dared.

"I guess it's cruel as anything else in life," he said, after considering the question from all sides. "These dogs only have one purpose in life, that's to fight."

Fanciers are not long on philosophy. They accept what they do with the same lack of introspection that they accept war and General Motors. Their sport is part of their life.

The October sun came through the Winnebago window, overexposing the pastiche of fanciers around the hay bales. From the swell of the crowd it sounded like a hell of a fight, then I realized it was Crater and Stout doing the cat number.

The cat number is traditional at dog fights, much like clowns at a circus or halftime bands at football games. What they do is throw live cats—which they buy for 50 cents a head from the city pound—to assorted dogs who aren't fighting that day but who need exercise, self-confidence, and a show of affection. J.K. and his daddy use cats for training. Some handlers claim you shouldn't run a dog, but J.K.'s daddy runs all of his beasts, using a homemade device consisting of an axle and crosspole on which he can leash one dog and one cat. The leashes are measured so the dog can chase the cat till doomsday and never catch up, which he usually will attempt to do. If a dog has worked well, J.K.'s daddy will toss him a reward—the cat of his recent ordeal. A cat who has had a run-in with a pit bulldog is something out of a wax museum—a statue frozen in terror, eyes wide with disbelief, front claws arched, fangs bared in a silly, final grin.

Several wax museum cats lay in the grass around the hay bales. Marvin Tilford's little boy walked by, swinging a dead cat by the tail.

I t was a few minutes after 2 p.m. when Stout and Annabelle brought Leroy down from the trailer.

They had changed his name to Tag. If he made it through the day, he would be Leroy again. He would return triumphantly to El Paso, but for now he was Tag, a dog with no past and an unenviable future. Tag looked more like a walking anthill of petrified Jell-O than any animal that might come to mind. He had so much scar tissue that you couldn't tell what part was the original dog. J.K.'s dye job was blatantly atrocious; it looked as if Leroy had been tie-dyed.

"He wants Cajun Rules," J.K.'s daddy told Marvin Tilford, who by previous agreement would referee the match.

"Yessir," Marvin said.

"He says, if you see a turn, call it. But let them maneuver. Don't let the handlers push their dogs out of corner. Check the handlers . . . make 'em roll up both sleeves, and make sure they taste their dogs' drinks. No sponges . . . no towels . . . all the handler can take in the pit is his dog's drink and a fan to fan him."

"Yessir," Marvin said.

When the handlers had carried the dogs to the pit, Mr. Maynard walked over and examined Leroy's teeth.

"Nice animal," he said. "Good head." If he thought the markings curious, or observed the stubs of two toes, one so recently cleaved the skin hadn't grown back, he didn't let on.

"Let's roll," he told Marvin.

Both dogs scratched hard out of their corners, and Bully took the lead, going low, forcing Leroy to bite around the nubs of gristle that had once been ears. Christ, he *was* strong. But there was no doubt Leroy was his daddy's boy; he just kept coming. "It's gonna be a long afternoon," Crater said. Unless you have more money than you can possibly afford riding on the outcome, a dog fight is about as interesting as a college wrestling match: the beasts hit, lock on, and hold fast, in endless repetition. The fight quickly settles into a test of strength, endurance, and gameness. Even the blood takes on a surrealistic quality after a while, like ghost shadows in a hall of mirrors.

After 45 minutes—when Marvin Tilford called the first pick up and broke the dogs apart by forcing his hickory wedge between their jaws and twisting counterclockwise—it was still impossible to say who was top dog.

While the handlers were cooling off their animals, Crater and I walked down by the old Indian mound. You could feel the excitement bouncing off the limestone walls of the creekbed: it wasn't watching the dogs that did it, it was *being there,* experiencing an almost-vanished culture of blood rites and a close familiarity with death.

Then we caught sight of Annabelle, coming out from behind some bushes, buttoning her pants.

"Damn," she said, "I'm so nervous I almost wet my britches."

"You think Mr. Maynard knows something?"

She shook her head: "I'd hate to find out. Old men like him can be real bad customers."

"He didn't say nothing when he looked at Leroy's teeth."

"That's not what worries me," Annabelle said. "Wait till his beast gets off on the acid."

"What's that suppose to mean?" Crater asked, squinting into the sun.

"Ask Stout."

"I'm asking you."

"We rubbed Leroy's chest with acid," Annabelle said. "Very shortly now Leroy's daddy's gonna take his first trip on LSD."

Crater watched the light hit and fracture off the creek walls.

"Oh, me," he sighed. "I get this awful feeling the center's not holding." Crater walked to his truck and got his gun. One of the fascinating things about Crater and his friends is the way they use the language. They are not educated, but they are amazingly literate.

At the second pick up an hour later, both dogs were bloody but strong. Bully's handler whispered something to Mr. Maynard, but Mr. Maynard shook his head and the handler told Marvin: "Let 'em roll." Leroy was bleeding from the chest and from the stifle of his left rear leg.

The battle was into its third hour when J.K. told his daddy: "His leg is starting to pump blood."

"I can't help that," his daddy said.

"He's making you like it, Leroy. You better eat!" Annabelle hollered out suddenly. At the name *Leroy*, both Stout and Crater felt for their guns, but Mr. Maynard didn't blink.

"Work him, *Tag*!" J.K. yelled.

Bully was clearly the top dog now. Leroy was losing blood and weakening noticeably, but Bully was zonked far past the limitations of fatigue and mere dogdom. The ploy of the LSD was backfiring. The hair and blood in Bully's mouth told him that he was a 60-ton gorilla at the Captain's Table reciting compound fractions in a tongue not previously heard on this planet. "Stand back," he said in his strange tongue. "This one will be for keeps." He took Leroy down by the front leg and chewed on the stifle, shaking hard, lifting Leroy off the ground and working him against the pit wall.

"Goddamn it, Marvin," Stout hollered, "keep 'em off the wall!" Marvin moved in with his hickory wedge, but before he could break the beasts Bully shook Leroy so hard he snapped off his hold and flew halfway across the pit. Then, by God, Leroy was on him, tearing at the soft part of his throat. This time Marvin called a pick up, which was the proper thing to do. Marvin had to help the handler restrain Bully and drag him back to his corner.

"Jesus, he's pumping," said Tarlton, the bicycle thief. "Don't let 'em roll again."

Marvin looked at Mr. Maynard, then at J.K. "You want to roll again?" he asked. J.K. answered by releasing his beast, who lunged straight at Bully and got him by the eye.

"No more pick ups," Mr. Maynard said quietly. "Let 'em roll."

"Let 'em roll," J.K. agreed.

So that would be it—one of the dogs would have to die or quit, and it wasn't difficult to project which it would be.

Three hours and fifty-eight minutes into the match, it happened. Bully was going for the chest, boring in like a jackhammer, when suddenly Leroy got a leg and flipped him easy as you turn a pancake. There was a wailing sound like echoes colliding, then Bully's eyes froze over. He lay still as Leroy tore out his throat. Leroy relaxed his hold, sniffed his dead opponent, then limped over and licked J.K.'s hand.

"If that don't beat all!" Otis Crater's old daddy said as they stood over the corpse of the late, great Bully. "It's like his old heart just give out on him."

J.K.'s daddy nodded, "Looks like he busted apart inside."

"That's just what happened," Mr. Maynard agreed.

"If that don't beat all!" Otis Crater's old daddy said again.

Mr. Maynard walked over to his Winnebago and returned with a .44 magnum and a sheaf of $100 bills. "Here's what I owe you," he told J.K.'s daddy.

Mr. Maynard turned the cold scars of his eyes on Stout, then on the others, taking his time.

"I don't know what you little bastards did to my dog," he said, "but you're the ones that have to live with it."

He walked over to Leroy, patted Leroy's head, then raised his .44 magnum to Leroy's head and blew it off. No one moved or spoke a word.

"If you boys ever get to Phoenix," he said, looking each of them over one more time, "look me up."

(August 1975)

"I was living in New York when I wrote this story, which I hand-carried to editors of five major magazines. Without exception, they liked the story but hated the subject. A guy I knew at *Rolling Stone* told me that five editors had threatened to quit if they published "Leroy's Revenge." An editor at *Esquire* said, "We can't print a story about dogs fighting!"

The only editor who would touch the story was *Texas Monthly* editor Bill Broyles. Maybe Broyles liked the story because the magazine was only two years old and desperate for good material. More likely, it was because he was a veteran of the Vietnam War and saw the tale for what it was. At the time, women, children, and old men were being massacred, and thousands of soldiers were killed each week in Vietnam; yet, in the view of these Eastern editors, Americans were not ready to read about dogs fighting dogs.

This isn't a story about dogs; it's a story about people, a Texas subculture known as Cedar Choppers, for whom life is a deadly crapshoot. I changed the names, but the story is true. The man identified as Crater died some years ago. I don't know what happened to the others, but I suspect theirs was not a happy ending.

Is Jay J. Armes for Real?

GARY CARTWRIGHT

Jay J. Armes was running short on patience and long on doubt. He was slipping out of character. It was possible he had made a mistake. The self-proclaimed world's greatest private detective, an internationally famous investigator who liked to brag that he'd never accepted a case he didn't solve, fast on his way to becoming a legend, was stumbling through a television interview with a crew of Canadians who never seemed to be in the right place at the right time, or to have the right equipment, or to ask the right questions.

Jay Armes calculated that his time was worth $10,000 a day, which meant that the three-man crew from Toronto had gone through $15,000 on the house. Pretty much ignoring his suggestions, the Canadians had concentrated on what Armes called "Mickey Mouse shots" of the "Nairobi Village" menagerie in the backyard of his high-security El Paso home, and on his bulletproof, super-customed, chauffeur-driven 1975 Cadillac limousine.

Worse still, the Canadians were not from the Canadian Broadcasting Corporation, as Armes had led himself to believe, but from CTV, a smaller independent network. He had badly overestimated the value of this publicity.

The seeds of discord had been scattered unexpectedly the previous day, at a corner table of El Paso's Miguel Steak and Spirits where Jay Armes sat with his back to the wall regaling the Canadians and two American magazine writers with tales of his escapades, or "capers," as he called them.

He talked of the long helicopter search and dramatic rescue of Marlon Brando's son Christian from a remote Mexican seaside cave where the lad was being held by eight dangerous hippies; of the time he piloted his glider into Cuba and recovered $2 million of his client's "assets"; of the famous Mexican prison break, another helicopter caper which, he said, inspired the Charles Bronson movie *Breakout*; of the "Onion King Caper" in which a beautiful model shot her octogenarian husband, then turned a shotgun on herself because Armes wouldn't spend the night with her—all incredible adventures of a super-sleuth, adventures made more incredible by the fact that both of Jay Armes' hands had been blown off in a childhood dynamite accident.

He raised one of his gleaming steel hooks, signaling the waitress, still watching the faces around the table. Too much, they said in admiration: how did he do it? "I read the book," Armes replied enigmatically, "and I saw the play." That was one of his best lines.

At another table strategically positioned between his boss and the front door sat Jay Armes' chauffeur-bodyguard, Fred Marshall, a large, taciturn man who used to sell potato chips. You could not detect the .38 under the coat of his navy-blue uniform. When they traveled in the limousine, which was a sort of floating office, laboratory, and fortress, Fred kept what appeared to be a submachine gun near his right leg. Armes claimed there had been thirteen or fourteen—the number varied from interview to interview—attempts on his life, a figure that did not include the six or seven times he had been wounded in the line of duty. He lifted his pants leg and exhibited what appeared to be a small-caliber bullet wound through his calf.

Concealed on his left hip, under his immaculate, custom-tailored suit with epaulets and belted back, was a .38 Special; implanted in the base of the hook on his right arm was a .22 magnum. What's more, he told CTV producer Heinz Avigdor, he held a third-degree black belt in karate—and that was the point of the ensuing argument.

"I want to show you what a black belt does, besides hold your gi [karate regalia] up," he smiled at the producer. "Look, I've been in a lot of films, I know what I'm talking about. Do it my way, I'll show you what it's all about."

Armes had called ahead and cleared the plan with the Miguel manager. It would be a scene right out of *The Investigator,* a proposed television series which, according to Armes, CBS would begin filming right here in El Paso, right here at the Miguel, in fact, on January 20, CBS planned a pilot film and 23 episodes, all of the stories adapted from Armes' personal files. Jay J. Armes, of course, would play the title role of Jay J. Armes.

This was the scenario Armes outlined for the CTV producer:

As soon as the Canadians had positioned their lights and camera, a telephone would ring. Armes would be paged. Fred would presumably go on eating his steak and chili. As Armes approached the lobby he would be confronted by a large Oriental who would grab him by the collar and say, "You've been pushing around the wrong people, Armes." Jay would project his thin smile, inform the Oriental that he was a man of peace, then flip the startled giant over his shoulder with a lightning-quick maneuver of his hooks. A second man would charge him with a pepper mill. Armes would deflect the blow with one of his steel hands, jump into the air, and paralyze the second assailant with a judo chop.

"Uh, Jay," producer Heinz Avigdor said feebly, "I think that is a bit dramatic for the purposes of our show. We're doing a documentary. I think perhaps a workout in your private exercise room, wearing your karate outfit, then some footage in your shooting range downstairs, and maybe a shot in your library. Something from real life, you see."

Jay Armes saw, all right: he saw that the producer was a fool.

"I'm offering you something from real life," he said, that edge of impatience returning to his voice.

"But, Jay, it's so . . . so staged," Avigdor argued. "W-5 isn't that sort of show."

"It's real," Armes snapped, and the pitch of his voice was much higher. "What you're talking about isn't real. There's nothing real about working out in a gym, with a body bag, wearing a stupid gi. This way, I'll be in a suit and tie in a public place doing my work, exactly like real life."

Avigdor protested that his crew didn't have the manpower or equipment for the scene Jay was suggesting.

Jay sighed, adjusted his hooks to the fork and knife. He changed the subject abruptly: he began telling the two magazine writers about his secret code, and about his dissolvable stationery that you could stir in a glass of water and drink.

But the affront hung in his mind, and he began to speak of the amateurish approach of the Canadians, about how when *60 Minutes* comes to El Paso in a few weeks to do the Jay Armes story the CTV crew would be eating tin cans. He estimated that the *60 Minutes* segment would be worth $2 million in publicity, and would probably get him elected sheriff of El Paso County, a post he covets not for personal gain but in the interest of justice. "When I decided to run for sheriff," he said, "I telephoned my producer at CBS and he said, great, what can I do to help?" The producer's name was Leonard Freeman, and what he agreed to do, Armes continued, was send the *60 Minutes* people to El Paso. The show would appear in January, a week before the election.

"Look," Armes told Avigdor, "I've tried to be patient with you guys. I wore the same suit two days in a row—I won't even look at this suit for at least a year now. I invited you into my home. I took time out from my work. I showed you around. I called my producer at CBS a little while ago, and, frankly, he advised me to blow you off."

Armes was smiling, but it wasn't his dark, boyish face and licorice-drop eyes that captured attention, it was those powerful, gleaming steel hooks. Each hook could apply 38 pounds of pressure per square inch, three times that of a normal hand. They were sensitive and deadly, these hooks, and he used them the way a surgeon uses his hands, picking rather than hacking, demonstrating, extracting, mesmerizing, proving precisely what it means for a man to turn a liability into an asset. Somewhere in those gestures was the message: I'll bet you couldn't do this. And yet what you saw was not an amazingly skilled man who could shoot and play tennis and paint and do pushups, what you saw was the dark bore of a .22 magnum inches from your forehead. It was rimmed with black powder and projected an even more deadly threat than the threat of the hooks—the threat of subconscious impulse, unchecked by distance or time—for the trigger mechanism of this weapon was connected by tiny wires to Armes' right biceps. The operation cost $50,000, Armes added, and was performed by a New York surgeon named Bechtol. Don't worry, he said, it has a failsafe: it can't go off by accident.

"It can only be fired by my brain," Armes had told us. "It's like . . . let me put this right . . . like opening your mouth. Your brain can tell you to open your mouth, but it doesn't just fly open by itself."

That was the same day that Armes asked Avigdor and his two technicians why it was that "Canadians condone concubines." Armes said he had known many cases, especially among French Canadians, in which prominent men "kept concubines [sic] of fifteen and even twenty women."

I don't know if Armes noticed, but Heinz Avigdor's mouth dropped wide enough to accommodate a jack rabbit.

The first thing you see when you enter Jay Armes' office at 1717 Montana in El Paso is a mural on the wall at the end of the hallway. The mural depicts a man in a trench coat and hat, cradling the world in one arm. Painted on the face of the globe are all the cities where Jay Armes operates branch offices. On closer inspection, the man in the trench coat turns out to be Jay Armes. It is a self-portrait.

There are other Jay Armes paintings throughout the office, and throughout his home, mostly of long, graceful tigers springing at some prey off canvas.

The office has a jungle motif. The rooms are dimly lit in eerie reds and greens. "Psychological lighting," Armes says. Armes says he employs more than 2000 full-time agents—600 right here in El Paso—but the only employees visible are a secretary who sits in the front office, and the faithful bodyguard Fred, who lurks nearby.

Armes escorts the visitors to his crime lab. On a long table under the weird green light, laid out like organs in an autopsy, is a curious assortment of detective gimmicks—the latest touch-tone portable telephone, its range worldwide; a de-bugger that Armes values at $10,000; a Dick Tracy–like wristwatch recorder; a tranquilizer gun that shoots sleeping gas; many small bugging devices; and two microscopes. Armes says he can do a complete laboratory breakdown here. In addition to his mastery of chemistry, Armes says he has degrees in psychology and criminology from New York University, as well as the ability to speak seven languages, including thirty-three dialects of Chinese.

Photographs on the wall and in the fat scrapbook show Armes in diving equipment, or playing with his lions and tigers, or firing on his pistol range. There is a photograph of his son, Jay Armes III, riding a pet lion.

Jay III used to have a pet elephant, but a neighbor shot it with a crossbow. In a rear room with a coffee pot and copying machine, Armes points out several bullet holes in the window and door, the marks of that night when an assassin sprayed the building with a .45-caliber grease-gun.

Armes leads the visitors to his private office and sits at his desk, his back to 71 volumes of *Corpus Juris*. On the wall are the framed diplomas testifying that Jay J. Armes is a graduate of a number of detective academies, and a member of detective associations. One of the academies is the Central Bureau of Investigation in Hollywood. Curiously, there is no diploma from NYU. But Armes tells a story about how his old mentor, Professor Max Falen, discovered Armes was working his way through NYU as a dishwasher. "He blew his stack," Jay says. "He said I was shortchanging criminology." Falen arranged for his prize student to receive a paid student assistantship and moved him into his own home. The years passed, poor Max Falen began hitting the bottle. NYU finally had to let him go. When Jay learned what fate had befallen his onetime friend and benefactor, he hired the professor and moved him to the Los Angeles bureau of The Investigators.

Although he graduated with honors at age nineteen, Jay Armes soon learned there were few openings for criminologists. That's when he decided to open his own detective agency.

"I wanted to clean up the image of the profession," he says. "In TV and the movies, private detectives are usually pictured as crooked ex-cops who keep a filing cabinet of booze and work both sides of the street." Jay pointed out that he did not smoke or drink (not even coffee), and was "deeply religious." Ten per cent of everything he makes goes to the Immanuel Baptist Church in El Paso. A secretary at the church later confirmed that Armes "attends regularly and gives generously."

Although Armes is seen regularly at church, at the El Paso Club and Empire Club, at the police station or courthouse, and cruising the streets in his black limo, he remains a mystery man to most citizens of El Paso. Most of what they know about him comes from recent articles in magazines like *People*, *Newsweek*, and *Atlantic*, or from national TV talk shows.

According to *Newsweek*, Armes "keeps a loaded submachine gun in his $37,000 Rolls-Royce as protection against the next—and fourteenth—attempt on his life. He lives behind an electrified fence in a milliondollar mansion with a shooting range, a $90,000 gymnasium and a private menagerie, complete with leopards that prowl the grounds unchained at night. He is an expert on bugging, a skilled pilot, a deadly marksman and karate fighter and, perhaps, the best private eye in the country."

The article in *People* was similar, except for a couple of discrepancies. According to *People*, Armes earned his degrees in criminology and psychology from UCLA, not NYU. And they referred to him as "recently divorced."

"My wife went through the ceiling when she read that," Armes said. His wife Linda Chew is the daughter of a respected Chinese grocer. She is a handsome, soft-spoken woman who seems to accept her husband's chosen role with traditional stoicism. "When I leave home in the morning," Armes says, "she never knows if she will see me again."

Armes doesn't especially enjoy discussing his childhood in Ysleta. The Lower Valley, as it is called, was a mostly lower-class, predominantly Mexican-American area of small farms and run-down businesses and ancient Indian teachings. It's now part of El Paso, but it was another town when Armes grew up. As Armes tells it, he was born August 12, 1939, to Jay Sr. and Beatrice Armes. His parents were Italian and French. His father ran a grocery.

"I was a tough kid, like the sidewalk types of Chicago," he recalls: "I had to fight for what I thought was right. I was always at the head of the class, captain of the football team, a boxer, a basketball player, a star in track. Even after I lost my hands I still played all sports."

Armes remembers that he was about eleven when the accident happened. An older boy of about eighteen found some railroad torpedoes beside the track and brought them to Jay's house. The older boy stood back and told Jay to beat the torpedoes together. He did, and they blew his hands off just above the wrists. The accident hardly seemed to slow him down. He recalled holding down four jobs, and running a loan-shark operation across the street from the school. "I'd loan a quarter and get back fifty cents," he said, and the memory seemed to please him. "If someone was slow in paying, I'd kick ass."

What he says happened next is straight out of the Lana Turner saga. Jay was drinking a milk shake in the Hilton Plaza drugstore when a Hollywood casting director named Frank Windsor strolled over and said:

"Hey, kid, you're pretty good with those mitts." The casting director offered Jay a part in a movie called *Am I Handicapped?*, starring Dana Andrews.

Jay was barely fifteen—he recalled that he had just started taking flying lessons—when he quit school and moved to Hollywood. The next few years are vague in his recollection, but they apparently weren't dull. He graduated from Hollywood High, landed roles in thirteen feature-length movies, studied one year (1959) at UCLA, moved to New York, did three years (or, as he sometimes remembers, six) at NYU, and returned to El Paso, a triumphant nineteen-year-old determined to change the image of his new profession. Somewhere in there he also graduated from the Central Bureau of Investigation in Hollywood.

Why El Paso, the visitor wonders? With that background, why go home again?

Jay says, "I am deeply religious. It says in the Bible that you will not prosper in your hometown. How could a carpenter's son become king of the Jews? Jesus had to go to Nazareth to be recognized."

Was he then trying to outdo Jesus?

"I was trying to see if this was a fact," he says. "And it is. I am recognized now all over the world more than I am in my hometown."

While the crew from CTV is setting up outside on Montana Street, I take another look around. There is something too deliberate about the way those crime-fighting gimmicks are laid out on that table under the green light in the lab, like toys under a Christmas tree. The holes from the .45 caliber grease-gun would be more impressive if they had smashed the glass or shattered the thin layer of wood instead of leaving clean, neat punctures. I glance through the Jay J. Armes Training Academy correspondence course, which can be had for $300. Sample question: "Eighty per cent of people do not see accurately because:

(a) they have a stigmatism

(b) there is too much smog in the air

(c) because they do not pay attention

(d) because they usually just watch the ground."

I wonder if the Central Bureau of Investigation was like this. Then something else catches my eye—the mural at the end of the hallway, the self-portrait. I didn't notice before, but Jay Armes has given himself blue eyes. And that's not a hook holding the world, it's a hand.

F red, the ex-potato chip salesman, stands at attention, holding the rear door of the limo open for Jay Armes and his guests. There are a few rules you learn in Jay Armes' company: you do not smoke, you do not swear, and you do not open your own limousine door. A New York book editor who was in El Paso a few weeks earlier recalled the door ritual as his most vivid impression. Jay Armes always got out first, explaining that "I'm armed. I can protect my friends."

As the black limousine pulls silently into the traffic and winds past the refinery adjacent to IH 10, Armes reaches out with his hooks and activates the videotape camera buried in the trunk lid of the car. On the black-and-white screen we can see the CTV station wagon trailing us. Sometimes, Armes tells us, he uses the videotape gear to follow other people. "While they're looking in their rearview mirror," he says, "I'm right in front of them watching their every move."

The limo is also equipped with a police siren, a yelper, and a public-address system, each of which he demonstrates. There is a front-seat telephone and a back-seat telephone with a different number, revolving license plates, and Jay Armes' crest on each door. You might suppose all these trappings would make it difficult to remain inconspicuous, but Jay has his methods. "I read the book," he says, "and I saw the play." Sometimes he uses a panel truck with Acme Plumbing on the side. Or the bronze Corvette with the Interpol sticker on the back. He even has a stand-in. Somewhere in El Paso there is another Jay J. Armes.

The limousine pulls off IH 10 and follows a narrow blacktop along rows of cheap houses, hotdog stands, and weed fields. This is not exactly your silk-stocking neighborhood.

Armes has been talking about his $50,000 fee for cracking a recent jewel robbery at the UN Plaza apartments in New York, and about a potential half-million dollar fee that he turned down on advice of his attorney. Working through his producer, Leonard Freeman, a national magazine that he is not at liberty to identify offered Armes that sum to locate Patty Hearst, which he boasted he could do in three weeks or less. "The FBI called and said, hey Jay, how can you find her in three weeks? I said: 'cause I know my business." In return for its money, the magazine wanted Armes to guarantee an exclusive 30,000-word interview with the mysterious heiress, and that's when Armes pulled out. "Even admitting to you now that I had her located," he said, "could subject me to criminal prosecution. But I'll tell you this much, that's a damn lie about her being in school in Sacramento. I'm writing a book for Macmillan, maybe I'll tell the true story. The FBI actually put a tail on my book publisher, thought maybe he'd lead them to Patty Hearst. I'll say one more thing. I'll bet you $10,000 that Patty will never be convicted."

Outside the eighteen-foot electrified fence that runs along the 8100 block of North Loop, Fred activates a small electronic box above his head and the gates swing open. He parks the car in front of Jay J. Armes' curious little mansion with its tall columns and flanking white stone lions.

A Rolls, a Corvette, and several other cars are parked in the driveway between the house and the tennis court. Gypsy, Armes' pet chimpanzee, screeches from her cage until Armes walks over and swaps her a piece of sugarless gum for a kiss. A pack of dogs hangs back, menacingly.

While the crew from CTV is hauling its equipment upstairs to the library, Armes conducts a tour of the Nairobi Village in the backyard. Armes stiffens when visitors refer to this as a "zoo," and with good reason: this place is right out of a Tarzan movie, except that most of the animals are caged. There are thatched huts, exotic plants, narrow trails through high walls of bamboo, and a lighted artificial waterfall beside a man-made lake. Though the lake is not much larger than a hockey rink, there is what appears to be a high-powered speedboat anchored against the far bank. And on the bank nearest to the house, inside a corral of zebras and small horses, sits a twin-blade helicopter. This is the chopper, Armes reveals, that he uses most often. He can have it fueled and airborne in less than half an hour. He also says he owns a jet helicopter (it's presently in Houston), a Riley turbojet, and a Hughes 500.

In the heart of the jungle, a telephone rings. Armes opens a box on the side of a palm tree and talks to someone. Then the tour resumes.

"When I was a kid," Armes says, "I couldn't even afford a good cat. I decided that when I got older and could afford it, I'd buy every animal I could find." So far he has found 22 different species, including a pair of black panthers from India, some miniature Tibetan horses that shrink with each generation, some ostriches, a West Texas puma, and a 400-pound Siberian tiger that roams the grounds at night, discouraging drop-in visitors. Many of his prize animals, he tells the visitors, are currently grazing on his 20,000-acre Three Rivers Ranch in New Mexico.

Armes opens the tiger cage and invites his guests inside. They politely decline. He smiles, having already detected the presence of fear in the tiger's movements. The tiger seems suddenly irritable. Armes talks to the tiger and strokes its head. The tiger rears back and Armes controls it with a skilled movement of his steel wrists.

Entering Jay Armes' mansion is yet another trip beyond the fringe: it is something like entering the living room of an eccentric aunt who just returned from the World's Fair. There is a feeling of incongruity, of massive accumulations of things that don't fit, passages that lead nowhere, bells that don't ring.

We wait in what I guess you would call the bar. The decor might be described as Neo-Earth in Upheaval. It was as though alien species had by some unexplained cataclysm been transposed to a common ground. Dark green water trickles from rocks and runs sluggishly along a concrete duct that divides the room. There are concrete palm trees, artificial flowers, and stuffed animals and birds. Two Japanese bridges span the duct, and the walls sag with fishnets, bright bulbs, African masks, and paintings of tigers. There is a piano in one corner, but Jay Armes does not volunteer to demonstrate that skill just now. Although neither Armes nor his wife Linda drink, the bar is well-stocked with Jack Daniels, Chivas Regal, Beefeater, and two varieties of beer on tap.

In an adjacent room, what appears to be a living coconut palm floats in a tub in the indoor swimming pool. Though the pool is small, it takes up most of the room. In one corner of the room, hidden behind a thatched bar, is a washer and dryer and a neat stack of freshly laundered children's clothes.

The room behind the swimming pool is Jay's exercise room. Steps lead down to his computerized target range in the basement. After his customary two-and-a-half hours sleep, Jay wakes around 4 a.m., dictates into his recorder, exercises with his karate instructor, practices on his target range, has a sauna and a shower, selects one of the suits with the epaulets from a closet that he estimates contains about 700 suits valued at $500 a pop, has a high-protein breakfast, and calls for Fred to bring the limousine around.

"Almost every day of my life," he says, "there is some violent or potentially violent incident. I have to stay in tip-top shape." His single vice is work. "The Lord has given us a brain," he says. "We only use one-tenth of ten per cent of it. The rest is dormant. That's because we are lazy. I try to use as much of my brain as I can." Armes claims that he personally worked on 200 cases last year, and that doesn't count the thousands of cases in the hands of his more than 2000 agents.

Like the other rooms, there is a disturbing incongruity to the exercise room. It's too neat, too formal. The equipment is the kind you would find at a reducing salon for middle-aged women. It's mostly the easy stuff that works for you.

Upstairs above the exercise room is the Armes' master bedroom. Scarlett O'Hara would have loved it. Flaming red carpet, flaming red fur spread, a lot of mirrors, and the ever-present eye of the security scanner. From the video screen beside his circular bed, Jay Armes can watch any point in or outside the house.

Armes is pacing like a cat: the CTV crew is still not ready in the library. He leads the two magazine writers downstairs again, to his shooting range where he demonstrates both the .38 and the .22 magnum.

"Yes," he says, "I have killed people. I don't want to talk about it. It's sad . . . no one has a monopoly on life. But it's like war. Sometimes you must take a life in the line of duty. I'm guarding some diamonds, say, my job is to protect my client's property. If someone gets in the way, maybe I'll have to kill him. But I don't like to talk about it."

Then he tells of a caper in which he rescued a fifteen-year-old girl runaway from an apartment somewhere in New Mexico. He kicked open the door and a hippie with a .32 shot him three times. The third bullet struck less than an inch from his heart. There was no time for the .38. Armes raised his right arm and killed the hippie with a single .22 slug square between the eyes. "Remind me to show you a picture of it when we get back to the office," he says. Bleeding like hell, Armes drove the runaway girl back to her parent's house in El Paso. Only then did he drive himself to the hospital.

"It's funny," he says, "but when I get shot, I seem to get super strength. I know the Lord is looking after me."

When the TV camera is finally in place, Armes goes up to the library and stands in front of a painting of a tiger which is actually a secret door to the children's room. On cue from Heinz Avigdor, Jay Armes shows off his gun collection, and tells a little story about each weapon. I had examined all this hardware earlier, so I excused myself and walked down to the bar where I telephoned a friend.

Through the fishnet and the porthole window I could get a closer look at Jay Armes' helicopter. From appearances, it hadn't been off the ground in years: its tires were deflated and hub-deep in hard ground, the blades were caked with dirt and grease, and the windows were covered with tape instead of glass. Armes had told us that the chopper had a brand-new engine. I wondered why he hadn't put glass in the windows.

I walked back upstairs and told Armes that I had to get back to town. I made up a lie about having dinner with my old college roommate.

"Say hello to Joe Shepard," Armes said with a thin smile.

"Is Jay J. Armes for real?" I asked Joe Shepard as we devoured the *grub du jour* of his favorite Juarez hangout.

"No way in hell," Joe said. At least that was his hunch. Like almost everyone else in El Paso, Shepsy (as he calls himself) knew Jay J. Armes only by reputation. He was that mystery man in the black limo. You'd see that big sinister Cadillac glide up in front of the police station or the courthouse, Fred would pop out, look around, open the door, and Jay Armes would hustle up the steps, his head low and his hooks locked contemplatively behind his back. They had all read about Armes and seen him on TV talk shows. He lived behind that eighteen-foot electric fence way out on North Loop, in a poor section of town, in that white mansion with the never-land facade, next to the parked helicopter, next to the miniature lake. They had heard that wild animals roamed the estate.

Shepsy had heard, too, about the repeated attempts on Armes' life and had concluded: "El Paso must have the worst assassins in America. If I wanted to shoot Jay Armes I'd sit across the street from the courthouse for an hour or two."

Shepsy is a licensed private investigator. He showed me his card. License number A-01123-9. True, he didn't know Jay J. Armes, but he knew enough to dislike him.

"I don't want to sound like sour grapes," Shepsy said, ordering another round of tequila and beer, "but it's not that difficult to run a magic lantern show in this business. The more sophisticated a client is, the easier it is to take them. They seem to feel an obligation to understand what you're doing. The wife of Dr. ———— [he named an El Paso surgeon] hired me to shadow him—I could have worked for her for 50,000 bucks, that's how sophisticated she wanted to be. But I didn't. I checked the doctor—there was nothing to it, so I dropped it.

"A good investigator will find out what a client

wants to hear. After that, it's no problem to write a report. The hell of it is, there are a lot of poor people getting ripped off, too. You have no idea how many poor husbands or wives will take everything out of their savings and hire a private investigator. They feel trapped, they *don't* know what's going on in their lives. . . . I guess they believe it's like it is on television."

Shepsy is 43, the same age as Jay J. Armes, although Armes claims to be 36. Shepsy has been frequently married, and his life is constantly in danger from his current wife, Jackie, a high-spirited, free-lance nurse anesthetist who supports his unorthodox lifestyle and sometimes heaps his clothes on the back porch and burns them. Shepsy drives a red VW and has never owned a gun in his life.

"If I carried a gun," he said, "sooner or later someone would take it away and shoot me. If someone is going to shoot ol' Shepsy he's damn sure gonna have to bring his own gun."

None of Shepsy's wives, including the pretty incumbent, Jackie, could get it through their heads that he was really spending all those lonely nights perched in a tree watching bedroom windows through binoculars.

They had been married about four months when Jackie hired Jay J. Armes to check out Shepsy's story that he was flying to Albuquerque on business. She paid Armes $300—she's still got the check to prove it—and he reported back by telephone. The entire substance of his report was that one of his "operatives" followed Shepsy and, sure enough, Shepsy had driven to the airport. He made a couple of "mysterious phone calls," then boarded the flight for Albuquerque, exactly as he said. Case closed. Fee paid.

"Nobody followed me," Shepsy said. "Not in a New York minute. I wasn't anywhere close to the airport that night. I *drove* to Albuquerque with my clients."

Shepsy had heard all about those fantastic fees that Jay Armes commanded, but he was skeptical. Nobody in the business charges like that—not half a million, not $100,000, not even $10,000. Shepsy works for $15 an hour, or $150 a day, plus expenses. One of his larger cases popped up just that morning when a distraught father paid him $500 to prove that his daughter was dating a homosexual, which in fact she was. What a price to pay for truth.

But this was a border town; the rules were a little different. Nothing was just what it seemed. So was everything. For $50 you could have someone killed. Any Juarez cab driver could arrange it. Investigators knew the rules of operating in Mexico—speak the language and have the money. They all heard about the 25 grand Jay Armes got for rescuing Marlon Brando's son. They believed it. They didn't believe the part about the three-day helicopter search in which Jay Armes survived on water, chewing gum, and guts, but they all knew the trick of grabbing a kid. You hired a couple of *federales* or gunsels. The problem wasn't finding the kid, it was getting him out of the country.

I told Joe Shepard what Armes had said as I was leaving. He'd said: "Say hello to Joe Shepard." I don't know how he knew I was meeting Joe Shepard.

The next night I had dinner with Joe and Jackie and some of their friends, and the entire conversation was Jay J. Armes. It turned out that Jackie had gone to Ysleta High School with Linda Chew, Armes' wife. Jackie recalled that Linda was shy and obedient, a hard worker. Jackie's friend, Guillermina Reyes, hired Armes a few months ago to substantiate her contention that the business manager of Newark Hospital was embezzling funds. Mina had been fired from her receptionist job by the business manager, but the hospital board had agreed to hear her story and she needed some hard evidence.

"This was last August," Mina told me. "I hadn't heard of Jay J. Armes at the time—I picked him out of the phone book. I went to his office and told him my problem and he said he would look into it for $1500. That shook me up. Then he said, how about $700? I apologized and said he was way out of my range, so he said, 'How much have you got?' "

Mina finally paid Armes $150, and several weeks later, Armes told her, "I checked it out. This guy is clean." That was the entire report. A few weeks later Mina and everyone else began hearing just how clean Ramirez was—the Newark business manager was arrested, charged with embezzling funds in the amount of some $21,000, and placed under $500,000 bond. Whatever the truth, Jay J. Armes hadn't exactly resembled the world's, or even El Paso's, greatest detective.

Brunson Moore, a lawyer and former El Paso JP, recalled a time when Armes had performed spectacularly in a domestic case involving a husband who thought his young wife was playing around. She was playing around all right—Armes gained entry into her apartment and produced some amazing movies. The wife's co-star turned out to be the pastor of one of El Paso's larger churches. The films were not admissible evidence, of course, but the pastor soon moved out of town.

Clarence Moyers, an attorney, had a Jay J. Armes story. This was a couple of years ago, when Moyers was getting a divorce. Jay Armes telephoned, very familiar, very friendly, saying, "Clarence, ol' buddy, I've been out of town and a terrible thing happened to you while I was gone."

"I had never spoken to Jay Armes," Moyers said, "but suddenly he's laying it on me how his agents didn't realize what great buddies we were, so they accepted an assignment from my ex-wife to do an investigation on me. Armes said he had a stack of pictures a foot deep. He said he was sitting there right then looking at one of me in a daisy chain. I asked him what a daisy chain was, and he told me. Well, I hadn't been in a daisy chain recently, but I was still worried. Then he got to the point: he said my ex-wife had paid his agents $300 cash, so if I'd put up another $300 he'd give me the pictures and return my ex-wife's money."

Moyers instructed Jay Armes what to do with his pictures and hung up. When he confronted his ex-wife later, she denied ever hiring Armes or one of Armes' agents.

There was a paradox, here. Jay J. Armes' stories didn't check, yet the man was absolutely larger than life. He didn't support his flamboyant lifestyle by misleading poor receptionists or working both sides in domestic cases. The riddle of Jay Armes hung in some dark passageway; tracing it back was like looking in old encyclopedias for new discoveries. The city directory, for example, first took note of Jay J. Armes in 1957, when he should have been in California. Armes operated the Central Bureau of Investigation, named no doubt for the detective course he took in Hollywood.

His office was in the Caples Building, an old seven-story warren of bail bondsmen, quicky finance companies, and ambulance chasers. "The Investigators" first appeared in 1963.

Joe Shepard nudged me with his elbow and motioned to follow him outside. We walked to a remote corner of the parking lot, and stood on a high ledge overlooking the lights of El Paso. Shepsy waited while a small aircraft passed overhead.

Then he said in a low voice, "The reason you're having trouble tracing Jay Armes is that's not his real name. He's really Julian Armas."

He pronounced it hool-*yon* are-*mas*.

Julian Armas was born August 12, 1932. His father was Pedro, not Jay Sr., and his mother was Beatriz. Pedro didn't own a grocery store as had been claimed, but he worked in one. He was a butcher at the P&N Grocery in Ysleta. "He worked hard and drank his beer," recalled Eddy Powell, who used to own the store. Like Professor Max Falen, Pedro had a drinking problem.

Pedro and Beatriz Armas and their five children were Mexican-Americans. Not Italians. Not French. Julian, a friend recalled, didn't speak English until he started to school.

Records in the El Paso County Courthouse show that Julian was nearly fourteen when he jabbed the railroad torpedoes with an ice pick and blew off both of his hands. A negligence suit filed against the Texas & Pacific Railroad on December 6, 1948, claimed 75 per cent disability and asked for $103,000 in damages, based on Julian's estimated total income for the next forty-six years. The case was dismissed. The way Armes, or Armas, tells it, he was awarded an $80,000 settlement, which he gave to his family. A lawyer connected with the case says Armas collected nothing.

"The boys didn't find the torpedoes beside the track," the lawyer said. "They broke into a section house. There was no evidence of negligence on the part of the railroad."

Margaret Caples Abraham recalled the day of the accident. It happened in the chicken yard behind her house. She was about seven at the time. It was her brother, Dickie Caples, who was with Julian. When Margaret and her family returned from a Saturday afternoon shopping trip, the boys were gone and the chickens were pecking on bits of flesh and small fingers. Dickie wasn't injured, but the trauma of that day still haunts him. Curiously, the Caples own the Caples Building where Jay J. Armes first started his detective business.

Van Turner helped Julian get fitted with his hooks. Van and Julian attended the same Catholic Church and were members of Boy Scout Troop 95. They also shared a paper route. Julian operated a motor scooter specially customed with two bolts instead of handle grips, and Van rode on the back.

"I never made any money from the paper route," Van Turner recalled. "I never knew what Jay did with the money. I felt sorry for him."

Van Turner remembered that the other kids helped Julian with his homework. After two years of high school, Julian split for California. "When he came home seven or eight years later," Turner said, "he had changed. He was always sort of a bully, but now he was very obnoxious."

"He came back with a different attitude," said Rudy Resendez, who also delivered newspapers with Julian Armas. Resendez is now principal of an elementary school in Ysleta. "It was like he had to prove himself. He was a strange person. Nobody could get close to him. He gave the impression that he was better than anyone else."

Old friends recalled well when he returned from California. Julian, or Jay J. Armes as he now called himself, drove an old, raggedy-topped Cadillac with a live lion in the back and a dummy telephone mounted to the dashboard. He would pull up beside the girls at the drive-in and pretend to be talking to some secret agent in some foreign land.

"He told stories about all the war movies he'd been in," recalled a doctor who asked that his name not be used. "He also told the story that he had lost his hands in the war. He had his hair cut very short. He wore a hat and sharp clothes. Yes, people in Ysleta were impressed at first.

"He had another wife back then. I don't remember her name, but I remember treating one of their daughters in the emergency room about 1962. Julian [the doctor used the Spanish pronunciation, hool-*yon*] said, 'Don't cry, honey, we'll watch our TV in the car on the way home.' He wanted everyone in the emergency room to understand that he had a television in his car."

The doctor, a one-time Golden Gloves champion and a Korean War veteran, was a few years older than Julian Armes, but he recalled that "he was very active, real smart, he had his finger in every pie. No, he never played football at Ysleta, but he was a pretty good touch football player, even without his hands. He had a competitive drive even before he lost his hands.

"There are many people in Ysleta who think of him as a phony, and by most standards perhaps he is, but I don't think so, because I understand the motive behind his behavior. I have respect for Julian. For most people, losing both hands would be the end of the show; for him, it was the beginning.

"The other things, the name change and claiming to be Italian, that's compensation . . . not only for his physical handicap, which is really an asset to him now, but for the psychological stigma of being a member of the much persecuted and chastized Mexican-American minority in Texas, which can be a problem even to the most intellectual of minds."

When you get down to it, the doctor said, Jay J. Armes isn't all that different from Julian Armas. He was always a braggart. He always demanded center stage. He always had a need to achieve, and a need to exaggerate his accomplishments. If he sold fifty newspapers, he would claim that the figure was two hundred. Even now, when he apparently has the wealth to live anywhere in the world, he built a fortress for himself located less than a mile from his place of origin. Why not one of the silk-stocking areas, you ask. Why not Coronado Hills, a section of El Paso that he openly admired?

The doctor's laugh was not sympathetic. He had a patient in the next room who manifested some of the same problems. This person had commissioned a sort of wood-carved Mount Rushmore in which his face appeared alongside Zapata, Villa, and Cortés. "The sine qua non," the doctor said, "is a departure from reality."

"Julian," he said, "lives here in the Lower Valley because these are the people he needs to impress. In a better part of town the rich gringos would just look on him as another crazy Mexican."

The Catholic church that Turner, Resendez, Julian Armas, and almost everyone else in Ysleta attended still stands, as it has since 1682. It was the first mission in Texas. From the Tigua Indian museum across the church grounds visitors can still hear recordings of the ancient ceremonial chants. Long before Europeans had crossed the Atlantic, the ancestry of these people— Julian Armas' forefathers—had perfected a civilization that the flock at the Immanuel Baptist Church might not yet comprehend. This was the heritage that Jay J. Armes denied.

Almost everyone I spoke with in Ysleta who was anywhere near Jay J. Armes' age, knew the story of Julian Armas. "He wasn't tough," a drunk Indian named Rachie told me, "but he was mean." Rachie recalled Julian's first job as a security officer—it was throwing Rachie and his friends out of the movie house where Julian worked. Rachie remembered how delightful it had been, shooting Julian in the head with chinaberries. Van Turner remembered the high school PE teacher made Julian take off his hooks when they played touch football. All of the old friends remembered that Julian liked to pinch the girls with his hooks. Or heat them red-hot in the popcorn machine at the movie house. One of his pleasures was heating up a 50 cent piece and throwing it to a younger kid. The doctor, Margie Luna, and several other eyewitnesses recounted the time he heated his hooks in the popcorn machine and grabbed Rosalie Stoltz by the arm. You can still see the burn scar 30 years later.

A few years ago when Jay J. Armes ran for justice of the peace, he failed to carry his home district of Ysleta. The prediction is he won't do much better running against Sheriff Mike Sullivan, who is also from Ysleta.

M ike Sullivan is half Irish and mostly Mexican. The people who know him think he's a pretty good man. Until very recently Jay Armes professed to think the same thing.

Sullivan made his department's criminal investigation division available to Armes, and helped Armes get appointed deputy constable last August, which is the reason Armes is permitted to wear a gun and maintain a siren and yelper on his limousine. Armes also claims to be one of three authorized Interpol agents working in the United States, but Sullivan has no knowledge of this.

Cynical talk has it that they are still friends, that Armes has volunteered his services as a stalking horse to ward off other potential candidates. Armes did this once before, in the JP race some years ago.

Whatever the motive, Armes sounds like a serious candidate. Lately, he has been speaking to labor and women's organizations, telling how he could find Jimmy Hoffa in a few days if the price were right, and spreading bad tales about his old mentor, Mike Sullivan. He called Sullivan a "figurehead" who allows prisoners to walk in and out of jail as though it were a resort motel, who permits his deputies to beat Farah picketers, who hires ex-cons and homosexuals, who gives his inmates amphetamines, which are "the same thing as tranquilizers, and also known as Darvon." But the most serious charge *was* serious, even by border-town standards. Armes accuses Sullivan of framing and even assassinating his enemies and credits several recent attempts on his own life to the Sheriff.

At the El Paso Club one afternoon when Armes was avoiding the crew from CTV, he struck up a conversation with a banker and an architect who were talking business at the next table. The El Paso Club is one of those phony-formal, itchy, squirmy private clubs frequented by movers and shakers, a place where you're embarrassed to cough unless someone winks first. So it was that everyone in the room (except Fred, who was having lobster salad at the next table) looked up when Jay Armes began to speak of Mike Sullivan as "the first dictator in the United States, except J. Edgar Hoover." He told the banker and the architect that Mike Sullivan was arranging small cells for his enemies, and when the cells got too small, he was arranging for them to be killed.

The banker puffed on his cigar and said, "I had no idea that situation existed." Then, as though the question naturally followed, he asked, "How's the TV series coming?"

Armes told them how his producer, Leonard Freeman, had leaned on *60 Minutes* to help him get elected.

"How is the media treating you?" the architect, asked.

"I'm more worried about the press than anyone else," the banker said. "If they can do it to the president, they can do it to anyone."

"Don't be surprised if a bomb goes off and blows me up," Armes said. Then he shrugged with his hooks, smiled, and said, "But that's life."

On the street outside the El Paso Club, Armes stopped to campaign with three gnarled loafers eating pecans on the curb. They didn't seem very interested. "I don't vote," an old man in a World War I campaign hat said. "I'm eighty-one. To hell with it." Armes shook his head and walked toward his waiting limo. "Can you imagine what this country would be like if everyone had that attitude," he said sadly.

Mike Sullivan refused to talk about his differences with Armes, except to say, "I knew the kid since he used to deliver my paper in Ysleta. I liked the kid. I helped him in many ways. Then something happened and he turned against me." What happened was a disagreement over just how Jay Armes could use the El Paso Sheriff's facilities. In the beginning, Sullivan had authorized his criminal investigation division to cooperate with Armes, and together they had solved some cases. Armes got the money, Sullivan pointed out, and most of the credit. From Armes' standpoint, the biggest case involved the theft of some men's slacks stored in the Lee Way trucking terminal. "We broke the case," Sullivan said, "but the kid took credit, and Lee Way was pleased. They hired him to check out a terminal in Oklahoma City where some TVs and stereos had been ripped off. I told him to go up there and work the same way he did here—work with the sheriff. Sure 'nuff, the goods were recovered. That led to even a bigger contract. He made better than a hundred grand off of that."

Then Armes became dissatisfied with Sullivan's criminal investigation division and started demanding the use of the patrol division as well. Getting Marlon Brando's son back from Mexico had been a good lesson. So had his authority as a deputy constable to serve subpoenas. Joe Shepard estimated that the right to serve subpoenas was worth at least $10,000 a year to a private investigator.

"He wanted our patrol cars for cover," said Captain S. J. Palos, one of Mike Sullivan's officers. "It was the same trick he pulled when he recovered Marlon Brando's kid. Brando's attorney already knew where the kid was. Jay Armes crossed the river, hired a couple of gunsels and got him out of Mexico. There was a similar child custody case here in El Paso. He got one of our marked patrol cars to park outside the residence. After that, all he had to do was knock on the door and say, 'I'm here for the kid. My backup is parked just outside.' The rest is automatic."

Captain Palos, a retired Army colonel, said, "Jay is not a scholar of evidence. We've had to reject several of his cases because the evidence just wasn't there. It appears to me that he lives in a type of fantasy world. He reads an adventure story, and a week later he tries to relive it."

"I liked the kid," Mike Sullivan repeated. "He came back from L.A. in an old Cadillac convertible with a dummy telephone, all fired up to be a private detective. I told him then, 'You do that work just like you do anything else: you take care of business, you do it by the book.' I said, 'You'll be living off human suffering, you had better stay on a straight line.' "

I asked Sheriff Sullivan about the submachine gun that Fred the bodyguard carries. Sullivan told me it was an M-1, hammed up to look like a submachine gun. A hype. Just like the helicopter at the side of the house. The same prop rusted years ago in front of Kessler Industries until Armes acquired it and had it shipped to his place.

Captain Palos had an explanation for Jay Armes' boast that he employs more than 2000 agents around the world, 600 of them in the El Paso office. There is an association of private detectives with about that number of members. They can all claim each other. "The are about 400,000 police officers in the United States," Palos said. "Sheriff Sullivan, as a member of the National Sheriffs Association, could claim all of them as agents. I seriously doubt if Jay's got two agents in El Paso, let alone 600. I have never seen them as long as I've been here. Put a pencil to it and figure up how much 600 full-time agents would cost a year."

I did, using the mythical poverty line as a pay base, but the figure was so ridiculous I threw it away.

If this were a real detective story it would now be time to confront the suspect, and with him the reader. It would be the place to pull in all the facts and discard all the red herrings and wrap the whole package with a red bow. But there won't be any neat red bows, because the true story of Jay J. Armes lies buried beneath the rubble of twisted stories, mistaken dates, and transposed facts: we may never know the true story, but it has little in common with what *Newsweek* and *People* and other periodicals printed, or with the B-grade plots and grand mystique that Armes projects for himself. The real story is of a Mexican-American kid from one of the most impoverished settlements in the United States, how he extracted himself from the wreckage of a crippling childhood accident and through the exercise of tenacity, courage, and wits became a moderately successful private investigator. There is more sympathy, drama, and human intrigue in that accomplishment than you're likely to find in any two or three normal studies of the human condition.

Who really understands the agony of Julian Armas? He wanted much more: he wanted the hands and blue eyes of his self-portrait, he wanted to be in the movies, he wanted his life to be *like* the movies. Maybe he didn't see the right movies. Maybe they didn't show them in Ysleta, or maybe he wasn't paying enough attention to see that the audience eventually woke to reality. What makes the story of Jay J. Armes, aka Julian Armas, so difficult to tell is precisely the Hollywood mentality in which nothing is what it seems, in which everything is an illusion.

There is no recourse then but to pare away the misstatements and exaggerations and attempt to fill in the blanks, but first I want to point out that I did not go to El Paso for the purpose of exposing Jay J. Armes. I had never heard of him until two days before I arrived, a bewildered guest, at his home. I hadn't read any of the magazine articles or seen him on any of the TV talk shows or even heard the mention of his name, although I soon discovered that half the kids in El Paso and even Austin knew him as that dude in the hooks who can do karate. The reader has discovered Armes the way I discovered him, and if the first part of this story overwhelms you, imagine what it did to me.

As the reader may have guessed, they never heard of Armes/Armas at UCLA. They never heard of Armes/Armas *or* Professor Max Falen at NYU. If this classic father figure, this teacher who first recognized his student's talents and took him into his own home, really is employed "as a sort of visiting fireman" in Armes' Los Angeles office, then he too has a serious handicap. Neither Falen nor the office is listed. Neither Falen nor Armes has a California detective's license.

The Federal Aeronautics Administration never issued a pilot's license to Armes or Armas. The Academy of Motion Pictures has no record of a film entitled *Am I Handicapped?*, starring Dana Andrews or anybody else. Old friends speculate that Armes may have made some technical films illustrating expert command of hooks, but no one knows for sure. He did appear in one episode of *Hawaii Five-O* as a heavy named Hookman, but some people who know Armes and have heard the sound track believe the voice is dubbed. Armes claims the Library of Congress selected that episode as the "best show ever on TV," an award the Library has never made or has any intention of making.

CBS isn't filming *The Investigator*, as the *El Paso Herald-Post* reported on November 29. That film crew that everyone supposed to be from CBS was a crew from Chicago doing commercial work for a toy company. A spokesman at CBS acknowledged that the series was a hot project of producer Leonard Freeman. But Freeman, the man Armes was repeatedly calling while I was there, died almost two years ago. The dog-eared script on Armes' desk is owned by Lorimar Productions, but it is not an active project. It is one of hundreds of scripts mildewing in Hollywood.

There is a staff memo making the rounds at *60 Minutes* suggesting a story on Jay J. Armes, but no decision has been made. Whatever the decision, it won't help

Armes to any election victory in January. The Democratic primary isn't until May, of course, and the general election is in November, as always. The wonder of it all is that apparently Armes himself is so wrapped up in his own myth that he doesn't realize what damage an investigative TV show like *60 Minutes* could do to him.

There was, to be sure, a dramatic Mexican jailbreak using a helicopter which inspired the Charles Bronson movie *Breakout*. The only authoritative account of it, *The 10-Second Jailbreak*, does not mention Jay J. Armes. Armes takes credit for this oversight: he claims that the pilot who got the publicity was a soldier of fortune from Jamaica whom Armes hired to take the heat off himself. Otherwise, Armes says he would be arrested the next time he put a foot over the border and be forced to serve out the remaining sixteen years of the sentence. Who knows?

Law officers in El Paso believe that Armes did bring Marlon Brando's kid out of Mexico, though they believe the circumstances were considerably less dramatic than the tale Armes spins. I saw a photograph of Armes and Brando, both exercising large smiles, but I also saw a photograph of Armes and Miss Universe. I couldn't reach Brando for his version. The UN Plaza jewelry caper, which came after Armes' recent spate of publicity, appears genuine, but there is no way to check the other claims—the Interpol connection, the third-degree black belt in karate, the glider caper into Castro Cuba, or the friendship with Howard Hughes; for that matter, Armes could have easily said he was a CIA agent or a UFO carrot farmer.

As for the obvious question, where does Armes get

all that money if he's not a big-time operator? I didn't see evidence of that much money. When you check the El Paso city tax records, Armes' "nine-acre estate" turns out to be 1.24 acres, although he does own 1.5 acres of adjacent property, as he claims. Most likely the net value of his estate is considerably less than the $1 million figure quoted in *Newsweek* (or the $1.2 million that he told me). The estimated replacement cost that appears on the city tax real estate card is about $50,000. Armes paid real estate taxes last year of $476.13.

Armes probably did earn a nice chunk for the Lee Way security job, and there is convincing evidence he collected on an $80,000 settlement from a bizarre law suit against the American owner of a Juarez radio station who hadn't paid Armes for his work in Mexico. Armes' friends trace a big part of his personal wealth to his friendship with an eccentric and reclusive multimillionaire named Thomas Fortune Ryan, who has supposedly cut Armes in on some lucrative real estate deals. The Three Rivers Ranch on the backside of White Mountain in New Mexico, which Armes claimed to own, is in fact Thomas Fortune Ryan's reclusory, although Leavell Properties picked up a purchase option a few years ago.

It is true that Jay J. Armes drives around El Paso in the damnedest black limo you ever saw, armed to the teeth. That pistol in his hook is the real McCoy; I watched him fire it. So is the loaded .38 on his left hip. Fred's "submachine gun" might technically qualify as a submachine gun: anyone with a knowledge of weapons can rig an M-1 with a paper clip and make it fully automatic.

Of all those incredible tales, at least two are fairly accurate, and they probably say more about our junk-commodity society, counterfeit-hero mentality, and burned-out consciences than all the fantasies and delusions of a poor boy from the Lower Valley.

The Ideal Toy Corp. is marketing a series of Jay J. Armes toys, designed along the line of the highly successful Evel Knievel series. "It's what we call our hero action figure," Herbert Sands, vice president of corporate marketing, told me. "Batman and Robin, Superman, that sort of hero, but like Evel Knievel, Jay Armes is a real live super hero doing what he really does." There will be Jay J. Armes dolls with little hooks for hands, Jay Armes T-shirts, a Jay Armes junior detective game. That film crew that the *El Paso Herald-Post* reported was shooting "The Midget Caper" with Armes and Mike ("Mannix") Connors in November, was in fact doing a trade film for Ideal toys.

And Macmillan Publishing Company of New York does have a contract for the Jay J. Armes story. I talked to Fred Honig, executive editor of the general books division, who got the idea for the book after reading the article in *Newsweek*. Honig immediately flew to El Paso and arranged the deal. He wouldn't confirm the price, but the contract I saw in El Paso revealed that Jay Armes would receive about $15,000 advance, and an extra-large break on royalties.

I asked Fred Honig for his impressions of Jay J. Armes.

He told me, "Here in New York we always think of someone from El Paso . . . in the wilds, you know . . . we think of them as being fairly unsophisticated . . . fairly unknowing of what's going on. But this man is fascinating. Very quick, very intelligent, able to grasp problems and solve them."

Yes, I thought, that sounds like Jay J. Armes.

(January 1996)

Contrary to what many supposed at the time, my exposé of Jay J. Armes didn't stop or even hinder his career. Not too long after the story appeared in print, a toy company produced a new line of Jay J. Armes dolls. Later, Armes was elected to public office in El Paso, and his private investigation business continued to thrive. Which only goes to prove that Hitler was right: If the lie is big enough, people will believe it.

The Girl, The Con Man, and The Massage Parlor King

GREGORY CURTIS

I first met Sam Corey during a time that must now seem like the high point of his life. His massage parlor in San Antonio, the Tokyo House, was doing well, so well in fact, that he had expanded to Irving and was engaged in a legal fight to open parlors in Dallas. At the same time he was running for mayor of San Antonio. His campaign had no importance politically and its main effect was that it produced a great amount of publicity for Sam. He adopted the slogan, "Let's put the nitty gritty before the city," had several masseuses run for city council on the same ticket with him, and promised voters that, if elected, he would hire a girl in hot pants to chauffeur the mayoral limousine. Sam also took a stand on such genuine issues as the completion of a freeway running through town and construction of a domed stadium. He even, in his first press release, claimed that in order to finance his campaign he would mortgage everything he owned and live in poverty, just as he had "successfully lived in the days of monastic existence as a Brother of Mary." All this, the whole campaign, was a mixture of hokum and bombast, of a need to be taken seriously combined with a perverse delight in acting not at all serious. Sam wanted to be mayor and had a few ideas, not many but a few, of things that needed to be done in San Antonio. But apparently, the real reason he wanted to be mayor was not so much to get things done as to cruise around town in a limousine driven by a girl in hot pants. Sam assumed the voters of San Antonio would find this idea endearing.

I found it, if not exactly endearing, at least intriguing and went to San Antonio to write a story about Sam, his massage parlors, and his political shenanigans. Never has a reporter had a more willing subject. When I returned a few days later with a photographer, Sam, who weighed over 300 pounds at that time, immediately agreed to my suggestion that he pose getting a massage. He stripped off the tentlike dark blue suit that he had worn especially for this session. Then, in only a pair of voluminous white boxer shorts that began at his rib cage and extended in yards of billowing white cotton below his knees, Sam crawled up on a massage table and lay there, giggling as foolishly as a baby in its crib, while a team of his masseuses kneaded his ponderous belly and rubbed his stubby legs and the photographer circled the scene clicking off shot after shot.

The candidate for mayor lying on the massage table, moaning in lugubrious pleasure, seemed incapable then of anything beyond low foolishness. But while Sam was busy posing for my photographer, two men were waiting for him in his office. One of them was Dr. Charles Guilliam, and he and his associate were there to sell Sam a credit-card service for his massage parlors. This Dr. Guilliam was neither a psychologist as he claimed nor was his name Guilliam. He was Claudius James Giesick, a 26-year-old rip-off artist, con man, and pathological liar, who less than a year later would take his bride of a few weeks, a young masseuse Giesick had insured for $351,000, to a lonely road outside New Orleans and push her under the wheels of a speeding automobile. Her skull and hips were brutally crushed, and yet she lingered for nine hours before she died. After a five-day trial, a New Orleans jury took only twenty minutes to decide that Sam Corey was the man who drove the car. Whatever cause far in the past or deep in their psyches made Corey and Giesick capable of conceiving and carrying out such a scheme, the direct series of events that led to the murder began when Sam, rosy-skinned from his massage and full of himself from being the center of attention for most of the afternoon, pulled his blue suit back over his boxer shorts and went into his office to talk about credit cards with this man posing as Dr. Guilliam.

I have seen Sam only twice since then. Once was a casual visit at the Tokyo House several months before the murder; the second was at Angola State Prison in Louisiana where Sam now waits on death row. Giesick, who testified against Sam in return for a lesser sentence, is serving his 21 years in another part of the same prison.

Angola is deep in the backwoods of Louisiana, not far from the southwest corner of Mississippi. The road that leads to the prison curves past ramshackle cabins, a logging mill, and a single tiny settlement grown up around a service station, before it dead-ends abruptly at the prison gate. Inside, the prison is all cement floors and pale green walls; my first impression was that life there would be rather like life locked inside a high school lavatory. A Cajun guard led me through barred doors that he opened and locked behind us and down a short hallway and through another set of doors to death row. The guard motioned me into a long, narrow V-shaped room with nothing in it but two metal folding chairs. After a few minutes, another guard brought Sam in. He was handcuffed to a thick leather belt which went around his waist and buckled in back. As the guard unlocked the handcuffs and unbuckled the belt, Sam looked over at me. He had not known until the guard had come to get him that I was coming to visit, and the news had obviously cheered him up.

Sam has always maintained his innocence. Just before my visit Giesick had told reporters that he had lied on the stand and related a completely different account of his wife's murder, one that didn't implicate Sam at all. Giesick's changing stories had given Sam new hope that he might be released and spared the electric chair. Seeing me now, Sam immediately assumed that I had come to help him. The look in his eyes as he gazed toward me was positively beatific. "Greg, I can't believe it," he said. "It's *won*derful to see you."

"It's good to see you, too, Sam," I said, but I was feeling more than a little uncomfortable. Sam assumed I was there to write what he called the real story, but I had no way of knowing whether the real story as I saw it would help Sam or not. I tried to mention this a few times but my small warnings were washed away by the torrent of Sam's enthusiasm for seeing me and his desperate hope for himself.

He looked miserable. He had lost, he told me, more than 150 pounds and now weighed 185. Instead of looking trim, however, he looked deflated. Skin hung in slack folds about his surprisingly small frame. His eyes were deep, black holes in a rather large head. He wore a T-shirt, blue-black gabardine slacks, no socks, and black brogans that were now, since he'd lost so much weight, far too large for him.

He smoked a small pipe with a curved stem. He would light it, take a few puffs, let it go out, then light it again. He kept all his burnt matches in a neat pile beside him so as not to litter the bare floor of the room we were locked in. Frequently as we talked Sam would rise from his chair, shamble over to the guard who was sitting just outside the door, and explain to him the important nuance of something he had been telling me. "No kidding," the guard would say patiently and I could tell that he had had to listen to Sam's story many times. Then Sam would shamble back to his chair and, distracted now, fiddling with his pipe, ask me, "Where *were* we? What were we talking about?"

He stuck to the same story he told at the trial, that when the girl was run over he was in his motel room with a prostitute named Linda whom he had met outside a massage parlor on Canal Street earlier that afternoon. Linda has never turned up and that, to say the least, put a crimp in his defense. Sam says he said good-bye to her in the parking lot of a Holiday Inn and hasn't seen her since. "I'd never have been with her at all," he told me, "if I'd known I was going to have to explain to the whole *world* what I was doing."

A television blared in the background. At one point, Archie and Edith singing "Those Were the Days" echoed down the cellblock. "It's two o'clock," Sam said. "*All in the Family.*" He went on to say how bored he was, that it wouldn't be so bad except for the boredom. He gets out of his nine-by-twelve cell only one hour every day so he can take a shower.

"If any good has come of this," he told me, "it's that this whole experience has brought me closer to God." He receives literature and letters from the members of the Full Gospel Business Men's Fellowship. He keeps a small altar in his cell, and a priest regularly hears his confession. Otherwise he is a debilitated man, desperate for the sympathy of anyone, pleading his innocence while the weight of his sentence pushes him farther and farther out of touch with reality. Just before I watched him get locked in his handcuff belt and led away toward his cell, he said to me, "But you know the *worst* thing about all this?" And without waiting for me to reply, he answered his own question, "It's ruined a perfectly beautiful city for me. New Orleans. I'll never go back there again."

But later, driving back to New Orleans from the prison, I remembered one moment with Sam different from the rest. He was telling me how he'd met Linda outside the massage parlor. He'd given her some money to wait for him while he had his massage. "I had a very good massage," he said. And his whole countenance, until then very serious and businesslike, changed completely. A wicked gleam appeared in his eye and, smiling and flushed, pleased with himself and giving me conspiratorial winks, he said, "I got a local there, too."

I knew what a "local" was. That is massage parlor jargon for a masseuse masturbating her client. But I didn't understand why this moment remained so viv-

idly in my mind or why it seemed so revealing of Sam
or what it had to do with murder.

Patricia Ann Albanowski, the masseuse who would
be run over and killed early one foggy morning in
New Orleans, was a girl who pursued love. She grew
up in New Jersey, but in September 1972, when she
was 24, she left her parents' home and moved to Dallas. She had come halfway across the country after a
dark and handsome pharmaceuticals salesman named
Roger. She had a broad flat face with rather thick features which she tried to cover with too much makeup.
On the other hand, she had long, slender legs, graceful
movements, pretty strawberry blond hair, and a pleasant, if slightly goofy, disposition. Roger indulged her
for a while.

They may or may not have been married. Trish later
told neighbors different stories. Sometimes she said
that she had never been married, other times that she
had, and still other times that she had been married
twice. Whatever their legal status, she moved in with
Roger in a large apartment complex in suburban Richardson. She worked at various jobs, in a food-process-
ing plant for a while, in a carpet company. One day she
came home to discover that Roger had moved out.
About the only thing he left behind was the message
that she could find the mailbox key in the manager's
office.

Whether the lack of money or lack of inclination,
Trish didn't return home, leave Dallas, or even move
out of the apartment. She still had her job at the carpet
company but was so alone and friendless that she was

forced, since she couldn't afford the apartment by herself, to advertise for a roommate in the newspaper.

Luckily, a girl who turned out to be pleasant and dependable answered the ad. When she came to see the apartment for the first time, Trish, instead of telling her potential roommate about the rent or the living arrangements or asking her any question about who she was or what she did, immediately began talking about Roger. She didn't call him by name but said that a guy had just moved out and left her all alone and that he had been in pharmaceuticals and now she was very sad. Trish talked on and on and her potential roommate didn't know what to say. She thought it odd enough to have a few second thoughts before finally moving in. But the explanation was simple enough—Trish didn't have anyone else she could talk to.

The roommate soon discovered about Trish what her neighbors and her succession of bosses always discovered, too. She was a cheerful, good-hearted, sweet girl, but hare-brained and empty-headed, someone so bewildered by the world around her she seemed to be living in a fog. She could not hold on to a job. Eventually even her boss at the carpet company, a man who liked her personally more than many people did, finally had to let her go. He could afford only one girl in his office, and Trish, despite her best intentions, had an aggravating tendency to work at her desk all day and leave everything more confused than when she started. Around the apartment complex she became an object of pity. Her neighbors told each other they felt sorry for her. They also agreed that she was a little strange, an impression that was most strongly reinforced when Trish was trying hardest to make friends. She would knock on someone's door and start talking to them on and on in a vague and confused ramble; she would lurk behind the floor-to-ceiling window at the front of her apartment and make what she hoped were funny faces at the people walking by; and she would stand at her kitchen windows with the curtains only inches apart and stare, sometimes for more than an hour, into the identical kitchen window of the identical apartment next door.

She made no secret about what she wanted, although it was obvious to everyone anyway. She wanted a husband or, lacking that, a man. She attended mass regularly, knew how to keep her apartment clean, liked trying to fix it up to look nice, could cook some, and enjoyed playing with children. But these wifely qualities didn't seem to appeal to the men she attracted. They came and went, a long string of them after Roger left, and none of them stayed with her for very long. Some were unsavory; one threatened to disfigure her and she lived the next weeks in extreme terror.

In the fall of 1973, about a year since she had come to Texas and nine months since Roger had left, she told the managers of the apartment complex that she was going to take a second job. That came as no surprise in itself since, needing money badly, she had recently sold some of her furniture to people at the complex for absurd prices—$30 for a nearly new console television. She told her neighbors, depending on her mood, that she was working as a model or as a hostess in a club. In the summer she lost her job at the carpet company, and after a brief stint at a food-processing company, she fell back on her new work for her total support. The only person who knew what she was really doing was a bachelor who lived in the apartment complex. She gave him a book of matches from her new place of employment: the Geisha House of Massage. Trish was neither a model nor a hostess but a masseuse. She began to keep very late hours and frequently arrived home with different men. When the bachelor asked her about one of the men he'd seen leaving her apartment, she replied, "Oh, him. He's a client." And the bachelor assumed she meant him to know exactly what she had implied.

Dallas had an ordinance that prohibited masseurs or masseuses from massaging anyone of the opposite sex, as did many of the suburban towns surrounding the city. Massage parlor operators tried to have the law declared unconstitutional by the courts, but while they were fighting that legal battle, which they were never able to win, they established their businesses in unincorporated county areas in the environs of Dallas. The first to arrive was Sam Corey, who opened his Tokyo House on a street just west of Irving, which is in turn just west of Dallas. Neighbors protested, not wanting what they took to be a den of prostitution in their midst, but their pleas to officials and picket lines outside Sam Corey's door weren't able to force Sam to close. On the contrary, the business looked so successful that a man named Jim Floyd opened a competing massage parlor of his own and named it the Geisha House. His first location was just outside Irving not far from Sam Corey's place. He soon opened a second parlor southeast of Dallas near Seagoville.

The Irving parlor may have been somewhat better, but the Seagoville parlor, the only one still operating, is merely a mobile home on cement blocks at the side of a highway access road. Inside two bored masseuses pass the time between customers by playing solitaire. They are surrounded by cheap furniture, dirty carpet, dismal wood paneling, overflowing ashtrays, empty soft drink cans, and half-empty cups of coffee so old the coffee looks solid. Trish worked here. She also worked in the Irving parlor. Whatever it seemed like to her, to anyone else it would seem like a place, even among massage parlors, where one would go only at the very end of the line.

About the time Trish started working full-time for the Geisha House, a man in his late twenties who said he was Dr. Guilliam, a clinical psychologist, became a regular customer of massage parlors in the Dallas area. He was a few inches shorter than Trish and had let himself get just slightly on the pudgy side, but he had a pleasant, open face, an easy and friendly way of talking, and always seemed to have plenty of money. Trish was still unabashedly looking for a man. All the other masseuses knew it; they thought she should have been smart enough to know that a massage parlor was the wrong place to look. Still, Trish wasn't shy about saying that she wished she could see something more of Dr. Guilliam.

Trish got a call one afternoon from another masseuse who had gone to a meeting with their boss Jim Floyd. She said Floyd was sending a man over and Trish was to give him a complimentary massage. The man turned out to be Dr. Guilliam. He took an immediate interest in her. They spent a long time together that first meeting. He seemed to understand her loneliness. He talked about his work and the money he made from it. She made love with him. After that he kept coming around to see her and, right from the start, began asking her to marry him.

At first she said yes, but then she changed her mind. He was nice and all that, but she didn't have any strong feelings for him and there were certain things about him that worried her. It turned out that his name wasn't really Guilliam but Claudius James Giesick. He told her he used Guilliam because he had helped apprehend some gold smugglers and, as protection from reprisals, the federal government had given him a new identity. He said he really was a psychologist; however, he didn't have an office, and he would disappear suddenly only to turn up again later. Trish had already had too much experience with disappearing men. Still Giesick-Guilliam kept coming around to see her.

Giesick, despite his glib and friendly manner, didn't seem to have many more friends than she had. The only one she knew about was Sam Corey, the owner of the rival massage parlor in Irving. Giesick had brought Corey with him several times and when Trish decided that she didn't want to marry Giesick after all, it was Corey who interceded and convinced her that she should. He said that Giesick really loved her and had enough money to take good care of her. She agreed a second time to marry him. At least it would be better than working at the Geisha House.

Nevertheless, Trish didn't feel completely comfortable with her decision. She went to see her former boss at the carpet company and talked to him about it. He said the man sounded a little suspect and gently asked her if she thought it was a good idea to marry someone she knew so little about. Neighbors at the apartments would occasionally ask her the same thing, but she took these questions as criticisms of her and responded by defending her decision. Only to her bachelor acquaintance did she say that she didn't love Giesick but that he was nice to her and made a lot of money and that was why she was going through with it.

Giesick told Trish that he had been married twice before. Once was to a former Miss Texas who, along with their child, had been killed in a hit-and-run accident. He had been married another time and divorced. That prevented them from being married in the Catholic church as Trish would have liked. It turned out, however, that Sam Corey had once been a novitiate in the Brotherhood of Mary and had now become a pastor in something called the Calvary Grace Christian Church of Faith. His motive in becoming a pastor was no more high-minded than the wish to escape police harassment of his massage parlors. He wanted to claim massage as a religious rite in his church, a rite whose practice would be protected under the Constitution. He had even taken steps to change the name of his business from Tokyo House of Massage to Tokyo House Massage Temple. Even so, Sam Corey had the legal right to perform marriages, and his old affiliation with the Catholic church made him seem to Trish something closer to a real priest than an ordinary minister. On January 2, 1974, he performed the ceremony in Trish's apartment. Only Sam Corey, Giesick, and Trish were there, although two other names were falsely added to the marriage license as witnesses. After the ceremony, Trish called her parents in New Jersey. "Hi, Mom," she said. "This is Mrs. Giesick." The new couple set up housekeeping in the apartment where Trish had been living since she came to Texas.

Before they were married, Giesick had promised that he would buy her a $100,000 house in Richardson and a yacht and take her on a long honeymoon trip. But after the marriage, the first thing her husband bought was life insurance. Losing one wife in an accident had taught him a lesson, he said. He wanted to be prepared in case, God forbid, anything should happen to either of them.

Their marriage had taken place on a Wednesday. The following Friday her husband had an insurance agent call on them at the apartment. The next Monday Giesick bought a $50,000 policy with a double-indemnity clause that covered both him and Trish. It seemed like a rather large policy to her, but her husband was a man who made lots of money and should know how much insurance to buy. When she signed the forms, she wrote "Patricia Ann" and was about to add her maiden name, Albanowski. She got as far as the "A" when she realized her mistake. She drew two lines through the letter and wrote "Giesick" after it.

Then her husband left town on what he told her was a business trip. He gave her a number where he could be reached but it turned out to be the number of an answering service. Trish desperately called Sam Corey and finally managed to reach her husband through him. Giesick told her he would be back by the weekend and she should start checking with travel agencies because they were going to take that trip he'd promised her. They would go to Florida, the Caribbean, home to New Jersey, perhaps to South America. When he reappeared that weekend he was sporting a new dark blue Chevrolet Monte Carlo with a black vinyl roof. He also presented Trish with a St. Bernard puppy as a wedding present.

Sunday afternoon, January 13, her new husband drove Trish out to the Dallas–Fort Worth Airport, which had just opened that day. They were leaving for New Orleans and he thought it would be a good idea to buy more insurance for the trip. He took her to the Tele-Trip insurance booth and asked specifically for the $300,000 annual policy. The woman in the booth explained that $200,000 of the coverage would be on vehicles, common carriers, and scheduled airlines, but the remaining $100,000 would only cover common carriers and scheduled airlines. Giesick immediately asked if that extra $100,000 covered automobile travel. The woman in the booth told him it didn't and Giesick said that he definitely was not interested in the additional coverage. The woman wrote out a $200,000 policy for Patricia Ann Giesick with Dr. Claudius Giesick as the beneficiary.

It was late in the evening before they were ready to leave. They planned to go to New Orleans first and from there to Florida where they would see Disneyworld and catch a boat for a Caribbean cruise. Trish insisted, although it was getting a little late, on taking the puppy down to the apartment of her bachelor acquaintance so she could say good-bye and let his young son, whom she had always liked, play with the puppy. When she introduced the two men, Giesick, normally so glib and outgoing, was coolly polite, remained in the background, and said very little. It was after nine o'clock by the time they left, but Trish now insisted on showing the puppy and saying good-bye to two girls who lived in a neighboring apartment. Again Giesick stayed quietly in the background. But when the visit dragged on, he interrupted, on this midwinter night, with, "Come on, Trish. Let's get going before it gets hot."

The vague unease about Giesick that had bothered Trish before their marriage did not go away. If she had hoped that his strange behavior would change on the trip, she was disappointed. They arrived in New Orleans Monday afternoon and the first thing Giesick did was disappear again. He told her the car, new as it was, was having transmission problems and he needed to see about having it fixed. Their motel was an isolated Ramada Inn far away from the center of the city on a road called Chef Menteur Highway. This road had once been the major thoroughfare entering New Orleans from the east, but when a new interstate opened, traffic on Chef Menteur dropped off drastically. The Ramada Inn and the Quality Inn next to it survived only because several large plants thereby brought in business. A few blocks away there was a shopping center with a grocery store, a service station, and a few small shops, but nothing that was very entertaining. Left alone in the motel, Trish had nowhere to go and nothing to do but play with the puppy.

Giesick didn't come back to their motel room for more than two hours. He said that he'd had to hitchhike from the dealer where he'd left the car. He acted very restless and upset. They watched television in their room for a while, but still he was restless. About 9:30 p.m. he suggested that they go walk along the highway for a while so they could talk things over. Trish said all right, although she was tired from the long drive from Dallas. It wasn't a pretty or quiet or easy place to walk.

Cars and trucks, noisy and belching exhaust, rumbled past. Their wheels frequently spit out gravel that had spread onto the asphalt from the narrow shoulders. It was dark and Trish and her husband stumbled along the side of the road. They couldn't really talk—it seemed like a car or truck went by every second—and Trish was soon ready to go back to the motel. But her husband seemed determined to stay out there. They walked up and down the same stretch of road several times before Giesick finally agreed to return to their room.

But he didn't stay there. He said the puppy needed walking and left her, almost exhausted, alone again in the room. Perhaps a half hour later he came back. He said he'd found a pretty bayou just on the other side of the shopping center down the highway and wanted to show it to her. Reluctantly, tired as she was, Trish agreed to go. They walked the four or five blocks to the shopping center and another hundred yards up a street called Michoud Boulevard. It led past the shopping center to a low four-lane bridge spanning the bayou and on to a new and now, since it was nearly midnight, quiet residential area.

In the parking lot of a service station near the bridge a Chevrolet Monte Carlo, the same year but a different color from the one she and her husband had driven to New Orleans, was parked alone. A police car, lights on and motor running, had stopped next to the Monte Carlo and a patrolman was shining his flashlight into it. They had hardly gotten to the bridge before her husband wanted to take her back to their room again. But once there, he said he needed some time by himself to think things over and went out walking once again.

Trish went to bed and her husband didn't return for several hours.

They slept so late that it was after one o'clock the next afternoon when Trish, alone, wandered into the motel lobby and asked if there was a good place to eat nearby, a place close enough to walk because their car was still in the shop. The only place, other than the motel restaurant, was a combination bar and restaurant across the street. She ate there and went back to her room. Her husband was gone again—he had said he was going to hitchhike to the dealer to see about the car—and she had nothing to do. She spent the time waiting in the room or playing with the puppy on the small lawn just outside their door. Once the phone rang and she answered it, thinking it must be her husband. "Hello," she said, but whoever was on the other end of the line hung up without saying anything. It could have been a wrong number, but the phone rang several more times that afternoon and each time the same thing happened. She was alone in a strange city, stuck in an isolated motel, married to a man she had known only a month, and now strange phone calls plagued her dull and lonely afternoon.

Her husband returned about six o'clock with the news that their car still wasn't ready. They sent out for some pizza and spent the evening watching television or, rather, she watched television. Giesick was even more restless than the night before. He took the puppy out for several walks and other times went out by himself. He told her something had come up in his business and he was going to have to catch a plane for the next day for a quick trip. He asked her to take some of his clothes to the desk clerk to see if they could be cleaned in time. Then he went out again because, he said, he needed to be by himself and think. She glumly gathered up her husband's dirty clothes.

It was just before 10:30 p.m. when she took the clothes to the desk clerk. Trish was despondent. She talked to the clerk a little and tried to make a joke about all that had gone wrong since they'd come here on their honeymoon. The brief conversation made her even sadder and, back in the room, she called her mother in New Jersey. Trish talked with her for half an hour. She told her about their difficulties with the car and said her husband was acting so strangely that she had begun to worry about something else—all that insurance Giesick had bought for her.

When her husband returned from his walk, it was well after midnight. Trish didn't want to be alone in the room anymore, but she was apprehensive about seeing him as well. For the first time, however, he was more like the way he'd been before they were married, more solicitous of her, filled with plans for what they would do together in the future. And he had seen something he wanted to show her. Down on the bayou they'd visited last night was a small family of ducks. They were right there near the edge of the road. The two of them could walk down there, discuss their future together on the way, and then watch the ducks on the bayou.

That wasn't much of an evening's entertainment for a honeymoon, but at least it was something. Trish put on a pair of old blue jeans, a red-and-blue-striped cotton jersey, and a heavy white sweater. Outside it was slightly chilly and there was a thick fog. Giesick had a flashlight which helped them see their way, but even with its light, it was very easy to stumble and impossible to see very far ahead.

Still, Trish was feeling excited. The combination of cool, damp fog and her husband's better attitude helped pick her out of her doldrums and she found the walk down the highway to the intersection and then down Michoud Boulevard more interesting than it had been the night before. With her new enthusiasm, she kept pointing out various things they passed to her husband and kept wanting to stop and examine trees and street signs and store windows more closely. He indulged her for a while but seemed determined that they should get to the place along the bayou near the bridge where he'd seen the ducks. They walked under the overhead lights along the short bridge. The fog, illuminated beneath the lights, was a shimmering, golden mist. Just across the bridge they walked down a short terrace to the bayou's edge. The grass, wet from the fog, was slippery. It was very quiet, the water making no sound, no one out but the two of them, no lights on in the houses nearby, and, except for an occasional car, no traffic on the boulevard. They spent several minutes down by the edge of the water until finally, when they were somewhat chilled, they began to climb the few slippery steps back up the terrace. During the climb a souped-up car with very loud mufflers drove by. The car was dark-colored and the driver looked very young. By the time they had reached the top, no longer than a few seconds, the car was out of sight, its mufflers a low moan resonating deep in the fog.

Her husband had fallen slightly behind and Trish waited on the sidewalk for a moment with her back to him. Then she started across the street. She had taken only a few steps when hands shoved hard against her back at the same time something tripped her. She sprawled face down in the street. She turned on her side and tried to push herself up on one arm to see what had happened. But a car traveling at high speed came at her out of the fog. One front tire hit her head; a rear tire, her hips. The car drove completely over her and kept on. She tried to lift herself on one arm again, then fell back against the pavement. If she saw anything before losing consciousness, it was her husband coming tentatively toward her.

Young Ricky Mock had just dropped his friend off at home. He was driving back down Michoud Boulevard, his loud mufflers roaring in the quiet night, when he saw the accident. A woman lay bleeding in the road. A man knelt over her. The man flagged Mock down and asked him to call for help. Mock gunned his '73 Dodge down Michoud, the car's mufflers roaring louder now, and turned right on Chef Menteur. Eight minutes later there were five patrol cars and an ambulance on the scene.

As ambulance attendants administered to the woman, the man walked over and sat on the curb. He had blood on his hands. An officer named Henderson came over to ask if he was hurt. "No," he said, "but she's hurt bad." Henderson asked him if he could describe the vehicle that had hit his wife. "I think it was a four door, a late model," the man said. "There was only one person in it and he was dark. I really don't know what kind of car it was." Henderson asked if he'd seen which direction the car took when it reached the highway. "No, I didn't," the man said. "The car never slowed down. In fact, after it hit my wife it picked up speed."

The ambulance was leaving by then and the investigating officers, Henderson and his partner Lesage, put the man into one of the patrol cars which would take him to the hospital. Henderson and Lesage stayed behind to take measurements and inspect the scene for whatever additional evidence they could find. The man had given his name as Claudius J. Giesick, Jr. He said he had driven with his wife to the bridge and now his car was parked in the supermarket parking lot nearby. The officers walked over and inspected his car—a 1974 silver-blue Monte Carlo with a black vinyl top. It had no license plates. There was nothing else to help them, no skidmarks, no gouges in the road, no mud samples or other physical evidence of any kind, and no witnesses except Giesick. Henderson and Lesage went on to Methodist Hospital to question him some more.

When they arrived, they saw Giesick in the parking lot outside the emergency room talking with a short, but very heavyset man. The heavyset man had his back to the officers. Giesick waved and walked up to meet them. The heavyset man, even as Giesick walked away, didn't turn around but stood exactly where he was and kept his back to the officers.

Giesick had apparently regained some of his composure. When the officers asked him if he could remember anything else that might help them in their investigation, Giesick said he remembered more about the car. "It was dark," he said. "I believe it was a late model. After it hit my wife, I think it took a right at the highway. And I remember one more thing. It had loud mufflers." He explained that just before the accident he and his wife were standing near the bridge looking at the water. They were getting ready to go back to their car in the supermarket parking lot when she said, "Let's race back to the car," and started to run across the street. She didn't see the car coming which by then was only a few yards away. It didn't have its lights on. It swerved to try to avoid her but it was too late. The car knocked her to the ground, ran over her, and never slowed down.

The officers took down where Giesick was staying and then left the hospital to join in the search for the hit-and-run car. They stopped numerous cars that night but to no avail.

At 1 p.m. on January 16, a priest at the hospital contacted Lesage to say that Patricia Ann Giesick had passed away at eleven that morning. The officer then tried to call Giesick at his hotel and, since Giesick wasn't in, left a message for him to come to the district station at 11 p.m. when Lesage came on duty. Instead of coming to the station, Giesick called. He said he was already back in Dallas and left a number where he could be reached.

By now the death was in the news. Reporters called it "New Orleans' first traffic fatality of the new year."

The next afternoon Henderson went to the Ramada Inn where the Giesicks had stayed. Giesick had registered under the name of Charles J. Guilliam. At the time of the accident he explained this by saying he didn't want anyone to know where he and his wife were staying on their honeymoon. Henderson now learned that Giesick had paid his bill with a credit card issued to Dr. Charles Guilliam. The motel clerk had checked the card and found that it was valid. Giesick told the clerk Guilliam was a good friend who had given him the use of the card as a wedding present. Giesick had signed Dr. Guilliam's name to the bill and then signed his own name below it. Henderson and Lesage turned in their report with the recommendation that Homicide Division question Giesick further and make a more detailed investigation of the accident.

That job fell to Detective John Dillmann, a young, intense, extremely serious investigator with the general size and build of a college halfback. He began by reviewing Henderson and Lesage's report and interviewing them personally. Dillmann shared their doubts about Giesick but became especially determined in his task after reading a letter the New Orleans Police Department received about ten days after the accident. It was written on behalf of Trish's mother by her lawyer. From this letter and from telephone conversations with Mrs. Albanowski, Dillmann learned that Patricia had called home only a few hours before her death and said she was worried about the large amount of insurance on her. She had also complained about their car still being in the shop. But Giesick, when he talked with Mrs. Albanowski after Patricia's death, at first said they had driven to the scene of the accident. When Mrs. Albanowski questioned him about the car being in the shop, he had changed his story to say they'd walked. She didn't know how much insurance money was involved, but she was extremely concerned that Patricia's death might not have been accidental.

It is one thing to suspect, as Dillmann already did, that this accident was really a murder. That suspicion combined with his immediate sympathy for Patricia's parents made Dillmann very determined about his investigation. But it is another thing, sympathy aside, to find whether those suspicions are true, and still another to develop the evidence to prove those suspicions in court. Dillmann began with very little solid information. He knew two names, Giesick and Guilliam, knew from motel records when Patricia and her husband arrived in New Orleans, and knew from Mrs. Albanowski her daughter's address in Richardson, the date she and Giesick had married, and the make of their car.

Beginning with the car, he canvassed Chevrolet dealers in the vicinity of the motel and discovered the one where Giesick, using the name Dr. Charles Giesick, had taken his Monte Carlo on January 14, the day he and Patricia arrived in New Orleans. Giesick claimed the car had transmission problems, but the mechanics found nothing wrong with the transmission. They made a few minor repairs and called Giesick. He picked up the Monte Carlo shortly after 5 p.m. the next day. Yet, Dillmann noted, later that night Patricia had complained to her mother that their new car was still in the shop.

Dillmann returned to his desk at the station and soon received a call from a representative of the Farmers Insurance Group who wanted to talk to the officer investigating the accident. One of Farmers agents had just contacted the home office. This agent had sold the Giesicks a $50,000 policy with a double-indemnity clause and Giesick had recently registered a claim to collect the $100,000 for Patricia's death. This information confirmed Mrs. Albanowski's statements about the large amount of insurance on her daughter.

Dillmann had been assigned to the case on a Tuesday. The following Saturday, February 2, he flew to

Dallas hoping to question Giesick. Unfortunately, Giesick had disappeared, but Dillmann took the opportunity to interview Patricia's neighbors. He learned that she had come to Texas about a year and a half earlier and had known Giesick only a short time before marrying him. She had worked at several jobs, and according to one neighbor, had recently been working as a masseuse in "one of Sam Corey's places."

Dillmann was unfamiliar with this name and ran a routine check on it. Corey turned out to be well known to the Dallas and San Antonio vice squads because he owned massage parlors in both places. He lived in San Antonio but flew to Dallas almost daily. His only real trouble with the law, however, was recent. Although free on bail, he was under indictment in Dallas County for the theft of some massage tables from another parlor. On Monday morning, checking with the Bureau of Vital Statistics, Dillmann learned from the Giesicks' marriage license, much to his surprise, that the presiding pastor had been the "Rt. Rev. Dr. Samuel C. Corey" of the Southwest Calvary Grace Christian Church, a church not registered in Dallas County.

Still, assuming Corey was actually ordained, there was nothing wrong with performing what appeared to be a legal marriage. Corey's involvement was peculiar and suspicious, but certainly not yet incriminating. For that matter, the same might be said, with only slightly less justification, about Giesick. But that afternoon Dillmann received a call from a representative of the Mutual of Omaha Insurance Company. They had written a $200,000 accident policy on Patricia Giesick. The insurance official suggested that he take Dillmann to the Dallas-Fort Worth Airport so he could interview the employees who had sold the insurance to the Giesicks. These interviews, which Dillmann conducted during most of the following day, revealed that Corey was involved in aspects of the case rather less religious than the rites of holy matrimony.

Dillmann talked with four employees of the Tele-Trip Company, a branch of Mutual of Omaha, which had issued the $200,000 policy on Patricia. From their statements he learned that two men had first come to the Love Field booth on January 10. One of the men was identified from a photograph as Corey; Dillmann had no photograph of Giesick, but the second man had identified himself by name and he matched Giesick's general physical description. When they first approached the booth, Giesick was holding a brochure that explained the various types of policies available. He asked about one called Plan C. Corey then prompted Giesick to ask about hit-and-run. After Giesick had asked, Corey again prompted him to say that he was interested because a friend had been involved in such an accident and the insurance company hadn't paid. Again, Giesick followed the prompting. Then he asked several more questions, all having to do with hit-and-run coverage and all prompted by Corey. He said he was interested in this coverage because he was planning a trip to Africa where the roads were very narrow and he wanted to be sure he was covered.

Two days later, on January 12, the two men returned and again asked about Plan C. This time Giesick was particularly interested in an additional rider of $100,000 that could be added to that plan to bring its total value to $300,000. On his earlier visit he had left the definite impression that the coverage was for him;

now he said it was for his wife. He returned the following afternoon with her and asked specifically for the $300,000 policy. When he learned that the $100,000 rider didn't cover accidents involving private automobiles, he said he didn't want it after all and bought the $200,000 coverage in his wife's name with himself as beneficiary.

Dillmann, at the end of a week's investigation, now had a choice. One option was to fly to San Antonio and question Corey about the marriage and his trips to the insurance counter. But Dillmann, like a halfback, favored end runs over plunges through the center of the line. Obviously Corey was, in some strange way, linked to Patricia's death. But he still had nothing that linked Corey directly with the events in New Orleans. And he thought he was more likely to find that in New Orleans than in San Antonio.

Back in New Orleans he returned to the Ramada Inn on Chef Menteur. He talked to two desk clerks, the manager, a waitress in the restaurant, and a maid. They had all seen Corey with Giesick the morning after the accident and identified him from a photograph. According to their statements, Giesick had returned from the hospital about 10 a.m. that day. He was covered with blood and a little later gave his clothes to a clerk to send to the laundry. About 11 a.m. he entered the motel dining room with Corey, whom these witnesses, like the Tele-Trip personnel, all described as heavyset and very shabbily dressed. A few minutes later a priest from the hospital phoned to tell Giesick his wife had died. Giesick talked with the priest for several minutes and then left the motel with Corey.

Late in the afternoon one of the clerks went back to

Giesick's room to tell him his clothes wouldn't be back from the cleaners until the next day. Corey was with Giesick in the room. The two of them were packing suitcases into a maroon car with a white roof. Giesick said he'd pick up his clothes later and asked if he could leave his Monte Carlo in the motel lot until he came back for his clothes. The clerk nodded but when she looked for the car the next day, it was gone.

Two days later, on Friday, January 18, Corey appeared at the Ramada Inn again and asked for Giesick's clothing. The police had requested the motel staff to notify them if anyone should come by to pick up this cleaning. The manager stalled Corey by saying he'd have to wait a few minutes as the clothes weren't back from the cleaners. Corey, suddenly very nervous, didn't wait. He got back in his car and sped out of the parking lot so fast that his rear wheels spun up a sheet of gravel. He stopped in the parking lot of the motel next door where he talked to a man waiting in a late-model blue car. The two men then drove off toward town.

The last person Dillmann interviewed was a maid who had seen Corey when he came back for Giesick's clothes. She said he was the same man she had seen walking across the street toward the Quality Inn next door the day before the accident. Dillmann walked straight next door and, from the motel register, discovered that Corey had checked in about 2 a.m. on January 15, about 24 hours before the accident. Not only had Corey been in New Orleans when Patricia was killed, but he also had been staying right next door.

The same night clerk who had checked Corey into the motel, a young student with the unfortunate name

E. J. Swindler, had seen Corey the next night around two o'clock, only about fifteen minutes before the accident. Corey had come into the lobby asking for a place where he could buy aspirin. Swindler had no idea where to suggest at that late hour, but Corey came back about 25 minutes later to tell Swindler he'd managed to find an open doughnut shop down the highway where he'd made his purchase. Swindler said Corey was in a happy, expansive mood and seemed very pleased with himself.

Dillmann also noted that one of the calls Corey made from his room was to the residence of a Dr. Charles Guilliam at an address on Tuxford Drive in San Antonio. And, exploring one final nuance, Dillmann checked back with the Ramada Inn to see if they had rooms available on the night of January 15. They had. Even though Corey knew the bride and groom well enough to have married them, he stayed out of sight in an adjoining motel.

Whatever Dillmann may have suspected at this point, all he could *prove* was that they were both in New Orleans on the night of Patricia's death. He had yet to talk with either Corey or Giesick to see how they would explain their actions; nor had he talked with this Dr. Guilliam to see where, if anywhere, he fit in. And he could not identify the murder weapon. Had it been Corey's car, or Giesick's or Guilliam's?—had he, by the way, been in New Orleans, too?—or had the weapon been some other car entirely?

A week later, Giesick was arrested in San Antonio on an old charge of passing worthless checks. That was enough for Dillmann to catch a plane in the hope of getting to San Antonio and interviewing Giesick before he got out of jail. And the way he'd gotten arrested was the first sign that, while Dillmann was trying to crack the case from the outside, the case might be cracking from the inside, too.

Giesick had contacted a San Antonio police detective with a story that he had spent the last two years keeping out of sight because his life was under constant threat from a criminal named Zent. Now, Giesick said, his wife had been killed in an accident down in New Orleans and the police from there might be making some inquiries about him. Would the detective tell New Orleans that Giesick had disappeared because he was a police informer in San Antonio? The request was so strange that the detective simply ran a computer check on Giesick, discovered the warrant, and arrested him. Dillmann wasn't sure, either, what Giesick was trying to do except throw up a smoke screen to hide himself from inquiries out of New Orleans. And Dillmann didn't get to ask Giesick what he was up to. By the time his plane landed in San Antonio, Giesick had been released on bond—posted by Sam Corey.

Dillmann had arrived in San Antonio early Sunday morning, February 17. Although thwarted in seeing Giesick, he asked Corey to come to the police station at 10 a.m. and took a formal statement from him. Much of what Corey said was untrue. He "emphatically and positively" denied knowing whether Patricia had worked in a massage parlor; he said he had seen Giesick only one time since his marriage and that was in Richardson; he claimed he had first heard of the accident when Patricia's mother called him at his massage parlor in San Antonio on the morning of January 16 and that he talked with Giesick long distance later that day; he said he had not been in New Orleans for several months; and he said that, although he had just posted bond for Giesick, he didn't know his address.

Then, having watched calmly while Corey lied to him at every turn, Dillmann drove out to the Tuxford Street address of Dr. James Guilliam. A woman in her middle twenties with long, straight blond hair came to the door, said she was Dr. Guilliam's wife, and that he was out of town where he couldn't be reached by phone. She claimed her husband was a consulting psychologist and a business associate of Giesick's. The only contact he had with Sam Corey was an occasional visit to his parlor for a massage. No, she had no pictures of her husband to show Dillmann. She became very nervous and insisted that her husband answer any more questions personally. As Dillmann left the house, he noticed a small detail that led him closer to what he had already begun to suspect—that Guilliam and Giesick were the same person. Patricia's neighbors in Richardson had told him that Giesick had given his wife a St. Bernard puppy. There were several St. Bernard puppies in the Guilliams' yard.

That growing suspicion was confirmed later that evening. Sitting in his motel room, Dillmann got a call from a San Antonio police officer who had known Giesick for six years. Giesick had asked the officer not to tell the New Orleans police he was now using the name Guilliam. This was, Dillmann thought, an obvious attempt to continue the confusion that Giesick's double identity had created during all the investigation. It also meant that Giesick was getting more and more worried about Dillmann finding him and was taking greater chances to try to prevent it. The San Antonio officer

told Dillmann that Giesick was living on Tuxford Street
with his wife Kathi, a woman with long, blond hair.
She was the same woman Giesick had been married to
for the six years the officer had known them. He didn't
think they had ever been divorced although Giesick
now was asking him to say that they had been divorced
for several years.

Dillmann went to the Bexar County Bureau of Vital
Statistics and found that Giesick had married Katherine
Kiser in September 1969. There was no record of their
ever being divorced. He talked with several neighbors
near the Tuxford Street house who, from the mug shot
taken when Giesick was arrested, identified him as
their neighbor Dr. Charles Guilliam. Dillmann tried
again to interview the blond woman he now knew to
be Kathi Giesick, but she wouldn't talk at all without a
lawyer.

That evening, February 18, after Dillmann had been
working on the case for three weeks, he got to interview Giesick at last. It was Giesick, finally, who contacted Dillmann and, while he refused to come to
police headquarters, agreed to meet at Sam Corey's
massage parlor. During the interview Giesick claimed
he was working with retarded school children in Dallas
and had degrees from universities in Brazil, Germany,
and Mexico. None of this turned out to be true. Giesick
also volunteered, and subsequent checking confirmed,
that he had been married four times: once from 1966
to 1967, which ended in divorce; once in California, a
marriage that was annulled after three days; once to
Katherine in 1969; and then, bigamously, to Patricia.
His version of the accident was essentially the same
story he told New Orleans police: he and Patricia had

gone out by the bayou to look at ducks and she raced into the street where she was hit by a speeding car. Then, he said, the evening after the hit-and-run he'd flown to Houston and on to Dallas. He didn't mention seeing Sam Corey until the night of January 17 when he flew to San Antonio. Toward the end of the interview Giesick began acting extremely nervous, insisting that he had to catch a plane to Dallas and didn't have time to talk any longer. Dillmann pressed on. If he'd flown from New Orleans, what happened to his car? Well, he'd flown back to get it and on the way had stopped at the Ramada Inn to pick up his clothes. And yet, Dillmann knew, it was Corey who had tried unsuccessfully to pick up Giesick's clothes. Why had he listed himself as a widower on his marriage license? Giesick said he'd lied about that to Patricia and was simply keeping up the lie. After that Giesick insisted on leaving to catch his plane.

Dillmann himself then flew to Dallas, where he told police what he'd found, particularly the new information that Giesick was already married when he married Patricia. They had a justice of the peace issue a warrant for Giesick on charges of bigamy. On February 22 San Antonio police arrested him in front of his house on Tuxford as he tried to flee in his Monte Carlo. Dillmann had thought this car was possibly the one that killed Patricia, but a thorough examination by the police lab found nothing that could prove the car had hit anyone.

Although disappointed—after all the time he'd spent on the investigation, the best case he could make against Giesick was bigamy, not murder—Dillmann returned to New Orleans and tried, in the hope he could find additional evidence, to discover more about Giesick's and Corey's activities while they were in New Orleans. He learned that Giesick, far from losing all means of transportation when he took his Monte Carlo in for repairs, had immediately rented another Monte Carlo from Avis. In fact, Avis had come to the dealership to pick him up. At two o'clock that night, exactly 24 hours before the accident, Giesick and Corey appeared at the Avis rental desk at the New Orleans airport where Giesick exchanged his rented Monte Carlo for another one that was identical except for color. He gave no reason for wanting to exchange cars and the attendant, when he checked the returned car, found nothing wrong with it. Dillmann was now disappointed to learn that the second Monte Carlo was out of the state and he would be forced to wait for its return before inspecting it.

He conducted several more interviews. A guard at the hospital had seen Corey there shortly after the accident. The doctor who treated Patricia said she had tire marks on the left side of her head and left shoulder. If she had been hit running across the street, as Giesick had claimed, she would have been struck around her waist and hips and thrown clear rather than run over. And Dillmann found Ricky Mock, the first person on the scene. When he heard the loud mufflers on Mock's car, Dillmann deduced that this was the car with loud mufflers Giesick had described as the hit-and-run car.

At this point he was stalled in his investigation until the Avis car turned up; but he managed to make some progress anyway with the unwitting help of Giesick and Corey. They were beginning to show more strain under the pressure of Dillmann's dogged pursuit. Corey resorted to a private polygraph examiner he had once employed to screen girls who worked in his massage parlor. Apparently Corey thought he knew enough about polygraphs to be able to beat the test. Instead the test showed deception or guilt when Corey answered no to the questions "Do you know who killed Patricia Giesick?" and "Do you know who was driving the car that struck Patricia Giesick?" Corey then pleaded with the examiner not to let the New Orleans police know the full results of the tests.

The examiner, of course, was legally obligated not to conceal possible evidence, and when Dillmann learned of the test he flew back to San Antonio. The examiner said he had concluded from the test that Corey was involved in Patricia's death or at least had knowledge that Giesick planned to take her life. Dillmann went straight to the Tokyo House where he told Corey that, because of his knowledge of Giesick's plans, he should voluntarily come to New Orleans and give a statement to police. Corey denied having any knowledge, but Dillmann told him what he'd just learned from the polygraph examiner. Flushed and nervous, Corey called the examiner, who confirmed that Dillmann was telling the truth. Corey then became mysteriously ill, complaining of severe pains in his chest. He said he would think about coming to New Orleans and tell Dillmann his decision the next day. But when Dillmann returned to the Tokyo House, the receptionist said Mr. Corey had suffered a stroke. Further questions were referred to Corey's lawyer, William Miller. Dillmann had no luck that day trying to contact Miller.

Unless Corey agreed to go voluntarily, Dillmann had no way of forcing him, so he returned to New Orleans himself and waited—waited for the Avis car to turn up, waited for something to break in San Antonio. Three weeks passed and nothing happened. But during that time Corey and Giesick were apparently feeling the heat of the investigation more and more. They must have met together in fear but not yet, judging from the plan that resulted, in mistrust. The first Sunday in May Giesick met in a Denny's with a San Antonio police detective and regaled him with a tale about the night of Patricia's death. The detective called Dillmann who in turn called Giesick so he could repeat the story.

It was the wildest and most desperate story yet. Giesick said he was ready to surrender himself in New Orleans and plead guilty to conspiring to kill his wife. Giesick said Sam Corey wasn't involved in this conspiracy, and, on the contrary, had been the one who prevented him from carrying out his plans. Giesick said he had met a "hippie" he knew only as Ronnie in Dallas. They had conspired to take Patricia to New Orleans where Giesick was supposed to beat her over the head with a rock and Ronnie would run over her with a truck to make her murder look like an accident. Corey learned of the conspiracy, came to New Orleans, and talked him out of it. Then he and Patricia went out walking by the bayou. He told her of his former plans. She became hysterical and ran into the street where, completely by accident, she was run over. Although he had planned to kill her, her death was purely coincidental. Giesick added that now he knew he was a habitual liar but was under psychiatric treatment and thought he was making progress. He was willing to confess to conspiracy now because he believed he was emotionally unable to serve the long prison sentence that would certainly follow a murder conviction. He repeated that Sam Corey was never involved in the conspiracy. Dillmann was somewhat less than greatly moved by Giesick's tender emotional condition. He assumed since Giesick had been so careful to exclude Corey from guilt, that Giesick was making his confession because of pressure from Corey.

Two days later Giesick called Dillmann again. The pressure had finally produced a break between the conspirators. Giesick said there had been an attempt on his life by, he believed, Sam Corey. He wanted to know, if he came to New Orleans, confessed everything, and agreed to cooperate, would he be granted a lesser charge than murder. Dillmann consulted the district attorney's office and called Giesick back to say his cooperation would be taken into account but if he came to New Orleans he would be arrested. Giesick declined to come. "I'd rather take my chances with Sam Corey,' he said. But the break was final. Two days later Giesick's attorney was in the DA's office trying to work a deal to get Giesick a reduced charge in return for testifying against Corey.

On May 13 the Avis car, the one Giesick had rented at the airport the night before the murder, arrived back in New Orleans. A thorough inspection revealed two nine-inch strands of human hair wrapped around and embedded in a spot of grease on a tie rod near the right front tire. Dillmann sent these hairs to the FBI Crime Lab. In order to obtain samples of Patricia's hair to compare with those on the car, Dillmann went to New Jersey where she had been buried near her parents' home, obtained a court order, and had her body exhumed. He took samples of her hair and sent them to the FBI. Hair, unlike fingerprints, does not have enough unique characteristics for one to say with certainty that it comes from a particular person. But there are some fifteen different traits by which hairs can be compared, among them color, texture, oil, types of scales, and various others. The hairs on the car, which had been crushed and ripped from the scalp as they would have been in an accident, matched Patricia's hair in all fifteen characteristics. Dillmann had found the murder weapon.

On June 6, 1975, a year and a half after he began his investigation, Dillmann told an Orleans Parish grand jury what he'd learned of Patricia Albanowski Giesick's death. After listening to four hours of testimony, they returned indictments against Jim Giesick and Sam Corey for murder in the second degree.

But the conduct of the trial changed many things. The maximum penalty in Louisiana for second-degree murder is life in prison. Sam Corey now awaits his execution on death row.

Ralph Whalen, the man who prosecuted Sam Corey, joined the Orleans Parish District Attorney's staff in 1971, immediately after graduating from the Tulane law school. He didn't seem like one of that school's most promising graduates. Not especially enamored of study, he had finished in the middle of his class and took a job with the DA as much from default as from choice. He spent his first week observing the trials in progress. That Friday afternoon, riding a crowded rush-hour bus home, he began to cry. The spectacle of defendants and victims and police and tales of horrible crimes and men and women hauled off to jail had overwhelmed him. He wasn't sure he was doing the right thing. Perhaps his deepest sympathies were opposed to the very office he was now serving. Hadn't he seen people go to jail that very week for smoking marijuana, an act he wasn't sure should be a crime at all?

The following Monday, however, he was given a handful of case files, a pat on the back, and the instructions that it was time for him to get in there and start prosecuting. The moment he stepped into a courtroom as a lawyer with a case to win, those tears became a relic of a past life. The courtroom battle intrigued and inspired him; he lost his doubts about whether the defendants he prosecuted deserved jail; and he became so skillful so quickly that by the time the Corey case came along—the most publicized criminal case in New Orleans since Clay Shaw—the newspapers were referring to Whalen as "the Whacker," and he had decided that a prosecutor's job was his life's calling.

Whalen found himself matched against a lawyer whose reputation was as old and established as Whalen's was new and promising. Irvin Dymond, the most famous criminal lawyer in New Orleans, the man who had defended Clay Shaw, had taken Corey's case. While Whalen was short, trim, neatly dressed, and aggressive and intense in the courtroom, Dymond had a calmer style, slower, and, in appearance at least, not at all flamboyant. About 30 years older than Whalen, Dymond had not only the benefit of longer experience in the courts but also a marvelous deep voice and a talent for a sonorous and compelling oratory that is seldom found outside the South. William Miller, Corey's San Antonio lawyer, also helped with his defense. He had, strangely enough, first been Giesick's lawyer. When Giesick abandoned him for C. David Evans, a well-known San Antonio attorney and former state legislator, Corey went to Miller. Dymond's responsibilities were to try the case while Miller's were research and investigation, a separation of duties that did not prevent the two lawyers from publicly disagreeing about the progress and direction of the defense.

The prosecution's case, despite all the evidence Dillmann had compiled, was weakened by the lack of witnesses to the crime. There had been two people, a man and a woman, in a car in the parking lot where Giesick had left his Monte Carlo. Officers at the scene questioned them and discovered that, though they were both married, they weren't married to each other. Both the man and the woman denied seeing anything. They pleaded with the officers not to take their names and the officers acceded. The prosecution could establish only that Giesick was present at the scene, but not what he did there; it could establish Corey's whereabouts before and immediately after the murder, but had no evidence that placed him precisely at the scene. The DA's office had no doubts that these were the guilty men, but juries were unpredictable. They might not convict without some direct evidence or testimony about exactly what happened that night. The events on Michoud Boulevard remained a large spot of white canvas at the center of an otherwise convincing painting.

At the same time, Giesick's attorneys had been trying to make a deal for a reduced sentence in return for their client's testimony against Corey. Giesick could be the eyewitness the prosecution needed. David Evans,

Giesick's attorney, also added another bit of pressure. He said he would fight extradition from Texas every step of the way. It was unlikely that, in the end, the Texas courts would refuse to extradite Giesick, but such legal maneuvering would tie things up in Texas for at least a year, perhaps longer. Eventually, the DA, who had come to believe that Corey was the instigator and mastermind of the plot, agreed to let Giesick plead guilty to manslaughter. Giesick surrendered himself and agreed to testify against Corey.

The case finally came to trial on November 6, almost ten months after Patricia's death. It had been scheduled once before, but Irvin Dymond, saying that he'd not had time to prepare his case properly, asked Whalen if he would agree to a continuance. Whalen agreed, but as the November 6 date approached, found that he was the one now not ready to go to trial. In the last ten months, important witnesses had moved or changed jobs and Whalen couldn't find some of them. He asked Dymond if he would agree to another continuance, but Dymond, thinking he had Whalen on the ropes, refused and insisted on going to trial. When the trial opened and Giesick and Corey stood stonily ignoring one another before the bar, Whalen shocked everyone by announcing that he was dropping the charges of second-degree murder against Sam Corey. A moment later he added, "Your honor, it is the state's position that a charge of first-degree murder more accurately reflects the crime and we intend to seek such an indictment." Corey walked out of the courtroom a free man only to have Dillmann arrest him once again.

Whalen, forced into a corner, had spent some time consulting the law books. Louisiana had recently revised its laws concerning the death penalty to comply with Supreme Court decisions. The result was a special and specific category of crimes that were defined as first-degree murder. That offense carried a mandatory death penalty. Part of the statute stated that murder is in the first degree "when the offender has specific intent to commit murder and has received anything of value for committing the murder." The Louisiana lawmakers probably had murder for hire in mind in writing that passage, but Whalen saw no reason why it couldn't be applied to Corey's case. Wasn't the state contending that his motive was more than $300,000 in insurance money? Would not obtaining that money be receiving something "of value for committing the murder"? One day after the second-degree murder charge was dropped, the same grand jury again heard Dillmann's testimony and returned a first-degree murder indictment against Sam Corey.

When the trial began late in April 1975, the prosecution began with the testimony of a pathologist who had performed the autopsy on Patricia. Then Whalen put Giesick on the stand to tell how he and Sam Corey had plotted murder.

Whalen had warned the jury in his opening statement that he had made a deal with Giesick whom he described as "a killer, a murderer . . . a man about as bad as they come." Though this might have seemed at the time like undermining his own witness, it was Whalen's attempt to lessen the effect of evidence the defense would surely introduce about Giesick's character. He had been diagnosed by a psychiatrist as a pathological liar with a lifelong history of anti-social behavior. He had threatened the life of the father of one of his former wives. He had been indicted for writing bad checks. He posed as a doctor of psychology. He had made much of his living for the past ten years by confidence games and insurance rip-offs, an occupation that had forced him to adopt a double identity. Under cross-examination by Dymond, he freely described a method he used to steal cars from airport parking lots. Everything he had, as he would also admit on the stand, he'd gotten by cheating someone. And the defense witnesses, the majority of them, were people called to discredit Giesick with testimony about actions he wouldn't admit so readily. A masseuse said he had suggested murdering her husband for insurance money. Another masseuse, one who had bought Sam Corey's parlor in Irving, said she'd hired Giesick as a psychologist to help two of her employees who were having emotional problems. Giesick treated them by prescribing frequent sexual intercourse with him. Later he propositioned the woman's fourteen-year-old daughter. Other witnesses testified to similar behavior.

Still, for a person as thoroughly bad as he was shown to be, Giesick made a good witness. He has an easygoing, soft-spoken manner and a glib tongue that, treacherous as it is, can also be charming. He does not, on first impression, seem like a killer or even, when he tried hard, which he did on the stand, like a liar. And in the end the jury chose to believe him.

The tale Giesick told on the stand was not so much of violence, although it was violent, and certainly not one of cleverness, but one of remarkable coldness, callousness, and cynicism. Giesick, using the name Guilliam, had met Sam Corey when he came to the Tokyo House in San Antonio to sell him a credit card service that day I was winding up my story. After that they saw each other occasionally and twice happened to run into each other's cars. (These accidents had all the earmarks of insurance frauds.) Around November 1973, while they were eating in a restaurant in San Antonio, Corey first brought up the possibility of Giesick marrying a girl and the two of them killing her for insurance money. Corey said he knew that Giesick was wanted for a bad check charge and threatened to turn him in unless he went along with the plan. Their conversation lasted about an hour and a half and at the end of that time Giesick had agreed to the idea.

He began frequenting massage parlors in San Antonio and Dallas looking for a girl. Before long he found Patricia and married her. She was the perfect victim. She was lonely, gullible, down on her luck, and desperate for both money and affection. He began insuring her. On at least one occasion Corey provided the money for the premium.

After the marriage, Giesick drove with Patricia to New Orleans and checked into the Ramada Inn on Chef Menteur. He immediately took his car to the shop for unneeded repairs and from there called his wife Kathi in San Antonio who told him where Corey was staying. Giesick rented a Monte Carlo from Avis and met Corey at his Holiday Inn. Then Giesick drove back to the parking lot at the intersection of Chef Menteur and Michoud where he parked his rented car. He walked the rest of the way back to the motel. The plan was to make Patricia think they had no car. This would confine her to the motel most of the time and force her to walk across the highway to the small bar and restaurant if she wanted to eat. They originally thought this might provide an occasion for her to have an "accident."

That night Giesick took the St. Bernard puppy out for a walk as an excuse to meet Corey. Corey signaled from his car by flashing his lights. They discussed possible locations and the mechanics of the crime. Then Giesick went back in, got Patricia, and walked her up and down Chef Menteur. Corey was on the road driving a Buick he and Giesick had stolen from Love Field in Dallas. But the traffic was too heavy to risk anything then.

Giesick took Patricia back to their room, took the dog out for another walk, and met with Corey again. They decided to try again that night on Michoud Boulevard near the bridge over the bayou. Giesick went back to the room and talked Patricia into coming outside with him once again. As they walked up Michoud toward the bridge, Giesick noticed a police car by his parked rental car. An officer was shining a flashlight inside. Giesick panicked a little, took Patricia back to their room, told her he needed time to think by himself, and, outside, told Corey the police had spotted his car. They both got in the rental car, Corey driving, and went to the airport where they exchanged that car for another one using the phony excuse about transmission trouble. On the way back, Corey checked out of his motel and moved to the Quality Inn next door to the Ramada Inn where Giesick and Patricia were staying.

The following afternoon Giesick picked up his car at the dealership and spent the rest of the afternoon and evening driving Patricia around and watching television in their room. (Patricia, however, later that night told her mother and a desk clerk that their car was still in the garage. The defense never questioned Giesick about this discrepancy.) Giesick took the dog out several times that night and met with Corey. Corey whispered through the door of his motel room, and Giesick stood facing away from him so Patricia, if she should happen to wander outside, wouldn't see him talking with anyone. They agreed on a time and place.

After midnight Giesick drove Patricia to Michoud Boulevard. (Here again his testimony conflicts with Patricia's comments about their car.) They walked across the short bridge and down to the edge of the bayou. Corey drove past, made a U-turn, and parked in front of the first house in the block after the bridge. He signaled with his parking lights that he was ready.

Giesick and Patricia walked up to the road. He stopped by a small tree. Holding his flashlight behind his back, he signaled three times. Corey signaled with his lights and then started toward them. Giesick waited for the right moment, grabbed Patricia, and shoved her and tripped her at the same time. Corey ran her down and kept on going. Sometime later, after the police and ambulance had arrived, Corey drove by the scene again. Giesick concluded his testimony by saying that he met Sam Corey on the roof of the hospital as Patricia lay unconscious below. "Don't worry about it," Corey said. "She's not going to live. Everything's fine. We're home free."

The rest of the prosecution's case was designed either to augment or corroborate Giesick's testimony. Whalen knew that Giesick's psychiatrist would testify for the defense that the prosecution's star witness was a pathological liar. But Whalen, by taking special courses and with a certain amount of study on his own, had learned rudiments of psychiatric theory and practice and how they applied to the law. He knew that the psychiatrist would also admit, as he later did during Whalen's cross-examination, that the testimony of a pathological liar could be believed if it was corroborated.

Whalen called Kathi Giesick to the stand and she testified about calls Corey and Giesick had made to her from New Orleans. Ricky Mock testified about discovering the accident after dropping his friend at home. Dillmann described what he'd discovered during his investigation. A criminologist from the FBI testified that the hair found on the rented Monte Carlo matched Patricia's hair. A guard at the hospital swore that after Patricia was brought in, he saw Corey in the hospital parking lot behind the wheel of a Monte Carlo. He was positive in his identification because a friend drove a car just like it "with the small windows behind the large windows." Employees of Tele-Trip, the Ramada Inn, and Avis all testified to the same information about Giesick and Corey that they'd provided Dillmann during his investigation. And Mrs. Albanowski, Patricia's mother, told the grim story of her daughter's funeral. Giesick, accompanied by Sam Corey, arrived somewhat late. Corey was dressed in a black suit and clerical collar. Mourners assumed he was a priest, and at a dinner after the burial, he strolled around accepting small donations to say prayers for Patricia's soul.

Whalen had another witness whom he could not decide what to do with. He wanted to wait to put this witness on the stand during his rebuttal to the defense, when the testimony would have the most impact. But he was worried that Dymond might put on no defense at all, simply rest his case, and proceed directly to final arguments. If that happened, this witness's testimony would never get before the jury, and it was, Whalen felt, the testimony that topped off the case he had so carefully built. Finally Whalen, holding his breath like a gambler who tosses his last chips into the pot and waits for the cards to fall, kept his witness back and rested his case.

Corey's attorneys had a continuing disagreement about whether to put Corey on the stand. This argument became so heated that they once came to words in the hallway outside the courtroom. Dymond, however, as the attorney responsible for trying the case, prevailed and the defense, instead of resting immediately, called several witnesses, including Corey. Whalen began to breathe somewhat easier.

First a series of masseuses told the stories about Giesick mentioned earlier. Their testimony, while hardly flattering about Giesick, did little damage to the prosecutor's case. Whalen asked each one of them whether they knew anything of the events on Michoud Boulevard around 2 a.m. on January 16, 1974. They all answered that they did not.

Then Dymond called Sam Corey and asked him three questions: had he killed Patricia; had he conspired with anyone to kill her; and had he conspired with Jim Giesick to kill her? To all three questions Corey answered, "No, sir, I did not." Dymond turned his witness over to Whalen.

Corey then weighed more than 300 pounds. He overflowed the witness chair, where he sat sunk in an extremely disheveled suit, wearing old scruffy shoes worn way down at the heels, and nervously popping mints in his mouth as he testified. He frequently mumbled in answer to Whalen's questions, many times answering that he couldn't recall where he'd been at a particular time or what he was doing. Whalen asked about the statement Corey had made for Dillmann when he denied being in New Orleans at the time of the murder. Corey was forced to admit he had lied then. Corey repeated his new story that he had come to New Orleans to patch up a lovers' quarrel between Patricia and Jim and had spent the night of the murder with a prostitute named Linda whom he had met in front of a massage parlor. Regardless of how many contradictions and unexplainable circumstances Whalen was able to reveal between Corey's story and all the other testimony—and there were many—here was where he made Corey look the worst.

"At that massage parlor," Whalen asked, "did you get a local?"

"Yes, sir."

"And what is a local, Mr. Corey?"

The would-be priest, the supposed minister, the man who solicited donations from mourners at the funeral of the girl he was now accused of murdering, glumly replied, "The genitals are massaged." If Corey's former priestly and ministerial poses had provoked any sympathy from the jury, this testimony destroyed it.

Then Whalen presented his rebuttal case. There were several witnesses but the last was the one Whalen had held back: E. J. Swindler, the desk clerk at the Holiday Inn whom Corey had asked for aspirin just before the time of the murder and who had seen Corey again about 25 minutes later when he returned to the motel lobby. Swindler's testimony placed Corey out of his room near the time of the murder, Linda or no Linda.

After closing arguments—Dymond's, eloquent and moving; Whalen's, powerful and persuasive—the jury retired to deliberate. The trial had lasted five days, but the jury returned in only twenty minutes with their decision.

Sam Corey was sentenced to death and Jim Giesick to 21 years in prison, the maximum punishment in Louisiana for manslaughter. But the story doesn't end there. As this is written Irvin Dymond is working on Sam Corey's appeal, and Giesick has, in interviews with reporters and from other forums, claimed he lied on the stand. He now says the real killer wasn't Sam at all but his wife Kathi in league with a man desperately in love with her, the mysterious hippie named Ronnie. The precise reason why his love should have driven Ronnie to murder his beloved's husband's other wife is a little complicated to explain. There is no evidence, however, to support this new version of the story.

In prison Giesick spends most of his time making plastic knicknacks which he sends to people along with an exorbitant bill. And he writes nasty letters. "Do try to write soon—Killer" was the way one to his wife ended. "Your secretary sounds nice. Does she have any life insurance?" was the postscript of a letter to Whalen. He is smug and unremorseful, and when I talked with him in prison, he maintained a rather breezy attitude about all that has happened. He has lost weight, has neatly styled and perfectly combed hair, and the day I saw him wore a gray T-shirt with "Jim" printed in fancy letters over his heart.

During the trial Giesick's mental instability received considerable attention. There was the testimony of his psychiatrist, his psychiatric discharge from the service, the history and habits of his life. But it seems to me now that Corey is the one with far worse delusions.

After our prison interview I kept seeing the way Sam's face looked—happy, conspiratorial, self-satisfied—when he told me he'd gotten a local in the massage parlor he visited the afternoon before the murder. For a while I assumed this was a new and private detail that, for some reason, he had decided to tell me, perhaps as a way of establishing a masculine rapport between us. But when I read the transcript of the trial and talked with people who had seen Sam testify, I discovered that it was one of the most public details in the case. Didn't Sam know how low and sleazy this testimony had made him appear? And yet he couldn't restrain himself from telling me. I could still see the way his face looked then—red, happy, his eyes alive with pleasure, and his whole body shaking with glee.

The crime itself, of course, reveals certain dark streams of the mind that lead directly into a psychological thicket: the gross, unattractive man brings a younger, handsomer, sweeter-talking man under his control; it is a woman they decide to kill; the marriage has an extremely voyeuristic aspect with the older man performing the ceremony and hovering unseen around the couple on their honeymoon; the actual killing requires their mutual cooperation complete with signaled contact in the night; rather than violate their victim's body with a bullet or knife they choose simply to crush her; the older man has religious delusions; the older man, it turns out, was rejected by his mother early in life and raised by an aunt.

I can do nothing more with that thicket than to say it's there. I do not know a clear path through it. But I do believe I now understand the look on Sam's face when he told me about the local. It was the face, surely, that E. J. Swindler saw when Sam, self-satisfied and gleeful, just back from killing Patricia, walked into the motel lobby to share with someone, however partially, his moment of greatest pleasure.

(July 1976)

Sam Corey died in prison on Saint Patrick's Day 1995. Jim Giesick was released after serving his sentence. Ralph Whalen practices law in New Orleans, handling mostly criminal cases. John Dillman has his own detective agency. He wrote a book about the case named *Unholy Matrimony*. It was made into a television movie. Fred Thompson, now a United States senator, played the role of the prosecutor.

The Madman on
the Tower

WILLIAM J. HELMER

It's like belonging to a fraternity that never meets: you are talking with someone and learn he was living in Austin in 1966, and pretty soon the subject of Charles Whitman comes up. Then for a minute or so, it's where-were-you time—that Monday, August 1, under bright skies with the temperature approaching one hundred. I was a University of Texas graduate student supervising student publications as a part-time job. Walking from the old journalism building on Twenty-fourth Street to the Union to get a sandwich for lunch, I could hear loud reports that had the *boom, snap* quality of rifle shots. They were coming from the vicinity of the Main Building, but I didn't see any unusual activity there and shrugged them off as the sounds of a nail-driving gun, which had been periodically banging away on a construction project there. Later I discovered that everyone hearing that noise was running it through a mental card-sorter until it found a slot that offered a perfectly ordinary explanation. One person, also mindful of the construction, decided that it was the sound of large planks falling over and slapping concrete. Another, closer to the mark, decided the

ROTC must be shooting blanks for some ceremonial reason on the mall in front of the Main Building with its 27-story Tower. Yet another saw a girl fling herself to the grass and assumed, having read a feature in the campus paper a few days earlier, that it was some kind of goofy crowd-response experiment being carried out by the psychology folks.

I was still operating on the nail-gun theory when some students standing behind a pillar of the Academic Center started shouting something about a guy on the Tower shooting people and how I should get moving. My first response was to resent being yelled at, so I just stood there in the middle of a grassy inner-drive area, squinting up at the Tower's northwest corner. Sure enough, I could see a gun barrel poke out over the parapet and emit smoke, followed an instant later by the boom I had been hearing. Now the computer was working a lot faster but still coming up with a bad readout: *Just look at that! There's some fool up there with a rifle, trying to get himself in one hell of a lot of trouble!* From my angle, it didn't look like the man was shooting downward, but was just trying to create a commotion.

So I turned around and started walking (don't show fear, they can smell it) the two hundred or so feet back to the protective corner of Hogg Auditorium, maybe trotting the last few yards. A student already there was pointing and jabbering about a girl who was hit in the side yard of the biology building, which I had just crossed coming from journalism. That bumped the alarm meter up substantially, and I joined him in yelling at a student strolling along the sidewalk past the old Littlefield Home, right behind us and to our left.

We nearly got the guy killed, for when he stopped to look at us in puzzlement, the sniper opened up on him with a semiautomatic rifle. That sent him scrambling to the protection of an alley as bullets whacked into the low limestone wall behind him, popping like movie squibs. Since then, I've wondered if he knew how lucky he was that Whitman had evidently emptied his two other rifles and was using his little open-sight Army carbine. With his scoped 6mm bolt-action Remington, it had been strictly one shot, one man, in the old Marine Corps tradition.

That bit of excitement convinced me that something not only very weird but very bad was happening. I had a queasy feeling that returned later that day when the paper said one Tower office employee looked out and saw "two young boys laying face down in front of Hogg Auditorium," and it came back a few days later, when a *Life* magazine aerial photo showed X's where people had been hit along the route I had just taken.

I had been a little slow in switching over to emergency, but my wits were supposedly about me as I made my way around the back of the auditorium to the Union, where I knew of a stairwell window that afforded a good and, I thought, safe view of the Tower. The window was wide open, and a girl in a white blouse was already sharing the right-hand side with someone, so I went to the left where only one student was standing and looked over his shoulder. Everyone was talking, and I could hear people downstairs in the Union lobby, babbling in confusion. Someone had come in from outside and was running through the lobby, crying, "That man is *dead!* That man is *dead!*" as though such a thing were entirely impossible.

I could see the sniper fairly well; he would lean out over the parapet, bring the rifle to bear on a target, fire, tip the weapon up as he worked the action, then walk quickly to another point and do the same thing. It must have been about that time that he hit an electrician next to his truck at Twentieth Street and University Avenue, a quarter of a mile away. It was about that time, too, that the Tower clock started chiming and then, with cold-blooded indifference, tolled the noon hour. And it must have been only moments after those echoes died that the sniper, evidently firing through one of the Tower's drain spouts, put a shot through the open window where the four of us stood gawking.

The bullet struck the edge of the window opening in front of the girl's face like an exploding stick of dynamite, filling the stairwell with glass, splinters, bullet fragments, and concrete dust. The blast put us on the floor, and the first thing I perceived was the girl, flat on her back, hands to her face, screaming. Which surprised me; I didn't think there could be any face left to scream with. I started crawling over to her, and my left hand slipped so that I partly fell forward into blood that was rapidly covering the floor of the stairwell. The blood wasn't hers; the bullet had fragmented, and a large chunk of it had pierced the right forearm of the guy on my side of the window. It had hit an artery that now, as he lay partly on his side, was pumping out blood in rapid squirts about three inches high.

It's strange what happens to time in situations like this. All motion slowed down and became dreamlike. I knew how to contend with arterial bleeding, but in the second or two it took me to get my hands to his arm it seemed as if I had ages to consider the neatness of the wound, the brightness of the blood, and its fountain-like behavior. I refused to think another shot might come through that window, because my legs were still exposed. I could still hear the girl's sobbing, and I could hear my own voice, squawking for someone to give me a handkerchief. The shooting victim used his good arm to pull one from his back pocket and hand it to me.

The girl had debris in her eyes but was otherwise okay. The guy would be okay once he was slid under the window and into the hands of other students who had come running up the stairs. I was okay but pretty blood-splattered and had trouble convincing one samaritan that the blood was not mine. Except for a tiny bit; while washing up in the basement men's room, I found that what looked like a shaving cut in my neck held a piece of the bullet's copper jacket, not much bigger than a pinhead. Realizing that that could have been the large chunk of bullet made it hard to breathe for a little while.

When I went back upstairs, no one had any real idea of what was going on—how many riflemen were up there or if the killing were part of something else that was happening. That feeling was enhanced by the absence of the police. Rarely does a person witness a car wreck or a fire or another emergency except in aftermath, when the scene is swarming with cops and firemen and spectators. To witness an emergency taking place is to realize that the cops don't come with it. After the first ten or fifteen minutes, I began hearing an occasional siren that ordinarily wouldn't have signaled anything more than a traffic problem here or an ambulance run there. But the shooting had been under way for nearly half an hour before the sirens of police cars and ambulances became obvious, blending into yelps and howls like a neighborhood full of dogs set off by a passing fire engine. That noise, punctuated by auto horns blown in panic and anger, blanketed the city. To that was soon added the garbled voices of newscasters blaring through more and more transistor radios. At least the radio reports were bringing things into sharper focus, describing a carnage far greater than anyone walking on campus could guess. Those early shots that had caused me more astonishment than alarm had, I now learned, hit their targets nearly every time, all over campus, up and down Guadalupe, at amazing ranges, killing people. Whitman hit running targets, bicycling targets, targets at ranges of up to five hundred yards; he even put a bullet through a light plane carrying a police rifleman. And his field of fire was so great that targets never stopped presenting themselves at distances they mistakenly thought were safe.

And something else incredible was happening. From about noon on, I had been hearing the occasional crack of return fire from the ground. I supposed it to be police, who at last were dashing around, revolvers in hand like pacifiers, looking helplessly officious. A couple of them had riot shotguns, which likewise could not have served much more than the psychological purpose of reducing frustration. But when I walked out the front door of the Union, staying out of Tower range, I felt the concussion of a high-powered rifle firing from somewhere nearby. I thought, "Ah, now we're getting someplace!" though I wasn't sure where. Minutes later I saw a man in street clothes with a scoped deer rifle in one hand and an Army surplus ammo can in the other, running in a crouch across Guadalupe toward the back of the architecture building, where he disappeared into bushes. I went back inside to find a safe route to the Academic Center, the only building between the Union and the Tower, and God help me if I didn't see a middle-aged man in a hunting cap and full camouflage hunting outfit, pockets bulging, standing in the Union's protected courtyard and squinting up at rooftops, apparently looking for a position from which to shoot. Later I heard some bizarre stories. A member of the Confederate Air Force antique-aircraft club in the Valley supposedly called the Department of Public Safety and offered to head north at full throttle in a World War II fighter, armed with privately owned .50-caliber machine guns. I somehow doubt that, but such a thing would not have been out of the question. Some friends of mine who were glued to a television set in the old San Jacinto Cafe a few blocks southeast of campus said that a man carrying a deer rifle rushed in, bought a six-pack of beer, and rushed back out.

About the only difference between police and citizens that day were uniforms and radios, and some cops had neither. Nobody seemed to know what to do except keep down, and I found out afterward that the officers on campus were angry and frustrated that no helpful suggestions were coming from headquarters, which had not even unlimbered the department's supply of fairly old .35-caliber rifles, which at least had the range. The only cops with useful weapons were those who went home and got them or those who came from home and brought them. One I knew, Lieutenant Burt Gerding, had headed for the campus with a .30-06

Army Springfield, scoped and sporterized from its World War I configuration, and several bandoliers of Army surplus armor-piercing ammunition. He took up a position on the roof of the business and economics building off the Tower's southeast corner and doesn't mind admitting now that before he got sighted in, the first shot went high and put the most conspicuous hole in the Tower clock's translucent glass face. After that, he hit a bag of cartridges that Whitman had set on the parapet and maybe one of Whitman's rifles, which appeared to have been struck by an armor-piercing bullet.

The ground fire was picking up, maybe a shot every five or ten seconds, which was causing me to think, "Just what we need—a bunch of loonies lobbing bullets all over the place, killing even more people." But I noted that as the ground fire increased, the shots from the Tower came less often. Peeking carefully upward from a corner of the Academic Center, I could see puffs around the Tower's parapet that were not smoke from the sniper's guns but bullets striking the soft stone, sometimes knocking out sizable chunks that seemed to waft slowly downward. At one point the shooting picked up in much the same way that kernels of corn begin to pop—sporadically for a time, then more and more often, until all of a sudden the popping blends into a roar before tapering off again.

I was trying to figure out what that barrage was all about when somebody pointed toward the mall in front of the Main Building, where a girl was stranded in the grassy area, squeezed behind the thick base of a flagpole, her face in her hands. A man's body was lying out there in the sun, cooking on the intensely hot concrete. Through the space between some large shrubbery I glimpsed someone running across the mall, fully exposed to the Tower. I found out later that some students had dashed out into the open, distances of twenty, thirty, maybe forty yards, to pick up the dead and wounded and carry them back out of range. The sniper wasn't firing because the fusillade from the ground was hitting the Tower's parapet like a slow-motion discharge from a giant shotgun.

I was watching part of this on live television in the basement of the Academic Center. One of the school's TV cameras had been rolled outside the door of some building and had been left there, unmanned, zoomed in on the top of the Tower and feeding a TV monitor in the lower level of the Academic Center. That was eerie—seeing the observation deck close up, seeing the little puffs of dust kicked out of the limestone by bullets, with the sound coming not from the TV but from outside, where it all was happening. A reminder of that was a wounded girl stretched out on a table in the same room. No one seemed to be looking after her when I walked in, so I asked if I could do anything or get her anything, and she shook her head no, as if she preferred to be left alone. I turned my attention to the TV and after a few minutes was perversely thinking that this show didn't have much action. Then, finally, something did happen—a piece of cloth waved briefly above the parapet, signaling the end.

I went outside to see maybe a thousand students emerging from everywhere and stampeding toward the Tower, nearly overwhelming several cops who were trying to keep them back. It crossed my mind that if the signal were a trick, the sniper had just cleverly replenished his supply of targets. But it was over, and I could hear a transistor radio calling for a halt to the ground fire on orders of the police. And now I was on the Academic Center breezeway, watching the crowd trying to turn itself into a mob, some overadrenalinized students starting to yell obscenities and words like "lynch" and "kill," as if more of that were needed. I found myself wanting to strike out at them as much as at whatever tortured creature had been in its death throes up in the Tower.

The accounts of Charles Whitman's death were pretty garbled at the time, and there was no way that those of us on the ground would understand what had just happened on the Tower. After the pilot of the small plane reported only one sniper, it seemed obvious to me that he had knowingly trapped himself, intending to die and to take with him as many others as possible. When the finale came, at about 1:25 p.m., it did so in a stroke that was at once a monument to official disorganization, dumb luck, and great personal courage.

The cops who had made it into the Main Building were trying to control the fairly panicky situation there, while others, deciding they were on their own, had taken the Tower elevator to the twenty-seventh floor, which gave access to the switch-back stairs leading two more flights up to the observation level. There they encountered new problems. Whitman, after lugging his gear up to the central reception area, had first killed the middle-aged woman who was well known to the campus for her insistence that everyone sign the visitors' register and not make jokes about jumping; then he had *not* killed a sight-seeing couple who came in from the outside walkway. Those two went on out, assuming that the man holding a gun who had cheerily said, "Hi, how are you?" was a school employee preparing to shoot pigeons. But six members of a tourist family who next came up were received with blasts from Whitman's sawed-off 12-gauge and four of them, two dead, were now lying on the stairs on top of one another in a great bloody mess.

Efforts to help those people and to push through the sniper's hastily erected barricades of furniture resulted in four men reaching the reception room at the observation level with no plan of action. Whitman was outside and unseen, but the sound of his shots seemed to be coming from the northwest corner of the outside walkway that circumscribed the clock tower. Luckily, that was exactly opposite the doorway leading outside, which was at the southeast corner.

The first man through the door was 29-year-old Ramiro Martinez, an officer who without discussion turned left and began working his way north along the Tower's east side, armed only with a revolver. Following him was Officer Houston McCoy, 26, armed with a revolver and a riot shotgun. Posted to guard the south side was a civilian, Allen Crum, the 40-year-old floor manager of the University Co-op bookstore who had asked to join the attack party; he was more or less deputized and given a rifle by a policeman downstairs. Joining him moments later was Officer Jerry Day, also acting as rear guard in case the sniper retreated in that direction.

Martinez and McCoy traversed the walkway on the east side of the building one after the other, hopping past drain spouts that were still funneling in bullets from the ground. Then, in a move of terrible courage that might now seem short on wisdom, Martinez leapt from cover and with one hand began firing his revolver at the young man with blondish hair who was backed into the opposite corner, about fifty feet away, holding a semiautomatic Army carbine. The carbine was swinging around to fire when McCoy delivered two bursts of double-aught buckshot to Whitman's head and neck, making up for the .38 bullets that appeared to be missing their target.

Later, neither cop went beyond a few clichés in trying to describe how it felt to climb over the dead and dying victims of a mass murderer and then confront the madman and his rifle face to face, but the psychic energy it took to do that thing displayed itself in ways that were not fully recorded in police reports. McCoy remembers that his colleague gave a war cry when Whitman was knocked backward by the blasts and that Martinez then slammed his empty revolver to the tiles, grabbed the shotgun from McCoy's hands, and ran to the still-jerking body to fire point-blank into its heart. After that he threw the shotgun down too hard to suit its owner and ran, shouting for the shooting to stop, toward the others on the walkway, who recognized him in time. Martinez doesn't recall being so rough on the guns but admits he was a bit rattled at the time and needed a hand getting back to the police station. That night he hid from the press at his brother's house, drinking an entire bottle of gin without—he said later—feeling its effects. McCoy stayed crouched by the body, searching it for identification, and spoke to it, warning it that if its spreading pool of blood ruined his boots he was going to heave it over the side. He likewise avoided reporters and spent the evening drinking.

Since neither cop claimed personal credit for killing Whitman, it went by default to Martinez, who was found more newsworthy by reporters pleased to have a genuine minority hero. He was widely honored and ended up a Texas Ranger, now stationed in New Braunfels. McCoy quickly faded from the picture and today works at a Boy Scout camp near Menard.

I t took time for the magnitude of August 1, 1966, to sink in and for the press to sort out what had happened. You don't get the biggest mass murder in the country's history very often, and whether this one qualified depended somewhat on definitions. Even the body count hinged upon the theological issue of a fetus that was killed but whose mother survived, and then there was the matter of Whitman's mother and wife, whom he had killed the previous night. Counting the latter and the fetus, the final toll came to 16 dead and 31 wounded, though it was possible that one or two others were treated for minor wounds at the height of the confusion and did not make the list. That Whitman, a 25-year-old architectural engineering student, was discovered to be a former altar boy and Eagle Scout provided delicious irony—the ugly duckling tale in reverse. That his marksmanship was astounding could be attributed to good Marine Corps training. Superficially he presented the image of a happily married college student and an all-American boy from the proverbial good family. But on closer examination, it turned out that his marriage wasn't happy, his family situation was thoroughly screwed up, and Whitman was a driven, pill-popping, self-flogging bully and all-around psycho with a talent for concealing it.

Exactly why Whitman snapped (and that seems to be the word) can never be known, but in the preceding weeks he had talked to a university psychiatrist about the emotional strain he was under, pressures that were building up, and his increasingly violent impulses, which apparently began to surface (or resurface) with the breakup of his parents' marriage a few months earlier. "I talked with a Doctor once for about two hours and tried to convey to him my fears that I felt come [*sic*] overwhelming violent impulses," Whitman wrote in a letter. "After one session I never saw the Doctor again, and since then I have been fighting my mental turmoil alone, and seemingly to no avail."

In fact, Whitman had told the psychiatrist that his urge was to go up on the Tower with a rifle and begin killing people. That was dismissed as fantasy, since thoughts of the Tower were not uncommon in the minds of troubled students, the doctor told a press conference the next day. I'm sure that's true, but I attended the press conference and was interested to see that the psychiatrist was the same one whom my wife and I had consulted independently a few months earlier when a pending divorce was causing us both some serious depression. My visit consisted mainly of listening to him talk on the telephone with the driller who was putting in a water well on his ranch, after which he gave me a prescription for Librium. My wife came back from her visit crying and said that after pretty much baring her soul, his advice to her was "Grow up." I won't hazard a guess as to what comfort and advice he gave Charles Whitman.

Whitman professed hatred for his rigid and authoritarian father in Florida, just as he expressed deep love for his wife and mother—feelings he described in remarkably lucid and introspective notes written the previous evening in the course of killing them both. In a letter dated "Sunday, July 31, 1966, 6:45 P.M." before his first step was even taken, the mixture of past and present tense suggests that a final decision had been made very recently by a compulsive man who placed great importance on following through:

I don't quite understand what it is that compels me to type this letter. Perhaps it is to leave some vague reason for the actions I have recently performed. I don't really understand myself these days. I am supposed to be an average reasonable and intelligent young man. However, lately (I can't recall when it started) I have been a victim of many unusual and irrational thoughts. These thoughts constantly recur, and it requires a tremendous mental effort to concentrate on useful and progressive tasks. . . .

It was after much thought that I decided to kill my wife, Kathy, tonight after I pick her up from work at the telephone company. I love her dearly, and she has been as fine a wife to me as any man could ever hope to have. I cannot rationaly [*sic*] pinpoint any specific reason for doing this. I don't know whether it is selfishness, or if I don't want her to have to face the embrassment [*sic*] my actions would surely cause her. At this time, though, the prominent reason in my mind is that I truly do not consider this world worth living in, and am prepared to die, and I do not want to leave her to suffer alone in it. I intend to kill her as painlessly as possible.

Similar reasons provoked me to take my mother's life also. . . .

At about that point in the letter, with his mother still alive in her apartment across town, Whitman remained true to his tightly scripted personality by scribbling in the margin, "Friends interrupted." The friends, a student and his wife, later described Whitman as acting "particularly relieved about something—you know, as if he had solved a problem." And he had. The exact nature of Whitman's madness is open to speculation— there were many family factors and possibly religious ones; there was a report of a small brain tumor whose possible effects are disputed. But most students of the mind would agree that he resolved some intolerable psychological conflict by turning over to his personal demon all responsibility for his actions and placing his skills at its disposal. With that came, evidently, the kind of relief psychiatrists and criminologists some- times see in prisoners for whom a single but exception- ally brutal killing has been the safety valve gone pop! Afterward those people confront their fate with an equanimity bordering on apathy. For them, death is only a further release—possibly the one they uncon- sciously sought all along but without Whitman's ability to turn it all into a prolonged drama. He returned to the letter and scribbled the matter-of-fact notation "8-1-66. Mon. 3:00 A.M. Both Dead."

Whitman spent the rest of the night and the next morning readying himself to depart life in a style reflecting the pressures that had been building for months, maybe years. He had several guns but bought two more, plus ammunition, without arousing suspicion, chatting amiably with clerks. Then he dressed in overalls, parked his car near the Main Building sometime after eleven in the morning and, giving the appearance of a maintenance man, dollied a duffel bag and a footlocker crammed with ordnance and supplies to the observation deck of the Tower. His encounter with the receptionist and the tourists may have caused him to miss the changing of classes at eleven, when the campus below him would have looked like a busy ant bed. About eleven-forty-five he fired his first shot from the parapet. An hour and a half later, he was killed.

I saw Whitman when they brought him out. When the shooting was over, my journalistic instincts revived, and I went to one of the back doors of the Main Building to avoid the crowd. The police, likewise avoiding the crowds at other doors, wheeled out a stretcher bearing the sniper's body under a blood-soaked sheet. My sense of time may be off, but it seemed as if they brought their bundle out quickly, as if they wanted it out of there before the mob could get to it.

I finished school in 1968, left Austin, and since then have worked in other cities, but the memories of that day are as lasting as the proofmarks on the barrel of a gun. I come back to Austin to visit friends and family, and I visit the UT campus often enough that it no longer affects me to walk around there, though I occasionally find myself idly figuring out the least-exposed route from one building to another. I don't actually go that way, of course. And I don't give more than a moment's thought to the things I saw and did that day. But if I'm walking from the Main Building across that wide concrete mall, say, or along one of the inner-campus drives, I can't quite shake an ever so slightly uneasy feeling that the Tower, somehow, is watching me.

                                                    (August 1986)

On August 5, 1966, four days after Charles Whitman's 96-minute rampage, a double funeral was held for him and his mother, Margaret, in Lake Worth, Florida. They are buried side by side. Though the University of Texas tower would always be associated with the Whitman massacre, it would take a series of suicides to close the observation deck in 1975. It remained off limits to the public for twenty-four years, until it reopened on September 15, 1999.

The Sins of
Walker Railey

LAWRENCE WRIGHT

Wife of anti-racist cleric is attacked, I read in the *New York Times* as I flew home from Los Angeles a few days after Easter. Margaret Railey, the 38-year-old wife of the Reverend Walker Railey of Dallas, was found beaten, choked, and unconscious on the floor of their garage when her husband returned from studying at the library shortly after midnight on April 22, 1987. The police had no leads in the case. "Dr. Railey, who is white, has been an outspoken critic of racial prejudice in this city," said the *Times*. According to the executive minister in Railey's church, Gordon D. Casad, Railey had received a series of threatening letters in the preceding weeks and had preached his Easter sermon wearing a bulletproof vest.

It took a moment for the realization to sink in that this bizarre episode had taken place in my very own church, the First United Methodist Church, on the corner of Ross and Harwood in downtown Dallas. This was the church I grew up in and angrily ran away from and retreated to on several guilty occasions. What I always had hated about my church was its instinctive fear of confronting society, but here was a minister who had spoken out against racial injustice and inequality in a city where such things are rarely said aloud. Here was a man threatened with death in that same sanctuary. And here was a man whose wife was strangled into what the doctors called a persistent vegetative state, for no other obvious reason than that someone wanted to punish Walker Railey for preaching the truth.

Was this Dallas? I asked myself. The open savagery of the Railey tragedy seemed oddly wrong in a city that is deeply preoccupied with appearances. From the beginning there was about the story a vague but haunting discordance.

And yet I was willing to believe that perhaps Dallas had returned to the racial violence of the fifties. Apparently Dallas worried about that too, for the next week the city was on its knees in prayer services and editorial self-reproach. It was a moment when people of various faiths and races stopped to pray for Walker and Peggy Railey and their two young children, Ryan and Megan. "Fight on, Railey family," cried the Reverend Daryll Coleman of the Kirkwood CME Temple Church in a rare gathering of the races at Thanks-Giving Square. "Fight on, soldiers of righteousness and truth. Thank God for today." The Baptists issued a statement that "the fact that a minister's clear stand against racial injustice and bigotry would jeopardize his life is an indicting commentary on our society." Rabbi Sheldon Zimmerman of Temple Emanu-El concluded that the Railey family had been "singled out because of his almost prophetic stance in regard to injustice in any form."

As Peggy lay in intensive care, hundreds of visitors came day after day to Presbyterian Hospital to pay homage to a woman few people knew well. The traffic was so great that volunteers from the church came to assist. Peggy's condition, at first critical, settled into an awful stasis. She was neither dead nor alive—it was as if she were waiting for some momentous resolution before she could either die or be released back into life. And as for her husband, his tragedy seemed unbearable. He had been the rising star of Methodism, as some called him, an electrifying preacher who had awakened the slumbering old church and infused it with his own extraordinary vigor. Now he was crushed by some unknown force too vast and heartless to be fended off by faith alone.

On the Sunday after the attack, the congregation of First Church returned to the sanctuary in a state of shock. There was an obvious show of security police, which added to the air of continuing menace. From the pulpit, Casad read a message from Railey, who remained in the hospital to be near his wife. "I do not know why senseless violence continues to pervade society, nor do I understand why the events of this past week took place," Railey's message said. "You have proven to me and all of Dallas that our church is a family. . . . I have been reminded once again that the breath of life is fragile but the fabric of life is eternal."

It is worth pausing to wonder at a city where a crime might assume such metaphorical power. When I was a child in the First Church, our minister, Robert E. Goodrich, Jr., used to speak about the "climate" of the city. It was one of his favorite sermons, one he turned to on that Sunday after John Kennedy came to town and became the 111th homicide of 1963: "There's no question about a relationship between physical climate and life. How about the spiritual and cultural climate of a neighborhood, a city, a home?"

In this allusive fashion Goodrich would imply that Dallas was not innocent of Kennedy's murder. There was something about the climate of the city that generated tragedy, that caused lightning to strike. Dallas is a city distinguished by clean, quiet, well-ordered suburbs; it is a pious town, with more than 1,200 churches and the highest-paid preachers in America. Many of the largest Protestant congregations in the world are in the Dallas–Fort Worth area, including seven of the top twenty churches in United Methodism. But all this piety and bustle hides another Dallas. It is number one among large American cities in the rate of overall crime. It has the highest rate of divorce. Dear Abby surveyed her readers last summer and concluded that Dallas–Fort Worth has more unfaithful spouses than any other region. One out of every six murders in Texas occurs in Dallas County. These grim figures describe the climate of the city today. Nevertheless, I felt hope and pride in a city that was painfully examining itself. It seemed to me that it was the special destiny of Dallas to have to grow through tragedy.

These were my thoughts until nine days after the attack. Then Railey locked himself in his hospital suite and ingested three bottles of tranquilizers and antidepressants, leaving a lengthy suicide note that said "demons" had been inside him for years and he was tired of trying to be good. By the time police broke in the following morning, he too had fallen into a coma. The focus of suspicion shifted from Dallas to Walker Railey himself. Civic introspection abruptly stopped: If Railey were guilty, then Dallas must be innocent. But

I wasn't so sure. It seemed to me that the Railey case went to the essence of Dallas, because it was a case of contrasting appearances. Who was Walker Railey—a holy, martyred minister or a depraved and perhaps insane villain?

Although First Church is not even the largest Methodist church in Dallas, it has a reputation of being the mother church of Methodism. Eight men who stood in this pulpit before Railey went on to become bishops; indeed, Railey's own election to the episcopacy was regarded as a certainty, perhaps as early as 1988, when he would have become one of the youngest bishops in the history of Methodism. Even his appointment as senior pastor of First Church in 1980 at the age of 33 was an "astonishment," according to eminent Methodist theologian Albert Outler: "He leapfrogged over two dozen of his elders who thought they were his equal." For ten years First Church had been losing members, as had many downtown churches all across the country, as had Methodism itself. "He breathed life into this church from his first sermon, when he literally blew into the microphone," remembers the choir director, John Yarrington, who became Railey's dear friend. Membership quickly increased, as did the budget, which more than doubled over the seven years that Railey held the pulpit.

New people came to First Church because they adored Walker Railey. "I've heard Harry Emerson Fosdick, Ralph Sockman, Ernest Fremont Tittle, and Norman Vincent Peale," says G. W. French, a lay leader in the church, "and I still feel that Walker Railey was the greatest pulpiteer I ever heard." For some of the older members, the personality cult they saw evolving around Railey took their breath away. Railey was a vigorous, outspoken advocate of certain social issues endorsed by the yuppie element, which had begun to make up a new, younger core of the congregation. He opposed capital punishment, supported equal rights for women and minorities, declared his ambivalence on the subject of abortion, and defended the rights of homosexuals. He preached an "open letter to President Reagan" calling for increased arms control. All of those stands, in the context of Dallas, seemed rather brave, although it is also true that many Methodist ministers in town had preached similar sermons, and Railey's social liberalism was pretty much what United Methodism had come to. Personal behavior, that is to say, morality and ethics, was rarely mentioned. Railey often inveighed against the disparity of great wealth and great deprivation that characterized the city, but he himself had grown comfortable with his $100,000 annual salary, his luxurious Lake Highlands home, and the many perks, favors, loans, and subsidies that come from being a high-steeple preacher in a wealthy Protestant congregation. For a young man who had grown up in the little western Kentucky farming community of Owensboro, the son of a sheet-metal worker, it had been quite a climb. "To a certain extent he was an existential man," observes Dallas city councilman Craig Holcomb, one of those who had been drawn to Railey's ministry. "He worked very hard and created who Walker Railey was going to be."

Because of the importance of First Church within the denomination, many of the congregation are ordained ministers who are retired or working in other areas of the ministry. Among that group Railey was a polarizing figure. The Reverend Howard Grimes, who taught Christian education at SMU's Perkins School of Theology for 33 years, calls Railey "one of the greatest, if not the greatest, Protestant preacher in the latter half of the twentieth century. He had become God for a lot of people and maybe me." The younger clergymen in the congregation—Railey's contemporaries—tended to look at him with less awe and with more than a little resentment. "His popularity at First Church was such for many people that they lost all sense that he had any imperfection," says Reverend Spurgeon Dunnam III, the editor of the *United Methodist Reporter.* Dunnam and Railey had jostled for power in the corporation that is buried inside the denomination. "The politics of the church are so subtle that only the most astute and discerning could understand what was going on. Walker was very analytical and perceptive; he took to that process very early. In the course of numerous different meetings it became clear to me his primary agenda was to be elected to the episcopacy as soon as possible. He campaigned for it by accepting speaking engagements here, there, and everywhere. He seemed incapable of saying no to serving additional outside responsibilities. His ambition was so completely unchecked."

Within a few years of his arrival at First Church, Railey had become one of the most prominent churchmen in town, rivaling even W. A. Criswell at the immense First Baptist Church a block away. "In the past, whenever something religious would come up, the press would ask Dr. Criswell what he thought of it. Pretty soon they stopped that and started asking Walker Railey," says the Reverend John Holbert, who taught

Railey Hebrew at SMU and who sings in the choir at First Church. Railey served as president of the Greater Dallas Community of Churches. He was on the United Methodists National Board of Global Ministries. He was selected to preach *Protestant Hour* sermons on a nationwide Christian radio network. Already his name was widely known among Methodists as a man destined not just for the bishop's chair but for something more—for greatness, in whatever form that might assume.

And yet there were extraordinary pressures that were at work and were already evident in Railey's personality. Several times he told Gordon Casad that the congregation at First Church "could never forgive even one bad sermon," so he slaved over his lessons, polished his delivery, choreographed his gestures, until each one of them was a characteristic Railey gem. Once, in the receiving line after the eleven o'clock service, a seminary student asked what it took to preach a sermon like the one he had just heard, and Railey answered candidly, "About thirty-five hours."

In a church with a congregation of nearly six thousand members and a $2 million budget, a pastor spends a considerable amount of time visiting hospitals, preaching funerals, counseling troubled youngsters, running administrative meetings, setting budget goals—it's a demanding occupation. Railey had a staff of 65 people to assist him, but just keeping the staff appeased was a full-time job. "He was the kind of preacher who knew everybody's name," says Diane Yarrington, John Yarrington's wife and Peggy Railey's closest friend. "He wrote hundreds of personal notes to people all the time—on your birthday you'd always get a handwritten note from Walker. He would make a special trip to a high school to see a play that one of the Sunday school children might be in. He spent hours and hours a day doing that kind of thing. And of course it wore him down."

Railey found in the church the loving family he himself had never known as the child of alcoholic and often neglectful parents. John Yarrington became "the older brother I never had." Howard Grimes was "a real father to me." Mrs. Knox Oakley was "my Dallas mother." It was typical of Railey to seek out such ersatz family members. He wanted to be loved and esteemed; he also wanted to return to his congregation the steady, attentive care he had craved as a young boy. By pouring that kind of love on the thousands before him, it was as if he were ministering to the angry and neglected child inside himself. He would not let them down, as he had been let down. When, in times of grief or trouble, a parishioner would stumble or his faith would fail, Reverend Railey was there—strong, certain, unwavering. His faith was a compass point by which others in the church could steer their fragile beliefs. In these ways Walker Railey became something larger than himself and, subtly, something other than himself.

Because behind the public face of this caring, highly blessed young man, with his beautiful wife, his charming children, his prestigious job, his important future, there was another Walker Railey. This was a man so besieged by the doubts and worries he held aside during the day that he seldom enjoyed an untroubled night's sleep. This was a person seen only occasionally by people close to him—his staff, for instance, who idolized him and were sometimes crushed by a volcanic temper that slept and slept then suddenly savagely erupted, usually over some small point such as the lighting in the sanctuary or the presentation of the budget. Nor were these eruptions followed by periods of remorse, which would have made them easy to forgive; instead, a certain cool satisfaction took hold of him. He would not call back the rain of shattering insults that led to tears or angry resignations. In the recent past when this other defiant, uncaring, self-centered Walker Railey had gained ascendancy, friends had talked him into seeing a psychiatrist, to help him "cope with the stress." Lately, however, when many of those closest to him had suggested that he go back to the psychiatrist, that he slow down, that he take a sabbatical, he had coldly cut them off.

When word of another Railey outburst circulated among the congregation, it was usually seen as more evidence of his temperamental genius. How insidious that must have seemed to him! Whatever fault he confessed to, whatever awful behavior he committed, only brought him new credit. Or perhaps—and this is the worst thing that can happen to a preacher, it is where he crosses the line between serving the forces of good and serving those of evil—perhaps he had begun to believe in his own perfection. Some of the other ministers in the congregation suspected that Railey had become one of those preachers who see themselves as God's special messengers, one of those who "become so convinced that they are so holy that they are above the standards they have to preach," as Spurgeon Dunnam observes. "The sin is to become as God, as one who would take God's place. Anytime a human being reaches that level he sets himself up for a fall."

O n Easter Sunday, three days before the attack on Peggy, Walker Railey preached what would be his last sermon. In the days to come, it would be reinterpreted in ways that no one in the congregation that morning could have imagined. On this holy day, which is set aside for hope, love, and rejoicing, the cast of characters who would figure in the tragedy were all in place in the sanctuary, about to begin a weird and—one could believe—demonic journey into a world of passion, violence, and madness. Just before the eleven o'clock service, the seventh of a series of threatening letters addressed to Railey was slipped under Gordon Casad's office door. "EASTER IS WHEN CHRIST AROSE, BUT YOU ARE GOING DOWN," the note said. There was already a police guard in the church, but the possibility that the author of those threats had walked unnoticed into the church offices left the staff and the police unnerved. They were even more surprised when an associate pastor, acting on a hunch, ran upstairs and typed out the same message on an IBM Selectric on the third floor. The typeface appeared to be the same. Whoever was sending the notes was probably a member of the congregation—perhaps even a member of the staff.

Railey, a medium-size, balding man with intense blue eyes, was pale and thin-lipped but apparently determined to preach. He borrowed an ill-fitting bulletproof vest from a woman police officer and strapped it on like a corset beneath his Easter vestments.

Few people in the congregation knew about the threats, but most sensed that something was wrong as soon as they entered the sanctuary. Councilman Holcomb noticed that Railey did not enter the procession behind the choir as he usually did. Instead, the choir came in alone, and the pastoral staff entered through a side door—without Railey. "I kept noticing these men standing beside the doors," Holcomb recalls. "I kept thinking I knew these men, but they're not from the church." Later he recognized Investigator Steve Torres as one of the officers who guard the city council. The congregation rose to sing the doxology, and when they sat down Railey abruptly appeared in the pulpit.

Looking out from the pulpit, he saw three thousand parishioners in their Easter finery, filling the sanctuary and spilling out into the hallway, where uniformed policemen had just arrived to guard the exits. It was no longer the predominantly elderly congregation that had greeted him on his first sermon in this pulpit seven years before. Who could deny that Walker Railey had put his stamp on this church and invigorated it with the force of his personality? And yet hovering over the sanctuary was a ghost that haunted Railey and would never let him feel entirely at home here; it was the ghost of Robert Goodrich. All the things Railey wanted, all the honors he sought, Goodrich had achieved. Goodrich had been elected bishop in 1972 and was succeeded in the First Church pulpit by Ben Oliphint, who also became a bishop eight years later. It was Goodrich with whom Railey was compared, however, and not always favorably. "In many ways I'll always consider that piece of wood up in front of the sanctuary as Bob Goodrich's pulpit," Railey would admit. Perhaps it was an act of charity or perhaps it was cleverness on Railey's part that he brought Bishop Goodrich back to Dallas in his final years of life, when he was ill and doddering, and placed him once again on the staff of his old church, where everyone could compare the frail old man with his lively young successor.

In the congregation on Easter morning was Bishop Goodrich's elegant widow, Thelma. I should note that she and her husband were close friends of my parents and that she is a woman whose dignity I have always admired. Thelma was sitting with Lucy, the second of her four children. Despite the mascara and frosted hair, one look at Lucy and you could see she was Bob Goodrich's daughter. She had that knotted Goodrich chin, his thin, drawn smile, and the dark eyes that were his most distinctive feature—eyes that seemed remote but also searching and intelligent. It was a strong face, like her father's, and if in some lights it appeared hard, in others you could detect a vulnerable and even wounded soul who had lived past the point where life surprised her. When she was younger, Lucy played the piano in the Sunday school class that my father taught. Now Lucy was 45, with two teenage children, but she was still slim and youthful, with the athletic carriage that was also a Goodrich legacy. She had been through two marriages before going off to California and becoming a clinical psychologist. She had come home to Dallas to set up a practice specializing in eating disorders. Along the way she acquired a new last name, one of her own invention: "Papillon," which means "butterfly" in French. Dr. Papillon once explained "the metaphor of the butterfly" to Reverend Railey when he interviewed her on *Faith Focus,* his weekly television show: "The caterpillar's crawling around, feels like the world's okay, but if they really want to fly, they've got to go through the darkest thing they've ever seen, which is the cocoon." According to the local press, soon after Lucy Papillon returned to Dallas, she became Walker Railey's mistress.

Mrs. Walker Railey sat in a pew halfway back, next to a woman police officer who happened to be a member of the church. It had become unusual to see Peggy in the congregation. Over the past year she had withdrawn from the choir and the children's Sunday school class that she taught, then from the board suppers and picnics and retreats, and finally from the main Sunday service. Walker explained her absence as illness or a need to be closer to five-year-old Ryan and two-year-old Megan. Although it was true that Peggy had suffered a bout of walking pneumonia earlier in 1987, she had recovered from that; and as for the children, other mothers in the congregation wondered why she couldn't leave them in the nursery, as they did. Peggy, however, always had seemed a remote personality—as introverted, friends said, as Walker was extroverted—so her retreat from church society was only partly noticed. "She was certainly much less visible than any other pastor's wife I've ever seen," says a member of the pastoral staff.

Later, while she lay in the hospital, fighting for the marginal edge of life that had been left her, people would describe Peggy as cool and distant, but to those few who she had allowed to know her well, she was a warm and devoted friend. The pictures that would appear in the newspaper did her no justice, because Peggy Railey was quite a beautiful woman. Where Lucy was strong and stylish, Peggy was frail and demure, but with a natural attractiveness, much like a fresh-faced milkmaid of her native Wisconsin. Peggy had a lovely singing voice—she was a second soprano—although her true talents were in her fingers. She had studied organ at SMU, obtaining a master's degree, and she might have pursued a career as a professional musician if she hadn't chosen to give herself over to the humbler role of being a minister's wife. In March, after she had recovered from her illness, she succumbed to friends' urgings and gave a small lunchtime harpsichord recital at the church, with John Yarrington joining her at the end of the program to sing a Bach cantata. She appeared wan and there was a new hollowness about her cheeks, but in many respects she had never been more lovely. And yet what was most striking about this performance was Peggy's trancelike behavior; she played robotically, and when the audience applauded her, she gave a sudden startled smile. Where was she? She seemed to be in some faraway sad place. Later people would remember that performance and wonder if Peggy had known about Lucy.

Another of Peggy's talents was sewing. She had made many of the elegant seasonal stoles that the ministers wore over their robes—Walker was wearing one now, a white stole with the Greek letters alpha and omega appliquéd on either side. Beneath the stole was Walker's black robe, and under the robe was his suit jacket, and under the jacket was the bulletproof vest, so as Walker stood in the pulpit his first action was to mop his bulbous forehead with a handkerchief.

He began his sermon with a discussion of a book written in 1965 called *The Passover Plot.* The premise of the book was that the Crucifixion had been faked. Of course Railey went on to dismiss *The Passover Plot*—"If there's ever a day you have nothing of substance to do, and you want nothing of substance to read, it would be a fine book to peruse." Perhaps he was only using the book as a provocative introduction to the standard Easter rejoicing; the questions that he was posing about Jesus, however, were exactly the same ones that would later be asked of him. Was he truly a martyr—the man who was now standing in Bob Goodrich's pulpit in a bulletproof vest, the man whose life for the next two weeks would be a march of catastrophe, from the attack on Peggy, followed by Walker's evasive testimony to the police, and culminating in his attempted suicide? Or was he orchestrating his own martyrdom, creating a myth of himself that would raise him higher and make the drama of his own small life into something grander, something divine?

One scarcely could call me an objective reporter. From the moment I got into the story, I had trouble holding on to my neutrality. I bullied my way into an interview with Railey's bishop, who said that I was "beneath contempt." I told preachers who refused to speak to me about the case that they were sanctimonious hypocrites. I excoriated the staff of First Church for not confronting the evil that had taken place in their own sanctuary. My behavior was hard to excuse and hard to explain.

In part it was anger at Dallas, a city where pious public faces often hid secret dirty appetites. But Dallas was an old war of mine, one that I had grown tired of fighting, to the point that I had subsided into an exhausted peace on the matter. The truth was that like any old contestant I had begun to sentimentalize the battles of my youth and had become grateful to Dallas for helping me learn who I am.

More than Dallas, there was Methodism. I have seen friends struggle to throw off the narrow-minded strictures of Southern Baptism or the ritualistic magic of Catholicism or the tribal creeds of Judaism. I have encountered religion in extreme forms, from Hare Krishnas and Amish farmers to snake-handling charismatics. And yet, with all my ambivalence about religion, what I feel about people who believe or disbelieve such stringent doctrines is a low-grade envy, for at least a hard-shell Baptist has the literalism of the Bible to react against, a Catholic has the pomp and mystery of the liturgy, and so on, but a Methodist struggles in a fog, not really knowing what is to be believed or disbelieved but learning in a subliminal way what is to be avoided.

I could not fairly hold Methodism responsible for the values of this city, because despite the fact that Dallas is a stronghold of United Methodism, only 7 percent of the population belongs to the denomination, a figure that represents less than half the number of Southern Baptists and is even behind the Catholics. This fact doesn't alter my opinion that Methodism is the state religion of corporate America, of which Dallas is the purest and most fervent example. Methodism began in the slums of eighteenth-century London and the British coalfields, where John Wesley began his ministry to the underclass. It settled the American frontier in the form of the lonely, tireless circuit rider. And thus it took root in an ambitious, desperately poor frontier people, and it grew with them as their cities grew, as their generations prospered, as their politics and their values changed. So had the church grown and prospered and changed, becoming essentially the same institution its founder had rebelled against.

Yes, I was angry at Methodism because I thought it had turned into Nothingism and was only in business to stay in business. My particular quarrel with Methodism began here in First Church, however, where for so much of my adolescence I had felt confused and bewildered and overlooked. It had seemed to me then that the special quality of my church was to float above the real world of lust and violence, passion and broken hearts, in a higher atmosphere of untroubled Christian behavior. Human failings were seldom addressed. I recall when the assistant pastor left his family and ran off to Colorado with a ski instructor. His name was never mentioned again. All that remained of him was some intoxicating vapor of sin and forbidden desire—an intimation of another world I was not supposed to know about. The church was like a timid old woman hiding behind shutters, shielding herself from confusion.

I had seen Walker Railey preach on Christmas Eve, 1984, when I was back in Dallas to see my parents. It was a tormented moment for me, a time when I had been confounded by my own behavior and eager to seek forgiveness. In that raw condition I experienced what so many would later speak of: the sensation that Railey was preaching to me, that those large and expressive blue eyes that swept across the sanctuary like a searchlight were looking for me.

Now, after the attack on Peggy Railey, I had come back inside the old sanctuary, had listened to another sermon that refused to acknowledge what had happened within the church's own family. Week after week had passed with one revelation after another and only the most oblique references from the pulpit about what was transpiring in the world beyond the stained glass windows. Nothing was said of Railey's attempted suicide. Nothing was said of the sensational revelations of Lucy Papillon's grand jury testimony, in which she talked about their affair, which had gone on for more than a year, their marriage plans, and their assignations "while he was out preaching"—they had even arranged to meet in England when Railey returned from a World Methodist Council meeting in Nairobi. Nothing was said of Railey's refusal to cooperate with the police or his decision to plead the Fifth Amendment before the grand jury. The church was in a state of delirium ("We're fine, the church is fine, everything's going to be fine," a member of the board assured me). I fought an impulse to stand up and shout Walker Railey's name out loud.

On the night of April 21, 1987, at 6:30 in the evening, Railey drove into the family garage. He says he found his wife working on a garage door latch with a bar of soap. The spring on the latch had been sticking, and Peggy was trying to lubricate it. According to Railey, he sat on the hood of Peggy's Chrysler for a few minutes, talking to his wife. She and the children already had eaten dinner, and Walker wasn't hungry, so the two of them shared a glass of wine. He then left, still in his business suit—ostensibly to spend the evening at the SMU libraries to write footnotes for his book on preaching.

At 6:38 Railey called the time from his car phone.

Everyone knew that Railey did not wear a watch; he had given it up when he came to First Church, partially because of his habit of wearing French cuffs, which frayed when he kept pushing up his sleeve to check the time. The phone had just been installed that day, at church expense. It was another of the many security measures the church provided him, including a home alarm system and a separate private telephone line. Railey says he spent the next thirty minutes at Bridwell Library at the theology school, searching for a biography of Anne Sullivan, Helen Keller's teacher. At 7:26 he was back in his car, calling Janet Marshall, a family friend who was going to baby-sit for the Railey children while Walker and Peggy went to San Antonio for the weekend. At 7:32 he called Lucy Papillon, then drove to her house, where he stayed for about forty minutes. He says he went there to get some relaxation tapes to help relieve his stress.

A librarian at Bridwell remembers seeing Railey sometime after eight, when the minister asked what time the library closed. At 8:30 Railey called Peggy from a pay phone, and she told him she was putting the children to bed. After that Peggy talked to her parents in Tyler until 9:14. Meanwhile, Railey had left the library. He purchased gas at a Texaco station on Greenville Avenue at 8:53 and also bought a wine cooler, which he says accounts for the fact that the police would later report him as intoxicated when they came to his house four hours later.

At 9:30 a jogger saw a man in a business suit running through a yard two streets away from the Raileys' house. Between 10:15 and 10:30 a neighbor heard rustling noises in the alley behind the Raileys' house.

Railey says he had gone to the Texaco station because he was thirsty and had returned to his research in the main library. The police say they have indisputable evidence that he was lying about his whereabouts from the time he left the Texaco station until a librarian saw him sometime between 11 and midnight. At midnight Railey attempted to give his business card to a Nigerian student at the checkout desk. On the back of the card was a message to the research librarian, asking for help in finding the Sullivan biography. He had also written the time, which was noted to be 10:30.

After leaving the library Railey phoned his home from his car, but this time he called the listed line, which was connected to an answering machine and did not even ring in the house. "I don't have my watch on," said the man who never wore one, "but it's about ten-thirty or ten-forty-five." Telephone company records show that the call was actually made at three minutes after midnight. "If you want to, go ahead and lock the garage door, and I'll park out front." At 12:29 he called his answering machine again, giving the correct time and saying he was on his way home. The theory of Railey's guilt presumes that Peggy was strangled sometime around 10:30 and that the calls were meant to establish both an alibi for himself and a reason for Peggy to go to the garage.

Eleven minutes after the second call Railey drove into the driveway and found the garage door partly open. The garage was dark; mysteriously, the bulbs had been removed from the overhead light of the automatic door opener. Railey said he left his headlights on and got out of the car. He found Peggy lying behind her Chrysler, writhing in convulsions. Her face was hugely swollen and discolored, yet her hair was scarcely mussed and her glasses were in place. At 12:43 a police dispatcher received a call from Railey, who said, "Uh, I just came into the house, and my wife is in the garage. . . . Somebody has done something to her." The dispatcher inquired, "Has she been beat up or what?" "I don't know," Railey replied. "She's foaming at the mouth or something."

"The phone rang about twelve forty-five," says Diane Yarrington. "It was Walker. He said, 'Diane, something awful has happened to Peggy. Come quick, come right now.' We literally raced over there. By the time we got there, the ambulance had arrived. Walker was inside holding Megan. Ryan was sort of sitting on the couch. I talked with Walker briefly, and then I said, 'I'll take the children,' and I asked the kids what they wanted to take with them. They each grabbed a pillow and a stuffed animal. Walker said, 'Don't leave me.' And John said, 'I'll be here. I'm like your second skin.'"

John Yarrington accompanied Walker to the hospital, and after he had gotten his friend settled, he went to speak to the doctors. "I did not know what had happened. I knew she had been hurt, but I didn't know how," he says. "At that point the doctors' assessment was that Peggy's neck had been broken. And I asked how would that happen? 'Well, she was strangled.' That was the first I knew."

John went into the emergency room where Peggy lay. "It's a terrible thing to see; it's Technicolor in my brain. I'll never forget her lying on that table, with that blotchy color, a terrible color, a terrible thing to see on someone you love."

For most of the seven years the Yarringtons had known the Raileys, they had been the closest of friends. Diane and Peggy were like sisters. They spoke several times a day on the phone and sat next to each other in the choir. Peggy accompanied John's rehearsals every Sunday night. Walker had been John's boss and also his spiritual guide and soul mate. Several months before the attack on Peggy, the couples had pledged that if anything were to happen—if one of the couples were to die in a plane accident or some other tragedy would befall them—then the other couple would take care of their children. John had made the pledge in all sincerity, but who could believe that so suddenly and so grotesquely it would come due?

The next day Railey went to the police station with a lawyer friend to talk to investigative officer Rick Silva. It is the only time Railey has talked to the police. His story then was that he had come home, spoken briefly to Peggy while she was working on the garage door latch, then spent the rest of the evening in the libraries. He said he had no idea who might want to harm her, except for the author of the anonymous letters. Silva indicated that he would like to set up a polygraph examination, and Railey said he would be happy to cooperate.

During the next week the police learned about the telephone call to Lucy, they listened to the tape on Railey's answering machine, they discovered a credit card slip from the Texaco station, and they examined the garage door, which seemed to work fine. They found no evidence that the latch had been lubricated; in fact, they learned that the Raileys had complained to the manufacturer and had had a new automatic door opener installed only a few days earlier.

In the meantime Railey stayed in his hospital suite, meeting friends and going through the mail. Lucy came to visit him, carrying a single red rose. One day he received telegrams from both Jesse Jackson and Billy Graham, and he went in to tell Peggy she had made "ecclesiastical history." She looked at him with open, unseeing eyes. Her brain was damaged but not dead. What she comprehended no one could even guess. Friends played videos of her harpsichord concert and papered her room with pictures drawn by Ryan and Megan. There was some hope, in those early days, that something inside Peggy would stir to life.

"Peggy, it's Diane." Peggy's face was still puffy and discolored the first morning Diane Yarrington got to see her. "The children are with me. It's just fine. It's all right." A tear rolled out of Peggy's eye. Later others would see her crying—Walker did, even Detective Silva—and they would wonder what she knew or felt. The truth was locked inside Peggy and could never be expressed, but that did not mean that it couldn't be experienced. What an unendurable tragedy that would be, to be alone with the truth.

The inconsistencies and omissions in Railey's story had accumulated to the point that Silva telephoned the hospital and told the officers guarding Railey's room that he wanted to question Railey. When they went to his room they found the door locked. They broke in and found Railey's unconscious body and his suicide note.

Once again John Yarrington would be standing in the same emergency room, this time over Walker's body as doctors pumped the drugs out of his stomach. Fortunately, Walker had not taken all the pills that were on his bedside table. Like Peggy, he had fallen onto that ledge of deep unconsciousness between life and death. Unlike her, he had not suffered a loss of oxygen and glucose to the brain, which doctors said probably would prevent her from recovering. She was wrapped in a cocoon from which few ever emerge.

For the next five days Walker lay in intensive care in a room opposite Peggy's. "It was bizarre and weird," says John. "You would go to your left to see Walker and go to your right to see Peggy. They essentially looked much the same." On the Wednesday after the Friday he had attempted suicide, Railey awakened, and the first thing he remembers is seeing his friend standing vigil at his bedside. He had absolutely no recall of anything. It was two more days before he fully resurfaced. Railey asked John then whether he could regain the pulpit. John was startled by the question. "I think it's very iffy," he said. Walker seemed surprised and wanted to know why. "Well, number one, you tried to commit suicide. And number two, a lot of people think you strangled Peggy."

The police had enough evidence to disbelieve Walker Railey but not enough to charge him. After he got out of the hospital, Railey checked into Timberlawn Psychiatric Center while his attorney, Doug Mulder, arranged for him to take a privately administered polygraph. The test indicated that Railey did not attack his wife and did not know who did. The next day at the police department Railey took a polygraph which proved inconclusive, although Railey "showed deception" about the threatening letters. Mulder and Railey arranged for a third polygraph, the results of which they have never made public. Norm Kinne, the frustrated chief criminal prosecutor in the district attorney's office, convened a grand jury investigation and warned Railey in front of television cameras to either "come before the grand jury" or "leave the country"—an odd injunction to be directed at the main suspect in the case. Railey appeared and took the Fifth Amendment 43 times. No indictments were handed down, but so much of the testimony was leaked to the press that it appeared that the grand jury was called for no other purpose than a public shaming of Walker Railey.

With the justice system at an impasse, a group of Methodist clergymen wrote a letter to Bishop John Russell, asking for a church inquiry into Railey's relationship with Lucy. The bishop began a lengthy private negotiation with Railey. On September 2 Railey surrendered his credentials, which voided the church's jurisdiction over him. That meant there would be no embarrassing church trial, but it also meant that Peggy's insurance would lapse after twelve months. In October Railey signed over guardianship of Peggy to her parents, who had placed Peggy in a Tyler nursing home. Peggy's father says that Railey has visited his wife "three or four times—that's about it." The Railey children continue to live with the Yarringtons.

I knew I was going to meet with Walker Railey because periodically he emerged from seclusion to proclaim his innocence to reporters and give his own version of the tragic events. The meetings were highly circumscribed, and when Railey finally answered one of my messages, I agreed to the same conditions: We would not talk about the case, and we would not talk about Lucy. "Are you a coffee drinker?" Railey asked cheerfully on the phone. He said he would have a pot waiting for me when we met in the morning in his Lake Highlands home.

There was no For Sale sign in front of the white brick house on Trail Hill Drive, although the house was on the market for $279,000. The sole business that was keeping Walker Railey in Dallas was the need to dispose of his property. He had gone through the police, the grand jury, the bishop, and the local reporters, and there remained only me.

Railey opened the door and greeted me. The house was comfortable and spacious, with the sun glinting off the pool in the back yard and making wrinkled shadows on the living room ceiling. Perhaps it was simply the absence of family detritus—toys and books and newspapers—that made the house seem so impersonal. Outside it was warm, but the house was unaccountably chilly—"like a mausoleum," as Railey observed while we sat at his kitchen table, drinking coffee.

He had been monitoring my presence ever since I had arrived in Dallas two weeks before. "I know that you have a couple of layers of subjectivity that are influencing your writing of this story, one having to do with your opinions about me and one having to do with your inner quarrels with the institutional church," he told me, quite accurately. I realized that we had been stalking each other with a growing sense of recognition and mission. His mission, old and by now habitual, was to get me to believe in the church—and in himself.

Mine was to tear away the many veils of falsity and hypocrisy and get to the truth, whatever that was.

He already knew who I was. But did anyone, even Walker Railey, know who he was? "I get depressed," he admitted. "I see my psychiatrist twice a week and have been doing that since May, and he helps me look inside myself." He spends his days now reading the psalms, playing golf occasionally, "trying to let my soul and my body get together." A few days before, he had enjoyed "kind of a joyous highlight" because he had played golf with former district attorney Henry Wade. "It was a fun time. And I thought he showed personal sensitivity to me." Railey said he was worried about the future, about his prospects for a job. "For the first time in my life, at forty, I have no earthly idea what, where, when, how, or anything else. So there's an element of fear."

He spoke of his ambition. "Most of the reports have written that I was drooling on my tie waiting to become a bishop, but that's not entirely true." Bishops are elected for life, he pointed out, and "you can only bless the opening of Sunday school units so many times until you get tired." His secret ambition was to stay at First Church another decade, then take early retirement and go to law school, so he could set up a practice in South Dallas to defend underprivileged minorities. I regarded that statement as gratuitous and unlikely; on the other hand, I never did understand the appeal of being a bishop.

"I had three books coming out in '88," Railey was boasting. "I was speaking all over the nation. I had been the *Protestant Hour* preacher—I'd just finished taping the sermons." Under Railey's tenure First

Church had become "one of the real turnaround stories in the nation." Everything that he had been working for was coming to fruition. "So you know, I was beginning to feel that my future was okay, but I was trying to get out of the future and more into the present—maybe for the first time in my life."

"And now, all that's lost to you," I observed. "You've resigned from the church, the books have been put on hold, your family has broken apart, and your future is in serious question. You're a man who's suffered tremendous losses. Why do you think this has happened to you?"

This question had been given to me by psychologists I had consulted, on the premise that Railey might be insane. If he is, he has done enough psychological consultation of his own to dodge the paranoiac response. "I've always tried to avoid asking 'why' questions because I don't think 'why' questions get you anywhere," he said, giving me his most defiantly honest stare. "If I'm asking any question, it's how I can feel the presence of God's healing power in my life right now, when, for the first time in my life, I can't even tell you where I'll be tomorrow."

He began to recount the events of Tuesday, April 21, leading up to the discovery of his wife's attack. "I went to the library and started at Bridwell down on the south part of the campus." He was checking footnotes for his book of sermons. When he finished there, he "walked up to Fondren," the main library. "On the way to Fondren I stopped by Lucy's house"—which is directly behind the campus—"for about forty minutes and back to Fondren after getting a Coke at a Texaco station and filling up the car. Worked at Fondren until a little after midnight, about twelve-fifteen or so, I had called Peggy to let her know that I was on the way. And I got home about twelve-thirty. I came into the garage and found her."

Until that point he had told the story in a rapid, shorthand manner—so fast that I completely missed the contradiction between his "walking" to Fondren and filling up his car with gas. He had said he would not talk about the case, and obviously he wanted to skate past this portion. I thought to myself: Here's a man who has avoided the police and the grand jury. I can't let him get by me that easily.

"The police said you had been drinking that night."

"Peggy and I had a glass of wine," he said.

"At what time?"

"Quarter of seven. And I had a wine cooler when I stopped at the Texaco."

"I thought you said you had a Coke at the Texaco."

"I said 'Coke' but that was just a Coke break, a coffee break," he replied. "I went up there to get something to drink. I refer to that as 'getting a Coke.'"

He would not be trapped. He started to talk again about finding Peggy. "Come here, I want to show you," he said, with a certain demanding eagerness. "I want you to see." We walked into the garage, which was large and empty of cars. Against the back wall were several storage closets. "I want you to understand that there's a freezer, there's a refrigerator, and there are toys that the children use, like the tricycle," Railey said, pointing out the clutter of an ordinary suburban family, which lined the side of the garage. "In the evening it was not uncommon—six, seven or eight times a night—for one of us to come out here." He showed me the latch he said Peggy was working on early in the evening of her attack. Somehow it had gotten bent. "How it got bent, I don't know." Railey's voice, even though it was nearly a whisper, reverberated in the vacancy of the garage. "Anyway, when I pulled in, the door was about up to here"—he indicated the height of his knee—"and Peggy was right here."

She would have been just behind her Chrysler, between her tool closet and the door that led into the house. As Railey explained how Peggy's body was oriented—"heels here, head here"—I thought what an intimate crime strangulation is, what a gruesome and prolonged dance. "I was actually horrified," Railey was saying. "I have never seen any such thing. Let alone my wife. Her face was purple and bloated, and her body was heaving from the waist up. Those were reflex actions, seizures, I later came to realize. I tried to shake her, tried to get some kind of response . . . and I couldn't get anything and ran in and checked on the children. Megan was lying down in front of the television." We walked back into the house. The family TV sat beside the picture window that looked out on the pool. "The TV was on and muted and she was on the floor and my first impression was that she was dead. I picked her up and she said, 'Daddy.' She had her little fingers in her mouth, and she was okay. She had evidently gotten up, looking for Mommy, and the TV was on and she laid down in front of the television."

"Had she found her mother?" I asked.

"I don't think so, but I don't know." We went through the living room to the children's rooms. "This is Ryan's room," Railey said. The room was still filled with Ryan's dolls and toys. "His bed's been moved over to the Yarringtons," Railey explained, "but his bed was here, and he was three fourths of the way asleep but kind of in a fog."

That was, I remembered, well after midnight, when the children would ordinarily be sound asleep. Perhaps the assailant had thought, as I did, that strangulation is a silent crime, but who knows how Peggy may have fought, what kind of racket she might have made. Did she wake the children? The awfulness of that scene played unhappily in my mind, along with the dreadful suspicion that the person who caused this tragedy was the same polite preacher who was giving me the tour of his home.

"So anyway," Railey continued, "I came in and called the police. I called the Yarringtons and I went across the yard and got my neighbor and he came over. He stayed with Peggy. I brought the children into the den, sat them down on the sofa with me and held them. Both were extremely quiet, 'cause they could obviously pick up on my panic. I was hyperventilating and scared to death."

Railey and I went up to his special lair on the second floor. As a writer, I have a particular interest in the places people make for themselves to write in. Two walls were covered with floor-to-ceiling bookshelves. There was an imposing desk of the sort that would belong to a bank vice president, and a more modest work area with a computer. One of Railey's manuscripts sat on the table. Under a dictionary stand was a copy of *The Plays of Eugene O'Neill*. It was a handsome office, but once again I noticed an absence of personal effects. Only two items in the room caught my eye. One was an SMU basketball on the window ledge behind

Railey's desk. He had bought the house from an SMU coach, it turns out, and had written into the contract that a basketball would come with the house. The other item was a three-foot-tall doll that resembled Big Bird. Railey said he had bought the doll for Ryan when he was in New York, and he recounted the spectacle of himself walking through the lobby of the Waldorf-Astoria with the doll under his arm. I laughed, but it struck me as curious that Railey, not Ryan, had the doll now. Railey sat in his easy chair, and I sat on a couch beside him.

"Tell me about your relationship with Peggy."

"Well, we'd been married sixteen years. Peggy was a lot quieter than me. We had a respect for one another. We were not the kind of couple that held hands and watched television on the sofa. When we went on vacation, before the children came, and went out on the beach, we'd both take a book and read and listen to the sea gulls and watch the waves.

"We were married eleven years before we had children, and once the children came, we became more and more committed to parenting. Peggy had a great love for the church, and the impression that she didn't enjoy being the pastor's spouse and stuff I think is unfair to her. She was a private person and didn't talk a lot about the inner parts of herself. I think her best friend on the face of the earth was her mother. I don't know how else to answer. We didn't have a lot of arguments."

"Did she know about your affair?"

"We—that never came up."

"She didn't know?"

"I can only say it never emerged."

"Did she suspect?"

Railey took a steadying breath. "I have no way of knowing, regarding that, that she suspected at all, about anything."

I knew I was crossing the line he had drawn. I started to press further, but he cut me off. "I've told you I would not talk about Lucy," he said.

"Do you plan to divorce Peggy?"

"That is not a question I will answer."

I observed that because of his stature in the community both the church, through the bishop, and the city, through the district attorney, had advised Railey to leave town to avoid being an embarrassment to them. "I guess you could interpret it like that," he said. "They don't really have to ask me to leave. I just feel like I got in a situation, and it's time for me to go."

"Would Lucy join you?"

"I don't care to answer that."

"You're going to California?" I asked. Friends of his had said that was his plan.

"No, not necessarily. I'm looking for a place to work, Larry."

More than once, Railey asked me for information about my business, which was unsettling to me because I already felt a greater sense of identification with him than I cared to feel. Several times he had even urged me to "push harder," to do a better job—the job he might have done on me if our roles had been reversed. We were the same age. In many ways the difference between writing and preaching was not so great; nor, really, was the difference between belief and disbelief—it was the intensity of the struggle that mattered. The lesson I had drawn from Walker Railey's life so far was that good and evil are not so far apart either.

They were both inside Walker Railey, warring for control—as they were in me as well. Whether or not Railey was guilty, he had caused me to look in myself and see the lurking dangers of my own personality.

"I'm surprised you haven't asked about my suicide attempt," he said, once again presuming on my role. He talked about it and began to cry. I found myself curiously removed. I began to tabulate the times he had cried so far. He had cried when he talked about the death of Bishop Goodrich. "What I was aware of"—here is the point that he cried—"was the death of tradition." He came close to crying when he spoke about having to leave this office we were in, which was dear to him. He had cried when I asked him about his recent return to First Church for a memorial service for his baby-sitter, Janet Marshall, who had suddenly died of lupus in September. "When I walked back into the sanctuary," he had said, "the first thing I saw was the pulpit, and I just kind of stood in the back, really, and at that point kind of lost consciousness of what was going on around me." Later in the day, when we were at lunch, he would cry when he remembered his neglected childhood. I didn't question the genuineness of those responses. These were real losses—of his tradition, his comfortable home, his profession, his childhood, and nearly his very life. But they seemed—what? Was it fair of me to compare his losses against Peggy's? against his children's? Why didn't he cry for them?

What interested me about his suicide attempt was the note he left behind, in which he had spoken of demons. In First Church there had been much speculation about what Railey's demons might have been—perhaps sex,

certainly ambition. This is the usual Methodist metaphorical construction of biblical language. I asked
Railey what demons meant to him.

" 'Demons,' " he said, "that's just not, that's just
not a word I use a lot. I've talked to you about depression, that's a demon. I've talked to you about a low
self-esteem, that's a demon. I've talked to you about a
great fear over the uncertainty of the future, that's a
demon. And there may be a lot more demons, but my
point is that several things I've struggled with would
fall under the category of demons."

"And yet your very first sermon was 'On Seeing
Satan Fall,' " I reminded him. "I wonder what your
opinion of Satan is. Is he a figurative creature or a real
force?"

"Well, first of all, I preached 'On Seeing Satan Fall'
because that was taken directly out of the text of the
Scripture. It was a sermon on the church. I do not see
Satan as some incarnated presence in life—who's over
against God and therefore the two are in a battle and
we're kind of little pawns in the game. That makes me
less responsible for my own actions. I think there is
evil in the world and I think there is goodness in the
world and I think that both the inclinations of good,
which would be godliness, and the inclination to evil,
which would be satanic, are inside of us."

"But you don't think that at any point in your life
you were controlled by forces that you couldn't—"

"No, no, I don't," he said abruptly. "I think that's a
theological and a psychological cop-out."

Railey turned the conversation back to the church,
back to the moment when he had stood in the rear of
the sanctuary at Janet Marshall's service. Several years

before, when Janet's illness flared up, she had summoned her pastor to her hospital room and demanded to know what he was going to preach when she died. She had him actually write out a sermon and read it to her. "Her death became the first occasion that I was not able to do something in an ordained way that I would have done," Railey remarked. Instead, he had slipped into the church at the last moment, hoping no one would see him but knowing that everyone expected him to be there. "There were some people who, I think—I can't be sure of this—but there were some people who went out of their way because they didn't know what to say. But there were a whole lot more people who did. They just squeezed, hugged, kissed, slapped me on the back. They could feel my pain," he said, crying again. "I wasn't able to conceal it; I wasn't trying to. I think everybody knew that I was there under a great price, just emotionally, to walk into that sanctuary. So there was a great combination of pain but also a sense of joy that the community was there, and I felt its love."

"Did you feel a sense of shame?" I asked.

Railey looked at me sharply. He is, of course, alert to insinuation. "I felt, probably, every emotion you could feel."

"But did you feel ashamed?"

"I felt a great need to be forgiven, if that's what you're talking about."

When he said this, it seemed to me as much of a concession as I was likely to get. We were still talking in generalities and metaphors—Methodistically, as it were—but I had the feeling that we were nearing the truth, as much as I was likely to see of it. On the other hand, perhaps I was merely twisting his words, finding more meaning than was really there.

"I felt a great need to . . . to . . . to be reaccepted," Railey offered.

"As who you really are?" This was a leap on my part.

"As who I really am," he agreed. "As someone who never wants to lose being part of the community that the church represents."

"And having had that experience, do you feel now that if you"—here I searched for another word, but none would come—"I'm going to use the word 'confess' to whatever you are not talking about now, that they would forgive you?"

"That's a pretty leading question."

"It's a hard question to ask."

"That . . . that really . . . you—that I wish you would ask it another way," Railey said, "because I'm not going to answer it like that. It's just too . . . it's too much of a setup."

I tried to think of another way to ask, but he cut me off. "Let me just make a statement," he said. "I was aware that night of the love that permeated the sanctuary—God's love—in their lives. God's love is both a judging love and a forgiving love; it's both a healing and a haunting love. And I experienced God's love in all four ways that night. Okay? And I think that's about the way I would say it."

Before I left, Railey wanted to know what I thought of him. "I don't know what your impression is, and you don't have to give it to me, but I've been real honest with you today," he said.

I admitted that I found myself relating to him, but I

also said that I could not construct an innocent man out of his behavior. I recounted his misleading testimony to the police, his avoidance of the grand jury, his inexplicable actions on the night of Peggy's attack, and so on. "I think you're a guilty person," I said.

"I hear what you're saying," he said.

Here he was, reflecting my feelings, while I was accusing him of trying to murder his wife. I didn't know what to think.

"I appreciate your even responding to that," Railey continued. "I'm aware that nobody can sit down with all the facts that are supposedly known . . . and just make it all fit. That's a frustration that everyone has felt, including me."

"Confess," I urged him. "It will haunt you forever, it will drive you crazy."

"I don't know if that's a word of advice, a backhanded comfort, or what," Railey said. "I am not guilty. I didn't do it. I don't feel tormented by the guilt of what I didn't do."

It would be the next day before I understood some of what disturbed me about my conversation with Walker Railey. There was, of course, the possibility of his innocence. If he was guilty of no more than infidelity, then what an awful fate for him to bear. How cruel of me to disbelieve him. But if he strangled Peggy and was going free, then what kind of person was he? I still didn't know.

I had been struck, in a literary way, by the metaphorical parallels between Peggy's condition and that of her children, who were in a custody limbo, and that of the congregation, which was still stunned and bewildered, and that of the crime, which continued to be unsolved, and that of Walker, who was, as I pointed out to him, suspended between one life and another. "Yes, yes!" he said with an eager intensity that surprised me. "Somebody asked me three or four months ago, 'How've you been?' And I said I kind of feel like I'm in an emotional coma. In that I'm breathing, existing, and living, but at that point—this is while I was still in the hospital—like anybody in a coma, like Peggy and others, I hear people around me talking and making decisions that affect my life, and at this point I don't seem to have any control over those decisions. So I'm kind of in a fixed state. I guess you could say the same thing now."

Perhaps it was the very eagerness with which he accepted this observation that chilled me, because of course there was no real equivalence between Walker Railey's tragedy and Peggy's. Soon after our interview he left to start a new life in California, but Peggy's life would never start again.

And what will become of the congregation he leaves behind? It is in many respects his congregation, much of it comprising people like me, who had felt let down by the churches of their youth and who had been drawn back to faith by Railey's radiant ministry. They shared a common belief in the goodness of Walker Railey. Now they were having to consider whether what they had taken as good was actually evil—or worse, far worse, that they would never really know the truth, and for the rest of their lives they would be bewildered, the truth would never be known, charges would never be filed, Peggy would neither die nor live again, and

Walker Railey would never be revealed as either hero or villain but instead would haunt them forever, asking, "Who am I?"

(January 1988)

In 1993, a San Antonio jury found Walker Railey not guilty of the attempted murder of his wife. Some jurors later told reporters that they believed he was guilty but that the Dallas prosecutors were unable to prove their case beyond a reasonable doubt. Railey has remarried and reportedly is living comfortably in Los Angeles. Peggy Railey remains in a vegetative state in a nursing home in Tyler, Texas.

Forgery Texas Style

GREGORY CURTIS

In March 1836 the Alamo had fallen and the Texas Revolution was in danger of collapsing. To bolster flagging spirits, the new Texas government commissioned the printers Baker and Bordens of San Felipe to print one thousand copies of the recently signed Texas Declaration of Independence and one thousand copies of William Barret Travis' Victory or Death letter from the Alamo. Texas patriots posted them in public places across the country, and then most of those broadsides, like political ephemera today, disappeared forever.

One hundred and fifty-one years later in Austin Dorothy Sloan opened a package sent to her from Dallas and removed a copy of the old declaration broadside. A dealer in rare books and manuscripts and a native Texan who had studied the history of the West at the University of Texas, she had been anticipating something like this practically all of her professional life. Here was a true piece of history that would be a coup for any dealer to sell. It would be profitable too. The collector offering her the declaration to sell had bought it for $21,500. Now the price should be even higher.

Instead of exhilaration, though, Sloan felt odd;

rather, she felt that something was odd about the document she held in her hands. She could not say exactly what. Perhaps it just didn't look old enough to her practiced eye.

She called her friend Bill Holman, a librarian and master printer, and the two of them went to the Barker Texas History Center at the University of Texas, where there was another copy of the declaration broadside. At first glance Sloan's copy and the library's copy looked identical. But after a more careful examination, Holman discovered that the dimensions of the type were different on the two copies. The type on Sloan's copy was narrower than that on the library's copy. The difference was slight but crucial. Lead type, the only kind of type in Texas in 1836, does not change. The difference in size meant that the two documents must have been printed at different times. That led to only one conclusion: One of the documents had to be a forgery, and it could not be the Barker library copy. Its provenance—or history of ownership—was known and proved it was genuine.

Sloan went home to call the collector, while Holman met another bookseller named Tom Taylor for lunch. Taylor was a master printer who produced fine editions for collections and also dealt in rare books. Holman told him about the two versions of the declaration. Although Taylor didn't say so at the time, Holman's story bothered him. He brooded on it all that afternoon, for he had sold copies of the declaration himself, one to the Dallas Public Library for $20,000, one to the museum at the San Jacinto Battleground for $30,000, and a third to a collector in Austin. Taylor knew Governor Bill Clements also had bought a copy. The news forced

Taylor to consider a question that had occurred to him while he was selling his declarations but that he had put out of his mind. The declaration broadside was one of the rarest items of Texas history. Before 1970 only five copies were known to exist. Now there were at least twenty. Where had the new copies come from?

Answering that question became an obsession for Taylor. He borrowed several copies of the declaration broadside and studied them letter by letter. He found that the copies either were identical to the copy in the Barker Texas History Center and thus were genuine or shared identical differences from the Barker copy and thus were forgeries. Taylor was even able to identify the specific genuine copy that had been used as a model for the forgeries. He began examining printed documents in libraries, museums, and private collections. By the end of 1988 he had identified more than fifty forgeries of thirteen original documents. All of the fakes had appeared in the marketplace after 1970, and none had clear provenance. Almost every one of the major libraries, historical museums, and leading private collectors in Texas found that they had been stung. The declarations Taylor himself had sold to the Dallas Public Library and to the San Jacinto museum were forgeries, and he had to return their purchase price. There were forged declarations at the University of Houston, the University of Texas at San Antonio, and the Star of the Republic Museum at Washington-on-the-Brazos. The libraries at Baylor, the University of Texas at Austin, UT-Arlington, and Yale all had one or more forged documents. Fakes were also in private collections, like those of Governor Clements and J. P.

Bryan, a Houston oilman who is a descendant of Moses Austin and a former president of the Texas State Historical Association.

Altogether there were at least nine forged copies of the declaration. But the most common forgeries, even more numerous than those of the declaration, were of the broadside of Travis' Victory or Death letter. There are only two known genuine copies, one at Yale and one that seems to have been stolen from the Texas Archives sometime in the sixties. Presumably, the stolen copy was used to make the forged copies. Ross Perot almost bought a Travis letter forgery but sent it back to the dealer when it was determined to be fake. Others were not based on historical documents but were complete fabrications. Although they were purported to be from 1835 or 1836, they were set in typefaces that Taylor knew had not been designed until around 1900. Undoubtedly, more forgeries than the fifty-some Taylor found will be discovered in time. It is no secret who made the fakes or who sold them, but a successful prosecution of anyone is unlikely. All in all, forging documents can be a highly profitable, successful, even gentlemanly business.

The forgeries might never have come to light if the prices for fine pieces of Texana had not increased so dramatically. Last year a genuine declaration broadside sold for $75,000, a price that would have been unimaginable even five years ago. For decades the most remarkable thing about Texana was the almost total lack of interest in it, even in Texas. Well into the fifties, there were few collectors and fewer dealers who concentrated primarily on Texas materials. The greatest collection ever built by a private individual was that of Thomas Streeter, an oilman from New Jersey who started coming to Texas on business in the twenties and thirties. But very few in Texas recognized the value of Streeter's collection. When he offered to sell it to the University of Texas in 1957, the university turned him down, and his hundreds of priceless documents, many of which are unique artifacts of our history, became the permanent property of Yale. (Streeter's *Bibliography of Texas, 1795–1845,* still the ultimate authority in the field, was published not in Texas but by Harvard University Press.)

Texas government showed a similar lack of interest in its own archives. Its records include not only the proceedings and papers of the state government but letters, land grants, minutes, and the like from the time of Austin Colony, the Texas Revolution, and the Republic. The manuscript of Travis' Victory or Death letter, for example, is part of the state archives. But over the years the valuable documents were guarded so poorly that it was easy for anyone to walk in and take what he wanted. Some people did just that.

During the seventies it became an open secret in the small world of collectors that items appearing for sale frequently had been stolen, either from the state archives or from libraries or county courthouses. Some collectors who were interested in Texana developed the habit of overlooking the provenance of prized items. Didn't these artifacts of history really belong to those who valued them the most? In the end that habit allowed the forgeries to be bought and sold undetected for almost two decades.

Interest in Texana began to grow during the early sixties. By then Texas was embarking on a period of prosperity that would not end for twenty years. The state had long been more urban than rural, and it was clear that, for better or worse, many of the old traditions and attitudes were dying out. Certainly the people who embodied them were. So a feeling of the past slipping away created a nostalgia among some Texans who had the money to indulge their sentiments.

At the same time, a group of young dealers began their businesses. Their work expanded the market for Texas rarities and created markets in new areas of collecting. One such dealer was John Jenkins, who grew up in Beaumont and became a coin dealer at a very young age. As a child he spent his weekends sorting through rolls of nickels and dimes on the kitchen table, hoping to find rare coins. Before graduating from high school he edited a book of his great-great-grandfather's memoirs. After receiving his degree from the University of Texas he started a business in Austin selling coins, documents, and rare books. By the mid-seventies Jenkins was proclaiming himself the largest rare-book dealer in the world. He ruled his empire from a corrugated-metal building on the interstate south of Austin. Not a particularly tall man, Jenkins sat behind a mammoth desk in a mahogany chair carved with snakes and dragons. Over the years he began to spend increasing amounts of time in Las Vegas, where he played poker under the nickname Austin Squatty.

In 1964 William Simpson opened a gallery on Main Street in Houston. He is a theatrical, good-humored man with a white goatee. He was once an acolyte of Ezra Pound, visiting the poet frequently during his internment in St. Elizabeth's Hospital in Washington, D.C., after World War II. Simpson sells few books. His trade is primarily in furniture, art, glass, rugs, linens, and crystal. But in the mid-sixties he began selling Texana, particularly historical documents and letters. His auctions became a regular gathering place for collectors.

By far the most interesting and important of the new dealers was C. Dorman David. The son of a wealthy, self-made man, David created the market for Texas historical imprints almost singlehandedly. At one time he had what was probably the greatest private collection since Streeter's. David had the best eye and the best taste of any dealer in Texas ever. The Bookman, the store he founded and designed on San Felipe in Houston, was a place of such stunning grandeur that it actually worked against the success of his business. Customers who wandered in were often too intimidated to buy. Unfortunately, his personal confusion and flaws of character overwhelmed even his perfect taste. He became a heroin addict. He was indicted for receiving stolen books. He was suspected to be the mastermind behind a ring of thieves who looted libraries and archives across Texas. And he became a forger.

These three men—Jenkins, Simpson, and David—all knew each other. They bought and sold from one another regularly for many years. That is important because every one of the fakes that Tom Taylor has traced was first sold by either John Jenkins, William Simpson, or Dorman David.

I know Dorman David made the forgeries because he told me so. We met in a house he was visiting in

Houston that had a collection of art so fine any museum in the world would like to have it. His dented old pickup, a distant echo of the exotic sports cars he used to favor, was parked toward the back, near the swimming pool. He was still, even at 51 years old, a tall, massive man with a bemused, wide-eyed expression. Despite his size he projected none of the tautness and aggression that had once made him his division's heavyweight representative in Army boxing tournaments.

It was the second time I had met him. The first was in the late sixties, when I had happened into his shop on lower Westheimer in Houston. At that time he was wearing boots and a Western jacket. I had recognized his name because I had worked as a shipping clerk and factotum at the Bookman, which David's mother then owned and ran. Leaning back in a chair with his boots up on a desk, his chin sunk down in his chest, mumbling almost inaudibly, he had seemed remote to the point of eeriness. I remember leaving the store rather quickly, with a combined sense of confusion and relief.

But this time our meeting was far more relaxed. He was married, had young children, and seemed to be making a go of things after years of drug addiction, life as a fugitive, and prison. We drove around searching for the lithographer's shop that had made the zinc printing plates David had used to produce his forgeries. It was out of business, we finally learned, but as we drove David explained in some detail the meticulous process he had used to make his fakes. It became clear that among the motives he may have had for forging, money was not the central one.

Earlier, David had shown me an ebony carving he

had made of two human torsos writhing in torment. He had sold it for $750, but obviously the money had not been the primary reason for his making the sculpture. It was made to express something. He had intended to sell his forgeries too—although not as genuine, he claims, only as a set of facsimiles of early Texas documents. But again money was not the real motive. The forgeries were made to express something. I believe that something was revenge.

Beginning in the early sixties David worked hard, in his way, as a dealer. He pursued books and documents across the United States and deep into Mexico. He was knowledgeable enough and persuasive enough to excite the interest of new collectors, who would then become customers. He recognized value, both historical and commercial, in items such as imprints, that others had passed over. But he did not understand money; it meant nothing to him at all.

David's father, a thick, knobby man from the backwoods of Louisiana, had made his fortune selling drilling mud. Henry David had little or nothing in common with his son or with his daughter, who ran an art gallery, or with his wife, who had the same eye for fine objects as Dorman. When Dorman made foolish decisions his family always rescued him eventually; thus he never had to make money in his book business, and he never did. Yet Dorman David would have liked nothing better than to have made great profits. In addition to whatever that might have done for his self-respect, it also would have brought him respect in the book world, where he was considered a rich curiosity. His nemesis was John Jenkins. The two were friends for many years and even issued catalogs together. They bought, sold, and traded constantly between themselves. David usually had the better things to start with, but Jenkins was the better trader. Too often after the heat of the trading session faded, David found himself on the short end of the bargain.

As in his dealings with Jenkins, David was frequently getting out-traded by other bookmen because he was really too gullible for the surprisingly Machiavellian world of antiquarian bookselling. There is in any business an expected rivalry between competitors. In bookselling that competition is intensified because rare books, precisely because they are rare, are difficult to find, so dealers must vie with one another for goods to sell. The most common source is not old attics but other dealers. When I worked at the Bookman, I was amazed at how much of the business—well over half— was selling books to other dealers. Of course, no dealer can know enough to understand everything that comes his way. Thus dealers talk about how they "beat" another dealer—sold something for more than it was worth or bought it for less.

All this buying and selling is carried on in an atmosphere of intense gossip. Booksellers like nothing better than to chatter about the minutiae of rival booksellers' professional and personal lives. Informal alliances spring up when small groups of dealers decide they don't like the ways of certain other dealers. Then these alliances fall apart over jealousies, misunderstandings, or occasionally even real betrayals, only to reform in different patterns of loyalty and hatred.

In that world David had few friends outside Texas and few enough in Texas. The bias against Texans as crude vulgarians trying to buy culture persists in parts of the book world today, but it was a major factor in the sixties, when David was most active. Tall and un-bridled as he was and rich as his family was, David fit enough of the Texas stereotype to earn the quiet contempt of many Eastern and Western dealers. Even within the state he was resented by booksellers trying to scrape by, because they believed that his father would rescue him from every poor business deal he made as well as from the messes of his personal life. He also bought the best items and then tripled or qua-drupled the asking price. Eventually, everyone learned to wait for David to overextend himself, get desperate for money, then lower his prices, often to below what he had paid. All of that combined to make dealers feel almost justified in taking advantage of him when they could. David knew he was getting beaten in trades and being ridiculed behind his back. But he couldn't ever change that. His frustration was a reason for getting back at the whole collecting world.

"I designed the Bookman to express my feelings toward books," David says. And what he had created in his store was an atmosphere both bright and reverent. Behind two massive wooden doors with brass knobs was a wall covered with old copper type and engrav-ings, themselves covered with a clear coating. To the right was a long, rectangular room three stories high and lit by skylights. Polished bookcases went from floor to ceiling. At one end of the room was a balcony and halfway up was a narrow wooden catwalk for reaching the higher shelves. An old movable pulpit with a spiral staircase stood in one corner. A long mahogany banquet table on luxurious oriental rugs completed the room.

David's attitude about life was not nearly so conservative. He was a founder of the 7th of April Club, a gentlemen's gourmet society that still meets. Its members were either wealthy or literary or both. In addition to books and fine objects, David liked sports cars, motorcycles, boats, and women, and he got into trouble with them all. Noticing the wide doors of one drugstore, he drove his car in to buy a pack of cigarettes. He brought an international debutante into Maxim's on the back of a motorcycle. He raced pursuing police cars down the Gulf Freeway to Galveston—and got away. He combined a brooding, nervous character, a pouting lower lip, and the wild abandon—and the money-to follow any impulse. John Jenkins says, "Nearly every woman who ever met him fell in love with him." David had six wives and so many girlfriends that he could not always keep them straight. He and a running mate once took two women for a cruise in the Gulf on David's sailboat. They ran aground in Galveston Bay. By the time they came ashore a television reporter was covering the story. David arrived home to find that his inflamed wife already knew about him and his girlfriend from the evening news. Sometime in the mid-sixties David bought an original Thunderbird and installed an eight-carburetor racing engine. Then he drove the car to Waco to trade books and documents. At three in the morning he fell asleep at the wheel and crashed into a farmer's pickup. He gave the farmer $1,000 and the car and hitchhiked to a hospital in Waco. As doctors sewed him up, David got on the phone and started trading, winding up with two antique six-shooters. He hired a plane to fly to Austin. Once in the air, blood seeping from his sutures, he pulled out the pistols and shouted, "Let's go to Cuba!"

David's taste, energy, and wealth carried him on a wild ride for almost ten years. He bought and sold thousands of books and documents as well as paintings, cigars, guns, furniture, and exotic cars. He traded with a network of friends and associates. In one trade that took two days of constant negotiation Jenkins got a Rolls-Royce, a Kentucky rifle, and a Bowie knife; Price Daniel, Jr., the son of the former governor and a book dealer before he became a politician, got a book collection; a car dealer who had owned the Rolls got an antique racing car; a restaurant owner got several thousand Cuban cigars; and David got $20,000 credit at Maxim's in Houston, which he traded for some rare wines, which he in turn traded to Jenkins for books and documents. What fun! David issued a series of catalogs for rare Texas books and some superb manuscripts, including letters by Sam Houston and Travis and the only known list of Mexican officers captured at San Jacinto. And as he bought high and sold low, he always turned to his family for more money until even they lost patience. He had to give up the Bookman to his mother and go to New Orleans, where he worked for his father in a cement business, an occupation for which he was totally unsuited. Meanwhile, he continued to deal in rare books and documents. He returned to Houston after a year or so and set up shop in a series of locations.

As it turned out, those years—about 1968 to 1972—were the devil-may-care days of selling and collecting Texana. David, Jenkins, and others were turning up books and documents. Simpson was having his auctions. Great collectors like J. P. Bryan, Sr., John Pease, and Jenkins Garrett were actively in the market. And there was suddenly a flood of new material to buy and sell. Some of it came from Mexico, where archives still held valuable documents concerning Texas from the revolutionary and pre-revolutionary era. Some items simply disappeared from the smaller *municipias* in northern Mexico and reappeared for sale on this side of the border. Somewhat later a dentist from Mexico City began bringing things for Simpson to sell at his auctions. David bought documents from a college professor who had somehow obtained them from archives in Saltillo. Even with all this new material, or perhaps because of it, prices began to rise. It was no longer unusual for items to sell for several thousand dollars or more. Those should have been great days for David, as they were for other dealers. Instead, what few restraints had held him before disappeared entirely. The drugs and thefts and forgeries had already begun.

I t is impossible to say when David made his first fake. In 1963 or 1964 he was involved in the sale of a letter that I believe is a forgery; it was purportedly written by a defender of the Alamo during the siege. David was aware of doubts about the letter at the time, but I think someone else was the forger. A former secretary and companion of one of David's best customers recalls going with her boss to see David in the mid-sixties. They found him baking paper in an oven. Without hesitating David volunteered that he was trying to make the paper look older. There are other stories of people coming upon him as he was drawing old maps or practicing calligraphy. But provocative as that may be, nothing is certain until 1971, the earliest date when it appears that fakes by Dorman David were on the market.

At the same time, a ring of thieves was raiding libraries and archives throughout Texas, and some people began to believe that the loot was going to David. In the light of all this skullduggery his early catalogs have an insouciant, bad-boy quality that is very curious. On the cover of a catalog from 1964 was an engraving of a stagecoach holdup; it was titled *The Bookman Offers for Sale Texas Books From a Recent Robbery*. Another cover around that time showed the only existing Wanted poster from the Republic period with "Dorman David" substituted for the name of the real outlaw. David's fourteenth catalog, issued in early 1966, was designed identical to a broadside, listed in Streeter's bibliography as #11, known as the Austin Declaration. Some copies of that declaration have since been identified as forgeries.

David himself dates the beginning of his decline from May 1971. He had taken about three thousand documents to show to a collector in Waco. Suddenly a Texas Ranger arrived with John Kinney, who was then the state archivist. They asked to look through the documents because they suspected some of them belonged to the archives. Eventually they found three or four that Kinney believed belonged to the state, although he could not prove it. Nevertheless, he announced that he was taking them back to Austin. The Ranger tossed David a receipt. Then he and Kinney grabbed the papers and took off. David had had a lifelong antipathy for the police, and the incident confirmed his prejudice.

As the story spread in the tight world of bookselling, it changed David's reputation from that of a foolish son of a wealthy father to that of a thief. It was a time of great emotional instability, even by David's standards. His finances were in disarray, as always. His parents were getting divorced for the second time. And his long-standing appetite for drugs had become voracious. Today David says, "After that I just didn't care anymore. I know one thing—I had never used any heroin before that. It all came after."

One month later, in June, David held an auction at the Warwick in Houston that intensified the suspicions and gossip about him. The auction was a small but, in the collecting world, glittering affair that earned a long paragraph in the *Houston Post* gossip column. The catalog stated that the auction would start "at exactly 8:10 P.M." Most of the leading collectors were there, and the letter, documents, and broadsides David offered for sale were rare and extremely desirable. There was a letter Stephen F. Austin had written from prison in Mexico City, orders Sam Houston had written at San Jacinto, a letter from Jim Bowie to Austin declining the offer of a command in the Texas Revolution, and much more, 77 items in all. But where had David gotten such platinum artifacts? Austin's letter from prison had been listed in the Austin Papers at the University of Texas. A letter from Peter Dimmitt from Fort Goliad, written October 21, 1835, which makes it one of the earliest letters of the Texas Revolution, also had been cataloged with the Austin Papers. Certain other items seemed out of place at the auction. Everyone wondered where they came from—or should have—but no one said anything publicly. The bidding proceeded quickly because knowledgeable collectors were there not to bid so much as to see if anything happened. Nothing did. Afterward, John Jenkins returned an item he had bought. In a letter to David he asked for his money back and added, "I still have doubts about the provenance of this large group of documents that you have come up with. Ten or twelve of the items in your sale were listed in Binkley, Gammel, or the Austin Papers. I hope you will have the good sense to check out your source very carefully before buying any more." Later, in his *Basic Texas Books,* Jenkins described the event euphemistically as a "memorable sale, in more ways than one, of spectacular Texana."

That summer a man we will call Thief A was arrested outside the Austin Public Library. In his rented car were valuable old maps, a contemporary road map with thirteen Central and South Texas county seats marked, and several pages of typed instructions, which said, in part: "1. Get as much as you can! 2. Get maps in these county clerk's offices. 3. Get all the old books you can. 4. Keep different counties separated." Then the individual counties were listed with instructions: "Fort Bend C/Seat—Richmond. Here the D/Clerk's office hasn't anything but a few documents. You can still get some stuff from it (plenty in the 1850's). Easy to get stuff out of here. In the C/Clerk's office you can get a brief case full but it'll take a couple of hours. I have gotten a lot of early items out."

Thief A also had a check for $650, written to him by a man we will call Thief B. Thief B was soon found. Both he and Thief A admitted to a Texas Ranger that they had been stealing from the state archives. They claimed that Dorman David had put them up to it and that they had delivered the stolen documents to him at his store in Houston. Thief A got a probated sentence, but the Rangers did not try to arrest David for receiving the stolen documents until the following June, more than a year after Thief A's capture.

The thirteen months or so between the Waco contretemps in May 1971 and the Texas Rangers' final descent on David in June 1972 was David's most active period as a forger. His heroin addiction was total. Old friends who might stop by would see him in the bathroom with a needle in his arm. Others would come in to find him sitting loopy-eyed in front of the television; he had twisted the dials to make the colors bizarre. He missed enough business appointments that even loyal associates finally gave up on him. In the midst of all this David did nothing to hide his fakes. He maintains that he was making facsimiles of historical imprints concerning immigration to Texas and thus had nothing to hide. Perhaps so. An addict, now reformed, who lived in a tent behind David's house, explains it this way: "There was so much else illegal going on around there that forgery didn't seem worth worrying about."

David's forgeries were so masterful that they fooled every dealer, librarian, collector, and other expert who saw them until Tom Taylor began his meticulous investigation. For someone like David, old paper was not hard to come by. Blank sheets could be cut from the endpapers of old books. Sometimes entire reams of old paper turned up in antique stores. David had a company in England make paper to the specifications of paper used in Texas during the Revolution and ship five hundred pounds to him in Houston. "But," he recalls, "the paper was so far off. It didn't have one hundred fifty years on it."

He found a lithographer with a camera that could make a negative many times larger than the original document. He carefully worked on the enlarged negative to restore any damaged or imprecise letters. Sometimes he made mistakes that altered the text; those errors are the surest way of identifying the forgeries now. Although the type on the original had crisp, sharp edges, those edges became slightly rounded in the negative. David tried to correct this on the negative in the places where it was most obvious. Then he went further than that, making tinkering changes that were needless. Had he not done so, his forgeries would be even harder to identify. The lithographer then made a zinc plate the size of the actual document from the retouched negative.

David had studied several books about forgeries and learned that the ink of today is not the ink of yesterday. He made his own. He lit a candle, then held a bag over it. With its oxygen limited, the candle began to smoke. David scraped the carbon from the smoke off the inside of the bag. He mixed the carbon with boiled linseed oil, working the mixture with a butter knife on a sheet of glass until he had a substance that would pass for period ink.

He believed that printers in 1836 had not rolled ink onto type but had tamped it with a leather tool. So he made a tamper and applied his ink to the zinc plate with it. Then he put a piece of paper on top of the inked plate, and with a small wooden mallet he tapped each letter one by one. He lifted the sheet after each tap to check the result. Sometimes he discarded his mistakes, other times he tried to repair them. Despite the tedious process, David says today. "I was never satisfied with anything I did." I believe he worked so hard to make the forgeries because the perfect fake would be the perfect revenge. If his fakes were accepted, he would beat everyone.

D avid's assertion is that he never sold one of his "facsimiles" as an original, although it appears that in at least one case he did. Still, of the fifty-some fakes that are known, few were first sold by David. Instead, they entered the marketplace through dealers John Jenkins and William Simpson after the police raided David's store and finally put him out of business.

On the night of June 14, 1972, two Texas Rangers, two detectives from the Houston Police Department's burglary-and-theft division, and an assistant district attorney raided David's store on Fairview, where he was also living. They expected to find the documents that Thief A and Thief B had admitted to stealing. An unnamed man had sworn that he had been in David's shop two days earlier and had seen the documents. The police found none of the documents listed in the warrant nor did they find any drugs. But they did find and confiscate so many books, documents, personal papers, and the like that the police inventory of their seizure was 54 pages long. In light of the forgeries, the most interesting items appear on page 49: an original copy of the Austin Declaration, a forged copy of it, a recent printing of another forgery called "Important News," nine sheets of old paper, and a negative of the Texas Declaration of Independence. But the police were looking for stolen documents, not forged ones, and took no special notice.

About two hundred books, including about seventy volumes of the *Southwestern Historical Quarterly*, belonged to the Lamar University Library in Beaumont and were returned to it. Representatives from the Rosenberg Library in Galveston claimed six books that belonged to that library. State archivist Kinney identified three documents that belonged to the state—all of them had stamps or some other identifying marks. David was indicted for receiving stolen property, but just as the case was to go to trial, the charges were dropped. David always insisted that he had bought those books and documents without knowing they were stolen. There was no absolute proof to the contrary, particularly since librarians testified in depositions that they often sold duplicates from their collections without bothering to remove their identifying marks.

The police returned all that they still had to David, but his days as a bookman were over. No one trusted him enough to buy from him. For his part, he was bitter and wanted out. He sold everything, most of it to William Simpson and John Jenkins, his old friend and rival. Soon afterward, David began getting arrested for drugs. He escaped from custody once and jumped bond another time. He lived as a fugitive, existing on menial jobs. "For seven years," he told me, "I was nobody." Finally, he conquered his addiction. In December 1980 he turned himself in and served a term in Huntsville. Even while a fugitive, he made sculptures. Because he was a wanted man, he signed his work by carving a fish hook, which stood for the first letter of his assumed name, "Jack." He still signs his work that way, a legacy from those black years.

From both his own admission and the items listed in the police inventory, it was clear that David had made a number of different forgeries and was probably making more. But where was his inventory of forgeries, and what happened to it? Only two forgeries were on the police list, but David must have had some material either outside his store or that the police did not discover. He sold a genuine copy of the Texas Declaration of Independence—the copy he used as the model for his forgeries—to a dealer in New York in October 1972, several months after the raid. That copy was not in the police inventory either. Perhaps the other forgeries were with the genuine declaration, wherever that was.

Simpson admits that after the raid he bought eight to ten large boxes from David that held approximately five thousand documents. David had not listed the contents nor did Simpson inventory them. Simpson says he then traded Jenkins the books and printed material, as he had done at various times before. Jenkins says all the fakes he sold came from Simpson, with the possible exception of one or two items that may have come directly from David in another collection that Jenkins had bought. Thus it seems likely that the stock of forgeries were in those eight to ten boxes whose contents ended up being divided between Simpson and Jenkins. As the two men sold the material bit by bit over the years, the forgeries entered the marketplace and made their way to museums, libraries, and private collections all across Texas.

Each of the men passionately denies knowing that any of the documents he sold were fake. Both point out that many other dealers and experts were fooled by the fakes over the years, that even Tom Taylor sold two fakes believing they were genuine. But apparently neither Simpson nor Jenkins saw any reason to wonder when six or eight or more copies of some of the rarest items in Texas history—there had been only two previously known copies of the Travis letter—suddenly turned up in their possession. In September 1987, Jenkins had a fire in his warehouse. He listed one of the fakes that had been returned to him in the insurance claim. He says that was before he knew the document was a fake and that he has since removed it from the claim. David maintains that he sold the plates he made to Jenkins, who says that's not true. But since David believes it was Jenkins who informed on him to the police—which Jenkins also denies—David might have his own reasons for naming him. It would be the last gesture in a long revenge.

O ne day last December David showed up at Dorothy Sloan's door in Austin, needing to cash a check. He had some beautiful antiques in his pickup. Sloan admired them, and then the two went inside and talked for a while about the forgeries. Soon enough David was on his way, but he paused on her porch steps and said, "You know, I think all of you owe me something."

Sloan said she didn't understand.

"Because of me everyone is having to look at Texas history a lot more closely," he said, and with a wave he was gone.

(March 1988)

The world of Texans has been free of forgery since this case, as far as we know. William Simpson retired shortly after the story was published and now lives in Florida. Johnny Jenkins's body was discovered in rural Texas not far from Austin in April 1989. He had apparently died from a self-inflicted gunshot wound. No one knows why he took his life. However, because of the ambiguity of the circumstances surrounding his death, the official ruling was that Jenkins "came to his death at the hands of a person or persons unknown." Dorman David is an artist living in Texas. Tom Taylor still occasionally designs books or authenticates documents, but following all the intrigue of discovering the forgeries, he grew weary of the rare-book business. He and his wife bought Lost Canyon, what he calls an "ecumenical retreat ranch," in West Texas, which is rented mostly by church organizations. He says his strongest selling point is that Lost Canyon is "forty-three miles from the nearest stop light."

The Work of the Devil

GARY CARTWRIGHT

Nobody could make sense out of what happened to Mark Kilroy. It was all mixed up with black magic, white magic, drugs, mestizo superstition, gringo hedonism, coincidence, and random selection. We had warned ourselves about this sort of thing many times and still didn't believe. It was the curse of *el otro lado*—the other side. Antonio Zavaleta, an expert on *curanderismo* who teaches at Texas Southmost College in Brownsville, was sometimes called to the other side of the border to supervise ghostbusting. "Look," said Zavaleta, who had taught sociology and anthropology to two members of the murderous gang responsible for Kilroy's death, "I'm a scientist. I have a Ph.D. in anthropology from the University of Texas. But when I went over there, I put a cross around my neck."

By the time Mark Kilroy's body was found on April 11 at Rancho Santa Elena, his disappearance had been the subject of fascinated media speculation for a month. The 21-year-old junior at the University of Texas had gone to South Padre Island along with thousands of other students during spring break and had simply vanished one night in the border town of Matamoros. From the beginning his disappearance seemed like an eerie and arbitrary event—a true mystery. When Kilroy's fate was finally known, the mystery was even greater, because few of us were conditioned to accept the reality of human sacrifice to Satan.

Officials on both sides of the border had begun to suspect black magic a couple of weeks before the bodies of Kilroy and fourteen others were discovered. A psychic had reported a vision in which Kilroy's body appeared alongside what looked like a witch's cauldron. A satanist in Brownsville had confessed to murdering Kilroy and burying his body on the beach—though under questioning, he recanted. When lawmen finally began to sort things out, the ritual killings seemed almost predestined. A map drawn two years ago by confessed mass-killer Henry Lee Lucas had predicted with inexplicable accuracy that the bodies of victims of satanic rituals would be found about where Kilroy and the others were found.

The beginning of the end of the search for Kilroy was suitably bizarre. Serafin Hernandez Garcia, a nephew of the cruel and clever gangster boss Elio Hernandez Rivera, ran a routine roadblock on Sunday afternoon, April 9, and stupidly led federales to the ranch that his family used for its smuggling operations. Serafin was no towering intellect—he displayed none of the savvy that had made his uncle the leader of a gang of smugglers and *pistoleros* who had terrorized Matamoros and the state of Tamaulipas for years—but he was no dummy either. Yet he went through that roadblock as if he believed himself to be invisible and bulletproof.

Later that same day federales started searching the

Hernandez ranch, Rancho Santa Elena. They had turned up thirty kilos of marijuana when one of them made a discovery that chilled his blood. To the unpracticed eye of a *norteamericano,* it appeared to be an ordinary storage shed with some melted candles, cigar butts, and empty bottles on the floor and some greasy cauldrons in the yard. But the Mexican cops saw something else. They saw a devil's temple, a place where black magic had been practiced. When they reported this astonishing news to their comandante, Juan Benitez Ayala, the investigation came to a screeching halt—much to the distress of American lawmen who believed that the smugglers knew something about the disappearance of Mark Kilroy. But Benitez was adamant: The search could not resume until the black magic had been neutralized.

Mexico has always been a country with a rich legacy of magic, born of the dynamic fusion between Christianity and ancient Indian religions. A visit to any marketplace reveals a tradition tracing back to the Aztecs—an enormous variety of strange and powerful herbs, potions, and amulets. *Brujos,* or shamans, work the villages, casting spells or relieving them for small fees. Even in cities as large as Matamoros ancient superstitions are a way of life; a *maquiladora* recently was spared being shut down only because a *curandero* was able to dehex a piece of expensive machinery with which a worker had been seriously injured. Magic is omnipresent; the plot of a popular mid-eighties primetime soap opera in Mexico, *El Maleficio* ("The Evil One"), revolved around the premise that a wealthy businessman in Oaxaca was able to sustain power by praying nightly to Satan. Magic is also double-edged;

for every evil there is a counterbalancing good. American lawmen who had visited the office of the comandante in Matamoros had noticed strings of garlic, strings of peppers, and white candles, articles commonly used in Mexico to ward off evil. It was no surprise then that Benitez called off the search until a *curandero* could be summoned to the ranch to cast out the demons.

After the *curandero* did his magic, things happened fast. On Monday afternoon a caretaker at the ranch identified a photograph of Mark Kilroy and remembered seeing him handcuffed in the back of a Suburban in the equipment yard. In an interrogation room of the Matamoros jail, Elio Hernandez Rivera, Serafin Hernandez Garcia, and two other suspects who had been arrested at the ranch confessed to kidnapping Kilroy and witnessing his ritual sacrifice. Serafin told investigators that he had buried Kilroy, and he led the way to Kilroy's grave, which was marked by a piece of wire sticking out of the ground. The other end of the wire had been attached to Kilroy's spinal column so that when his body decomposed members of the cult could pull out the vertebrae to make into a necklace. When Kilroy's body was uncovered the comandante noticed that his legs had been cut off above the knees and asked Serafin if that was part of the ritual. "No," Serafin said. "It just made him easier to bury." Serafin had a baby face, a weak chin, and a Zapata-like moustache that seemed stuck to his face by accident. He was no peasant recently arrived on a wagon of maize; he was a spoiled suburban kid with a taste for designer jeans, tinted sunglasses, and fast American cars with cellular phones. Serafin worked at gunpoint in the hot sun for hours, digging up bodies. He seemed to resent the forced labor but was otherwise nonchalant, remorseless—curiously without passion. By midafternoon a dozen corpses lay in a row.

The story hit the wires before the last body had been exhumed. In a few hours all the major television networks and most of the major news organizations on both sides of the border had dispatched teams of journalists. Several media outlets chartered planes. Agents for Geraldo Rivera and Oprah Winfrey were on the phone. On the highway between Matamoros and Reynosa, campesinos working in the corn and wheat fields of their *ejidos*—communal farms—stopped and leaned on their hoe handles as jeeploads of federales raced by, closely followed by a stream of media vans and television-satellite trucks. A boy herding scrawny Mexican cattle removed his hat until the procession had passed.

Officials on both sides went out of their way to accommodate the media, effecting coverage in their own peculiar styles. U.S. Customs agent Oran Neck was crisp and to the point. Drugs caused this to happen, he emphasized. Lieutenant George Gavito of the Cameron County Sheriff's Department was wry and laconic. When a reporter asked how the federales had gotten confessions so quickly, Gavito pointed to a bottle of mineral water—federales like to shake the bottle and squirt the water up the noses of reluctant witnesses. Press conferences were held twice daily in front of the courthouse in Brownsville, and politicians who had hurried to the Valley to assist and commiserate with the Kilroy family made their own agendas available. A

Port Isabel legislator announced that he was introducing a law that would allow the killers to be tried for capital murder in Texas, even though the murders had taken place in Mexico, where there is no capital punishment. Everywhere the cameras turned—the courthouse in Brownsville, the federale headquarters in Matamoros, the killing field—there was Jim Mattox, the attorney general of Texas, his face as grave as ashes, mumbling pronouncements on the horror of it all.

The real drama was on the Mexican side, and the young comandante damn well knew it. Benitez was a new breed of federal authority in Mexico—young, educated, tough, moderately honest. He had a perfect Indian face, Bambi eyes, and a shaggy haircut, and he usually wore jeans and a Philadelphia Eagles football jacket. Mexican officials had discovered that Benitez's predecessor and most of his top officers had squirreled away $5.5 million in cash and jewelry in confiscations and bribes. The violent border town of Matamoros was considered the end of the road for a comandante, but Benitez took to the assignment with unexpected zeal. So far the results had been spectacular: Drug busts had skyrocketed, and now he had captured practically the entire hierarchy of the infamous Hernandez gang. You could see in his eyes that the magic was working.

With a contingent of 250 international journalists jammed in the courtyard behind federale headquarters, the comandante appeared on the balcony with the four suspects in custody; warrants had been issued for the arrests of seven others. To the astonishment of American journalists, all four freely answered questions about their roles in the ritual murders. They seemed eager to confess. Elio Hernandez acknowledged that he had been ordained an executioner priest by the cult's high priest and godfather, the fugitive Cuban sadomasochist Adolfo de Jesus Constanzo. Constanzo had personally executed Kilroy: Indeed, the reason Kilroy had been abducted was the Cuban's explicit order to find an American college student for the ceremony. As TV cameras zoomed in, Elio proudly displayed the badges of his office—groups of satanic symbols branded on his arms, chest, and back. Even after two days in the Matamoros jail, Elio was undaunted. A Mexican reporter wrote that the young leader of the gang had challenged the comandante to shoot him: "Go ahead," Hernandez had said. "Your bullets will just bounce off."

Mexican journalists instinctively played to the morbid. From their point of view, death was far more fascinating than life. This wasn't a story about drugs, it was a story about magic. They described in grisly detail how the satanists cut the hearts out of victims much as ancient Aztecs had done. Editors of even the more traditional newspapers saw nothing distasteful in running photographs of the corpses—"*sin genitales,*" read one caption.

Forty-eight hours after the story hit the wires, journalists were still flocking to the Valley. There wasn't a vacant hotel room or a rental car to be had. A crew representing the Fuji network of Tokyo arrived two days late, just in time to film the most dramatic event of all—the discovery of the thirteenth body. No sooner had the Fuji crew set up its camera at Rancho Santa Elena than a truckload of federales appeared with one of the prisoners, Sergio Martinez, known within the cult as La Mariposa (the Butterfly), a pejorative term usually reserved for homosexuals.

The handcuffed Martinez led a squad of federales armed with automatic weapons to a spot just outside the corral fence. There he stopped and pointed to the ground. One of the federales handed him a shovel and a pick, and Martinez began to dig. The sun was high, and the humidity from a morning rain mixed with the unflagging stench of rotting hay and decomposed flesh that had permeated the site since the first bodies were uncovered.

Cameramen wearing surgical masks and kerchiefs over their mouths and noses moved in close, and a sound man dangled a boom mike over Martinez's head as reporters fired questions. Martinez kept saying he didn't kill anyone, he just kidnapped and buried them. After 45 minutes a knee and part of a foot protruded from the ground where Martinez was digging. There was a blast of putrid wind, and everyone backed away, even Martinez, who ignored the machine guns as he gagged and gasped for air. A cameraman removed his surgical mask and offered it to Martinez, who crawled back into the hole and continued digging. The body was that of a man in his thirties, blindfolded and gagged, his chest ripped open and his heart gouged out. *Sin genitales.*

The comandante warned the media to stay away from Martinez—which everyone took to mean "Don't get between him and our machine guns"—but the Butterfly seemed incongruously docile and harmless. As federales removed the thirteenth body, Martinez leaned against the fence, answering questions put to him by the Spanish-speaking assistant of a *New York Times* reporter. It was a lengthy interview, and from the emotion in the Butterfly's voice, he might have been describing the Mexican Revolution. But the translator returned, shaking her head.

"What was that all about?" asked the *Times* reporter.

"Not much," she replied. "He just said he didn't know why he did it."

The comandante pandered irresistibly to the media. For example, he made no attempt to seal off the crime scene. During almost any hour of the day journalists could be found stomping about the ranch, poking in mounds of dirt and in haystacks, looking for something—anything—that no one else had found. American camera crews intentionally overlooked two tiny tennis shoes discarded near a trash pile; they suggested something too horrible for the six o'clock news. A Mexican radio station, however, broadcast a rumor that cultists were still on the prowl and looking for children to kidnap and murder, causing a number of Valley parents to take their children out of school.

Reporters tied handkerchiefs across their faces as they stepped inside the devil's cathedral, a small shed with a tin roof and red tar-paper walls. The air was foul and thick. On the concrete floor were the remains of an altar and the accoutrements of black magic: black candles, cigar butts, bottles of a cheap cane liquor known as *aguardiente*. There were also white candles, peppers, and pods of garlic used by the white magician brought in by the comandante to purify the site.

Just outside the door—apparently arranged by the federales so that the media could not miss their significance—were the vessels and instruments of the sacrificial ceremony: four cauldrons and a machete. Three of the pots were small and contained chicken and goat heads, thousands of pennies, some bones, and some gold beads. The other vessel was a large iron kettle with a cluster of wooden stakes immersed in a thick, evil-smelling goo of blood and body parts, both human and animal. The iron kettle was surprisingly similar to the object described two weeks earlier by the psychic.

As the comandante related it, the ceremony went like this: First, the high priest offered up the sacrifice, cutting the victim's throat or, as in Kilroy's case, taking off the top of his head with a machete. The victims were usually killed first, then mutilated, though not always. Then the brains, hearts, lungs, and testicles were boiled in the iron kettle, and the resulting brew was passed among members so that they could drink and be sanctified. After that, laymen of the cult buried the remains in and around the corral behind the shed. The ultimate piety and conceit of the cult—its unforgivable stupidity—was the abiding belief that this act of unholy communion would make its members invincible.

Nothing during that whole incredible week since the bodies had been discovered was more remarkable than the show of faith demonstrated by the family of Mark Kilroy. At a press conference and later after a mass at St. Luke Catholic Church in Brownsville, the Kilroys spoke calmly and with deep conviction. "I don't feel any anger at all, to be honest with you," said James Kilroy, adding that he hoped that if and when the killers got to heaven, they would find his son and apologize. Helen Kilroy asked people to pray for her son's murderers. Maybe the Kilroys would fall apart later.

Maybe when they got home and started putting Mark's things away for the last time and knew that a part of their lives was gone forever, maybe then they would cry out and surrender to the agony of their loss. But there in the Valley, in the presence of an insatiable media feeding on the details of butchery and cannibalism, the Kilroys demonstrated a grace under pressure that few journalists had ever witnessed.

Mark Kilroy and Bradley Moore had been talking about spring break since the start of the fall semester. At least twice a week Bradley called Mark in Austin or Mark called Bradley in Bryan, and they talked about the deeper meanings of life—beer, girls, the beach, the Miss Tanline contest, and nights across the border, in Matamoros. Mark was a junior pre-med major at the University of Texas, and Bradley was a sophomore electrical engineering major at Texas A&M. Before college, they had been basketball teammates and good buddies at Sante Fe High. Both had made the spring break scene at South Padre Island the previous year but not together.

For Bradley Moore, who had finished his exams the previous day, spring break started Friday, March 10, at noon. That was when he left his mobile home in Bryan and drove his Mustang to Austin to pick up Mark. Then they headed for Santa Fe, where they would rendezvous with two other old pals, Bill Huddleston and Brent Martin. On the way, they talked about cars and school and what they planned to do this summer. "We talked about how it would probably be our last summer at home together," Bradley recalled.

Sante Fe is on Texas Highway 6 between Houston

and Galveston. It is a small, middle-class town with wholesome, middle-class values and a large interest in high school sports. Mark, Bradley, and Brent had played basketball, and Mark and Bill had played baseball. All four boys—young men, actually—were tall, athletic, and clean-cut. None of them used drugs. All were serious students. They were the kind of boys you would like your daughter to date and maybe marry, and Sante Fe was the sort of place where you'd like your grandchildren to grow up.

Shortly after midnight that Friday, the four boys started for South Padre Island in Brent's Cutlass, following the long Texas coastline to its end. There was heavy fog that night, and the going was slow. Counting the two times the boys stopped to eat, the journey took nine hours. It was mid-morning by the time they checked into the Sheraton on South Padre. The hotel had been fortified for spring break. All of the furniture had been removed from the lobby. The four boys from Santa Fe showered, ate, and hit the beach.

The big crowds hadn't arrived yet. This was the opening weekend of South Padre's five-week spring break season, and students from all over the country were beginning to pour over the bridge from Port Isabel. The island was about to become a gigantic stage on which competing forces struggled for the souls of a quarter of a million students. Beer companies were sponsoring an unprecedented variety of entertainment, including free movies, free concerts, free calls home, and surf-simulator rides. Religious organizations from as far away as Madison, Wisconsin, were handing out pamphlets and free suntan lotion and urging students to pray rather than party. A beer company offered the free use of a swimming pool to students who didn't mind being a part of a filmed commercial and the boys took advantage of it. Mark and Bradley used a free phone line to call their parents. That night they met some girls from Purdue who were sharing an adjoining room and partied until dawn.

By Sunday the boys had more or less established a daily routine. They would hit the beach early and spend the morning soaking up rays. After lunch they would wander back to the part of the beach behind the Sheraton where the daily Miss Tanline contest was held. The cops had warned the contest sponsors about nudity, but when the emcee tried to prevent the contestants from removing their tops, the crowd went berserk. Later in the afternoon the boys would return to their room and try to take short naps, usually without success. Then they would plan their evening's entertainment.

On Sunday night they headed for Matamoros. First, they dined at the Sonic Drive-In in Port Isabel, where they met some girls from the University of Kansas who also were on the way to Matamoros. The girls followed Brent's Cutlass along the narrow, dangerous 24-mile highway that cuts across the tip of Texas. They parked both cars on the Brownsville side of the international bridge and walked across. They spent the whole evening at a place called Sgt. Pepper's, then the boys and the girls went their separate ways.

Monday was another glorious day on the beach. Mark struck up a conversation with one of the contestants in the Miss Tanline contest, a coed from Southwest Texas State University. In the early evening the boys checked out a condo party that some of Mark's former frat buddies at Tarleton State were throwing—

Mark had attended TSU before transferring to UT. About ten-thirty they decided to go back to Matamoros. Again they parked on the Texas side and walked across.

That night the border town had gone mad. The full wave had hit, and 15,000 spring breakers jammed the narrow sidewalks and spilled into the streets. The nightclubs on the main tourist drag, Avenida Alvaro Obregon, had placed sandwich boards along the way, advertising specials on margaritas and beer. Once within the first block past the bridge, the boys looked for the bar with the shortest waiting line. They selected Los Sombreros, a spot with a lot of neon and music loud enough to shatter brick. They didn't know it, but Los Sombreros wasn't exactly your old college inn. In July 1988 the son of the owner of another nightclub had been killed in a shoot-out at Los Sombreros, supposedly by a Hernandez gang member known as El Duby. A Matamoros cop who had been following El Duby had disappeared and hadn't been seen again. Barroom shootings were not novelties in Matamoros. Neither were people disappearing off the street. That happened every night, though usually not to gringos.

From Los Sombreros the boys wandered deeper into the madness, to the London Pub, which for the purposes of spring break had renamed itself the Hardrock Cafe. It was even louder and wilder than the first place, and the boys stood at the bar, dodging beer cans thrown from the balcony. Mark met some girls, and for a while the others didn't see him. It was nearly two o'clock when Bill Huddleston suggested that they head back to the island. When Bill, Bradley, and Brent walked out of the bar, they saw Mark leaning against a Volkswagen, talking to the girl from the Miss Tanline contest.

All up and down Avenida Alvaro Obregon, people were leaving the bars, most of them heading back to the bridge, but some moving aimlessly in the other direction or ducking down side streets to smoke a joint. Making progress in any direction was like swimming in a whirlpool. Bradley and Brent had walked ahead of the other two boys and were waiting in front of Garcia's, the gringo watering hole and gift shop, adjacent to a wooded area where vendors get their last shot at tourists crossing the bridge. Mark stopped in front of the steps of a private home to say goodbye to the girl from the Miss Tanline contest, then waited for Bill to catch up. Bill remembered Mark asking him if something was wrong. "I'm just tired," Bill replied. "Just not in a partying mood." Then he ran ahead and ducked behind a tree to relieve himself. When he joined Bradley and Brent in front of Garcia's two minutes later, Mark had vanished.

The three searched for their friend until long after the bars had closed and the streets had emptied. But there wasn't a trace. It was as though Mark Kilroy had dropped off the face of the earth.

Sitting in his pickup truck watching the spring breakers flow along Avenida Alvaro Obregon, Serafin Hernandez Garcia might have pondered the irony of his new religion, if he hadn't needed to pee so badly—and if he were the type to ponder. Nobody had mentioned this part. Nobody had told him that one of his jobs was to kidnap people so that his uncle Elio and the Cuban could sacrifice them to the gods. The gods were insatiable. True, the Hernandez family's marijuana smuggling business had recovered from last year's series of misfortunes. Things had never been better on that front. Also, since embracing the Palo Mayombe religion, Serafin's grades had improved. (He was a law enforcement major at Texas Southmost College and proud of it.) Serafin had converted to Palo Mayombe to please Elio, who was only two years older and more like a brother than an uncle. He had also done it because he thought it would bring him luck. Now it was too late to back out.

There were dozens of Hernandezes on both sides of the border—brothers, cousins, nephews, in-laws. Twenty-year-old Serafin represented a new generation: middle class, relatively well educated, conditioned to a life of plenty. For as long as he could remember, the drug business had provided. Poverty was something the old people talked about, something long before Serafin's time. His father, Serafin Hernandez Rivera, and grandfather and most of the others had been born and raised on an *ejido* near the village of San Fernando, on the highway between Matamoros and Ciudad Victoria. Ejido Ramirez was as poor as they came until Saul Hernandez Rivera came up with the idea to use the *ejido* as a marijuana area. Ten years later they were rich. They owned ranches and villas all over Mexico, drove expensive cars, and were able to educate their children. Serafin was born in Mission, Texas, and educated at Nimitz High in Houston, where his father ran the Texas end of the family's business. For the past seven years his family had lived in Brownsville.

Serafin Senior was the oldest of four brothers—5 years older than Saul, 17 years older than Ovidio, and

23 years older than Elio. But Saul was the one with balls. That's what it took to run marijuana out of Matamoros in the early eighties. U.S. drug interdiction in the Caribbean had caused traffic to be rerouted through Mexico to Texas, greatly enhancing business—and murder—in Matamoros. Dealers and second-echelon mobsters killed each other regularly, usually by way of machine-gun attacks on downtown streets. In 1984 a team of assassins in a homemade armored truck attacked a clinic where a minor mob boss named El Cacho was being treated, killing six innocents. The raid allegedly was ordered by another mob boss, El Profe, whose pistol had put El Cacho in the clinic in the first place. Though the Hernandezes were small-timers, they had the protection of a prominent and powerful Matamoros businessman who, according to reports in the newspaper *El Popular,* was the boss of bosses of organized crime in the border town. In July 1986 the publisher and a star reporter of *El Popular* were gunned down in front of their paper. The chief suspect was Saul Hernandez. Six months later Saul was cut down by machine-gun fire in front of a restaurant. His assassins were said to be drug rivals.

When Saul died, so did the moxie, skill, and connections that had made the Hernandez family successful. For the first time in memory, the family found itself bitterly divided. As the eldest brother, Serafin Senior tried to assume leadership, but he was hopeless. A month after Saul's murder Serafin Senior was arrested in the U.S. after a bungled attempt to land a load of dope on an airstrip in Grimes County. He hasn't yet been brought to trial, but his arrest compromised the Texas end of the business. On the Mexican side, meanwhile, Elio had seized power. Though he was the youngest of the brothers, Elio was most like Saul—ruthless, clever, ambitious, and willing to try new things. Some of the Hernandez cousins, nephews, and in-laws remained loyal to Serafin Senior, but many more fell in with Elio, including Serafin Junior and Ovidio.

Then there were other problems within the family. One of their *pistoleros,* El Duby, was wanted by authorities for questioning in the July 1988 shoot-out at Los Sombreros. Ovidio was feuding with a cousin, Jesus Hernandez, over a dope transaction in which Ovidio apparently pocketed $800,000 that belonged to Jesus. In the summer of 1988 a frightened Elio notified the police that Jesus had kidnapped Ovidio and Ovidio's two-year-old son and threatened to kill them unless the money was repaid. When his loved ones were released unharmed, Elio refused to press charges.

What the family needed, Elio decided, was protection. In the world of the Hernandezes, the best protection was magic. Witches and *curanderos* were as much a part of their daily lives as lawyers and doctors were to, say, the Kilroy family. How a simple man like Elio hooked up with a prince of darkness like Adolfo de Jesus Constanzo is still a mystery. There are three theories, all plausible: (1) Constanzo had connections with powerful drug lords in Central Mexico and had worked with the Hernandezes on previous deals; (2) El Duby knew Constanzo through his own connections in Mexico City; (3) Elio's girlfriend, Sara Aldrete, dabbled in black magic and had met Constanzo through friends in Mexico City's Cuban community.

Aldrete had read books on Santeria, an Afro-Caribbean religion that relies on animal sacrifices to achieve power and punish enemies. Constanzo had grown up in a Cuban neighborhood near Miami, where the practice of Santeria was common. His mother was said to be a witch who placed hexes on neighbors and left headless chickens and goats on the doorsteps of her enemies. When Constanzo was eighteen his mother sent him to study another Afro-Caribbean religion called Palo Mayombe. But whereas practitioners of Santeria used animal parts in their rituals, practitioners of Palo Mayombe used human parts that were stolen from graves.

Elio contacted Constanzo at a luxury apartment in Mexico City that the Cuban shared with a circle of male companions. Constanzo was a shadowy, duplicitous, charismatic young man who frequented the gay bars of the city's Zona Rosa and affected a flashy lifestyle. He was 26, older and far more sophisticated than Elio and others in the Hernandez gang. He was glib, relatively well educated, and highly persuasive. There was a Manson-esque intensity about him, an aura that was partly rehearsed, partly instinctive, and fully evil. The Cuban offered to act as the Hernandez gang's high priest, protecting its members from all enemies and promising riches beyond their dreams—in return for a share of their drug profits.

It was less than a mile from Rancho Santa Elena to the Rio Grande. Periodically, the Hernandez gang gave thanks to the Palo Mayombe gods, then smuggled hundreds of pounds of marijuana into Texas. The Cuban apparently made up the gang's religion as he went along, using various aspects of Santeria, Palo Mayombe, and voodoo as the mood struck him. Members of the cult smoked ritual cigars, drank ritual rum, slaughtered ritual chickens and goats, and prayed to various dieties including Oshun, the god of money and sex. Constanzo insisted that his followers call him El Padrino—the Godfather—and introduced various forms of mind control in the guise of religious mumbo jumbo. As Charles Manson had used the Beatles song "Helter Skelter," the Cuban used a movie called *The Believers,* in which a father and his son are caught in a web of black magic.

The tie that bound members of the Hernandez gang was drugs, not religion, but as the ceremony got stranger and their involvement got deeper, that changed. The Cuban was probably the first to suggest using human sacrifices, but it also may have been Elio or even Sara Aldrete. Of all the converts, Aldrete was the most zealous and the most mysterious.

An exceptionally tall woman with long brown hair and an athletic build, Aldrete lived an uncanny double life—honor student at Texas Southmost College by day and witch by night. Those who knew her as a cheer-leader for the soccer team and a nominee for TSC's Who's Who found her courteous, friendly, and always eager to please. There was nothing to suggest her dark side. Antonio Zavaleta, who knew Aldrete well, said: "She sat in my anthropology class all semester, an A student, always present, always friendly. I never saw her wear an emblem, an amulet, a talisman, any sign of black magic—and I'm trained to watch for such things; never heard her ask a weird question, even when we talked about weird religions." And yet Aldrete drove across the international bridge every night in her new Ford Taurus, went to her private room at her parents' home in a middle-class Matamoros neighborhood, and prayed before a blood-splattered altar. The police believe she took part in at least one human sacrifice, that she personally selected the victim (a man who had insulted her), lured him to the ranch, and supervised a slow death that included cutting off his nipples with scissors and boiling him alive.

At first the victims were selected from the ranks of enemies—rival drug dealers or dirty cops who had gone back on an agreement—strictly business to Elio's way of thinking. The Cuban made Elio, and later El Duby, executioner priests, branding their arms, chests, and backs with a red-hot knife. Elio was a real sweetheart of a priest. He was said to have cut out one rival's heart while the man was still alive. The planned execution of a Matamoros cop named Sauceda produced fireworks when Sauceda pulled out a gun, and Elio had to shoot him before the ceremony began. The cop's sudden and untimely death left the gang without a victim to sacrifice. Elio sent three of his men out to grab the first person they could find, who happened to be a fourteen-year-old boy looking for his lost goat. They threw a gunnysack over the boy's head and took him to Elio, who promptly decapitated the boy with a machete, never bothering to look at his face. As the headless body flopped across the floor, Elio was struck by something familiar. It was the boy's gray-and-green football jersey. Terror flooded Elio's dark eyes as he reached for the gunnysack: He had just executed his own nephew.

Though Mark Kilroy was selected at random, there may have been something about him that attracted Serafin Junior and his three companions. The Cuban had told them to find a typical gringo, and Kilroy's blond good looks and wholesome manner must have been irresistible. They grabbed Kilroy and wrestled him into the pickup between Serafin and another gang member named Torres. A few blocks down the avenue, Serafin stopped to relieve himself and Kilroy escaped, but a second carload of gangsters caught the student and handcuffed him in the back seat.

They drove through the back streets of Matamoros and past an industrial district. After a while the number of small bars and vendors' huts began to thin out and newly planted fields stretched off into the distance. The country air smelled musty and overused. There was a quarter moon, and by its light Kilroy might have had a chance to see that his kidnappers were his own age. Serafin had graduated from Nimitz in 1986, the same year Mark graduated from Sante Fe. Both of them had played baseball. They could have been on the same field, playing by the same rules.

Around a long, sloping curve, the car turned onto a narrow dirt road that snaked between two cornfields. Presently, the car's headlights caught a barn with some farm equipment on one side and an irrigation levee on the other. The gangsters left Mark Kilroy handcuffed in the back seat of a Suburban. He didn't see them again all night. An aging caretaker came around after dawn and gave him something to eat—some eggs, bread, and water.

Roughly twelve hours after Kilroy's abduction, the Cuban and his disciples came for him. They wrapped duct tape over his eyes and mouth and took him across a field, his hands still cuffed behind his back. Then they guided him through the door of a shed, where the air smelled like rotting meat. It was early afternoon, the time of day when the boys would have been drifting down the beach to watch the Miss Tanline contest. Whatever was going through Mark Kilroy's mind, whatever he imagined would be his fate, it wasn't nearly as terrible as what was about to happen.

By Friday, the fourth day after the discovery of the bodies, the story had lost steam and dropped off page one. The Kilroys had gone home, and so had the politicians and most of the media. Nobody had claimed the $15,000 reward, though an extortionist in the Galveston County jail had tried to hit on the Kilroys for ransom. Few noticed and fewer stopped to record the activities of the peasants and campesinos who had come down from mountain villages or traveled, sometimes hundreds of miles, from their *ejidos,* looking for lost loved ones among the rows of mutilated corpses. They stood on the sidewalks in front of funeral homes, not sure what to do next, or in small groups at the ranch, where the search for more bodies continued.

In the shadows of the sacrificial shed, while bulldozers and backhoes excavated the putrid black soil that had been the devil's graveyard, a priest prayed. Nearby a woman from Ejido Ramireno waited with her two sons, watching and wondering if a sixteen-year-old friend from her *ejido* would be among the victims. Seventy-six-year-old Hidalgo Castillo wondered the same thing about his 52-year-old son, Moises Castillo. Moises lived in Houston, but once a year he went to Ejido Morelos to work his cornfields. He had disappeared in May 1988, and in light of all that had happened, the old man feared the worst. He was right. Two days later Mexican authorities found the bodies of Moises Castillo and another man in shallow graves across the highway—victims number 14 and 15.

In the lobby of a Matamoros funeral home, Isidoro and Ericada Garcia waited while one of their daughters slipped behind a curtain to view the remains of a boy who had been decapitated and whose lungs and brain had been cut out. Devout Evangelicals, the Garcias worked a farm two miles from Rancho Santa Elena. Their fourteen-year-old son, Jose Luis, had vanished on February 25—three weeks before Mark Kilroy had disappeared. There had been no press conferences for Jose Luis, no rewards, no attorneys general or network TV. The Garcias didn't even have enough money to buy a body bag to bury their son, if the body behind the curtain proved to be their son.

It was Jose Luis, all right. "He had no head," his sister reported. "It was chopped off on the side. But I knew it was him by the shirt he was wearing. It was gray and green, his favorite football shirt."

The Garcias seemed almost relieved, which, strangely enough, was the same reaction the Kilroys had when they finally learned their son's fate. Now they were at peace. Now the white magic could do its work.

When Ericada Garcia spoke with Tom Ragan of the *Brownsville Herald,* it was without a trace of bitterness or irony. "If it weren't for the Kilroy boy," she said, "none of the other men, including my son, would ever have been found."

Adolfo de Jesus Constanzo may have been more twisted and evil than anyone suspected. While promising to protect the Hernandez gang, he was using

their connections to steal from other drug dealers. The
police weren't the only ones looking for the ill-fated
gang. Constanzo had a group of followers separate and
apart from the Hernandezes. It included an inner circle
of Mexico City friends who may have been involved in
the ritual killings of at least eight additional victims.

When Serafin Hernandez blundered past that roadblock and doomed the Matamoros sect, Constanzo suggested a vacation to Mexico City. He flew out of
Brownsville the day the bodies were discovered, accompanied by Sara Aldrete, El Duby, and four or five
others. When police discovered some of Aldrete's
clothing in the abandoned safe house, they assumed
that she had become the newest victim of the Cuban's
murderous ritual; the so-called witch was the most ex-
pendable member of the cult. But the final twist was
more demonic than even the Hernandez gang had
imagined.

Three weeks later, when Mexico City police surrounded the building where the gang was hiding, the
Cuban went berserk. He began firing his machine gun
and tossing bundles of money out of the fourth-floor
window. Constanzo had taken the precaution of ordain-
ing El Duby and transferring to him the power to make
human sacrifices; now he commanded El Duby to perform the ultimate ritual—Constanzo wanted to die with
his lover and bodyguard, Martin Quintana Rodriguez.
El Duby hesitated, but the Cuban slapped him and
warned him that failure to carry out this last assignment would make it hard on him in hell. Constanzo sat
on a stool in the closet and positioned his lover beside
him, then he nodded, and El Duby squeezed the trigger
of his machine gun. When police stormed the apart-

ment a few minutes later, El Duby, Aldrete, and three others surrendered quietly.

As for the devil's ranch where Kilroy and the others were sacrificed, it remained a citadel of black magic until there was a proper purification ceremony. One quiet Sunday afternoon, when no one was looking, the federales slipped out there with a *curandero*. He went inside the shed, mumbled incantations, sprinkled salt on the floor, and made the sign of the cross. Then federales sloshed gasoline over the shed and burned it to the ground.

(June 1989)

Long after the drug-crazed killers of Mark Kilroy were arrested and sent to prison to rot—and people had forgotten the satanic events in Matamoros—Kilroy's parents traveled the country at their own expense, telling anyone who would listen the fatal lesson of drug abuse. James and Helen Kilroy aren't zealots, just good Christian parents who suffered an unimaginable loss and dealt with it the way Jesus might have. I've never met better or more decent people than the Kilroys. I still get a lump in my throat remembering how straightforward James Kilroy was when he told a group of journalists, "I don't feel any anger at all, to be honest with you. If and when they [the murderers] get to heaven, I hope they will find Mark and apologize."

I Loved The
Dapper Bandit

MARK SEAL

I am a hardworking hooker in a perpetually horny town. I've been turning tricks professionally for seven years, working my way up from the Kit Kat Club on Industrial Boulevard ($20 for twenty minutes) to the Mansion on Turtle Creek ($200 an hour from a television joke writer in 1989). In the last few days I've seen an Indian, a Taiwanese, a Chinese, an African, a Saudi Arabian, two Greeks, and a German. Whoever thinks Dallas isn't an international city should talk to me.

Have I ever been in love? That's usually the first question my tricks ask me in the Motel 6, eager to get the most out of my average $60-an-hour fee. Let's answer this one right up front. Yes. I fell in love with a trick named Mark Reeves, the Dapper Bandit, the most notorious Texas bank robber since Bonnie and Clyde. I was his steady squeeze for a year and a half without knowing that when he went to work—which wasn't often enough for me—he traded his jeans and T-shirt for a wig, a moustache, sunglasses, gloves, and a gray J. C. Penney suit. That's why they called him "Dapper." With a yuppie briefcase in one hand, a .38-caliber stainless steel revolver in the other, and a Browning

9-millimeter pistol tucked in his belt, my lover knocked off banks, vaulting over bank counters in rubber-soled Hush Puppies. He confessed to robbing 25 banks in Dallas, Houston, San Antonio, Austin, and Tarrant County from 1978 to 1988. His take? More than half a million dollars. His strategy? He never fired a shot, and he never kept a dollar. No matter how much he made, he would be broke in a few months. I wondered how he got his money, which he brought home either in a shoe box or not at all. I thought he was a dope dealer or a gun runner. That shows how good I am with my serious relationships.

Hooking is a loony way to make a living. But nobody was crazier than Mark Reeves, the Dapper Bandit, the man who wanted to buy me out of the business and make me respectable. What a joke.

I met Mark in September 1984, about two and a half years after I started tricking. He was high on cocaine. I usually stay away from cocaine calls—they're not my style. A cocaine call is when somebody has drugs and they would love for you to say two magic words: "Gimmie some." Tricks on cocaine offer it to you every five minutes, which is really annoying, especially for a reformed coke junkie like me. Cocaine calls don't really get into sex; they just want to work you for twelve hours. They're just trying to play vampire. Misery loves company. I've been there a million times. To these guys, saying "I've got some cocaine" is like saying, "I've got the Hope diamond."

The call was through an escort agency. I didn't have my own agency then. I had a beeper, and I was working for these people who were ripping me off, lying to me about the money I had coming through MasterCard. It was the old story: Get a green girl, give her one cash call a day so she'll have gas and hamburger money, then put the rest on credit cards, so the girl gets paid once a month. You work two or three weeks. Call mania. Anything that breathes. Until the agency owes you like $3,000 and won't pay. When you finally demand your cash, they say, "Well, you didn't turn those vouchers in" or "The bank has questions." Finally you have to quit since you can't take the problem to the police or anything.

One Friday night they told me, "Go see this guy who's been seen before." That means it's a good call, a regular, not a cop. He sees four hookers a week. Pays cash. They gave me his vital statistics: name, telephone number. I had just finished a domination call, tying up an Arlington businessman between two desks. I was a nervous wreck. I called Mark Reeves at four in the morning, just after leaving the pervert in Arlington.

"What's your description?" he asked.

"Five six, brown hair, brown eyes. 35-24-35. Weight 120 pounds. I *like* my work."

"Come on over," he said. "Here's the address."

I told him it would be $150 cash—$50 for the agency fee, $100 for the tip. When I got there, he looked like a cocaine call. A guy about thirty, living by himself in some boring apartment on Park Lane with rented furniture. Motorcycle by the front door. Shorts. Hawaiian shirt. Good body from daily workouts. A great tan. A guy you'd spot at the pool and feel your sap rising. Cute. Real casual. He was the last guy you'd take for a notorious bank robber. But by the time we met, the police later said, Mark had already knocked off at least eight banks, his latest being Plaza National Bank of Dallas in July and American State Bank in Fort Worth for $65,000 that February. Like a lot of guys, Mark would get a hooker whenever he had money in his pocket. The minute I saw him, smiling at me from his balcony, I thought, "Not my style." Dumpy apartments and cocaine—I've spent too many years wallowing in both.

We sat on the couch. I told him if he wanted me to stay, I had to collect first. We started making out. He kept going into the bathroom to do more cocaine. After an hour, I got up to go.

"I want you to stay longer," he said.

"Okay," I said, "So let's collect again."

He was tired. And wired. He kept talking about race car driving. "I spend three thousand dollars a weekend, racing cars," he said. He showed me some trophies. And he kept doing cocaine. The best thing about him? He didn't push the coke on me. So he had some manners. Then he started in on his fantasies.

"If I get good enough in racing, it would be really neat if you would come to my races, and we could be in love," Mark said.

In love? Mark was into this whole fantasy trip. I just said, "Okay." He told me that he liked me. And I said, "Yeah, okay." A lot of people say that. They go, "Wow, you've got a great body. I'm in love." It's nothing new to me. I always agree with everything—"Sure, we can live on a desert island, whatever you say." I'll go with the fantasy, unless it's something really morbid.

I stayed with Mark for about three and a half hours. But I told my agency I had gone home after the first hour. So I made about $350 off of the call. He was a good call. I gave him my home number when I left. "Call me at home sometimes, and we'll bypass the agency," I said.

The next Sunday at six in the morning, he called me at home. On my mother's phone. At that point, I didn't have my own trick phone yet. I was living with my parents. Sure, they knew I was hooking. They were just thrilled that I was off the drugs, proud of me for working. *Any* career was better than being a junkie. After all, when I was on drugs, I was stealing from them like crazy. Guns. Silverware. Jewelry. I even stole all my dad's anniversary pins from the LTV Corporation, prying out the diamonds and trading them for a shot of junk. I figured that my parents had brought me out of the womb and deserved to suffer for their creation. Talk about a twisted mind. But when I became a hooker, I straightened up overnight. I realized what a bitch I'd been. My parents were thrilled. I paid them back every dime I had stolen. My mother dreamed of me marrying a rich trick, who would whisk me off to the land of suburbia, babies, and soap operas.

"Are you on that white stuff again?" I asked Mark.

"Yeah."

"Look, let me get my act together, and I'll come over."

But then I felt funny about it. I called a girlfriend who was also a hooker. Marilyn talked me out of going. You're too weak, she said, and if you do cocaine calls, you're exposing yourself back to that old phase of drug addition.

Mark called again about ten.

"Where are you?" he pleaded.

He sounded sexy, charming. Real nice. And stoned.

"Look, I'm not coming over," I said. "Leave me

alone. I don't need calls like this. If you call me back, I'll call the police."

"What did *I* do?" he asked.

I hung up. Mark Reeves didn't call back—for a year.

How did I ever get into this business? That's another question I get asked, usually between the last kiss and the cigarette. Born and raised in Cockrell Hill—which I have always called Cockroach Hill—I was a bookworm and honor student, a real egghead, until I lost interest in school, dropped out, and became a dedicated rock groupie and champion coke snorter and speed shooter.

I had done the bar scene for years, winding up every night in a different guy's bed, waking up to find some jerk who refused to talk to me or take me home, a guy who mumbled, "Can't you call a cab?" before rolling over and going back to his snoring. I'd done freelance whoring since I was nineteen, working at massage parlors, taking out personal ads, seeing a sugar daddy at a Hilton hotel. I've done it all. But I never made enough money to think of hooking as a profession until I followed a friend's advice: "Pick up the Yellow Pages, and look under 'Escort Service.'" I got hired over the telephone right off the bat, without even an interview. I was sent to the Wyndham Hotel. Within half an hour, I was drinking champagne and eating shrimp cocktails with some traveling salesman in room 484. Not a bad way to make a quick $50.

A long time ago, I made up my mind: It takes money to live right and eat well. It takes a lot of jing to go to aerobics and the tanning salon every day and to Paul Neinast once a month for a $400 beauty treatment. I've always had expensive tastes. These days, at 31, I'm addicted to my career. Total workaholic.

I don't have a pimp, and I don't want to stand on the street. I prefer going where I'm invited. So, like everybody else in Dallas, I use a car. My old 1984 Subaru had 100,000 miles in four yours of service. I cover the Metroplex. I'm listed in the Yellow Pages under "Escort Service," and I had two telephones with answering machines. Ten calls an hour, 24 hours a day. Like clockwork. And that's what turning a trick is: dealing with some nut with a problem.

Dallas men? A good definition would be "hard up for sex." They do a lot of explaining—about their wives, their girlfriends, the women who won't do anything except on Easter Sunday. Some of them are just hooked on paying. That was the story of the Dapper Bandit. Mark had a nice bunch of straight, normal, hardworking friends. But when it came to sex, he liked hookers. He figured, why spend all night in a bar talking to some floozy who would soak up $60 in drinks only to eventually tell him, "You don't get none," when he could have somebody like me panting on his doorstep in twenty minutes? It's like calling Domino's Pizza. Guys like Mark don't want dates. Either they're too shy or they feel their date won't be nasty enough. Some of them are such closet cases with sex that they just lose it. A lot get emotional. Their mother just died or their wife just walked out. I've entered a lot of empty houses, just some guy sitting in the dark with a bottle of Scotch. I'll ask, "Where's the furniture?" And he'll say, "She took it all."

Sometimes they tell me, "You must have a really neat life. It must be great making money on your back." I go, "Uh-huh." And then I'm off to the next call, thinking, "Is this next guy going to rob me? Is he going to be on the level? Is he a vice cop who has a good line of bull and video cameras hidden behind the blinds, trying to get me to tell him what we're going to do before we do it, so he can flash his badge and ship me off to a $5,000-a-night suite in Lew Sterrett Justice Center (which all the hookers call Lew's Place)? Or is he a decoy for some goon in a gas mask, who's going to leap from the closet, shoot me up with heroin, then sell me for $15,000 to China, where I'll be the star of a snuff film?" I'm told that actually happened to a hooker friend of mine. Talk about a fatal attraction. Sometimes the cops will run you all the way out to Red Oak, just to jack with you, or a guy will call four hookers at once, then try to short us on the fee. Some of the girls get really P.O.'d when that happens. They'll call pizzas and cabs on the guy all night or throw a brick through his window. But I always say, "Girls, let's be civilized." After all, we're professionals.

Guys call all the time from all the major hotels and downtown office buildings: 500 Ervay, Southland Life, the Infomart (I call it the Nymphomart). Usually, it's closing time or lunch hour on an off day. They'll just lock the door of their office. Airline pilots are another big market sector. The Byron Nelson Golf Classic wears me out. I've been with dozens of Dallas Cowboys and practically every rock band that has played Reunion Arena. About a dozen preachers have said grace over me. Once a year I tiptoe through the pup tents at Boy Scout training sessions at the Flagship Inn in Arlington.

I have hundreds of regulars. Sometimes I'm glad

when they can't get me. I get burned out if I see some-body over and over. It just gets old. It's like I'm his wife. If there's no hassle, it's okay. But if he's on a weird trip or if he puts out love vibes, that's when I cut him off. I can't afford to fall in love. I'm a working girl, not a debutante.

I don't worry about AIDS. I get four tests a year, and I'm clean. But my tricks put me through mental torture about it—"Are you sure you don't have anything? Are you *sure?*"—and I say, "I'm a hooker, not a killer. I practice safe sex." I've made millions for the Trojan company. More than AIDS, I worry about weirdos. Nothing will protect you from them.

I've done tricks in parked airplanes, limousines, $8-an-hour Harry Hines Boulevard motel rooms with porno movies on TV. I've done it in the back of a dump truck behind Tom Thumb with a drunken driver who flagged me down on Fort Worth Avenue. Some guys are too cheap to get a motel room. I've had only one who gave me $500 when I asked for only $200. He was a dedicated husband. His wife was dying of leukemia, and he said he didn't believe in screwing around. But he had a prostate problem, and his doctor told him, "You gotta have sex, or you're gonna die." He told me he was seeing me for medical reasons, and he had an extreme guilt trip about his wife.

You don't get many like that. Most of them want to pay $60. That's the magic word: "sixty." Oh, fabulous, they say. Or they'll try to talk you down further. $52.50 is the lowest I will go. I used to be the only escort service listed in the GTE Yellow Pages in Las Colinas, which brought swarms of realtors, insurance agents, and rock stars. But there are just as many traveling salesmen and truck drivers at some Best Western motel. Like the rig driver I met recently. I pulled up at 6 p.m. on a Sunday and told the guy, "I need to collect first." He opened up his wallet and shut it. Real weird.

"I pay when I'm done," he said.

"No, you won't," I answered. "I'll leave."

He got up off the bed, put his hand against the door. He was a real big stocky guy. And he pulled a knife from a sheath behind his back. A Rambo knife. He stuck it to my throat.

"You're not getting out of this room," he said.

I was sweating, thinking, "I've got a real lunatic on my hands." He told me he'd been up on speed for days. I cased the room and saw Uzi machine guns. Sawed-off shotguns. Everything. He made me pull my clothes off and do the trick. I was shaking the whole time, kinda crying. When he got off, he fell back on the bed, dazed, real tired. Finally, he said, "Look, my kids love me. But my wife hates me," and I ran out of the room into the motel parking lot. Buck naked.

My trick phones ring constantly. "This is Joe, Sammy, José, Doug, Bill, Johnny," they say. "Remember me?" I'll say no, and they get real insulted. But the names just mean nothing. Every voice sounds the same. "Hi, this is Randy, Craig, Malcolm, Bobby."

"Who?" I'll say.

"I can't believe you don't remember!"

When Mark Reeves called me again, it was August 1985. I didn't know it, but the Dapper Bandit had had a successful spring and summer. He later confessed to five robberies in 1985, including $17,000 from Houston's Allied Bank in April, $67,000 from the Arlington State Bank in May, $23,000 from Dallas' Swiss Avenue Bank, and a smaller amount from the Medallion National. But when he called me again, I didn't know him from the thousands of other voices on the telephone.

"Do you remember me?" he asked.

Right, Jack.

He called at ten every night for two weeks before I finally went to see him. I was still working my tricks out of my parents' home. They were still happy about it. Better hooking than shooting. I was tricking like a madwoman, saving up to buy a house. That was my dream: to own my own home. I had my trick phone, but Mark always called on my parents' line. They would be watching Johnny Carson, and my dad would say, "It's that Mark guy, and he's drunk again." But I was always too busy to see him.

Finally I thought, "Better go see this Mark guy, get him out of the way." On the phone he told me that I hadn't seen him for a while. He gave me an address on Slopes Drive, and I said, "I don't know you. I remember addresses, and I've never been to this one before." He said he had moved.

"Okay, I'm coming over," I said, thinking in the back of my head, "Watch for cops. Watch for a weirdo."

When I got to his apartment, he had one of those security gates that you have to be "buzzed" through. He buzzed me inside, and when I walked into the apartment and saw him standing on the balcony—shorts, T-shirt, Panama hat, big "Hello! How are you?"—I thought to myself, "Oh, no. This is that crazy race car driver, that cocaine addict. Why didn't I pick up on that when he called?" My first instinct was, get out. But I was already locked inside the apartment gates. So I just thought, "Get a grip. Do the call. *Do not do any drugs.*"

"Are you on coke?" I yelled up to the balcony.

"No, I quit six months ago," he said. "Now all I do is drink."

He was smashed. We sat on the couch. I liked the apartment. It was expensive-looking. Pictures of his race car on the wall. Jacuzzi bathtub. All the modern conveniences. Mark went into this long thing about what he'd been doing for the last year. He talked on and on about his car racing—he was a car freak! He told me about the trips he'd been taking. He was stuck on Colorado, especially Durango. He went there dozens of times. He said that was where he wanted to live. All during the conversation he kept saying, "Do you remember me? I'm the guy from the other apartment."

How could I forget?

"I'm racing formula Fords, and I spend most of my weekends going off racing," he said. "I've been thinking about you a lot. I've wanted to see you again."

He went on for about 45 minutes, until I finally said, "Look, Mark, we've got to do the call. I've got other calls to do." But he didn't really want sex. He said, "Well, I don't even know if I can do anything."

"Well, what did you call me for?"

"Okay, okay," he said. "Let's go in the other room and do something. But before we do, can you stay the rest of the night?"

I told him it was going to cost him. He pulled a $100 bill out from under his clock-radio. But he was real reluctant about the sex. I took him to bed, got him undressed, and afterward he passed out cold. He was just so drunk and tired. But I was getting wider and wider awake. I thought about my phones ringing and how much I needed the money. I looked at him and thought, "This guy is dead to the world." I felt something for him, especially when he said he'd been thinking about me for months. He was just so serious and cute and a *race car driver*! But I couldn't relax. I wasn't prepared to do an all-night call, and it's not good to sleep with a trick. They might steal their money back, or you might wake up naked, by yourself, not knowing if you're in Highland Park or Haltom City.

I was ready to work. So I split, did a call at the old Mandalay Four Seasons in Las Colinas, and went home. I started feeling strange vibes about Mark wondering where I went. So I called him and said that I just had to work, that it was my life. He asked when I could see him again.

"As a client or not as a client?" I asked.

"Not as a client," he said. "I just want to see you."

I told him I'd see him in two days because I needed to get some work done first. I was attracted to him. But there's little time for romance when you're seeing forty johns a week. On the evening of the third day, I went to Mark's apartment. We got drunk. But then we got off. I'm talking great, passionate, wild, hot sex. Incredibly handsome and romantic, Mark could have qualified for the Grand Prix in the sack. He just had charisma. He was the best I'd ever had. Mark Reeves blew my mind. After that night, I was hooked.

"Remember the first time we met, when I told you we would be in love someday?" Mark said in bed that first dynamite night. He was right: I felt the twang. I felt like I'd been hit with a magic wand. In the weeks to come my clothes accumulated in his apartment, panty by panty. I couldn't stay away from him. My psychic of fifteen years, David Russo, had told me just before I met Mark that I'd soon be in love. I was skeptical. My girlfriends figured that after doing calls day and night for three years, I needed a change and just didn't know it.

When Mark came along, I was ready to throw the agency away. I hardly answered my trick phone. I just hung around and watched TV with him—I hadn't done that in years. I was real happy. I thought I had this exotic race-car-driving boyfriend. I was soaking him up like a sponge: a hooker acting like an SMU girl with this guy who looked like a North Dallas white-trash yuppie.

I even introduced Mark to my parents. One day he took me to the Filling Station, got me drunk on margaritas, and talked me into going camping. "If we don't go pack this very minute and leave for Colorado, you'll try and back out," he said. I said, "Okay, let's go to my parents' house and get the gear," and we drove out drunk to Cockroach Hill. My parents were sitting, as usual, in their twin La-Z-Boy recliners before a booming big-screen TV that's too large for their living room. When we walked in, Mom's eyes went directly from *Family Feud* to Mark's legs.

"Boy, he *is* good looking!" she shouted. "He's got great legs!"

Dad just sat there, shaking his head. "Whaddya do, son?" he asked.

Mark told him something like, "Well, I loan money at a high rate of interest, and I'm a race car driver."

I went to get the camping equipment, and Mark tried to get out of talking to my folks. He washed his car. Sat on the front porch. Anything to get out of parental conversation. Buy Mom still thought he was Mr. Wonderful. "Marry him!" she whispered as I was leaving. "At least he'll get you off the streets."

But beneath his great looks, Mark was a walking hunk of problems. He was born on March 4, 1953, in Kassel, West Germany, where his dad was in service. His problems started when his parents divorced; he never talked about his mother, who later died, and he was estranged from his father. When Mark was four, he was shipped off to Dallas to live with his aunt, who's just like Granny in *The Beverly Hillbillies*. She nicknamed him Bucky and raised him until late grade school, when he went to live with his father again. His dad was strict, military-style. He would lock Mark in his room and make him do like two thousand push-ups. Soon Mark was back with his aunt. He felt like he was being dumped all the time.

He was the captain of his high school football team, a pretty good swimmer, and an all-star car thief. He would take his aunt out for lunch in one stolen car, then in another a week later. She got wise and told him to quit. But he kept on doing it. When he finally got busted for the cars and was sitting in his attorney's office, he said all he could think about was his aunt's voice, a voice in his head that kept saying, "I've never seen a guy so smart and act so stupid." That really bothered him.

He went to Huntsville for a year, and he got an extra

seven months because guys kept trying to mess with him. They had one dirty magazine, and they would take turns with it. That was sex: magazines or another man. So Mark would fight. And you're not allowed to fight in prison. You get more time. He beat one guy up pretty bad because the guy would not leave him alone. Mark didn't slow down much when he got out. He got probation for a couple of petty thefts, constantly got speeding tickets, and walked away from two motorcycle accidents. Just another handsome Dallas hustler, trying to live life in the fast lane with no visible means of support.

He liked being alone, watching TV, drinking, cooking steaks on a grill, or telling me, "I'm gonna make some macaroni and cheese in my special way." I would go to the Jacuzzi or swim, and when I came back, dinner would be on the table. Lust was blooming into love.

Every other weekend during racing season, Mark flew to Canada or Colorado to compete in races, returning home like a champion, raving about racing with Paul Newman or somebody. But he was all talk and few trophies. The more I got to know him, the less I liked him. He wasn't like a regular guy. He slept late. He drank every night. Tremendous drinking. Gallons of Crown Royal. Tequila straight out of the bottle. He even drank rum straight out of the bottle, and I've *never* seen anybody do that. Every night he'd work out at the AKA Fitness Center on Greenville Avenue, then drink a dozen beers.

We'd spend the night together, but soon I'd wake up and say, "I really need to be working." He would say, "Let's go rent a boat on Lake Lavon." He'd come up with different options. "We could ride the motorcycle, then go look at new motorcycles, then go jet skiing on Lake Lavon." He knew how to tap me, and I'd just blow off my work.

We took trips to Hot Springs, then Durango, then Ruidoso, then Cripple Creek. Mark paid cash for everything. And we spent plenty. As much as $8,000 per trip. My motto? Let the good times roll! He kept his cash in the trunk of his Camaro IROC-Z, with personalized license plates that read, "SWIFT 1."

"You know what's the most stolen car in America?" he asked me on one trip. "The Camaro. It's the easiest to hot-wire."

Later, the papers said Mark had stolen Camaros to do his bank jobs. But at the beginning of our affair, I didn't care who he was or where he came from. Love conquers all. After several months I moved into his apartment. I said, "Look, we're together all the time. I just need to bring some stuff over here and move in or something."

And he said, "Move in! Move in!" We made this deal: We would live together for a month, see how it went. He signed a contract I wrote, in which he agreed to give me about $20,000 a year for my personal expenses while we were together. In return, I agreed to forget about my trick phones for a while. When I moved in, I said, "I'm going to have to have some money to go the hairdresser and blah, blah, blah." He gave me $2,000. "You caught me completely off guard," he said. "I hadn't planned to have a girlfriend; I'd planned to stay alone. And now my life is going through this big change because I'm going to *get married*!"

"Why do you love me?" I asked Mark one day. "Because we're equals," he said. "You're the best at what you do, and I'm the best at what I do." I assumed he was talking about racing.

He kept bringing up marriage. He had this dream of us moving to Colorado, having a baby, and buying a llama farm. There's big money in ostriches and llamas, he said, because you can sell the ostrich skins for cowboy boots and the llamas as pets. He kept telling me that I was so smart and that all the other girls he was seeing were so stupid. He was a chick *magnet*. He had to beat them off at the pool. It was that race car image.

After exactly fourteen days of live-in monogamy, I got drunk, moved out, and started tricking again. Why? Because Mark wasn't living up to this contract. Yeah, he had given me the $2,000. But besides that, I wasn't getting a dime. And my motto's like the old blues song—"If I Can't Sell It, I'll Keep Sittin' on It." Mark soon got disgusted with my career, telling me I was in a sleazy profession and that I was going to die. One night I had just returned from Reunion Arena, and I had this big rug burn on my back from this monster monkey musician. Mark wanted me to quit, but he wouldn't offer me a better deal. I said, "The man who gets me out of this is going to offer me a better way."

But I guess I still loved him. Because the day after I moved out, we were back into daily dating. I dragged my clothes back and forth from my parents' house to Mark's apartment, sometimes crashing at his place for several days at a time. While I was tricking during the day, Mark worked out at the health club. By four in the afternoon, I would call him up, and we'd meet at his apartment and start drinking and watching TV. He watched TV constantly: *The Andy Griffith Show, Leave It to Beaver, The Munsters, The Real McCoys.* He would quote things about Aunt Bea and her pickles or Goober trying to get a date, telling me how he thought those things related to life. But his favorites were *Miami Vice* and, most of all, Tom Selleck in *Magnum, P.I.* He loved Magnum. He dressed like him, and he acted like him. Hawaiian shirts, cut-offs, guns, and fancy cars. Going to gun shows and coming home with two or three Uzis for sport shooting.

Once every two weeks I'd explode, telling him that he was a jerk, that he was keeping me from working, that he was a professional time-waster, that I really liked him a lot but he was nothing but a stud. Our early problems centered on the racing. I was under the impression that he was a *professional* race car driver. So I thought it odd when he took me to meet a banker on the $40,000 loan he'd taken out for his race car. That was when I started wondering about his financial stability. Mysteriously, money would appear for trips, for dinner, for fun. But you wonder about a guy who says he's a professional racer, then comes home from the Dallas Public Library with a copy of something like *How to Get a Race Car Sponser* under his arm. He later told the cops that he hung around the library, studying everything from FDIC bank directories and getaway routes in the Mapsco to really heavy books like *The Anarchist Cookbook*, learning how to make bombs. It turns out that twice in 1988 he hid bombs in banks, planning to demand cash before telling where the bombs were. But both the bombs and the extortions fizzled.

I got wise to his real racing situation when I heard

him on the phone one day, asking, "How much is the car gonna cost to be fixed this time?" When he hung up, he said, "God, this is costing me a fortune."

"I thought that *you* got paid!" I said, freaking a little.

"Well, I put some money in it," he said.

"How much is this gonna cost?"

"Twelve thousand," he said. "The car needs a new nose and a new fender."

I went wild. "You're spending this kind of money to go racing?" The first year we were together, he had a bad year racing, a horrible year. Plus I was screaming about all the money. I was just throwing fits. Finally I flipped out. I told Mark I couldn't handle it. I didn't like sitting around getting drunk every night and not making any money. I said, "Look, either make some money and get me off the street or I'll show your aunt my escort-service ads." He'd flare his nostrils and start making excuses. "Being involved with you makes it hard for me to work," he said.

What work? I couldn't figure out what he did. My psychic told me that Mark's business was covered in blackness, that he would never reveal his occupation to me, and that he was trouble with a capital *T.* Just like all men, I figured. Mark and I would have these question-and-answer sessions about his mysterious career, which quickly escalated into knock-down-drag-outs if I didn't drop the subject.

"Is what you do illegal?" I asked.

"No," he said.

"Well, if it's not illegal, why can't you tell me?"

"I just can't tell you. I have to be real careful with you because you're so smart. You'd pick up any clues or evidence I might leave around. You make my life a challenge. All I can say is that when I was twenty-five, I was a construction worker eating off a catering truck, and I came up with a plan and it worked."

"When do you work?"

"When they call me. I have a boss, and there's other people involved. The people I work with are guys I would never be seen with outside of work, even in a 7-Eleven. I'm talking *thugs*!"

"Are you Mafia or CIA? You must be in some secret organization, where you can't tell anybody. Or are you the Atlanta child murderer?"

"Look, I work, and I have no problem with my job."

"You must have a problem since you can't tell anybody what you do."

"It's not *me* with the job problem. It's you! How can you go from man to man, doing whatever they tell you, degrading yourself with all of these people?"

We went on like that at least once a week. I'd go, "You don't seem to be working very much. You need to work!" And he'd go, "Yeah, but this thing that I'm doing, it's just harder and harder to do now that I've got you around, and it could affect you if something happened to me." And I'd say, "Whaddya mean, it could affect me? Am I gonna get shot?"

"No, no, no. You could be affected if something happens to me. You'd be alone and in love."

One night, while watching *Magnum*, Mark turned to me and said, "I can't tell you what I do for a living, but I will tell you this much: If I ever get caught, it'll be front-page news. Headlines. I'll be a legend. Like Clint Eastwood. I'm an outlaw, a real outlaw."

When he left the room, I called one of my girl-friends.

"This guy is retarded," I said. "He's walking around acting like Clint Eastwood. Totally living in a dream world."

When I told my tricks about my mystery man, they'd guess that he was a "mule" for a drug runner. Or a hit man for the Mafia, getting a call and flying across the country to blow somebody's brains out. A wise guy. But to me, he seemed like just another lunatic, messing with my mind. I remember returning from a trip with him early in our relationship. Mark sat down to count his money. When he was finished, he looked up and said, "Oh, my God, we've *overspent*!"

"Overspent!" I screamed. "I didn't think we were on any certain travel budget."

Mark said he had to go to work. This was maybe October 1985. We'd been together for a little over two months.

The next day we went to lunch at the Vickery Feed Store. "I've got a favor to ask you," he said. "I need to borrow two thousand for a week. The race car just cost more than I thought, and with all the trips, I'm broke. Think about loaning me the money, and I'll give you my Rolex. If something happens to me, you'll have the watch, and it's worth fourteen thousand."

He loved his Rolex. That was his main piece of cloth-ing. He said it was the best one he'd ever seen. It was a pretty watch, with a blue lapis face. One night he thought he lost it in his apartment, and he became sui-cidal. Crying. Mumbling, "I'm a worm without that watch. That watch signified my arrival as an important person." That night he cried that he thought he was functionally insane, somebody who could get up and go to McDonald's and the library, then come home and barbecue steaks like every other joker, but who's really crazy.

"I don't think you're crazy, but I do think you've got two monkeys on your back—your job and your race car," I said.

When I told Mark I didn't have the money to loan him, that the $20,000 I had when I met him was down to $5,000 and that was my "bust" money for attorney's fees, he was flustered, depressed, flushed. I didn't like the way he looked when he was broke. I went home and told my father that Mark wanted me to loan him money. Dad's opinion of him went down to zero after that. But Mother still loved Mark and constantly begged me to marry him and move to Colorado.

Many months passed. Mark said he was going to work. But first we had to take one more trip to Ruidoso. We camped out on some mountain, staying four days. He seemed real quiet and clammy, drinking all night, riding rented Jeeps all day.

"You act real weird," I said finally.

"What I have to do when I get home is just hard," he said. "I'll be okay once it's over."

When we got back to Dallas, he dropped me off at my parents' house and said he'd see me when he finished working. A week later he called. "What are you doing?" he asked.

"I just got through turning a trick. How did everything go?"

"Oh, it went great," he said. "Everything went down just like it was planned. C'mon over!"

When I got to his apartment, I found a different

Mark Reeves. He was naked, with open porno magazines all around him. Very weird. Scratching himself
on his head, his arms, everywhere, with a big hairbrush
like he had lice. I looked at him and said, "What the
hell's wrong with you? I'm gonna go work."

"I'll get rid of all this," he said, grinning. "I know
I'm kind of a mess."

He led me to the kitchen counter, where there were
two shoe boxes filled with neatly stacked cash. He later
confessed to the cops that he had bagged $50,000 from
the RepublicBank in San Antonio on February 10,
1986. All I remember is a big wad of cash sitting on
his kitchen counter after he got back from Ruidoso.

"On this job, I made over forty thousand dollars," he
said proudly. "I did real good. No problems. I handled
everything like a piece of cake."

He was in such a weird state. Scratching his head,
touching himself. I just shook my head and said,
"Look, maybe I better leave and come back later."

"You're right. I'm still a mess from what I did," he
said. "I'm still kind of shaky. I'll get it together."

A couple of hours later he was back to his normal
schedule: drink, cook, eat, screw, pass out. That was
our routine. After a few days he was ready for another
trip.

"What I did was so horrible, so traumatic, so dangerous, that I need a month's vacation before I even *think*
about working again," he said. "Let's go to Durango!"

M ark would cry sometimes, telling me, "I can't
quit my work because I'll only get a four-dollar-
an-hour job. That's all I'm qualified for."

I'd go, "Oooh, that does sound bad."

"You won't hang around me. You have to have somebody with money around you, with all the things *you* like."

"Damn straight there, buddy," I said. "That four-dollar-an-hour job's not going to work out very well with me. And you need to get out of debt."

Soon he returned to a familiar subject: shooting himself. He always told me that he carried a gun and that he'd shoot himself if things ever turned out badly at work.

"Shoot yourself?" I screamed, "Oh, my god! What do you mean, shoot yourself? Here I am, in love with you, and you're talking suicide! It sounds like whatever you're doing, you'd get a thousand-year prison term or the electric chair."

"Nah," he said. "It's not that bad. I just don't want to spend another day in prison. Not one more day."

Then I shifted the subject back to money, my favorite nag topic. "You're a genius at making money, but you don't have a clue of what to do with it! You're blowing it, and you're throwing me out the window too." I was sick of watching him throw away thousands on lottery tickets, hundreds a week on Crown Royal, $70,000 or more a year on racing. And investing in the stock market! Sometimes he would go down to Charles Schwab and throw his money at those maniacs.

But the racing was the worst. Finally I demanded, "Quit racing!" I told him that if he quit, we could take more trips. That's how I got him to stop.

Eventually he consented. He had been racing for seven years. He traded his race car for a red Porsche 911, then sold that for $30,000. With the money from the car and some other cash he had on hand, I had him buy his rented furniture, pay his bills, pay off his bank loan. For once, things were looking up. But then he turned into a trip-aholic! He went from one addiction to another. We were like an episode of *Lifestyles of the Rich and Famous*. New Orleans for lunch. Entire months in Colorado, looking at houses, dreaming of moving, hitting sixteen ski resorts on one vacation. Camping in the Ozarks. We were rental freaks: acrobatic airplanes, bikes, jet skis, helicopters and $300-per-hour airplanes, gazing down on the elk in the Rockies. Fourteen or fifteen trips in a row. All he wanted to do was travel.

I got sick of the trips. I was going broke. I would get home from another vacation, pay my bills, and I was down to almost nothing. Being a hooker is not cheap, after all. My ad in the Yellow Pages is $3,000 a year. When people ask me if I have a pimp, I say, "Yeah, Southwestern Bell." And state comptroller Bob Bullock. I pay sales tax on every call I make. Then there's rent on my office—a desk in a Mexican mechanic's shop with a telephone that I forward my trick phones at home—since you have to have a business address to get an escort-service listing. My business was going down the toilet, and Mark was showing me everything in the world except that he could take care of me. My dad asked me, "How can you keep on living like this?"

I flipped out on a camping trip in the summer of 1986. I got drunk and realized that I was wasting my life on this mysterious schmuck. Reality hit. I pounced on him, beating him up, breaking his glasses, calling him a "worthless lowlife." I was a screaming banshee bitch. I threw all the wienies and marshmallows in the fire. Then I grabbed the hatchet, slashing everything—

the tent, the ice chest, the air mattress Mark was trying to sleep on. I staggered off into the woods, got lost, and eventually had to call the cops from a gas station to take me back to the campsite. When we got there, they made me give them Mark's I.D. They did a big search on it and told me that although they couldn't prove anything, I'd best stay away from Mark Reeves.

When we got home, I told Mark he'd better get serious about earning a regular living. "What do you want to do with your life?" I asked him. He sat for a long time and thought about it.

"A stockbroker," he said. "I think I can predict the stock market."

"Well, go for it!" I said, thinking anything would be an improvement over whatever he was doing in his present career. He later confessed to three bank jobs during the summer of 1986: two in Fort Worth and one in San Antonio.

After our first year together, Mark still wanted to get married. Sometimes so did I. Twice I got him in front of the courthouse. But I wouldn't go in. I'd been married before, to a guy named Mike Brock, whom everybody called Mikey Vee. He was a day laborer and the lead singer for a punk band called the Vomit Pigs. The minute I got him across the threshold, he changed, saying, "I'm gonna quit my job and lay around and do drugs. That's the way it's gonna be. Tough cookies." He wanted to buy dope with our $1,000 of wedding-gift money. I kicked him out. The marriage lasted two days. A year later, just after he went to sign the divorce papers, Mikey dropped dead from a drug overdose.

The thought of marriage does crazy things to people. So when Mark met me in the front of John Neely Bryan's cabin, all ready for matrimony, I looked at him and had bad vibes. "He can't take care of you," I thought. "You don't know what he does for a living. This is gonna be another Mikey Vee." A two-day marriage ending in divorce and death.

"C'mon, get in the car," I said. "Let's go have a drink first."

"I can't let you go, or I'll never have you," Mark said when I told him I wanted more time. But then we went to the Stoneleigh P, had lunch, and spent the day getting drunk, forgetting all about the wedding. I just left like I deserved better than this guy who said, "Honey, I'm going off to work, and I may not come back. There's a will in the mailbox, and you're in it." What made me even look at him as a possible husband I'll never know. Everything I wanted, he didn't want. He didn't want to save any money. He didn't want a house. He kept saying, "I'm going to be the one who takes care of you. I just can't do it today." Someday, someday, someday—that's the mantra of Dallas men.

By now it was November 1986. I'd been tricking hard and had finally bought my dream house, a nice stone gingerbread in Oak Cliff. But instead of moving in, I had leased it out. My girlfriend Marilyn told me the best way to get rid of Mark was to move into my house, which Mark hated. So I left the nut on Slopes Drive for good.

Alone at night in my new house, I'd have nightmares about Mark's work, seeing him as a cat burglar or a maniac blowing up houses. I'd wake up scared, sweating. Mark had switched roles on me. I had become the trick, the love slave. So one day that November I decided to reverse the roles to their proper place. When Mark called, I told him, "Look, I'm not taking any more trips. If you want to see me, the price will be a thousand a day."

"I can't pay a thousand," he said, flustered but not shocked. "How about five hundred?"

I'd take the $500 and time with him—24 hours. No more. Everything worked out pretty well. We'd shoot guns at the Yello Belly Drag Strip rifle range or fly kites or do a hot-air balloon ride or go to the Dallas Zoo. Lots of day trips. One day a guard caught us screwing in the dinosaur tracks in Dinosaur Valley State Park near Glen Rose. I guess I still cared for him because I started getting really P.O.'d that he would pay the $500 only once a week. It bothered me that he could go so long without seeing me. He'd make me jealous, telling me about all the other women he was seeing while we were apart.

But when he called again, I cut him off for good. The next week, he showed up at my front door at six in the morning, carrying flowers and candy and $500 in cash and wearing a three-piece suit. It was the only time I'd ever seen him in a suit, which he apparently reserved for his bank jobs. I came to the door screaming, being a bitch, which was my technique for cutting him off.

"You weren't invited over here! You're just jacking with me again! You just want another five-hundred-dollar date, and then you'll leave me beat up emotionally! You'll never get serious! You're just wasting my time! Leave me alone! I hate you! You're a lousy lay!"

He started sobbing. Just bawling.

I threw the flowers on the ground, broke the vase, stomped on the Godiva chocolates, then slammed the door in his face. After he'd gone, I took the broken roses, the chocolates, and the $500 and sent it back to him by Federal Express, deducting the shipping charges. He called constantly for the next few weeks, begging me to go traveling. "Please go with me to Yamafest!" Or, "Come to Daytona with me."

Eventually, in December 1986, I agreed to go with him to Hells Gate in Colorado for old times' sake. We argued the entire time. The biggest problem? He didn't seem interested in me sexually. Whenever that happens, I know the party's over. In a motel room, over an open bottle of Crown Royal, I told him, "My New Year's resolution for 1987 is to stay away from Mark Ervin Reeves."

The last time I talked to Mark was in August 1987, nine months before he was arrested. I was in the middle of talking to a trick on the telephone. It was five in the afternoon, happy hour, when the phones ring every two seconds, and a dozen girls can't handle all the prospective clients. Then Mark's voice came over the receiver, using the pet name he had for me.

"Glowworm?"

I'm like still sick of the guy, embarrassed that he wasted all my time. I said, "Whaddya need? I told you never to call me."

"Look, you just have to talk to me for a few minutes, Gloria. I decided I'm gonna kill myself."

"Kill yourself?" I said, hearing the same talk he blabbered when he lost his Rolex or when I wouldn't move with him to Colorado. "Why kill yourself?"

"Because you won't have anything to do with me. Because you won't date me anymore."

"Damn right, I won't date you anymore," I said. "You're not offering any security for me. And now I've got to do millions of tricks, do hard labor, just to get back the money I lost after wasting all that time with you. How are you going to kill yourself?"

"I'm going to shoot myself."

"Do you have a loaded gun? You do? Well, take the telephone into the bathroom, pull the shower curtain shut, and blow your brains out. I'll listen."

He was crying, mumbling, "I think I'll just go out and work until I get caught. You won't see me anymore. I have absolutely nothing to live for."

"You need to be working anyway," I said. Apparently he took my advice. After we broke up in January 1987, he hit six more banks in Dallas and Arlington in 1987 and 1988.

On May 4, 1988, I was watering the pansies and marigolds in my front yard when Mother called. A couple of months before, she had told me that she thought Mark was the Dapper Bandit. I just laughed at her. "Good grief, Mother," I said. "Mark couldn't rob a bank. He can hardly get his next beer open."

This time Mother said, "You're not going to believe this. They caught the guy they think is the Dapper Bandit. The police surrounded his stalled El Camino, after he robbed a Bright Banc in North Dallas. I don't think it's Mark, after all. But the strangest thing happened. When they caught him, he pulled a pistol and shot himself in the head. But he's still alive."

"He shot himself *in the head*?" I screamed. "Mother that *is* Mark! He told me that's what he would do if he ever got caught." I turned on the TV. The story of the Dapper Bandit led the local news. Big time. By the ten o'clock broadcast, they had identified him as Mark. I was talking on the telephone like a chatterbox. "That guy I was dating with the El Camino and the Camaro, remember? He's the Dapper Bandit!" It was like discovering Jesse James in your bathroom. The most celebrated bank robber in modern times. I kept thinking about what one newspaper article said: "The Dapper Bandit is what legends are made of."

I think about Mark all the time, whenever I pass a bank or ride by his old place on Park Lane. He lived like an outlaw who thinks, "If you get caught, you blow your head off." That's what he tried to do, but he screwed up, ending up in a wheelchair instead of an outlaw's grave. He confessed to robbing 7 of his career-total 25 banks during the year and a half we were together, from September 1985 to January 1987. Now he's doing 22 years without parole; he is recuperating in the U.S. Medical Center for Federal Prisoners in Springfield, Missouri. His fine was $1.7 million and $750,000 in restitution. Talk about a financial problem. But I gotta hand it to the guy: he went out like Clyde Barrow. His only words in public? "I'm sorry for all this."

Of course, he spilled his whole story to the police. A friend got his confession and told me what it said. Mark told them that he had stolen at least fifty cars from auto dealerships across Texas, using two getaway cars per robbery. He cased out each job by buying a money order at the bank a day or two before the heist, he said, and he hit only banks insured by the FDIC, so the depositors wouldn't get hurt. "The idea of working at a job for the rest of my life did not appeal to me," he said in his confession. "I decided I could finance my lifestyle by robbing banks." He added, "I have no stolen bank money left. I spent all of the money on my living expenses." At least that part sounded familiar.

After he shot himself, he had a series of strokes while he was in the hospital. Now he's partially paralyzed, although he was able to spill his whole story to the cops. I thought about going to see him. But let's face it: My career severely inhibits my appearances around the authorities. I loved the guy, but what was I going to do—walk in and say, "Hi, honey. You know I'll be true until you get out"?

Somebody once told me that when you have sex with somebody, you spiritually bond with them and it takes seven years for you to get them out of your system. I guess it will take me an ice age to get over all of my lovers. Sometimes I think I'm still in love with Mark. But then the phone will ring, and I'll be off on another call, another trick, another crazy guy with a problem.

(September 1989)

Mark Ervin Reeves (inmate registration number 18427-077) was sentenced to twenty years and eleven months on November 23, 1988, for bank robbery, carrying a firearm during a violent crime, and extortion. After stints in federal correctional facilities in Marianna, Florida; Atlanta, Georgia; El Reno, Oklahoma; and Three Rivers, Texas, he is now serving out his sentence in the U.S. penitentiary in Beaumont, Texas. His projected release date is February 21, 2007.

The Cheerleader
Murder Plot

MIMI SWARTZ

When Houston winters are grim, they are that much grimmer in Channelview. Heading east out Interstate 10, the big city's stately pines, designer skyscrapers, and tasteful suburbs give way to pockmarked asphalt, ramshackle churches, and rusting ship-channel businesses. When the cold, steady winter rain starts to fall, as it did unrelentingly last January, Channelview seems drenched in a dingy futility. The only color seems to be the perilous orange of the refinery gas flares; at the Dell Dale highway exit, the white elephant rearing above the flea market looks hopelessly grimy, and off the road the rain soaks the yards of the tract and trailer homes to a dirty brown. In such weather, people lose their resolve: In the Baptist temples, they turn to hymns of salvation but do not keep time with the melody; in the pawnshops, they hock their baby furniture, stub out their cigarettes, and think about looking for work out of town. Winter in Channelview can bring menace and breed hopelessness, two qualities with which Wanda Holloway, who had spent most of her life here, was more than well aquainted.

This January, however, was going to be different.

Slight and pretty, with dark shoulder-length hair
brushed off her face, Holloway, 37, had the tight perm
and tighter jawline of so many women who start with
little but the determination to better themselves. She
had certainly done that. Holloway had worked as a secretary, she was a gifted pianist at her church, and she
had married well. Holloway, in fact, had made herself
into a well-regarded member of the Channelview community. She was, in local parlance, "a lovely person"
in a place where that was not so common; she was, in
the words of her daughter's junior high school principal, "very refined, spoke good English, and was beautifully attired."

But unbeknownst to almost everyone, Wanda Holloway was also a brooder, and, law enforcement
sources speculate, she had spent years brooding on a
problem for which she had finally found a dark solution. The story has since made headlines in everything
from the Channelview *Sentinel* to the British tabloids:
Holloway believed that by hiring someone to kill 38-
year-old Verna Heath and her 13-year-old daughter,
Amber, she would assure her own daughter, Shanna, of
a place on the cheerleading squad at Channelview High
School. For help, she turned to one Terry Harper, her
first husband's brother, who would later recall that
when ordering the hit, Wanda was calm: "She wanted
it done. She said she could handle it." As has also been
reported, Terry Harper, fortunately, could not. He took
her scheme to the police. The two officers who arrested
Holloway on January 30 would remember that when
they told her that she was charged with solicitation of
capital murder, she showed no reaction at all.

She was, most likely, the last person to respond in

such fashion. This was, after all, before the story of the
Pom-pom Mom would cause an international sensation, before the value of cheerleading would be as hotly
debated as the Gulf War, before every major player in
this drama would receive a call from *Geraldo,* before
the people of Houston and beyond would open their
morning papers to find that, thanks to the strange,
seemingly inexplicable dreams of one formerly anonymous, innocuous woman, their winter doldrums were
over and a true story of Channelview had begun.

"**T**his is a made-for-TV movie, not a feature
film," one lawyer remarked dismissively a few
weeks before Holloway's February indictment. He may
or may not be right, depending on which production
company eventually wins the rights to whose story, but
his remark still speaks to some essential Channelview
truth: Here, a smaller, diminished view of life has a
way of eclipsing larger ones. If, far away, Holloway's
story is viewed as an aberration, closer to home it
makes more sense. To those who know Channelview,
Wanda Holloway's story is a story of place, and to understand the place is to understand almost everything.

"God created Channelview so the people of Pasadena would have someplace to look down on," said
criminal attorney Mike Ramsey, who was born and
raised in Channelview. Physically, it straddles I-10 just
outside of Houston on the way to Beaumont, though it
has less in common with other faceless suburbs than
with distinctive small towns. The brochure for the
North Channel Chamber of Commerce depicts the area
as one where new brick mansions nestle in pine groves,
complete with ponds populated with regal swans, and

the streets have pastoral names like Woodforest and Sterling Glen, but Channelview is in no way bucolic. The brochure also asserts that lights from tankers on the ship channel glisten just as brightly as those of the Houston skyline at night, but Channelview is in no way romantic. It is instead unabashedly rough, taking a defensive posture against the world. Neighboring communities like Deer Park and Baytown were created and dominated by Shell and Exxon and so maintain a corporate courteousness that Channelview lacks—the place has no sponsor. One tabloid TV show got it right when it focused on a welcome sign that announced, "Don't Mess With Channelview."

Mostly white, resolutely working class, it was, even as late as the seventies, a Ku Klux Klan stronghold. In the sixties and seventies, when Wanda Holloway was coming of age, the high school students could be evenly divided between dopers and ropers. Mike Ramsey and most of his friends grew up on better than nodding terms with the bars on Market Street. One of his friends had an ear torn off in a fight, and when an emergency room doctor told Ramsey that he could reattach the ear if Ramsey could retrieve it, the lawyer returned to find a scroungy dog sniffing hungrily for more remains. You don't see "Yard of the Month" signs in Channelview; instead, particularly on the south side of I-10, you see homes guarded by German shepherds, rottweilers, or mastiffs. People here have even steeled themselves against the very air they breathe, laced as it is with industrial toxins: "We don't trust air we can't see or hack off a chunk and chew on it for a while," joked one resident.

As is true of many places where passions lie close to

the surface, so too does the desire for redemption. Though one Channelview resident gaily tells the story of the Baptist preacher caught "doin' a parishioner" in the back of the church bus, the portable signs in Channelview announce that Jesus is Lord, and on Sundays, the churches, mostly Baptist, are full. The ministers preach against aspiring to wealth, against sex, and now, even against cheerleading. Punishment is severe; hell is no abstract concept here. "I believe if people are going to this place, it deserves to be preached on," the pastor of Holloway's church warned his congregation one Sunday. Still, the fear of eternal damnation would not necessarily have stopped someone like Holloway from plotting a murder one day and playing the piano in the church the next—Jesus, she would have learned since childhood, forgives all who are saved, and she had been.

In fact, the sin that preoccupies most Channelview residents is the sin of pretension. Because so many daddies work in the petrochemical plants, most families make the same amount of money. Alice Johnson Junior High, which Amber Heath and Shanna Harper, the daughter of Wanda and her first husband, Tony Harper, attended, had been named after a custodian. In spite of Channelview's toughness, its residents are unfailingly polite—even those who've moved away slip back into yes and no ma'aming here—and the loyalists can think of no better place to live. Parents wonder why their kids want to go into Houston when Baytown has a mall that's just as good. It's not a place for strivers—"If Tony Harper had raised those children, they'd of been at our level," sniped one person who found Shanna's Liz Claiborne purses to be a bit much. For the most part, people in Channelview know just how harsh life can be and so have learned to keep their dreams modest, in check. Most often, they pass them on, unfulfilled, to their kids. In this way, Wanda Holloway was both of Channelview and desperate to escape it, for she believed in a future that was much grander than her past. She could not see that her life story was one in which all Channelview truths applied.

Wanda Holloway was the best-dressed woman at her February arraignment, a distinction that is not difficult to achieve at the Harris County criminal courthouse but that, regardless, would not have surprised those who knew her. The first thing people said about her was that she was always nicely dressed or impeccably dressed or beautifully dressed, which was not necessarily a compliment but was definitely Channelview code for the fact that she had a tendency to hold herself above others. "People with our backgrounds typically do not have the money to dress like that, or if we do, we don't, because it's not that important," explained one person who grew up with Holloway. "You would never see Wanda outside bathing a German shepherd or digging in the dirt."

Indeed, the day that she would plead innocent, Holloway was smartly dressed, the high level of concentration required to produce her ensemble clearly evident. For that courtroom appearance, she wore a black-and-white houndstooth skirt under a black jacket, along with a white shirt with a black-and-white polka-dot collar. Her black purse matched her black pumps, which, decorated with slyly sexy black-and-white piping, came from Dillard's. She had accented her nails in a deep red, which matched the wallet from which she extracted pictures of her kids to show a friend seated next to her. She giggled once or twice and marveled at the doggedness of the press; the only sign that she was nervous was the way she anxiously swung one crossed leg back and forth while waiting for the proceedings to begin.

It was this prideful nature—the other quality consistently ascribed to Holloway—that rubbed people in Channelview the wrong way and caused them to reexamine her ambitiousness in less than generous terms. "She has a very bad craving for money, and she loves to dress the part," said someone who knows her well. "She was always, always wanting this and wanting that."

Holloway grew up on the south side of I-10, the rougher stretch of Channelview. Her father was a tester at a concrete plant, and her mother worked in the high school cafeteria. "Wanda felt people looked down on her," recalled Tony Harper. If she felt some shame at her station, Wanda inherited from her father, Clyde Webb, a drive that she might one day use to propel herself beyond it. Tony described Webb as "headstrong" and, by way of example, said that when Webb lost a power struggle at the church to which he and his wife belonged, he left with a splinter group and started a new one. The Webbs did not have any more money than anyone else in town, but they always seemed to stretch for their kids. Their son was not remembered as being exceptional; Wanda, however, was consistently referred to by those who knew her as an overachiever. As a young girl, she took piano lessons and, in high school, was zealous about her business courses, at which she excelled. "She was very hyper, very active, she always wanted everybody to like her," says Tony of their high school days. But Holloway never could get the acceptance she wanted. She longed to try out for the cheerleading squad or the drill team, but her father found the activities an affront to his conservative religious beliefs. The costumes, he said, were too skimpy. Whorish.

Other dreams slipped away more gradually. When she married at eighteen, Holloway abandoned her business education; her husband did not want her to work, and she wanted to start having children. Tony, whom she had known most of her life, came from a family that was not wealthy but was wealthier than her own: His father owned three gas stations, and his mother had her own business, Peggy's Cameo Boutique, a lingerie store. Tony and Wanda settled into the classic Channelview life. "I thought you got married, got a job, had kids, and that was it," Tony said simply. "We had a good life; we were going in the right direction." Wanda may have coveted her mother-in-law's Cadillac—she wanted her own Lincoln Town Car—but in those days, Tony, a sturdy-looking man with a solid, somewhat obdurate air, had a modest job at a railroad warehouse, and the couple lived in a house on the same street as the rest of the Harper family. It was when her children were born that Holloway's hopes seemed rekindled. Her son, born in 1973, she named Shane, after the heroic loner in the movie of the same name. When her daughter was born four years later, Wanda stressed the point, naming her Shanna. Though Tony prospered, opening Harper's Insurance ("Insurance With a Personal Touch"), the marriage foundered. The divorce in

1980 was testy but far from acrimonious: Wanda got the house and most of the furnishings; Tony cleared out with his water skis, recliner, and pickup truck.

It was Wanda's next two marriages that caused talk in Channelview. The first was to an older, wealthier man living in Beaumont, and when that ended, after a brief try at a reconciliation with Tony, she married another older, wealthier man from Channelview, C. D. Holloway. C.D. had his own oil-field service company. Though he was twenty years her senior, the two had been attracted to one another when he was the choirmaster and Wanda was the pianist at the Missionary Baptist Church. C.D. and Wanda made their home in Sterling Green, a tony subdivision by Channelview standards, and eventually, Wanda got her Lincoln Town Car. Local gossips took note of C.D.'s airplane; Wanda took to talking about diamonds and moving to River Oaks or Memorial. But like so many people from Channelview, the couple never made the break. They stayed in the modest tract house with the sloping roof and pink burglar bars. "Maybe he just gave the appearance of cutting a fat hog in the rear," said one Channelview native of Holloway's wealth.

Still, with C.D., Wanda seemed to have found a measure of peace. A friend once asked her if all that money made her happy. "Well," Wanda said, smiling, "we're havin' fun."

After Wanda Holloway's arrest, much was made of the differences between her and her nemesis, Verna Heath. The police and the press painted Verna and her daughter, Amber, as winners, while Wanda and Shanna were assigned the roles of also-rans. Verna had been a twirling champion and was the daughter of a well-known twirling teacher; Wanda had never been allowed to set foot on the field at halftime. Even the economic differences between the two families were said to be profound—Jack Heath managed a Gerland's Food Fair in Deer Park, while C. D. Holloway had his own company. (The two families actually live around the corner from one another, and their houses have the same floor plan.) But as with so many competitors, the similarities between the two women far outweighed their differences—for a time at least. When Verna stood behind her screen door, her stocky body tense, her arms folded over her chest, her chin thrust forward, and told one reporter that Wanda Holloway "is a mother who goes 150 percent in everything she does," it was possible to believe that she was also talking about herself. Or, as Tony Harper put it, "Verna is the same caliber woman as Wanda is."

Wanda's ambition would naturally lead her to Verna Heath. Verna, after all, had succeeded in a realm where Wanda had been prohibited. Those who dismiss cheerleading as trivial and vapid miss its essential and enduring reality—that it is still one of the best ways a young woman can advance herself socially, not just in school, but beyond. If it remains important in a place like Plano, where a child can have many options, it is doubly so in a place like Channelview, where feminine beauty is short-lived and harshness is the norm. Verna learned this lesson at home. "My first twirling experience was with a stick with a cork with my father's trotline painted silver," said Joyce Brown, Verna's mother. Brown, who grew up poor in Huffman, recalled that the school drum majorette was one of the most beautiful girls she had ever seen: "She rode my bus, and whenever she put her stick down, I picked it up." Fiercely intense, Brown made three of her four daughters into twirling champions (her other daughter and son triumphed in 4-H), just as today she tries to mold the talents of the daughters of refinery workers. In her cinder block studio in Highlands, she offers not only twirling but also tap dance and modeling.

Verna absorbed her mother's lessons well, channeling her competitive instincts into the family tradition. "I remember, in twirling there were girls who liked it just because they liked being in front of the band," she said of her school years. "But it was my life—I loved it." She learned about jealousy too: "In high school, one girl would not even stay in the band because I got drum major and she didn't."

But when it came to her own daughter, Verna abandoned her mother's old-fashioned quest for beauty and poise for something more contemporary. Both Verna and Wanda sent their daughters to the Alpha Gymnastics studio, a towering gym in Pasadena just across Spencer Highway from Gilley's. There, the girls could learn cheerleading from teachers certified by the National Cheerleading Association, as well as tumbling and gymnastics, skills now demanded of most cheerleaders. ("A lot of these girls think they'll be a cheerleader in a month," said one teacher of this new professionalism. "They can't understand why they're not going to make it.")

At Alpha, parental sacrifice is powerfully evident. Often, the kids are better dressed than their mothers, and there is more tension in the viewing area than on the floor. Mothers invoke Mary Lou Retton and sound like professional handicappers when they talk about how much more demanding the physical requirements of cheerleading have become. They wince when a child blows a somersault and snap at a son who needs help with his long division while his big sister does flip-flops on the mats below. They shell out $36 an hour for private lessons and then coach the coach, politick the school sponsors, demand that the newspaper run their daughters' cheerleading pictures, and even, some-times, float nasty rumors about the competition. Last year there was a bomb threat at the cheerleader tryouts at Alice Johnson Junior High, though it has not been tied to Holloway's case. "This has probably happened before, and the people just didn't get caught," half-joked one woman who knew of the rivalry between Verna Heath and Wanda Holloway, as well as the cheerleading milieu.

Among these moms, Verna and Wanda were well known. Each had the reputation of going all out for her daughter. Amber, who inherited her mother's opulent brown curls and her father's pale-blue eyes, had ac-companied Verna to her grandmother's twirling studio since she was a small child. She had been winning twirling contests since she was three. By the seventh grade, Amber had become a yearbook star, having been named friendliest and most spirited. Shanna, an honor student like Amber, was also popular and talented. She was vice president of the eighth grade when Amber was president. (The two did not compete—they ran for different offices.) Both girls were pretty, though both could affect a fussed-over, far from casual style. It is not surprising that, like their mothers, they both were considered snappy dressers. "Shanna always mentioned that she would like to be Amber's friend because they were so much alike," one of Shanna's friends said. Too often, however, her best friend was her mother. Perhaps driven by her own dreams, Wanda saw to it that Shanna had private cheerleading lessons, a modeling stint at San Jacinto Mall, and mother-daughter outfits that further blurred the distinction between Shanna's life and her own—one of the outfits was even a cheerleader suit.

The relationship between Verna and Wanda began when their daughters were sleep-over friends in elementary school. Like many friends, they shared coffee and car pool—"My wife had braided Wanda's hair before," Jack Heath told the *Dallas Morning News,* offering proof of their intimacy. But they were never the best of friends. "I've always been so busy, I never had time for close friends," Verna said of her role as a mother. It may be, too, that Wanda underestimated the force of Verna's ambitions for her own daughter.

The first sign of trouble appeared in 1989, when Shanna was scheduled to try out for seventh-grade cheerleader at Channelview's public junior high school. Wanda had planned for the event—she had taken Shanna out of Channelview Christian School, a private elementary school, and enrolled her in Alice Johnson Junior High to assure her eligibility. What she had not foreseen was that Amber, who was still at Channelview Christian, would be one of Shanna's competitors. Verna, intending to send her daughter to Alice Johnson when she reached seventh grade, got the principal's permission to let Amber try out, and during the three days during which campaigning was allowed, Verna picked Amber up at the private school and drove her to the junior high to meet, greet, and lobby her future schoolmates. This was a carefully orchestrated campaign—Verna even had flyers printed with peppermint candies attached. In response, Wanda was "severely bent out of shape," according to one observer. It is possible that this particular competition made her feel like a Channelview nobody all over again—it wasn't just her daughter who was threatened but her own hopes of advancement. As Tony Harper noted, "She couldn't be a cheerleader, but she could be a cheerleader's mom." And perhaps she felt betrayed by a friend.

Wanda complained about Amber to the school board; she pestered other parents to urge their children not to vote for "the outsider," as she came to call the girl. She even talked about getting a lawyer. However, she could not save her child, or herself, from disappointment: With two slots open and three competitors, Amber won but Shanna did not. Wanda was devastated. "Wanda went through a lot when Shanna didn't make it," said one school administrator. "Had they not allowed Amber to try out, Shanna would have made it."

In deference to Wanda—and, it was said, her powerful husband, C.D., who was then on the board of the Channelview Bank—the school later amended the rules so that potential cheerleading candidates would have to spend one semester in the Channelview system before trying out. For Wanda, it was small consolation. "She felt so helpless," the administrator continued. "She was so desperate. She felt her child had been cheated."

The next year, Wanda worked even harder to get Shanna elected. Months before the event, she called on her ex-husband Tony and told him that she wanted to create something special to guarantee victory for Shanna. In what would become known as the Ruler Incident, Tony came up with the idea of handing out wooden rulers and number-two pencils printed with "Vote for Shanna Harper for Cheerleader." "I thought it was a good idea because most kids couldn't afford them," Tony said. Wanda thought it was a good idea too and offered to split the cost with him. Anxious and excited, she called him every day until the supplies arrived. Then, when the campaign began, she took them to school. Later that day, Harper got a tearful call from his ex-wife. "They're not gonna let me do this," she told him.

The handouts did not comply with the school-election code—rules that Wanda would have been familiar with, according to Tony—and the vice principal had confiscated them, with the support of the cheerleading sponsor. When Wanda continued to pass the rulers out a few days later, a meeting was called at the school. The sponsor asked the parents of other cheerleader candidates to attend. One member of the group was Verna Heath. Afterward, Shanna was disqualified. When Wanda learned of the decision, she was mortified. She begged the vice principal to reconsider, as did Tony, to no avail. "She did it because the Heaths and other parents had had such luck the year before," said one person close to the Heaths. "She thought she could make up for last year." Sometime after that, Shanna told her father that she didn't want to be a cheerleader anymore. Her mother, however, was not about to give up the fight. "Wanda," the source continued, "had personalized it."

People in Channelview wondered why Wanda chose to involve her ex-husband's brother, Terry Harper, in her plan. He was not the luckiest member of the Harper family; "Lots of rain hits him," explained Paula Asher, Tony Harper's attorney. Married several times, Terry had had some minor brushes with the law; he had been charged with several misdemeanors including drunk driving. Around Channelview, that just made him rough around the edges. To the police, however, Wanda's choice was less mysterious. "You don't just go to Kmart and hire a hit man," said Sergeant Flynt Blackwell, who worked on the investigation. Most ordinary people lack the underworld connections of, say, Colombian drug dealers. When they go looking for a hired killer, they turn to the first person they know who has the slightest criminal history. But, as Wanda would learn, trouble with the law does not a criminal make—one reason why so many people who shop for killers wind up talking to police informants and, in turn, undercover cops. Such was the case with burly, blue-eyed, gap-toothed Terry, 36, a sandy-haired construction worker who lived in a trailer. He had decided in the fall of 1990 to quit "cussin', drinkin', and going to clubs" and had instead put his faith in the Lord. Wanda Holloway would be the first to test his resolve.

Cheerleader tryouts for Channelview High School were not scheduled until March 1991, but Wanda had begun to stew on the event several months in advance. She had taken a job doing clerical work in the high school band director's office and had asked at least one administrator for advice on advancing Shanna's chances. Should she try to cozy up to the sponsor? Was there any way to get Amber or another competitor disqualified? Eventually, however, her quest led her to Terry's trailer: She pulled up outside, honked the horn, and when he came out, said that she wanted to talk to him but not at home. The two met at a nearby convenience store called Bo's. Though Terry would later describe Wanda's mood as "no different from normal—she's a very outgoing person," Wanda had a probing question for him. She wanted to know just how much he loved his niece and nephew. "Well," Terry told her, "I love them with my life." Wanda was glad to hear it and then told him that she wanted two people taken care of and she didn't care how. Terry, appalled, had a straightforward answer to Wanda's straightforward request. "I said, 'I don't do anything like that and I don't know anyone who would do a thirteen-year-old child.' " Wanda said that she would get back to him. "I thought, fine," Terry recalled. "I just wanted to get out of the car."

He heard nothing more from Holloway until Christmas Eve, when, opening presents at his parents' house, Shanna asked to speak with him privately. "Mom wants you to call her at this number," she said. Terry figured that Wanda wanted one of two things: to call off the deal or to push him to find someone to pull it off. When he discovered that it was the latter, he tried to reason with her, Why didn't she just let Shanna try out for cheerleading, and if "she doesn't get it, she don't get it?" he asked Wanda. She had her answer ready. "No," Terry said Wanda told him, "she'll be too devastated and never try out again."

Realizing that Wanda intended to go through with her plan, Terry went to his brother, Tony, who directed him to the Harris County Sheriff's Department. When he was asked later by one reporter why he had come forward, Terry's explanations were both metaphorical and practical. A man of aphorisms, he quoted the two pieces of advice he liked to live by. The first was, "Your mind's like a parachute, it only works when it's open." The second was, "Truth's like iodine, it only helps when it hurts." But the main reason Terry went to the police was that if anything should happen to Verna or Amber Heath, he wanted to be sure that he was not considered a suspect.

Convincing the cops that Wanda was serious, however, was tougher than he had expected. That was partly because Terry was put in touch with Detective George Helton, a lanky and garrulous chain-smoker. Hits were a sideline, not a specialty of this seventeen-year law enforcement veteran and Harris County Organized Crime/Narcotics Task Force member. He was happier busting dope dealers. Besides, Helton had worked the ship-channel area for more than a decade and was all too familiar with the dead-end weirdness that characterized it. The last hit he had investigated near Channelview involved a husband who wanted to get rid of his wife. "I don't care if you hit the bitch in the head with a hammer," he told Helton right before he paid him the $5,000 fee. The police arrested the man and informed his disbelieving spouse while she was shopping at Kroger. The husband went to trial and got probation; the couple remain reconciled to this day. Then, too, Helton had just bought himself a new pair of $300 lizard-skin shoes, and he did not want to ruin them by traipsing around in the rain for surreptitious meetings that might go exactly nowhere. "No shit," he said without enthusiasm when Terry, over coffee at

McDonald's, said that he knew someone who wanted two people killed.

With the assistance of Sergeant Flynt Blackwell, Helton put a wire on Terry and showed him how to record his phone conversations with Wanda. Over the next three weeks, Helton came to believe Terry's story: The police became convinced that Wanda did intend to go through with the crime and that she was no longer shopping for a killer—she had settled on Terry's choice of a murderer for hire. Then they haggled over price: The $2,500 that the police quoted to assassinate Verna, coupled with the $5,000 quoted to do in Amber, was, in Terry's words, "just too much money for her." Wanda had to settle on only one murder and figured that killing Verna would leave Amber too distraught to compete. On the day that she was to make the down payment that would lead to her arrest, Wanda dropped Shanna off at church and then passed on a pair of diamond earrings as payment to Terry. Removing them, she said, "I couldn't pull the trigger myself, but I can sure do it this way." When Flynt Blackwell went with Helton to arrest Wanda the next day, he noticed that she was impeccably dressed.

As spring progressed, it became much harder to remember that the lives of several people—including those of two teenage girls—had been so adversely affected. ("I felt numb and I felt hurt and I just sank into the couch," Verna said of the day the police told her of Holloway's intentions. "You've really got to dislike someone to do that.") The story was simply too entertaining, too ripe for exploitation. As Alice

Johnson principal Jim Barker noted, "The farther you get from this building, the bigger the story becomes."

It appeared to have everything, at least as far as neighborhood gossips, news directors, and movie producers were concerned: It had Texas, it had cheerleading. (*A Current Affair* neatly linked the two by asserting that "the bizarre murder-for-hire scheme" was "unfolding in the back yard of the most famous cheerleading squad in history, the Dallas Cowboys Cheerleaders.") It had indisputable evil: "I just hope we never experience anybody in this country doing this again," Terry Harper's attorney, former district attorney Mike Hinton, huffed to a camera crew for *Inside Edition*. "Over a cheerleader, for God's sake! Our country cannot tolerate this—period." It was also a cautionary tale of parental love gone awry, complete with an inarguable moral: The police's casting of Wanda Holloway as the ultimate stage mother inspired *Houston Post* columnist Bonnie Gangelhoff to write, "The lesson here, perhaps, is that for children to grow into confident adults, honors must be their own and so must the pain of losing cheerleader competitions." Wanda's story may have been played as a grotesque aberration, but it was quickly reduced to archetypal—and predictable—components, which meant that it gave everyone a chance to feel smug. Once again, people in Pasadena—and elsewhere—had a place to look down on.

Naturally, the case of the Pom-pom Mom sparked much tortured and unnecessary debate on the value of cheerleading, which in turn embarrassed many Texans who had hoped that they had put cheerleading behind them. "Cheerleading," posited the *Dallas Morning*

News cautiously, "is a big deal to some in Texas. To them, the ideal boy plays football and his girlfriend twirls a baton on the field or waves pompons on the sidelines. And it is seen that way in Channelview." The *Houston Chronicle* was more bullish on the activity: CHEERLEADING 'NOT THE ISSUE' IN ALLEGED MURDER CONTRACT was one headline. (Perhaps the most-subdued coverage was the local Channelview paper's: MURDER-FOR-HIRE CASE CALLED 'REALLY STRANGE' was its headline a few days after the story broke.) The national press, of course, had no qualms about blurring the carefully constructed distinctions the rest of Texas put between itself, cheerleading, and Channelview. *A Current Affair* drew the logical, time-honored conclusion: "At one time or another every girl in America dreams of being a cheerleader," intoned the reporter. "That's especially true in Texas. Pom-poms are a major part of the Lone Star legend."

It was only a matter of time before the rest of the press dropped any pretense of seriousness, largely because the story was such a tabloid-TV natural. Representatives of Sally Jessy Raphaël, Oprah, and Geraldo holed up at the Galleria. A gutsier team from a British newspaper bunked at the I-10 Holiday Inn, much closer to Channelview. Their targets were the drama's stars: Verna Heath received roses every day from a producer for *A Current Affair* and, after refusing to go on camera, was supposedly ambushed by another reporter wearing a hidden microphone. Verna briefly agreed to do the Sally Jessy Raphaël show—until the topic was changed from stage mothers to people who have been the targets of hired killers.

When the major players proved elusive—Wanda's

besieged lawyers, it was stated on the evening news, had refused interviews from "around the world"—the press set out to create other stars: *Inside Edition* offered to fly to principal Barker's home, for instance, and then turned to Terry Harper, who appeared on camera in jeans, boots, a new duster, a pink bandanna, and a gimme cap. Casting him as the hero of the story, the reporter asked how he felt. "Tired," he said, sighing deeply. That was not a universal feeling. Virtually every character in the drama—including a *Houston Chronicle* reporter—was contacted by a movie company. "I cannot answer any questions unless they are submitted in writing," one newly savvy player joked. The press coverage even produced a bonanza for Alice Johnson students: Yearbooks containing pictures of Shanna and Amber, which once sold for $15, started going to reporters for $50.

It was, then, not surprising that what had initially been shaped as a tragedy became a comedy. A report on the incident that appeared in a Bowling Green, Ohio, paper ran under a heading of THE LIGHTER SIDE. The story was also featured humorously in *Newsweek* and in the *Sports Illustrated* swimsuit issue. A series of *Scotty* cartoons in the *Houston Post* linked it to the war in the Middle East—a main character headed for a peace demonstration not in Washington but in Channelview. It was a source of some pride in Channelview that Johnny Carson added the topic to his monologue. (Wanda, he asserted, wasn't hard to find: "She was out on Main Street, saying, 'Gimme me a *g,* gimme a *u,* gimme an *n,* gimme a *g-u-n.*' ")

Before long, this seemed a story with only one loser, Wanda Holloway. "I'm gonna sic Mrs. Holloway on you" became a running joke at Alice Johnson Junior High.

By the time of cheerleader tryouts on March 22, school administrators had had more than enough. They had tried to keep the date and time from the press, and now, administrators in shirt-sleeves patrolled the grounds, their arms folded, their eyes fixed on the crowd like Secret Service men. The one reporter who found her way into the boys' gym, where the event was held, was summarily ejected.

On this day, Verna Heath looked like a woman who had had more than enough too. She had lost weight, and her jaw was firmly set; she fixed a steely gaze on strangers who ventured into the gym. She sat high up in the bleachers with other cheerleading parents, who held video cameras and silver balloons emblazoned with the words "Good Luck." Her ensemble made you think of Wanda Holloway, and how natural she would have looked, sitting proudly in the stands: Verna's opulent mane was coiffed superbly, her purple jacket matched her purple pumps, which coordinated nicely with her aqua slacks and her print blouse, which contained both colors. Once, she left the bleachers to place a steadying hand on Amber's shoulder. Dressed in black shorts and a chartreuse T-shirt with her name in cursive across the back, Amber looked less like the vamp of her newspaper photographs and more like a gangly teenager, with long skinny legs and her thick, coarse hair barely restrained by two hair clips. Everyone hoped that she could put the chilling times behind her, though it hadn't been easy—during the tryouts campaign, someone had defaced Amber's photograph on one of her elaborate posters by writing "bull's-eye" on her forehead. But, in the gym, the audience acted as if nothing had happened. There was no special applause for Amber, and the program went off without a hitch. With four candidates for four places on the freshman cheerleading squad, everyone could be a winner. "Amber did make cheerleader and she was happy and her mama was happy," recalled one person there. "Everyone met in the hall and cried and hugged afterward." Shanna did not perform that day.

It was a more arduous time for Wanda Holloway. People turned on her. She was no longer a lovely person, but one who looked far too comfortable in front of the television cameras. A more penitent performance was called for (just as, at school, Shanna was being scorned by her fellow students for acting as if nothing was wrong). When Wanda refused to get counseling for her children, Tony Harper sued his ex-wife for custody, which for a time gave credence to an alternative theory of the entire narrative—that Terry and Tony had framed Wanda in order to get custody of Tony's children, an interesting notion but one that was not supported by any prior attempts at custody on Tony's part. In eleven years he had made no effort to modify his custody or visitation rights. Now, with the trial date approaching, Tony and Wanda share custody of their children, though Shane, an honor student himself, has shown a clear preference for his father. His college money will now go to his mother's defense: "It's all down the tubes," he told Tony, disgusted.

As the June trial date approached, people began to turn aspects of the case into a kind of parlor game. "This case has so many ironies," they said, shaking their heads and smiling. They speculated that if the Channelview High School band director had not forbidden ninth-graders to do so, Amber would have tried out for twirler instead of cheerleader. They said that if Wanda had just let things be, Shanna's talent would have won her a spot on the cheerleading squad this year. They might have also said that in setting out to destroy Verna, Wanda had managed to hand her enemy the kind of victory she sought to avoid at all costs: The agony to the Heath family notwithstanding, they are sure to realize some fame and fortune from the movie offers that are coming their way. Meanwhile, Holloway may lose virtually everything if she is found guilty. "She created a scenario where her own daughter will be deprived of her mother," said Tony's lawyer, Paula Asher. "What she sought out to do to Amber Heath is what she created for her own child."

But losing should be nothing new to someone from Channelview, which is, of course, who Wanda Holloway has been all along. In her desperate attempt to escape it, she has come to embody it; as victim and villain, she has made herself into a true heroine of Channelview, putting herself in her place for good.

(May 1991)

In September 1991 Wanda Holloway was convicted of solicitation of capital murder and sentenced to fifteen years in prison and fined $10,000. The conviction was later overturned, however, because one of the jurors was under indictment and should not have been seated. Five years later, just one month before her second trial was to begin, Holloway pleaded no contest to the charges and received a ten-year prison sentence. After just six months she was released and placed on probation for the remainder of her term. She has since remarried and still lives in Texas. The case, which gained worldwide attention, was made into two television movies, one in 1992, called *Willing to Kill: The Texas Cheerleader Story,* starring Lesley Ann Warren; and one in 1993, called *The Positively True Adventures of the Alleged Texas Cheerleader-Murdering Mom,* starring Holly Hunter.

Benny and the Boys

GARY CARTWRIGHT

They say it was hard for anyone to dislike Benny Binion, unless, of course, Benny had his gun in that person's ear and was in the process of blowing that person's brains into West Dallas, which Benny was known to do when displeased. Even then it was nothing personal, just business. The man had thousands of friends, a fair number of enemies, and the good sense to tell the difference.

Benny Binion lived the first half of his life in Texas and the last half in Las Vegas and became a legend in both places. They called him the Cowboy; for reasons that had to do with guns, not horses. He was maybe the most popular gambler in America and certainly one of the few ever cast in bronze. There is a larger-than-life statue of the Cowboy near the rear entrance of Binion's Horseshoe Hotel and Casino, the no-limit, no-frills gambling joint in downtown Las Vegas that Benny opened in 1951 and his family still owns.

The Cowboy was as generous with friends as he was malevolent with enemies. Politicians, judges, cops, entertainers, rodeo cowboys, robbers, and *pistoleros* from Dallas to Vegas owed him debts of gratitude, and sometimes debts of hard cash, which Benny was inclined to forget, rationalizing that if somebody owed him money it was his own damn fault. For Benny's eighty-third birthday party, in November 1987, 18,000 friends and admirers showed up. The crowd included Willie Nelson, Hank Williams, Jr., Gene Autry, Dale Robertson, and other celebrities and underworld characters.

Though Benny claimed that he never went to school a day in his life, never learned to read or write, to multiply or subtract, he knew about numbers. He wasn't much of a gambler himself, but he became, in the idiom of the trade, "a square craps fader," square meaning honest and fader being the one who covers the crapshooter's bet. He learned his lesson early, from an old-time Dallas racketeer named Warren Diamond, who operated a no-limits craps game in the twenties in a room at the St. George Hotel, near the Dallas County courthouse. Benny worked for Diamond, parking cars and running errands, and he never forgot the day that an oilman from Texarkana threw an envelope on the line and said, "Diamond, I'm gonna make you look." Diamond gave the oilman a glance and said, "Pass him the dice," meaning that he didn't need to look, that he was ready to cover whatever amount was in the envelope. The oilman crapped out in two rolls, and Warren Diamond opened the envelope and counted out 170 one-thousand-dollar bills. The margin favoring a craps fader is small, something like 1.4 percent, but in the long run that fractional edge can make a fellow rich. By the time Benny died in December 1989, he was worth at least $100 million.

Benny had a talent for knowing exactly who and where he was and for sensing when it was time to fold his hand and go home. If his son and grandson had inherited this talent, they wouldn't be facing federal racketeering charges today.

B enny was a product of turn-of-the-century Texas, when gambling was an accepted occupation and killing was a proper way of settling things, Old West style. It was an era that placed enormous value on individual initiative. The moral collapse that started with Prohibition and accelerated into the Great Depression made criminals out of people who were not otherwise inclined, fostering a disdain for law, an obsession with betrayal, a willingness to do almost anything to get by. The mind-set of the times was compressed in a saying that Benny repeated all of his life: "Never holler whoa or look back in a bad place." When Benny thought of the Depression, he thought of what his pal Red Nose Kelly said one Thanksgiving Day when the bartender at the C&W poolroom asked him what he was thankful for. "Chili's a dime and I still like it," Red Nose replied straight off.

Born in Pilot Point in Grayson County in 1904, the son of a layabout who drank up the family inheritance, Benny left home at fifteen, bumming around El Paso and the Dallas–Fort Worth area, punching cattle, trading horses, gambling, bootlegging, getting in a little trouble but nothing he couldn't handle. Toward the end of World War I, Benny settled in Dallas, apprenticing himself to Warren Diamond. Seldom had ambition and opportunity been better matched.

Despite the smug, pious, self-righteous image that Dallas has courted for the past half-century, there has always been a lascivious twinkle in the old girl's eye.

For most of her history, in fact, Dallas was a wide-open town. Her power daddies in the thirties and forties, particularly downtown bankers Bob Thornton and Fred Florence, not only tolerated vice, they competed with Fort Worth publisher Amon Carter to see which town could be the most wicked. Dallas landed the 1936 Texas Centennial celebration because of its reputation as a swinging town.

Though gambling was technically illegal, the systematic revenues it generated helped sustain city government and, in a curious way, helped forestall corruption. Bribes in Dallas during Binion's reign were infrequent, usually in the form of personal loans to cops whose families had fallen on bad times. The true unit of exchange wasn't money but information and influence. Benny wanted a rival shut down, he called Sheriff R. A. "Smoot" Schmid or deputy sheriff Bill Decker, his longtime friend and the lawman who really ran Dallas for most of three decades. Decker wanted some character run out of town, he called Benny. Rather than bribing individual cops, Binion and other gamblers cheerfully paid regular fines. Two times each week, an officer from the vice squad visited all the gambling houses and did a head count of customers. The next morning the gambling-house operators, or their attorneys, marched down to city hall, pleaded guilty, and paid fines of $10 a head. The charade was basically a taxing and licensing procedure, the perfect compromise between the dictates of piety and the doctrine of laissez-faire.

During World War II, there were 27 casinos in downtown Dallas and no telling how many whorehouses. Every weekend thousands of troops poured into town.

"The downtown bankers and the big law firms believed that having an open town was patriotic," recalls Will Wilson, who became the district attorney of Dallas County at the end of the war. In this milieu, Benny Binion was bound to succeed, his business being the city's pleasure and vice versa.

Benny cut ties with his mentor, Warren Diamond, in 1926 and opened his own permanent craps game in room 226 of the Southland Hotel, just west of the Adolphus in the heart of downtown. Challenging a racketeer like Warren Diamond was a bold move for a 22-year-old, but it was exactly the sort of risk that energized Benny. He'd get a glint in his cool blue eyes, a sort of hard edge that told adversaries he was coming through, like it or not; Diamond was either too wise or too old to challenge his protégé. The Southland, owned by Galveston mob boss Sam Maceo, became the headquarters for Binion's gang, known as the Southland Hotel Group. In 1928 Benny expanded his business to include the numbers racket, also known as the "policy" business. When Diamond killed himself in 1933, Benny became king of the racketeers.

Benny allowed other gamblers to operate craps games for a 25 percent cut of the action, but where the policy racket was concerned, he enforced a monopoly. Even during the Depression, the policies netted hundreds of thousands of dollars a year. The Southland Hotel Group ran several different policy "wheels," so called because winning numbers were drawn lottery style twice daily from wire-mesh wheels; the word "policy" was there to suggest that a ticket was in some way insurance. Most customers were poor blacks from the Fair Park and the South Dallas areas, playing their hunches and dreams. Benny distributed free booklets on dream interpretations and gave the wheels fanciful names like the Harlem Queen or the Horseshoe. Benny's gang kept 80 percent of the take and paid out the other 20 percent to the lucky winners.

Since runners picked up and delivered sacks of cash twice daily, employee theft was a big problem. Hard times called for hard measures. Benny once poked a pencil through the eye of a runner who held out on him. The bullet-riddled bodies of policy runners were found from time to time beside railroad tracks or in fields of weeds near the Trinity River bottom, but lawmen didn't bother to investigate.

For the most part, Benny was generous to his employees and considerate of his clientele. When a Jewish immigrant lost his dry cleaning business and everything else playing the numbers, Benny arranged for him to receive a modest lifetime pension. At Christmas the Binion gang passed out turkeys to regular customers. Not long before Benny died, some aging Dallas blacks, in Las Vegas for a class reunion, stopped by the Horseshoe to pay their respects to the Cowboy.

King of the racketeers was a title that had to be defended almost daily. The rule was, Do your enemies before they can do you, and Benny often found it necessary to arbitrate business differences with a .45 automatic. Murder was also *technically* illegal, but in the spirit of those times it was usually easier to beat a murder rap than to get exonerated for breaking and entering. Officially, Benny was charged with only two homicides, a black rum-runner named Frank Bolding, who was gunned down in Benny's back yard in 1931, and a rival racketeer named Ben Frieden, who was am-

bushed in September 1936 as he waited in his parked
car on Allen Street for a policy pickup. The area of
Ross and Allen was the heartland of Benny's territory.
Killing Bolding was how Binion got his nickname;
when the rum-runner charged at him with a knife,
Benny tumbled backward from the crate where he had
been sitting and came up shooting, cowboy style.
Benny got a suspended sentence for that killing. An
accommodating district attorney ruled that Frieden's
murder was self-defense, Benny having had the fore-
sight to give himself a flesh wound before the cops arrived.

The danger to high-stakes gamblers was from robbers, not cops. Hijackers loved to prey on poker and
craps games because players probably had more pocket
money than banks had deposits and were not inclined
to report their losses. It was necessary, therefore, to
retain the services of freelance gunsels, the most dependable being Jim Clyde Thomas, Tincy Eggleston,
and Lois Green. Green was the nastiest, most depraved
hit man of his time. He would take the subject for a
ride in the country, march him to a pre-dug grave, strip
him naked, shoot him in the guts with a double-bar-
reled shotgun, kick him into the hole, cover him with
quicklime, and bury him while he was still alive,
screaming for mercy.

Another dependable gunsel was Ivy Miller, who
bushwacked a gambler named Sam Murray after he
made a move on Benny's territory in 1938. At the time,
the rubbing out of Sam Murray must have seemed like
just another shooting, but it touched off a gang war that
blazed across Dallas and Fort Worth for the next twenty
years. Even after Benny departed for Las Vegas in

1946, he remained a major presence in the Dallas and Fort Worth underworld. Every time a body was discovered in a shallow grave of quicklime near Lake Worth or at the bottom of a vat of coke acid at a steel mill in East Texas, someone was sure to bring up Benny Binion's name. He always said he had no part in any of the killings, but then Benny would say that, wouldn't he?

B enny's longest-running feud was with a gangster named Herbert "the Cat" Noble, so called because a dozen attempts were required to kill him. The feud was like those old Tom and Jerry cartoons, except the bullets and bombs were real.

Noble was the classic nemesis for a man of Binion's temperament. He was everything Benny wasn't— suave, debonair, a dashing figure who wildcatted in the oil patch and flew his own small fleet of airplanes. He was something of a ladies' man too, and fairly well educated, at least by Benny's standards. Noble was a city boy, raised in West Dallas, which also spawned such infamous outlaws as Clyde Barrow, Bonnie Parker, and Raymond Hamilton. By the late thirties he was a bodyguard for Sam Murray. After Murray was killed, Noble recruited one of Benny's most valued men, Ray Laudermilk—he was Binion's "steerman," the guy who steered clients off the street and up to room 226. The two of them took over Murray's operation. Noble and Laudermilk set up several lucrative policy wheels and a downtown craps game at a joint called the Airmen's Club, near the intersection of Pacific and Ervay.

This was a betrayal that could not go unchallenged. Laudermilk knew all of Benny's regular pistolmen, so he wasn't suspicious when a skid-row bum named Bob

Minyard walked up to his car window, drew a pistol, and shot him dead. Noble accepted his partner's death as a business omen and promptly shut down his policy wheels. He was able to retain the craps game at the Airmen's Club, however, when he agreed to give Benny his usual 25 percent cut. As for the skid-row bum, Bob Minyard, he became one of Binion's regulars after that.

During the boom brought on by World War II, Benny expanded his operation to Fort Worth and bought an interest in Top O'Hill Terrace, the notorious gambling hideaway just west of Arlington. Everyone in the rackets was making big money by this time. The Airmen's Club was doing so well that in January 1946, Benny decided he deserved 40 percent of the action. Noble refused, in effect challenging Benny's rule, and a day later the cops closed Noble down. Noble lived in Oak Cliff, but he also had a ranch just north of Grapevine, and as he was driving to the ranch the following night, three men in a car drove up behind him and started shooting. Pretty soon the two cars were careening down country roads at speeds of ninety miles an hour, exchanging gunfire. Noble managed to stop and flee on foot, but a slug caught him in the back as he escaped into the woods. Hiding under a farmhouse until help arrived, Noble was able to recognize his assailants: Lois Green, Bob Minyard, and a thug named Little Johnny Grissaffi. A few days later, while Noble was in the hospital recovering, three of his boys bushwacked Minyard in his back yard.

"With Minyard's murder Benny was on the spot," a former Dallas police captain explained later in an interview with the authors of *The Green Felt Jungle*, a book about Las Vegas. "It was the first time someone had actually defied him and lived. He was losing face with everybody in the rackets."

The rackets themselves were in trouble. World War II was over, troops were coming home, people dared again talk about the future. Winds of reform blew across the land, not just in Dallas but all over America. Ambitious young veterans, presenting themselves as reform candidates for political office, preached a gospel of growth, prosperity, law and order; red-light districts and gambling houses fell to their onslaught. In the elections of November 1946, Benny's perennial choice as sheriff of Dallas County, the amiable old duffer Smoot Schmid, lost his job to a 33-year-old ex-GI named Steve Guthrie. The district attorney vacancy was captured by Will Wilson, who beat out another reform candidate, Henry Wade, for the job, then hired Wade as his first assistant. Nobody had to tell Benny Binion the party was over.

A month after the election, Benny packed two suitcases full of money and headed for Las Vegas. Las Vegas was just a wide spot on the map in December 1946—there were only two casinos in town, the El Rancho and the Frontier—but it was about to blossom into the gambling capital of the world. That same month, Bugsy Siegel opened his "fabulous" Flamingo Hotel and Casino. As usual, Benny's timing was perfect.

Benny did not cut his ties with Dallas, however. Though he now lived 1,500 miles away, he continued to control the policy racket, and he got a share from all craps games. Herbert Noble, of course, was a problem still to be resolved. Benny posted a reward of $10,000 for Noble's scalp, then bumped it to $25,000, and then to $50,000, with a craps game thrown in as added incentive. A lot of gunsels sniffed at that proposition, and a lot of them ended up dead. Noble was no patsy.

In May 1948, as Noble drove through the entrance gate of his ranch home, gunmen riddled his car with bullets. He escaped with a bloody and mangled arm. On Valentine's Day 1949, Noble discovered dynamite wired to the starter of his car, which was parked near the Airmen's Club. The following September, another high-speed chase ended when Noble's car overturned. Miraculously, the Cat limped away with just a few bruises and a leg full of buckshot.

Noble was in Fort Worth negotiating the purchase of an old Air Force training center called Hicks Field when the fifth attempt was made on his life. As fate would have it, he had driven his wife's car that day. So it was that when 36-year-old Mildred Noble climbed into her husband's car in front of their Oak Cliff home and stepped on the starter, an explosion blew parts of the car over the treetops. Mildred's body was found one hundred feet from the twisted, blackened frame, her face crushed and one foot blown off.

After his wife's death, Noble went a little crazy, spending hours alone staring at a photograph of her flower-bedecked coffin. Rightly or wrongly, he believed that the bomb that killed his wife was planted by Benny Binion's gang, and revenge became his solitary obsession. On Christmas Eve, less than a month after Mildred Noble's death, 31-year-old Lois Green, the depraved gunman who liked to bury his victims alive, walked out of the Sky-Vue Club in West Dallas and was ripped apart by the blast of a shotgun. Everyone

assumed that Green was done in by Noble's number
one hitter, a gunsel known as the Groceryman. A day
or so after Green was killed, the Groceryman arrived
in Las Vegas to assassinate Benny but was captured
instead by some of Benny's gangsters, taken to the desert for rehabilitation, and returned to Dallas—
ostensibly with a mission. On New Year's Eve, exactly
a week after Lois Green was cut down, Noble walked
out onto his front porch and into the beam of a spotlight and the hail of automatic rifle fire.

Again the Cat escaped with his life, but his odds
were diminishing fast. As he recovered at Methodist
Hospital, a bullet shattered the window glass of his
fourth-floor room and lodged in the ceiling. After his
release from the hospital, Noble moved from his house
in Oak Cliff and moved to the ranch, where a floodlit
yard and six vicious dogs offered some security. Attempt number eight came in June 1950, when an assailant hiding in a duck blind opened fire with a machine
gun. This time Noble was saved by the armored plating
of his bulletproof car.

Paradoxically, during all the bloodletting, there was
no organized crime in Texas, not in the sense of the
Mafia or a Capone-style operation. Our gangs were
strictly homegrown. But Benny Binion was now part
of the Las Vegas establishment, which meant that his
feud with Noble—and particularly the publicity generated by the brutal murder of Mildred Noble—put a lot
of heat on national crime organizations. New York
crime boss Frank Costello reportedly canceled plans to
move into oil-rich South Texas. By 1951 the Kefauver
Senate Crime Committee was holding hearings in Los
Angeles, and Benny was on the committee's list of wit-

nesses "wanted but not (yet) found." Meanwhile, back in Dallas, Benny had been charged with operating a policy wheel and income tax evasion and was fighting extradition.

In an effort to negotiate a peace treaty between Binion and Noble, Flamingo Hotel president Dave Berman, a front man for the Eastern syndicate, sent a scumball named Harold Shimley to Dallas for a secret rendezvous with Noble. Meeting at a tourist court near Love Field (and speaking into a hidden microphone planted by the Dallas police) Shimley assured the Cat that no one was more grief-stricken by his wife's death than Benny Binion, that Benny had sworn on the lives of his own wife and five children that he had nothing to do with the bombing.

Noble didn't buy Shimley's story. If anything, the meeting only escalated the violence. In February 1951, Noble attacked an associate of the late Lois Green outside a West Dallas grocery store and got his earlobe bitten off. Five days later somebody threw a bomb through the front door of the Airmen's Club. The Cat was away that night. Two months after that, a nitro bomb exploded in the engine of one of Noble's airplanes, but he was saved by a steel-plated instrument panel. A few days later Noble found another bomb in another airplane. Like all the previous attempts, number eleven failed; but the Cat must have known he was living on borrowed time.

Hell, the attempts themselves were killing him. Once thickset and muscular, Noble had lost at least fifty pounds and looked like a piece of overcooked bacon. His silver-blond hair, once thick and wavy, was now limp and snow white. Though he was only 42, Noble could have passed for 60. He slept—or at least he tried to sleep—with a shotgun next to his bed and carried a carbine everywhere he went. His mind was slipping too, and he had started drinking heavily and taking pills.

And yet in the Cat's grief-twisted brain a fantastic plot was fomenting. He was planning an air raid on Benny's home in Las Vegas—kill 'em all, Benny, his wife, his five kids, his dog, his cat. Noble had bought a stagger-wing Beechcraft with extra wing tanks, a bomb rack, and two large bombs, one an incendiary and the other a high-explosive. He even had an airmen's map of Las Vegas, pinpointing the Binion home on Bonanza Road. Noble might have pulled it off except that Dallas police lieutenant George Butler, who was on temporary assignment to the Kefauver committee, happened to drive up to the ranch just as Noble was doing his final checkout. Noble made a grab for his carbine, but Butler beat him to the draw. At that point Noble crumpled to the ground, blubbering like a baby and sobbing that Benny got all the breaks, that nobody but nobody gave a damn what happened to poor Herbert Noble.

That wasn't entirely true. Someone still cared. On a hot August day in 1951 a land bomb, planted two feet from the mailbox and directly under the spot where a driver stopping to pick up his mail would sit, blew Herbert Noble into an almost infinite number of pieces. Nobody ever found or even looked very hard for his killer—though gangland rumor had it that the shock waves of the explosion knocked Jim Clyde Thomas, one of the premier hitters of the time, out of a nearby tree and broke his arm. Dallas County sheriff Bill Decker, the longtime deputy who had replaced the hapless Steve Guthrie in 1950, summed up the official take on Herbert the Cat this way: "He was folks. He lived here, and it takes all kinds of people to make a city."

The good ol' boy network that Benny Binion helped create in Las Vegas—a cabal of entrepreneurs, lawyers, cops, prosecutors, judges, and politicians— was nearly impregnable. But in the end it was no match for the tenacity of Dallas' postwar crusaders or their lust for vengeance.

Vegas was Benny's kind of town, businesslike and practical, the way Dallas had been in the thirties, only more direct, less hypocritical. The business of Vegas *was* gambling, which meant that everyone could be more out-front. Semantic distinctions concerning loans, gifts, and contributions were not the sort of thing that got people confused or caused them to lose sleep. When Benny loaned $30,000 to Clark County sheriff Ralph Lamb, for example, he didn't expect Lamb to repay the money, but he expected Lamb to be there for him when he needed a favor. And Lamb was, just as Benny was there for Lamb when the sheriff was tried for bribery in 1977. Testimony appeared to establish beyond a doubt that Lamb had taken bribes. Nevertheless, U.S. district judge Roger Foley, Sr., whose son Thomas was one of Benny's lawyers, dismissed the case. Thomas Foley and his brother Roger Foley, Jr., eventually became judges themselves, as did Benny's other chief lawyer, Harry Claiborne.

The network was a living thing, as solid as gold. In 1951, even while Benny was fighting extradition to Texas, the governor of Nevada and the Nevada Tax Commission saw no reason to deny the Cowboy a license to operate his new casino, Binion's Horseshoe. State senator E. L. Nores, who appeared before the commission as a character witness for Binion, claimed that Benny's only limitation was his unbounded generosity. It was a subject on which the senator was well qualified to speak, Benny having gifted him with a new Hudson Hornet automobile a short time before.

Back in Dallas, Henry Wade had moved into the district attorney's office when Will Wilson was elected to the state supreme court, and was plotting a strategy to get Benny behind bars. Work through the federal courts, Wade reasoned, nail Binion on charges of income tax evasion, then hit him with gambling charges after the feds had returned him to Texas. Wade had plenty of evidence, which he shared with the feds. Documents and records seized from the Harlem Queen policy headquarters on Texas Highway 183—and from Benny's safe-deposit box at the Hillcrest State Bank—showed that in 1948 Binion had netted more than $1 million from the rackets in Dallas, hardly any of it reported to the Internal Revenue Service. Juries found Binion and his partner Harry Urban guilty of tax evasion. But while the judge in Dallas sent Urban to prison, Binion's case was transferred to Nevada jurisdiction, and he got off with probation and a small fine.

Outraged by the light sentence, Wade traveled to Washington, where he consulted with U.S. attorney general James McGrannery and other high officials of the Truman administration. According to one report, orders to get Benny Binion were issued the following summer from the Democratic National Convention. McGrannery sent two attorneys from the Department of Justice to Dallas to supervise a new grand jury, and the FBI and the IRS made the investigation a priority. Wade was so determined to get Binion that he had an assistant DA furnish the FBI with an extensive dossier outlining Benny's criminal history, real and alleged. The FBI showed the dossier to a federal judge, who, as Wade recalls, read it and was incited to remark, "I'm gonna get that S.O.B. back to Texas."

In June 1953 Benny had his chauffeur, a large black man who went by the name of Gold Dollar, drive him from Las Vegas to Dallas, where he surrendered to his old friend Bill Decker. The following December, he pleaded guilty to federal charges of income tax evasion and state charges of operating an illegal policy wheel. By previous agreement, the sentences would run concurrently: five years in the federal prison at Leavenworth, a fine of $20,000, and a payment of $776,000 in back taxes, penalties, and interest.

Benny paid his $20,000 fine on the spot, peeling the bills from a much larger roll he had brought along to bribe the judge. Benny apparently was under the misapprehension that U.S. district judge Ben Rice was prepared to give him probation in exchange for a gift of $100,000. "The FBI threatened him and scared him off," Benny claimed later. Binion did 42 months of hard time and was released in October 1957. Wade warned him to stay out of Texas or face additional prison time, but a few months later the Cowboy was riding in the Fat Stock Show parade in downtown Fort Worth, as sassy as ever.

Never again would Benny Binion be allowed to hold a gambling license in Nevada, not that it really mattered. His wife, Teddy Jane, and his eldest son, Jack, were much better able to handle the daily affairs of the casino and hotel business. Teddy Jane was a good, hard-headed woman, not easily influenced by the gamblers and gangsters who took advantage of Benny's generous nature. As a young woman she had predicted, "If I marry Benny Binion, I'll spend my life in a room above a two-bit crap game." She was half right. She spent her life in a room above Binion's Horseshoe. Teddy Jane ran the casino as though it were a mom-and-pop cafe, trusting no one but herself to make bank deposits. She was a familiar sight on Fremont Avenue, this scrawny old lady with dyed hair and a cigarette between her nicotine-stained fingers, trudging from the casino to the bank with hundreds of thousands of dollars stuffed in the pockets of her trench coat.

Prison took something out of Benny and maybe put something else in its place. He got religion in Leavenworth from a Catholic priest. "Religion is too strong a mystery to doubt," he said. Benny was 52 when he got out. His face was gentler and rounder, his blue eyes cloudy and not so hard, his waist and hips going to fat, his voice husky but good-humored. He still loved to talk—God how he loved to talk!—and he held court every afternoon at a corner booth at the Horseshoe, telling old war stories. Hell, yes, he remembered gunning down Ben Frieden in '36. There had always been a dispute over how many bullets were fired from Benny's .45. Was it one, as Benny maintained at the time, or three, as Bill Decker told the grand jury? "Weren't no mystery to it, don't you see," Benny would cackle. "I shot once and hit him three times right in the heart."

And yet there was no question that the Cowboy had mellowed. When a preacher from North Carolina lost $1,000 of his congregation's money shooting craps at the Horseshoe, Benny gave the money back. "God may forgive you, preacher," he said, "but your congregation won't." Life was a crapshoot, that's what made it exciting. In 1980 a high roller from Austin walked into the Horseshoe with two suitcases, one full and one empty. He took $777,000 from the full suitcase and slapped it on the "don't pass" line. Benny nodded: Damn right he'd fade the bet. Three rolls later the man walked out, this time with both suitcases full. Life in the fast lane wasn't all that different from life anywhere else, was it? Nobody got out alive. Benny's eldest child, Barbara Binion Fechser, was a drug addict and died from an overdose in 1983, an apparent suicide; and his youngest son, Ted Binion, pleaded guilty to a drug charge in 1987.

The stigma of being a convicted felon made Benny uncomfortable, and obtaining a presidential pardon became his final obsession. He almost got it in 1978 when his friend Robert Strauss, then the chairman of the Democratic National Committee, brought Benny's plight to the attention of the Carter administration. By now his application for pardon had been denied four times, but Benny proposed a deal. He claimed that he could deliver a vote in the U.S. Senate on the Panama Canal treaties in return for three presidential favors. One was a federal judgeship for Benny's friend and lawyer Harry Claiborne, the second was an exemption from interstate trucking regulations for a business acquaintance in Oklahoma, and the third was a pardon for himself.

It might have come off too, except Benny couldn't keep his famous mouth shut. The Senate ratified the treaties; Benny never made public *which* vote he delivered. Claiborne got his judgeship and was later impeached for income tax evasion. Trucking regulations became irrelevant when Benny's friend went broke. And just as the Justice Department was ready to move on his application for pardon, word of a Binion wisecrack reached Washington. Mafia hitman Jimmy "the Weasel" Fratianno had testified that Benny had hired him to kill a gambler named Russian Louie Strauss, which the FBI knew was not true. But rather than issue a simple denial, Benny replied that, "Tell them FBIs that . . . I'm able to do my own killing without that sorry son of a bitch!" So much for pardon application number five.

During Ronald Reagan's first term, Nevada senator Paul Laxalt suggested to Benny that a contribution to Reagan's campaign treasury might help. Benny sent $15,000, and two days later his pardon was denied. In the old days such a perceived betrayal might have tempted the Cowboy to call Lois Green. But a mellower, more mature Benny was content to buy a newspaper ad calling Laxalt a welsher. Benny said that he intended to live long enough to piss on Reagan's grave, but he finally crapped out.

W hat made Binion's Horseshoe such a success—at least in Benny's opinion—was adherence to two bedrock rules. First, the casino catered to hard-eyed, no-nonsense gamblers. No limits, no entertainment, no gurgling fountains or fancy decor. Until recently, the dealers wore jeans. The specialty of the house was (and still is) generous drinks and Benny's greasy, fiery chili, made not from Chill Will's recipe as advertised but from Smoot Schmid's old Dallas jailhouse recipe. Second was Benny's promise that cheaters and thieves would be escorted to the alley, where their arms and legs would be broken by security guards highly qualified for the assignment. Frank Sutton, a detective sergeant with the Las Vegas metropolitan police department, says, "The Horseshoe was the only casino in town that didn't believe in calling the police. They took care of trouble their own way."

The Wild West motif worked in Las Vegas for many years, just as it had in Dallas, but again times were changing. By the mid-eighties, Las Vegas was trying to recast its image as a sort of adult Disneyland, and the Horseshoe's vigilante tactics were an embarrassment. After the Cowboy suffered two major heart attacks and surrendered even a pretense of control, the rough stuff got out of hand. A casino employee chased down a drunk who had thrown a brick through a window, calmly shot him to death on a street a few blocks from the police station, then strolled back to the Horseshoe as though nothing had happened. Two men assumed to be cheating at blackjack were hauled into the security office, beaten, and robbed.

In January 1988, Benny's grandson, 33-year-old Steven Binion Fechser, and two security guards were convicted of assaulting the two blackjack players. But instead of passing sentence, district judge Thomas Foley took it on himself to overturn the jury verdict, an action within the power of a Nevada judge.

That didn't end it, however. In April 1990, Fechser, his uncle Ted Binion, and six guards were indicted on federal charges of conspiring to kidnap, beat, and rob customers of the Horseshoe—particularly blacks and other people considered undesirable by the Binions.

The case will be tried starting October 8 in the court of U.S. district judge Philip M. Pro.

Teddy Jane Binion will no doubt be among the spectators, as she was at her grandson's trial three years ago. During a break in the trial, she approached chief deputy attorney general John Redlein, who was prosecuting the case.

"Haven't I seen you in the hotel?" she asked.

"I used to have lunch over at the Horseshoe fairly often," he replied, "but I guess I won't be welcome after this, heh?"

"Not at all, honey," she told him. "This is just business."

(October 1991)

Eight years after I wrote this story, I wrote another (*Texas Monthly*, November 1999) about the murder of Benny's youngest son, Ted Binion, and the ugly legal battle waged by the Binion siblings over control of the Horseshoe Casino. Coupled with Ted's death, the battle destroyed the family and permanently altered the legendary casino. Benny's children grew up as aristocrats, at least by Las Vegas standards, and failed to learn the lesson that I'm sure Benny tried to teach them—the price of wealth and privilege can be greed, betrayal, and cold-blooded murder.

The Killer Next Door

GAYLE GOLDEN

The knocks came after midnight. We were in bed upstairs, sleeping so soundly that the noise seemed, at first, just part of a dream.

"That's the door?" I asked, turning to see my husband already heading downstairs. I followed. Standing on the stoop outside was Richard Lyon, our duplex landlord, holding a baby monitor. His face was pale; his eyes were deep and tired. He spoke in a low, hoarse voice: Nancy, his wife, had been vomiting for hours. He was taking her to the emergency room. Could we please look after his daughters while he was gone?

We took the monitor without a thought. In the nearly six years we had lived side by side—sharing, as we did, a wall, a front porch, a back yard, and the cramped conditions of middle-income Park Cities housing—we had come to rely on each other for life's little emergencies: electronic baby-sitting, pet care during vacations, newspapers retrieved from the rain. During the past year, especially, as their marriage crumbled and Richard was frequently gone, we had often come to Nancy's aid. We helped when she was sick, collected her mail, listened for her phone. Now this.

"Don't worry about the kids," I said, as Richard headed back to his door. "And tell Nancy I hope she feels better."

Six days later, she was dead.

Within two months, the official word was that Nancy Dillard Lyon had been poisoned. The Dallas County medical examiner, who ruled her death a homicide, found lethal concentrations of arsenic in her body. Richard, then 34, was arrested and charged with her murder. Less than a year later, he was convicted and given a life sentence.

From the start, the Lyon murder attracted national publicity and attracted national publicity and local curiosity. The victim was the daughter of a prominent Highland Park family and a partner in one of Trammell Crow's residential companies. From her death on January 14, 1991, to Richard's trial in December, there was a constant flow of new twists: suggestions of other suspects, rumors of incest, revelations about chemical purchases, and Nancy's own suspicions that she was being poisoned.

Throughout those eleven months, I did all I could to believe that Richard had not poisoned his wife. At every opportunity, I turned distrust and fear into doubt and denial. I refused to follow the tide of opinion about my neighbor, refused to convict him without proof of his guilt. I knew Richard, I thought. We had lived so close—close enough to hear, as I did the night he took Nancy to the hospital, his last tender words to her in their bedroom. "I'm warming up the car," his voice crackled through the monitor, inches from my ear. "Do you think you can make it downstairs? I'll carry you."

But what did I know? What does anyone know about

anyone, even those who share your walls for years? You see their lives, hear them, only in fragments— steps on a stair, casual glimpses through a window, doors closing and opening, the sound of running water, a child's cry or laugh. The pieces of their lives enter your consciousness, become as much a part of you as your own life. But in the end, you can only imagine what's in their souls, even if it is unimaginable.

When I decided to write about Nancy's death, many who knew her wouldn't talk to me. They worried that I would take Richard's side, or that I would expose too much, having lived so close. Am I violating some neighborly code of privacy? I only know I wouldn't be writing this if Nancy had not died as she did. If anything, I would have written some nice little testament to the loss of a good neighbor. Maybe it would have inspired some nice little neighborly acts.

But this is not a nice little story. It is a story of lies and betrayal, ugly accusations and cold, calculated murder. And there is no inspiration in any of it.

I t's hard to say when my suspicions began. My sense is that I felt inklings of a sinister aura over Nancy's illness from the start, but they were deep, intuitive, ill-defined. I couldn't pin them down.

Maybe it was nothing more than the shock of it all. A 37-year-old woman, in seemingly good health, was suddenly lying in an intensive care unit with a team of doctors unable to stop her swift decline. At 1:50 a.m., when Nancy first entered Presbyterian Hospital's emergency room, the doctors tried several medications to stop her vomiting. By 8 a.m., she was no better. She had been retching uncontrollably; her pulse was racing at 144; her blood pressure had dropped to 50 over 18.

When she was transferred to the ICU, doctors first suspected toxic shock syndrome. For more than a week, Nancy had complained of vaginal itching; two days earlier, she had begun taking Zovirax capsules for pimplelike lesions on her cervix. But she lacked the rash and high fever of toxic shock. Food poisoning looked doubtful too. Although she said she had eaten old pasta the night before, her symptoms had lasted too long. Puzzled, her doctors began to test for infections.

Within hours, family and friends gathered. Eventually, they would fill the waiting room and spill out into the hall. Most had known Nancy's parents, Bill and Sue Dillard, for years. They had watched them bury one of their four children, thirty-year-old Tom, who died of a brain tumor in 1985. But nobody expected that Nancy would not make it. As she thrashed in pain, her family members urged her to fight. To boost her spirits, friends played tape recordings of her daughters, four-year-old Allison and two-year-old Anna, singing and talking to their mother.

Only when she continued to deteriorate did tensions escalate. On January 10 a friend of the Dillards' showed up on our doorstep and suggested that we visit Richard in the waiting room. "There's a lot of anger," she said. "It's the Dillards on one side, Richard on the other. What he really needs is friends."

I went to the hospital that afternoon. The anger toward Richard didn't surprise me. I knew the Dillards thought he had put Nancy through hell for the past year.

Nearly everyone was surprised, especially Nancy, when Richard grew so unhappy with the marriage. When we first became their tenants in 1985, they seemed a compatible, warm, active couple, with a homey friendliness and virtually no flash or friction in their lives. We never once heard them fight. Nancy was bright, ambitious, and full of cheerful energy, a small woman with short dark hair and a pretty face marked by jet-black eyes, alabaster skin, and large white teeth. Richard, a short man with wavy brown hair and chiseled features, was congenial, calm, conservative, and relentless in his puttering around the yard.

They had met six years earlier at Harvard University's Graduate School of Design, where they studied landscaping and development together, and had come to Dallas at the crest of its land boom. They were intent on working hard, but they also freely took help from Nancy's real estate developer father—Big Daddy, as his children called him—in the form of loans and business clout. In 1982, Nancy accepted a management job with longtime family friend Trammell Crow's residential company. She rose quickly and made partner in a year. In 1984, in part from Bill Dillard's recommendation, Richard was hired by developer Kenneth Hughes to oversee construction of his firm's largest projects.

The couple busied themselves nearly all the time: sprucing up their property, directing family Christmas pageants, making Allison's dollhouse shingle by shingle. At Harvard, they had teamed up on all their projects, working through the night until collapsing together in the single bed they shared. According to friends, Nancy had the ideas, Richard the speedy execution.

The constant activity bridged the striking differences in their backgrounds. Nancy had grown up among the manicured lawns and large brick homes of Highland Park, a rarefied world of close-knit, affluent, churchgoing families whose children sang Christmas carols together and spent summers at the country club pool. Richard had none of that breeding. He grew up in a middle-class neighborhood in small-town Connecticut, where his father sold insurance and his mother was a teacher's aide. When he met Nancy in 1979, he didn't even own a suit. At their wedding three years later, his relatives were daunted by the Dillards' money and what they perceived to be their in-laws' clannish ways. It bothered them that Richard didn't quite fit in. His parents bristled when Nancy's older brother, Bill Junior, jokingly toasted Richard at the rehearsal dinner as "a Yankee and a yardman."

If Richard resented his wife's family or her success, however, he never let on in those early years. The couple ate burgers at regular Dillard picnics by the Dallas Country Club pool and went on Dillard family vacations each summer. Richard worked with Nancy on her Junior League philanthropy projects. Particularly after Allison's birth in 1986, the couple's life meshed easily with Highland Park expectations: They hired a full-time nanny; they got their children on waiting lists for the best preschools; they taught in the Sunday school nursery. Yet they were never blatant materialists. Their life in the 1,100-square-foot duplex appeared simple and earnest. They spent weekend nights at home, renting old movies. On their own they transformed the once-scrawny back yard into a little paradise, planting trees and wisteria, driving bricks into sand to make a patio, hanging chimes and a hammock.

But my husband and I could see the stresses build. By 1988 the real estate boom had gone bust. Richard's work with Hughes was slowing. In January 1989 their second daughter, Anna, was born with a hip problem. Their cramped space seemed nearly intolerable. All through that summer, we would listen to Anna's crying in their bedroom. Richard was gone on business often.

In the fall of that year, we had heard only hints that the marriage was troubled, that Richard had met another woman and wanted out. The first real sign of their break came sadly and quietly the day after Christmas. We awoke to see their tree already stripped of its ornaments and lying on the front sidewalk to be hauled away. Richard was crouched in the driveway with a packed duffel bag on the ground beside him, his face bitter and unhappy as he held an arm around little Allison and spoke softly in her ear. Then he threw his bag into his red 1966 Mustang and drove off.

The separation left Nancy dumbfounded and distraught. He had told her he was going to a family counseling program in Arizona, but he ended up joining his girlfriend on a ski trip. Two weeks later he was back—only to move out again within a month. Yet through the next year, Nancy was endlessly willing to endure Richard's occasional, always short-lived attempts at reconciliation, much to the increasing chagrin of her family and friends. "I know the real Richard," she used to say. "This isn't like him. He's a family man. He's sick, but I know he'll come around."

By early summer 1990, the separation was taking a physical toll on Nancy. She grew alarmingly thin. One morning she knocked on our door, handed us Anna, sat down on our front step, and vomited. We got a bucket and called her parents. Later that day I took her some soup. Her doctor attributed the illness to antibiotics, she said. Two weeks later she told me that she tried taking the same pills again and again got sick.

The incident became, for me, a metaphor for the sense of rot I began to feel at the duplex that summer. Maybe it was just the image of their garden—which, once lavish, was now withered and infested. I began watering and tending it. Each night, I straightened up the yard and washed off the porch.

When Richard filed for divorce in September, I was actually relieved. The finality seemed to strengthen Nancy. Her attorney requested that she get sole custody of the children, child support, and rights to as much as $260,000 in separate assets. One settlement proposal suggested that Richard was willing to give Nancy most of what she wanted. For the first time, I heard her speak hopefully about herself. She mentioned moving to Washington, D.C., to work.

Then, by mid-November, Richard began appearing at the duplex. We were surprised and skeptical at first. When I asked Nancy about it, she told me that Richard wanted to reconcile and that she had asked him to prove it. Suddenly the place came alive. The couple began planning a new back yard, including a playhouse that Richard was building himself, working late into the freezing nights to finish it before Christmas. He put a wood-burning fireplace in the living room and, at Nancy's request, painted the downstairs walls a funky red. In the evenings he built pillow forts with the kids and played his guitar. The atmosphere was so lively that my 21-month-old son, Shawn, began yearning to visit. One morning, without my knowing it, he wandered out of our door. I found him eating apple slices at their breakfast table.

So that was my view on January 10, 1991, when I decided to visit Richard in the hospital waiting room. I had a certain amount of compassion for him. If there was anger, I thought, it was because the Dillards didn't understand how much he had been around, how so much had seemed to change.

I entered carrying a bag of deli sandwiches. The waiting room was crowded. Richard was sitting in one corner with a group, looking pale but refreshed from a shower. I went directly to him, gave him the sandwiches, and hugged him.

"I'm so sorry," I said.

"About what?" he asked.

I flushed and paused for a moment, unsure of what to say. "Well," I said, "I'm sorry Nancy's so sick."

S ix hours after I left, Nancy's lungs failed. She was sedated and placed on a respirator. She never communicated again. By the time she was taken off life support on January 14, she was a bloated, unrecognizable figure. The intravenous attempts to bring up her blood pressure had pumped nearly forty pounds of excess fluids into her body.

At the time of Nancy's death, the doctors still didn't know the exact cause. But hours after she was admitted on January 9, her father told Dr. Ali Bagheri, the resident overseeing her care, that the family suspected Richard had poisoned Nancy. A few days later, her brother Bill told the Dallas County district attorney the same thing.

Nancy, it turned out, had suspected Richard of poisoning her four months earlier. She had related her fears to her divorce lawyer, Mary Henrich, and to her sister-in-law, Mary Helen Dillard. In early September, she told them, she found a bottle of wine on her porch with an anonymous note to her; the cork looked as if it had been tampered with. Soon after, Nancy said, she and Richard went to the movies. When Richard brought her a soft drink, she took one sip and immediately spit it out because of a foul taste. She then saw a white powder floating on top. According to Henrich, Nancy said Richard "threw a fit" because she didn't drink it. She said she was sick that night.

It's hard to say why Nancy would have reconciled with Richard in the face of such suspicions, which apparently continued. Henrich urged her to have the wine tested, but Nancy never followed through, saying it would embarrass her to accuse her husband. Then, in late October, friends saw Nancy with a collection of unusual "health pills" Richard had given her. In December, after she and Richard went on a ski weekend in Colorado, Nancy told Mary Helen she had stayed in the bathroom vomiting for an entire night during the trip. Richard, she said, never once got out of bed to check on her.

After Nancy's father talked to Bagheri, it was at least ten hours before the doctor did anything. Bagheri later testified that his patient load was busy that day and that he was waiting for Richard to leave Nancy's bedside so he could talk to her alone. Finally, around midnight, he saw Nancy in her room. She told him about the soft drink, about the wine and the health pills. When Bagheri left Nancy that night, he recalled, she was writhing in pain, pleading with him to find out what was wrong with her. "I remember what she said," he testified. " 'Please help me. Help me. Don't let me die.' "

Early the next morning, Bagheri asked the Dillards to search the duplex. Later that day, they returned with a red bag. Inside was an eight-compartment container filled with various pills and an open bottle of wine. The bags had been in the car trunk of Allison and Anna's nanny, who said she saw Nancy place them there amid sundry garage sale items a few months earlier. Richard, meanwhile, apparently knew nothing of the Dillard family's suspicions. Shortly after Nancy was admitted to the ICU, he himself asked doctors if tainted food could have made her ill. He said she had been drinking foul-tasting coffee the morning before she got sick. He brought in a bag of food from the house to be tested.

By this point, I later learned, observers were clearly divided into two camps. Doctors viewed Richard's efforts with skepticism, and Nancy's family and friends were quick to catalog his misplaced gestures, indifferent responses, and odd refusal to leave her bedside. Yet others saw nothing strange about Richard's behavior. They saw him pray with his minister. They saw him barely sleep. When Nancy died, he appeared as bereft as any husband would be.

Gary Perkins, a business associate and close friend of Richard's, came to the hospital just as Nancy's life support was being turned off. At first Perkins was directed to an upstairs waiting room where the Dillards were congregating separately from Richard. When he walked off the elevator and asked for Richard, he felt a discernible chill. A woman showed him downstairs to a room where Richard's parents sat alone, waiting for their son to exit Nancy's room. "Richard came out, and he was crying real hard," Perkins recalls. "He was surprised to see me, and he hugged me. It upset me, because I'd never seen him upset like that."

Perkins ended up driving Richard home. It wasn't until they were in the car that he learned Nancy had died. "I cried and told him I was sorry," Perkins says. "He had her pair of shoes there in his lap and he kept rubbing them in his hands. Man, it just ripped me apart. I couldn't stand it. and he kept saying, 'How am I going to tell my girls? How am I going to tell them?' "

The day before Nancy died, I took down their Christmas lights. I raked and swept the back yard, picking up pieces of wood shavings, screws, and nails while my son played.

In the center of the small lawn stood a stone statue of a curly haired angel playing a harp. Richard had given it to Nancy for Christmas. For some reason, my son knew it was hers and would occasionally point to it and call out her name. When he did, I felt a loss of surprising depth. I hadn't known Nancy as a close friend; although we had talked nearly every day, our relationship was seasoned with a cordial neighborly distance.

For a long time, in fact, Nancy was nothing more to me than a good neighbor. She practiced that art well. When we first moved in, she would bring us gifts of soup or ice cream. If she borrowed a dish, she would always return it filled with something she or Richard had cooked. She remembered us every Christmas with a gift of raspberry vinegar or a basket of fruit. My husband—who is rarely hyperbolic about anyone—began calling her "the nicest person in the world."

Admittedly, Nancy could be aggravating. Often we would step over dirty dishes or half-full coffee mugs that she would leave for hours on the front stoop. When her children painted on the upstairs porch, globs of red or blue would drip onto the stroller we kept near our door. And in conversation, she could be infuriatingly optimistic, addressing problems with empty platitudes about how everything would work out. Even after Richard left, even as her world fell apart, she tried to hang on to her rosy views.

Yet when she couldn't, she seemed more approachable, softer, more real. She had quit her job shortly after Richard moved out, intent on giving her daughters stability through the marital chaos. I was home with a child too. Together we began to forge a silent household alliance. On warm days and evenings our doors would swing open and our children would run back and forth, playing together as Nancy and I stayed on separate sides working or cooking. We would take turns keeping an eye on the kids. On some days we would borrow sugar, noodles, or milk from each other with an almost comic style.

As the months passed, our reliance on each other grew. At times she would say how grateful she felt with us living so close, how comforting our mere presence was to her, how safe she felt. For me, too, Nancy's movements became etched into my daily routine. The sound of her step at night. The slamming of her door. The smell of her cooking. The sight of the toys strewn on her living room floor. The music she played.

Then, suddenly, she was gone.

I mmediately after Nancy's death the police advised the Dillards to keep up appearances with Richard. In retrospect, it amazes me how convincingly they played their roles. They received scores of guests at their home. During the funeral, which drew hundreds, Richard sat in the front pew next to Nancy's mother. The two wept with their arms around each other as they sang "Amazing Grace." At the grave site, her family calmly watched Richard hold Allison close.

In the weeks that followed, Nancy's father came by the duplex nearly every other morning with a box of fresh-baked muffins. He sometimes helped with the household tasks or the children until Richard drove them to school. My husband and I tried to help Richard too. We baby-sat when he went to a grief-recovery program. We cooked him dinners. We tried to offer him chances to talk, although we knew he didn't bare his feelings easily. But it seemed to us that Richard was finding a way to cope with his wife's death. With his old energy and industriousness, he took up the backyard work he and Nancy had begun. He built a greenhouse. He bought rabbits for his daughters and made an open bunny hutch. He moved the angel statue into the center of the vegetable garden and planned to put a little washtub fountain in front of it—a makeshift memorial to his dead wife.

As I write this now, it seems almost absurd that I held so firmly to the idea that Richard was above suspicion. I am not—as few in Dallas are, I suppose—naive about spousal murders. I know that seemingly fine, upstanding men in our community are capable of strangling, smothering, or otherwise mutilating their wives to death. But I could see no such capacity for evil in

Richard; nor could friends or co-workers. "Nothing ever suggested Richard could do this kind of thing," said one of Richard's former employers. "Richard would get mad, sure, but it was never, never carried out in the form of retribution."

As a child, Richard was, according to his parents, always quiet and independent, rarely outwardly emotional but always amiable. He was drawn to art and music, did well in school, and showed signs of being a perfectionist. By age 28, he was competently directing multimillion-dollar construction projects and, all the while, earning the affection of colleagues, who saw him as generous and honest. He once gave his secretary $500 to help with a down payment on her house; he paid his associate Gary Perkins $5,000 from his personal account when a company check was late. Perkins, who worked nearly every day with Richard through 1989, describes him as a gentle man who never lost his temper on the job. "Richard would get angry, and he would voice his anger," Perkins says, "but he always maintained control."

By all accounts Richard also impressed the Dillards with his creativity and work ethic. As Nancy's father wrote in 1989, recommending him for membership in the Dallas Salesmanship Club, "I have had ten years to observe his personality, drive, wit, and determination. Richard is hard-working, serious, and dedicated, but he can laugh at himself and has a great appreciation for the simple pleasures in life."

"He was the Pied Piper of all times with kids," says an acquaintance. "He'd get out on the lawn at these picnics, and all the parents would be eating and drink-

ing, and Richard was just there frolicking with the kids
and having a good time."

When Richard left Nancy, however, her friends saw
him change; he became disdainful, cold, and angry. Yet
Nancy would always defend him, saying he was simply
having an acute mid-life crisis. "Richard has always
been so compliant in his family," says Emily Com-
stock, a longtime friend of Nancy's. "I think Nancy felt
like he just hit a point where he didn't want to be a
good boy anymore."

I first saw Tami Ayn Gaisford at the duplex just a few
days after Nancy's funeral. Her car was parked in
the driveway, with the same "94.5—The Edge"
bumper sticker that had appeared on Richard's Mustang shortly after he had left Nancy. As I walked to our
door, I glanced briefly through Richard's window and
saw a blond sitting at the dinner table with Richard and
the girls.

She appeared every two or three days after that, once
lazily reading while he worked in the back yard. At
first I didn't recognize her as the "other woman" that
Nancy had mentioned. She was not, as Nancy had said,
a sultry, miniskirted hussy who frequented bars. She
was fit and attractive, with a demeanor undoubtedly
sensual but not at all cheap. The daughter of a residential contractor in Dallas, Ayn Gaisford was an intelligent, reasonable woman who had met Richard in the
summer of 1989 while both worked on the renovation
of the Saks Fifth Avenue Pavilion in Houston.

As I later learned, the affair had not been a casual
one. For Christmas 1989, Richard had bought her a
$4,900 ring. And their affection appeared mutual and

deep, lasting even through Richard's attempts at reconciliation with Nancy. "Richard knew he was in love with Ayn," says one business associate who knew them. "What to do about it was the confusing part. He loved his kids."

Obviously it was awkward seeing Ayn at the duplex so soon after Nancy's death. It was unseemly, really—particularly late one night in early February, when I heard laughter in the back yard and saw her, Richard, and another couple having a dinner party. One early February morning I opened our dining room blinds at the exact moment she walked out of Richard's back door, carrying a small overnight bag.

Yet I continued to give Richard the benefit of the doubt. He had few close friends, I thought; who was I to decide what he needed in his grief?

There was, after all, so much I didn't know.

On January 15, one day after Nancy's death, an autopsy was conducted by the Dallas County medical examiner's office. It would show lethal doses of arsenic in her liver and kidneys. Her blood had as much as one hundred times more arsenic than normal. Her hair showed as much as forty times the normal amount at the root. That day, Detective Don S. Ortega of the Dallas Police Departments' homicide unit met with Nancy's father. Ortega told him the investigation would take a while. In most cases Ortega questions his prime suspect within a day or two, but this one was trickier. This time he would wait.

The Dillards had told him that during 1990 Nancy had seen a canceled check from Richard to General Laboratory Supply, a chemical distributor in Pasadena.

Apparently worried that Richard was using drugs, Nancy had mentioned the laboratory's name to her sister. Ortega subpoenaed bank records for Richard's accounts and asked General Labs to search their files. Within a month he obtained receipts showing Richard had bought several toxic chemicals in powdered form, including barium carbonate and sodium nitroferricyanide, from the supplier throughout 1990. None showed an arsenic purchase.

In late February the duplex grew quiet for days. Richard had told the Dillards he was going fishing in Mexico with a friend named John, and he left his daughters with Bill Junior's family. While he was gone, Ortega checked airline records and discovered Richard had flown to Puerta Vallarta with Ayn Gaisford. Their return date was February 25. Ortega picked up Richard for questioning two days later.

Richard, pleasant and cooperative, spent five hours downtown with Ortega. During their talk, Ortega recalls, Richard's eye contact never wavered. He answered questions calmly, without obvious emotion—even at times when Ortega felt emotion was warranted.

Ortega already knew that in the 44 days since Nancy's death, Richard hadn't once called the medical examiner's office to ask about the autopsy results. When he told Richard that Nancy had been poisoned, Richard barely reacted. "He remained calm," Ortega testified. "He didn't say anything and did not appear upset. No response at all." The most telling moment, in Ortega's view, came when he asked Richard if he had any poisons at the duplex. Richard mentioned that Amdro, an ant killer, and Vapam, a herbicide, were stored in the garage. When he then asked if Richard had ever bought any chemicals, Ortega testified, Richard "thought for a moment and then said, 'No.' "

"Right then, I knew I'd found my suspect," Ortega told me after the trial. "I knew that he killed her. He lied to me, and I let him lie to me."

In Ortega's view, Richard's lies only continued. When he asked if Richard had ever bought chemicals "from a laboratory outside Houston," Richard said he had: mercury and lead to repair a battery, along with cyanide and "arsenic acid" to kill fire ants. At first Richard said he didn't recall what he had done with the poisons; later he said he had put them in a trash bag and thrown them away. After the interview, Richard allowed police officers to search the duplex and his car. They turned up no evidence—no tainted food, none of the chemicals purchased by Richard, and no medication in Nancy's name, not even the Zovirax capsules prescribed by her gynecologist just two days before she got sick.

As it happened, Richard *had* ordered arsenic, in both liquid and powder form, on November 19, 1990, from General Labs. On December 26, Richard called the company to ask about its status and was told it should arrive within two weeks. The package was delivered to Richard's office the next day. Early that morning, Richard, Nancy, and the children had left Dallas on a flight to Connecticut. A receptionist signed for the package and placed it in the mail room. The earliest Richard could have picked it up was January 3, six days before Nancy went to the hospital.

At the trial, when Richard took the stand in his defense, he told a different version of his talk with Ortega. He said he initially answered no to the question about chemicals because he thought Ortega was asking about pesticides. And he testified that he never told Ortega that he had received the December 27 delivery of arsenic.

In fact, nobody was ever able to prove Richard had actually picked up the arsenic at his office. Shortly after Richard's arrest in May, he contacted the receptionist who signed for the delivery and asked her if she remembered him complaining that he hadn't received a package. The receptionist said she didn't recall any such complaint—yet neither she nor any other witnesses saw Richard take the package from the mail room.

It was nearly three months after Richard's trip downtown before Ortega arrested and charged him with first-degree murder. In that time Dallas County toxicologists had analyzed the "health pills" that Nancy said Richard had given her. Most were benign vitamin formulas, but two of the sixteen capsules contained pure barium carbonate—one of the toxic chemicals Richard had ordered in August.

O n a cold Sunday in early March, four days after his initial interview with Ortega, Richard knocked on our door and asked to see my husband. Richard told him about the police investigation and said Bill Junior had filed a temporary restraining order to gain custody of his daughters. As my husband recalls it, Richard began hinting at a Dillard conspiracy—a family effort to pin Nancy's death on him, to take away the girls. Maybe the hospital screwed up, Richard said, or maybe someone else killed his wife. As they talked, my husband sensed concern and fear in Richard's voice but no

anger at the apparent injustice of the police accusations. "He looked serious and shook up," my husband
later told me. "He looked more scared than outraged."

Ayn Gaisford stopped visiting after that. Richard
hired lawyers and was gone often. I started a journal.
Three days after Richard talked with my husband, I sat
in the back yard, struck by the stark contrast of two
weeks earlier. Then, the yard had been full of life, with
Allison, Anna, and Shawn running after the bunnies
while Richard sawed and hammered and potted plants.
"Now," I wrote, "the plants have been strewn about,
upturned by the wind or the rabbits. A light had been
on for several nights in Richard's tool shed. No one has
been in to turn it off. The face of Nancy's angel has
streaks of light brown muck on it—sap, rusty water,
bird crap for all I know. All life has gone, suddenly,
except for the bunnies. Even they are thin, shaking, and
hungry. Shawn and I feed them every day. Sometimes
they run wild in the alley. The other night, their hutch
collapsed in the wind."

That night, I was awake in bed when Richard's car
pulled into the driveway. I heard his key in the door,
his step on the stair six feet from my head. I felt, for
the first time, a naked and nauseating fear.

Maybe it was Rosemary Lyon, Richard's mother,
who made me feel better. Within a few days she had
left her job in Connecticut, moved in, and was washing
and ironing his shirts, opening his mail, and cooking
his meals. "I finally got him to eat something last
night," she said to me. "Now I can't fill him up."

Rosemary had a gritty, comforting, no-nonsense
warmth about her. A second-generation Lebanese
American, she seemed to be a woman who orders life

by simple rules. She believes in the power of saints and is deeply loyal to her family and friends. I never heard her doubt Richard's innocence. As she saw it, whoever killed Nancy was out to get Richard too. When she arrived, she emptied all of Richard's spices in the trash. She looked warily at bottles of vinegar Nancy had kept above the sink.

Through Rosemary, I began to see Richard as a mother's son. I found myself, once again, warmed to him, able to view him with uncertainty—a feeling that was far more comforting than the terror I had felt days earlier. My trust was still tenuous. One night Rosemary came to our door with a plate of apple pie Richard had made that day. I could never bring myself to eat it. Yet I remember, too, the beautiful, sunny, cool, windy afternoon when Richard and Rosemary came back from the first day of the custody hearing. I sat on the front porch while Richard complained about having to plead the Fifth Amendment on nearly every question, which his lawyers had advised. He said his stomach felt like it had "a hole in it" after he heard the Dillards' testimony against him. "It hurts when you see your family, or what you thought was your family, saying you did something so horrible," he said. He looked so sad, so sincere in his stated incredulities. In that moment, I felt genuine sympathy for him.

The Dillards never struck me as conspiring people. If anything, the manner of Nancy's death left them stunned, outraged, and somewhat mortified. They were also scared. "I was sure that once Richard knew the jig was up, he would do something crazy, like kill the girls and then kill himself," Bill Junior told me months later. "I had a lot of fear, a lot of fear."

At the time, though, I didn't know what to believe about Richard's hints of secrets in Nancy's family—secrets, he said, that tied into the mystery of her death. I found it hard to imagine. But by this point, nothing would have surprised me—or so I thought.

I hadn't heard the testimony in the custody hearing. Richard's lawyer had subpoenaed me as a witness, but after two days of waiting outside the courtroom, I was never called. Faced with no hard evidence proving Richard an unfit parent, the court gave the Dillards visiting rights but temporarily returned the girls to their father. After Richard and Rosemary returned, jubilant, from court that day, I knocked on their door. Richard ushered me in. He had loosened his tie; his face looked more relaxed than it had in months. He had seriously hurt the Dillards' case, he said, by testifying about the incestuous relationship Nancy had had with her brother Bill while the two were adolescents.

According to Richard, Nancy first told him about the incest in late spring 1989, when they and other Dillard family members spent a "family counseling week" at Sierra Tucson, a psychiatric facility in Arizona, where Bill Junior was undergoing treatment for alcohol and drug abuse. While there, Nancy and Richard saw a sex therapist. The incest came out at that session, and as he said later, it left him "disgusted" and "repulsed."

What actually happened between Nancy and her brother 25 years ago is disputed. After Richard's trial, Bill Junior spoke to me frankly about it. There was never any intercourse, he said, and no one victim or perpetrator. He and Nancy cooperated in fondling games that confused physical closeness with emotional intimacy. The two had even talked forgivingly about it months before she died, he said.

But as I sat in his living room that day, Richard painted the ugliest of pictures: that Bill Junior would "pounce" on Nancy with advances she escaped by mentally withdrawing—by reading, in one instance, even as it happened. According to Richard, Nancy's parents only discovered the incest when she complained of vaginal bleeding. I sat, speechless, at his descriptions. He looked back at me calmly. "Now you know," he said.

That evening, when Richard drove his daughters back to the duplex, he got a police escort. Even though the day was wet, Richard brought out his guitar and began singing Raffi songs out back. The atmosphere was very festive, and it stayed that way for days. I remember, most clearly, one evening when Shawn brought out his toy guitar for another sing-along. Allison hung on Richard's back, holding her blanket, while Anna played in the sand nearby. At the end of one song, Richard reached down and stroked Shawn softly on the cheek. For a moment, in that warmth, it was if the whole matter of Nancy's death had disappeared.

We moved out six weeks later, into a house we had bought before Nancy died. In that time, we felt close to Richard. We shared dinners. When Anna was hospitalized with a rare viral syndrome, I watched how tenderly he cared for her. From time to time, Richard frolicked with my son. Their favorite seemed to be a tickling game, which Richard called "typing torture." It always made Shawn giggle wildly.

Before we left, Richard gave us two bonsai trees.

"Please keep these trees," he wrote in a note, "as they will survive for decades with the same care that you give each other."

We heard about Richard's arrest in May. I felt helpless, seeing his picture on the front page. I went to his bond hearing and embraced Rosemary when his bail, originally set at $2 million, was reduced to $50,000. We didn't see them much after that. We became, like so many who knew Nancy and Richard, intent on escaping the ordeal.

But escape was impossible. I had mistakenly taped the news report of Richard's arrest on my son's favorite *Barney and the Backyard Gang* videotape. I could barely listen to Raffi music. When one of the two bonsai trees died, I couldn't stop seeing Nancy in its thin, withered trunk. and Shawn began having bedtime fears of men coming to "type" him. One night, months after we had moved out, I cradled him close and asked him, "Who types you?"

"Richard," he answered.

The hallway outside state district judge John Creuzot's courtroom was packed when I arrived on December 2 for Richard's trial. It was an unusual scene from the start. For three weeks nearly everything in the courtroom, including the white-collar jury, masked the carnality of murder with a veneer of North Dallas propriety and aesthetics.

Richard appeared clean-shaven, in finely tailored suits, always carrying a briefcase full of legal pads and files. His lawyer, Dan Guthrie, a former assistant United States attorney with a reputation for defending savings and loan executives, was tall, handsome, and impeccably dressed. The state's case was led by assistant district attorney Jerri Sims, whose elegant skirts, spiked heels, and waist-long blond hair effectively disguised her hard-nosed reputation for winning convictions. And each day, scores of well-scrubbed Dillard supporters came: elderly benefactors, young women with hankies pinned to their sweaters, Episcopalian ministers, ladies doing cross-stitch. Richard's parents, and sometimes a friend or two, sat quietly apart from that crowd.

I sat with the journalists, believing I could watch Richard's trial with their dispassion. I acted the part well, recording every minute of testimony in my little notebooks. Only later did I realize that I had never been dispassionate.

I had hoped Guthrie would show me that his client didn't kill Nancy. He had pledged as much in an unusual press conference nine months earlier, which he called after University Park police named Richard as a suspect. Then, Guthrie declared Richard innocent and promised that if the case went to trial it would be a "real Perry Mason whodunit." I was hoping it would be, I suppose, for the same reasons I had continually denied Richard's guilt. It wasn't just my belief in his right to a fair trial. I also didn't want to admit that I had put my faith in a man who had coldly killed his wife.

What I saw instead was the state's carefully laid-out case, which implicated Richard at every turn. In testimony from Nancy's father, her doctor, Detective Ortega, and others, the state fashioned a picture out of her suspicions of Richard, Richard's apparent lies to the police, the autopsy report, the health pills packed with barium carbonate, and the paper trail of chemical purchases that ended with the December arsenic delivery. I was stunned, too, by the testimony of a man who, in January 1991, repainted and cleaned the apartment Richard had lived in while he was separated from Nancy. Among Richard's belongings the man saw several empty clear gelatin capsules—the same as those containing the two tainted health pills. There was also the subsequent tenant at the apartment, who testified that while cleaning the back of a bathroom cabinet, she found a prescription bottle in Nancy's name. Along with the pills inside were two antibiotic capsules laced with sodium nitroferricyanide—another poisonous chemical that Richard had bought from General Labs in August 1990.

Money, not just his romantic liaison with Ayn, appeared to be the motive. Nancy was worth about $1.2 million, including $500,000 from her life insurance policy. Four months before her death, she had removed Richard as beneficiary, naming her children instead. The children's nanny, Lynn Pease-Woods, had signed as witness to the change. According to Lynn's testimony, it seemed as if Richard didn't know about the switch, even after Nancy's death. The defense's attempts to counter Lynn's testimony looked suspicious. Guthrie introduced a typewritten note, addressed to Richard, dated November 1, 1990, and signed "Nancy," which mentioned the beneficiary change. But Lynn testified that Nancy didn't know how to type and even took pride in that fact.

Through his cross-examination of other state witnesses, Guthrie deluged the jury with a muddle of doubts. He suggested other suspects: Bill Junior, for instance, or Nancy's former boss at Crow Development, David Bagwell, who had been sued by the Crow companies for misappropriating $720,000. Nancy had been a potential witness against Bagwell and had received a death threat relating to the case in 1989.

Guthrie also hinted at suicide. But that scenario seemed unlikely when the state introduced a nine-page letter from Nancy to Richard, written four months before her death in powerful, intelligent, eloquent prose. When read aloud, it was as if Nancy's voice had suddenly come into the courtroom to state her own case:

> My nature has always been to be so optimistic, so positive, so charged up about my life, and over this last year, in losing what I valued most in my life, I have let myself be so consumed by fear, unhappiness, heartache, and misery that I have compromised my values and principles and lost sight of myself, my needs and my dreams . . . I can see clearly that the children and I need and deserve so much more. They need a loving, consistent parent who is there for them day and night . . . They need stability and predictability and a promise that no matter what, they will be defended, protected and safe, every moment, every day . . . I no longer have any desire to hold you to your marriage commitment. Not only are you free to go, but I need to demand that you go before even more damage is done to the children and to me.

I watched Richard cry as the letter was read. I will never believe, as some suggested, that his tears were just a ploy to win the jury's sentiments. But I could feel my focus changing. I no longer wondered if he had killed her. I wondered, instead, what twisted passion had carried him through the months of premeditation, through the hours of her retching at home, through the days of her decline and death. I cannot pretend to know what happened between Richard and Nancy, but I believed then, as now, that Richard loved her once—as deeply as he must have grown to hate her.

On the day the state rested its case, Richard came over to me in the courtroom. He asked about Shawn and told me about Anna's funny antics. As we talked, I had trouble looking into his eyes. I could feel the Dillards' friends staring at us. When he asked how I thought the trial had gone, I shrugged and said nothing. "Just wait," he told me. "All the facts will come out."

When he took the stand two days later, Richard never denied ordering the arsenic. He said he bought the poison to kill fire ants at the duplex and at a job site. Although his testimony drew snickers of disbelief that his supposedly all-organic company would sanction arsenic as a fire ant control, I knew the duplex had an ant problem. In late summer 1990 it had gotten so bad that I asked Nancy about it. "Richard's working on something," she told me. As Richard described it, he planned to bore into the mounds and then spray poison. Nancy had worked with him on the scheme, he said; in fact, it was Nancy who suggested buying arsenic in the first place.

Richard's testimony also put him 250 miles from Nancy during the hours on January 8 when she would have gotten the fatal dose of arsenic. Airline tickets, restaurant receipts, and eyewitnesses all confirmed that he had been in Houston since early that day and had arrived home around six, about the time Nancy began feeling sick. He portrayed his wife as a vulnerable, sickly woman. All through the fall of 1990, he said, Nancy had called him often, complaining of illness. Her calls always drew him back to the duplex, he said, to check on the children or to help her.

As proof he offered writings he said were Nancy's—pages of notes, which Richard said he found in a file box three months before the trial. Nancy had been in counseling nearly all of her final year. I knew she wrote often about her therapy; once, I had seen the walls of her bedroom covered with sheets of paper. Two pages offered by the defense particularly played into suggestions of suicide or other suspects. One described how Bill Junior had incestuously "violated" Nancy for years, how her family had denied it, and how Richard had tried to help her—"tried to save me," the note said, "with his sincere heart and his unending patience with my 'hang ups' about sex." On the bottom of another page was written, "fears of Bill and what his desires are—sex—sick sex-incest issues with me?—my girls?"

The defense had hired a handwriting expert, who had said the writing was Nancy's. Later, they would put on the stand James Grigson, the psychiatrist known as Dr. Death for his controversial death-penalty testimony. Solely on the basis of the notes, Grigson described Nancy as deeply troubled, calculating, controlling, and manipulative. He suggested that she had made herself sick with poisons to lure Richard back to the marriage.

By itself, the theory seemed preposterous. Arsenic poisoning is a painful, prolonged, and agonizing way to kill oneself. What's more, Nancy hadn't acted one bit suicidal in the weeks before her death. She made her usual Christmas gifts and planned trips for the coming year. Her daughters seemed far too important to her. And why would she have cried out for help in the hospital if she had known, all the while, what was killing her?

Then Guthrie produced the receipt. It was dated September 6, 1990, from a company called Chemical Engineering in Dallas. It listed purchases of four chemicals: barium carbonate, lead nitrate, cyanogen bromide, and arsenic trioxide. It was signed "Nancy Lyon," with her driver's license number beneath her name.

As Richard stood before the jury, pointing to a blowup of the receipt, the change in the courtroom was physical. He testified that he had found it stashed in the same files with her private writings. For the first time during the trial, Rosemary leaned forward and tried to catch my eye. "Can you believe it?" she mouthed.

It was hard to know what to believe, particularly when the president of Chemical Engineering, Charles Couch, testified later that his firm specialized in recycling old carpeting. But Couch, a large man with a cocksure manner, also acknowledged he was "known in the business" as someone who could devise chemical formulas. In September 1990, he testified, a woman had called him to discuss fire ant poison. According to Couch, the woman never identified herself, but she told him that she and her husband were trying to inject poison into the mounds with a long drill. When Couch offered to look up a formula for her at the Southern Methodist University library, the woman asked if he could drop the notation by her house—which, she said, was right next to campus, as our duplex was.

Couch testified that he did look up a formula, which matched the items on the receipt. But he never dropped it off. Instead, the woman apparently came to his plant the next day to get it. He testified that he never saw her: He was on the phone in a back office at the time. Through one of his employees, he passed on the formula, which he had jotted on notepaper with his company's logo. But Couch called the receipt a forgery. It had no invoice number. It was typed, while all his are handwritten. And, oddly, it had a notation to call Keith or Charles on the bottom—names of contractors who transport huge quantities of chemicals for the company. Couch said he remembered inadvertently jotting their names on the bottom of the notepaper with the formula right before the woman came to pick it up.

Yet even if Richard had forged the receipt, it was hard to explain the call Couch had gotten. Equally puzzling were the results of additional forensic tests on Nancy's hair, which the medical examiner's office had requested in May. Bundles of the hair had been sent to Vincent Guinn, a chemist at the University of Maryland, who uses a technique called neutron activation analysis to detect various chemicals in hair. Before analyzing the hair, Guinn had sliced it into tiny segments, each representing roughly two weeks' growth. The results showed that in addition to the lethal dose in early January, Nancy probably had ingested arsenic at least two other times before that: a sizable dose sometime between mid-December and New Year's Eve, and a much smaller one in mid-November. Both were before

Richard could have received the arsenic from General Labs.

There were theories to explain the evidence. Richard might have gotten arsenic elsewhere. Maybe Nancy's hair grew faster than normal. Maybe shellfish or hair coloring caused the small November dose. Yet the autopsy also showed Nancy's fingernails had at least five times more arsenic than her toenails—a result that suggested she might have handled the chemical, either by touching poisoned food or the arsenic itself.

Two days before the end of the trial, it seemed Guthrie had achieved reasonable doubt. That day, Shawn visited me at the courthouse for lunch, and Richard chatted easily with him in the hallway. As I watched, it seemed that more harm would come from a conviction than from an acquittal.

I lost all faith less than two hours later. On rebuttal, the state produced Hartford R. Kittel, a retired document examiner from the FBI. Unlike the defense's handwriting analyst, Kittel compared all handwritings in evidence not just with Nancy's known samples but also with Richard's.

I had always marveled at how similar Richard's and Nancy's handwriting was. In graduate school, I later learned, they had actually worked to make their writing look alike for design projects, giving it the same angular *n*'s, the same long loops below their *g*'s and their *y*'s. But Kittel pointed out their differences. Richard's *i*'s were a straight line down; Nancy's were framed by little cross lines. Richard's *f*'s sometimes had a backward loop; Nancy's never did. Nancy's *s*'s were always serpentine; Richard's were sometimes scripted.

And then I saw how, in the most powerful of Nancy's personal writings—in the pen scratches that spelled out "Bill violated me for years," "sick sex" and "Richard . . . with his sincere heart"—in nearly every word that damned Nancy, there were Richard's handwriting peculiarities. To my eyes, the call wasn't even close. Kittel also questioned the authenticity of the signature on the insurance note and couldn't identify the one on the receipt from Chemical Engineering.

The jury returned its verdict less than three hours later. As the courtroom doors opened, I saw an ashen Richard looking back at the crowd filing in. When the foreman read, "Guilty," Richard's eyes widened. Then he stared straight ahead, hung his head, and sighed.

"I can't believe this has happened," he told Guthrie minutes later, as they sat in a holding cell. "I'm innocent." Outside, amid a flurry of television cameras, the Dillards were whisked away. In the emptiness that followed, journalists milled the halls, looking for someone who would comment on the case. I walked toward the elevators and left.

Soon I was driving up Central Expressway in a pouring rain. As I had done so often in the years before, I turned off at Mockingbird and zigzagged past SMU to the duplex. The shutters were drawn. The Christmas lights were hanging in the same loose way as the year before, when I had taken them down as Nancy lay dying. Sitting there in my car, it seemed absurd that after all these months, my doubt about who killed Nancy should have fallen apart based on the shape of an *i*, an *f*, and an *s*. But that was all it took. Mere markings of a pen had become, for me, the desperate imprints of a very convincing liar.

O n New Year's Day, I went to see Richard in jail. He wasn't expecting me. I didn't quite know how to alert him that I was coming, so I simply showed up. Richard entered on the other side of the bulletproof glass dressed in white jail overalls. An orange ID band encircled his wrist. He looked pale but lively. He sat down easily and picked up the phone. He looked as even-tempered and pleasant as I remembered him. There was no desperation in his voice or face.

"How are you doing?" I asked.

"Not great," he said. "But we're working on getting a new trial now . . ." His talk quickly moved into a litany of reasons why he should have been acquitted, especially with what the forensic evidence showed. "You tell me how I could have given her those prior exposures," he said. "You tell me, and then I can sit in a jail cell and think about it. But you *can't* tell me. That's reasonable doubt."

I was blunt with him. The handwriting analysis had hurt him. So did his apparent lies to the police. And it simply didn't make sense that Nancy would beg for help in the hospital if she had killed herself. "I don't understand it either," he said. "I lived with her, and I don't understand it. All I know is that she bought arsenic. That receipt is real. . . . Why would I forge that stuff?"

As he talked, he looked me straight in the eye, and I found myself searching his pale green irises for some hint of the truth. All I saw was calm, logical analysis. He had an answer for every question. The thought crossed my mind, at one point, that Richard was delusional, thoroughly evil, or innocent. And at that moment I really could not tell which it was. "You know me," he said. "You know I would never do anything to hurt the girls. I would never have taken away their mother. Why would I need to kill her? I would have walked away from the marriage."

I was hoping my visit would give me some closure to the matter of my neighbor's death. It did not. What was I expecting, after all? That Richard would suddenly break down, confess, set forth the story without ambiguity, allow me to walk away that night satisfied that at least I knew the whole wretched truth? Instead, as the guard came to get him, Richard left me with this: "I can only pray that the truth will come out someday," he said, "because it didn't at the trial."

I cannot say Richard Lyon killed his wife beyond all possible doubt. Like the jury, I believe he is guilty beyond a reasonable doubt, but my knowledge will always be in fragments, like the glimpses I had during the years I lived under his roof, like the pieces of evidence that became the court record.

Or, as I thought driving back from the jail that night, like the way I saw his eyes shift downward only twice during my visit with him.

The first time was when I asked about his daughters.

The second time was when I suggested that maybe Nancy got her poison in the Zovirax capsules she had been taking at the time.

(April 1992)

In March 1992 Richard Lyon's request for a new trial was denied, and he was sent to prison in Huntsville to serve out his life sentence. His story was dramatized in the 1995 made-for-TV movie *Death in Small Doses,* which starred Richard Thomas.

See No Evil

SKIP HOLLANDSWORTH

Charles Albright patiently waited behind an unbreakable glass wall, watching as the prison guard escorted me through three sets of steel-barred doors. "I apologize for not being able to shake your hand and say hello," he said, formally rising as I approached his window in the visiting room. "They do not allow me to have face-to-face visits."

The steel doors clanged shut. Then the man whom the Dallas police had called the coldest, most depraved killer of women in the city's history gave me a long gentle stare, his dark deep-set eyes never wavering, an encouraging half-smile on his lips. At 59, he had a finely sculpted face and carefully groomed gray hair. Even in his prison uniform, he looked positively distinguished. "Ask me anything you want," he said. "I'm not going to tell you anything that's not true."

Throughout his life, Albright had been described by many who knew him as the portrait of happiness, untroubled and troubling no one. He was, they said, a kind of Renaissance man—fluent in French and Spanish, a masterful painter, able to woo women by playing Chopin preludes on the piano or reciting poetry by

Keats. It was simply impossible to believe that he could have viciously murdered three Dallas prostitutes in late 1990 and early 1991. The person who should have been arrested, Albright's friends and lawyers insisted, was Axton Schindler, a paranoid, fast-talking truck driver who lived in one of Albright's rental homes. The evidence pointed to him, they claimed, not to their beloved Charles Albright. Perhaps Albright was a touch eccentric, but he was certainly harmless; he was even squeamish when it came to violence.

"You won't find any woman who'll say anything other than that I was always a perfect gentleman in their presence," he said softly. Behind the glass wall, he wore an almost childlike expression—weak and perplexed and, yes, oddly appealing. "I was always trying to do things for women. I would take their pictures. I would paint their portraits. I would give them little presents. I was always open for a lasting relationship."

In most cases, serial killers are brutal, woefully uneducated young men, lifelong sadists who kill for their own twisted reasons. How, then, could someone so charming, so exceedingly polite, suddenly decide in the later years of his life to become a blood-thirsty sex monster? "Look, I've known Charlie for thirty years," sighed one Albright friend, a retired Baptist minister. "In all that time I think I would have seen his dark side slip out at least once. Believe me, if he really was a psychotic killer, he couldn't have kept it a secret all this time—could he?"

December 1944: Life With Mother

He was known as the most good-natured, eager-to-please of children, a precocious boy who could do just about anything: name all the constellations in the sky, catch snakes without getting bitten, even perform a tap dance routine onstage at the famous Texas Theater. "Charlie was like a Pied Piper to the rest of us kids," a childhood friend recalled. "We always wanted to see what he would do next. He was just so much damn fun."

In 1933, when he was three weeks old, Charles was adopted by a young dark-haired woman, Delle Albright, and her husband, Fred, a Dallas grocer. The Albrights lived in the all-white middle-class neighborhood of Oak Cliff, then a beautiful residential area across the river from downtown. According to the story Delle would later tell Charles, his birth mother was an exceptional law student, just sixteen years old, who had secretly married another student and had become pregnant. When the girl's father found out, he demanded that she annul her marriage and give up the baby for adoption; otherwise, he would cut her off from the family.

Delle Albright made sure that Charles knew she would never abandon him. She pampered her boy. She kept goats in the back yard so he could drink goat's milk, which she said was better for him than cow's milk. Yet sometimes her mothering went to extremes. When Charles was a small child, she occasionally put him in a little girl's dress and gave him a doll to hold. Two or three times a day she would change his clothes to keep the dirt off him. Afraid that he might touch dog feces and get polio, she took him to Parkland Hospital to see the polio patients locked in huge iron lungs. "You can spend the rest of your life here," Delle would solemnly tell her son. Delle put him in a dark room as punishment for chewing on her tape measure. When he wouldn't take a nap, she would tie him to his bed. When he wouldn't drink his milk, she would spank him.

Indeed, people around the neighborhood talked about Delle Albright's odd, grim nature. No one could ever remember her buying herself a dress. She kept a scarf over her head and wore clothes from Goodwill. Although she and Fred were far from poor, she usually scrimped at mealtimes, even picking up the old bones the local butcher threw in a box for his dogs. She could use them, she would say, for soup.

Not that Charles ever openly complained. He always appreciated that his mother taught him manners. Delle told him to speak politely about other people or "say nothing at all." She told him to respect women, especially when it came to sex. She lectured him about the way his father acted "greedy" with sex: Whenever Fred saw her in the bedroom in her bra and panties, he tried to grab her. She was going to have none of that, and she was going to make sure Charlie never tried anything like that with his girlfriends either. As he grew older, she insisted on chauffeuring him every time he was on a date. She would even call the girl's parents to let them know that her son would not do anything untoward.

If Delle seemed overprotective, friends said, surely it was because she had never raised a child before. Charles himself recognized how fiercely she wanted him to succeed. Each morning, before the school bus arrived, she had him practice the piano for at least thirty minutes. She taught him so much reading, writing, and arithmetic that he was moved up two grades in elementary school.

Delle also introduced Charles to the world of taxidermy. When he was eleven years old, she enrolled him in a mail-order course—the Northwestern School of Taxidermy, taught by Professor J. W. Elwood. "You are beginning to learn an art that is second only to painting and sculpturing," Professor Elwood wrote in the first book of lessons Charles received. "A true taxidermist must be an artist." As Charles set to work on the dead birds he found, Delle was right beside him. She showed him how to use all the tools: the knife used to cut the skull, the little spoon used to scoop out the brains, the scalpel required to cut away the eyes from their sockets, the forceps that pulled out the eyes. She even skinned the first bird for him, teaching him not to cut too deep.

Dutifully, Charles spent hours on his taxidermy courses, stuffing and mounting his birds, making them look as lifelike as possible. Then he would be ready for the crowning touch—the eyes. He used to go to a taxidermy shop and stare at the boxes and boxes full of gloriously fake eyes: owl eyes, eagle eyes, deer eyes. He loved their iridescent gleam. He wished he could collect them the way other boys collected marbles.

Yet Delle wouldn't let him. Taxidermists' eyes were too expensive, his frugal mother would say; there was a better, cheaper way. She would open her sewing kit, look for exactly what she needed, and get to work. Then she and her son would place the birds in the oak china cabinet in the front of the house.

They were, indeed, Charles Albright's first works of art, just as the mail-order booklet had promised. Everyone who came to the house would peer into the cabinet to see what he had done. And there, peering back, would be his birds, beautiful, lifelike . . . and blind.

The birds had no eyes. Instead, sewn tightly against their delicate feathered faces, were two dark buttons, each shimmering dully in the living room light.

"You never knew a prostitute in Dallas?" I asked.

He shook his head, baffled by the question. "Never! I knew absolutely none of them. At the time I was arrested, I couldn't tell you the names of the motels they stayed in, any of the motels' locations, or anything else. It is a crime that the police never put me on the lie detector to find out what I did know and what I didn't."

"Could the prostitutes possibly have seen you somewhere?"

"None of these girls had ever seen me. They never saw me drive slowly by like I wanted to pick somebody up. Believe me, if I had anything to do with any prostitutes in Dallas, I would tell you."

December 1990: Mary Pratt

The first victim turned up in an undeveloped, almost forgotten lower-class area of far south Dallas. She was a large woman, 156 pounds, naked except for a T-shirt and a bra, which had been pushed up over her breasts. Her eyes were shut; her face and chest were badly bruised. Apparently, the killer had thought it best to beat her before firing a .44-caliber bullet into her brain. A resident of the neighborhood was so horrified by what he saw that he rushed inside his home and brought out a flowered bed sheet to cover the body.

A police officer on the scene immediately recognized the woman as Mary Pratt, age 33, a veteran prostitute who worked the Star Motel in Oak Cliff. While it was not unusual for the "whores of Oak Cliff," as the police called them, to get their share of beatings—almost nightly, a girl would complain about a trick "jumping bad" on her, punching her, kicking her, even trying to run her over with a car—for a whore to be murdered was unusual, especially when it happened to someone as well liked as Mary Pratt. Mary wasn't one of the brazen hookers who stood in the street and flagged down tricks. Because she rarely had any extra spending money—the money she got usually went for drugs—she never bought sexy clothes. Standing quietly on her corner, she wore blue jeans, tennis shoes, and small T-shirts that showed off her breasts. Occasionally, at the end of a night, she asked one of her regulars to drive her to her parents' home in the south Dallas suburb of Lancaster. Mary's parents—older retired people—never knew about her other life. They would call out good night as she climbed into her childhood bed.

Pratt's file was handed to John Westphalen, a short, ruddy-faced homicide detective at the Dallas Police Department. With his thick East Texas accent and a wad of Red Man chewing tobacco permanently packed in his cheek, Westphalen looked more like a rustic county sheriff than a street-smart urban cop. In homicide circles he was something of a character: Defense attorneys loved to complain about his blustery, intimidating interrogation tactics. But Westphalen was also one of the department's most tenacious investigators. He took one look at the Pratt file and realized the case would depend more on good luck than on good detective work. Pratt's killing was a "dumped body" case—one of the hardest types of murders to solve. She had obviously been killed in one location and dumped somewhere else. There were no witnesses to either the killing or the dumping, no murder weapon, little forensic evidence, no fingerprints, and no apparent motive. Considering the kind of felonious characters who nightly swing by the Star Motel, Mary Pratt could have been shot by just about anyone.

Accompanied by his partner, homicide detective Stan McNear, Westphalen drove to the Dallas County medical examiner's office to watch the autopsy of Mary Pratt. It was a routine trip; both men knew the autopsy would show a gunshot wound as the cause of death. As Dr. Elizabeth Peacock, one of the staff's younger pathologists, put down her coffee cup to begin the examination, Westphalen and McNear stood a short distance from the blue plastic cart where Pratt's body lay. Peacock noted the needle tracks on Pratt's arms, the Playboy bunny tattoo on her chest, the bullet hole in her head. She opened Pratt's right eyelid. Then she opened the left.

"My God!" she exclaimed. "They're gone!"

There were no eyeballs, no tissue—nothing. Mary Pratt's eyes had been cut out and removed so carefully that her upper and lower eyelids were left undisturbed. Peacock was dumbfounded. This was not an operation taught in medical school. The killer had to know how to slip a knife around the eyes, making sure not to injure the adjoining skin, and then cut the six major muscles holding each eye in the socket, as well as the rope-tough optical nerve. With the eyelids shut, it was impossible to tell the eyes were missing. Surely, whoever did this had to have had a lot of practice on someone, or something, else.

Quickly Westphalen contacted the FBI's Violent Crimes Apprehension Program unit. Through its computers, the FBI keeps data on the nation's most unusual, depraved mutilations—bodies chopped up, organs removed, even eyes punctured with a knife as a result of a frenzied attack. But an FBI agent told Westphalen that he found no listing anywhere of such a surgically precise cutting.

Longtime Dallas cops take pride in acting utterly unaffected by anything that comes their way. But this time, Westphalen couldn't help it.

"What kind of person," he asked McNear, "would want a girl's eyeballs?"

September 1952: Class Clown

When Charlie Albright transferred to Arkansas State Teacher's College in Conway, Arkansas, it didn't take him long to become one of the school's most popular students. He was remarkably well rounded: president of the French club, business manager of the yearbook, member of the school choir, halfback on the football team. When he signed up for a drawing course, the art professor was so impressed with Charlie's good looks that he made him the class model.

Yet Charlie wasn't known as just a goody two-shoes. He was the all-American fraternity boy, a great college prankster. One time he sneaked into the home economics building, got a load of food out of the refrigerator, and cooked a steak dinner for his buddies. Another time, on a dare, he broke into a physics professor's office in the middle of the day, picked the lock on his cabinet, stole what was known around school as "the unstealable physics test," raced downtown to make a copy of it, and had the test back in its place within an hour. The professor, who was teaching a class next door, never suspected a thing.

Frankly, Charlie Albright had to feel some relief in being away from home. He was considered a very bright boy in Dallas—he graduated from Adamson High School at fifteen—and he was something of a celebrity. When Charlie was fourteen, Delle and Fred purchased a piece of property in their neighborhood and gave it to Charlie. Charlie sold it to buy more lots, and the *Dallas Times Herald* published a story about him under the headline WORLD'S YOUNGEST REAL ESTATE MAN AMASSING NEST EGG FOR COLLEGE. Yet Charlie's love for mischief had tainted his reputation. He had received bad deportment grades in school for shooting rubber bands and crawling out of study hall. He had "accidentally" set fire to his chemistry teacher's dress. And he had flunked a few courses because he was "too bored" to study. (Of course, if his mother had found out, he would never have heard the end of it. So he sneaked into the school office, filched some report cards from a desk, filled them in with all A's, and proudly showed them to his parents—his teachers' and principal's signatures perfectly forged.)

It was minor stuff, really. It wasn't like he went to jail. As Charlie himself would later explain, "I just didn't know what I was doing. If anybody tells the truth, they will say I never did a mean thing in all my life. But I did a lot of mischievous things just to show off for the older kids."

Well, there was the time he was caught breaking into a neighborhood church. Then there was the time he was caught breaking into a little store and stealing a watch. And there were the visits he and his mother received from Alfred Jones, a twenty-year-old psychology student working part-time as a Dallas County juvenile probation officer. But what did Jones know back then? And what right did Jones have to say, forty years later, when he was a well-known psychologist in Dallas, that of the dozens of juveniles he saw back in the forties, the one he remembered most clearly was Charlie Albright? "He could divorce reality sufficiently from his value system," Jones said, "so that he could tell you something false and at the time actually believe he was telling you the truth."

Maybe, one of Charlie's relatives said, he pilfered things from stores because his mother was so stingy. Or maybe he just wanted to rebel against her. Granted, Delle Albright did whatever she could to keep a close watch on her son. She took him to the Methodist church each Sunday. She made him go to bed, even when he was in his teens, at eight each night. Whenever she chauffeured him on a date, she watched him so closely that he would joke about the way she drove "with her eyes on the rearview mirror." Charlie loved his mother—that much was clear. But there were little things that sometimes bothered him. He was never certain, for example, that his biological mother had been the brilliant law student that Delle claimed she was. He so hated Delle's cooking that he would stuff his food on a ledge under the table or give it to his dog. Delle fussed over him so regularly, he said, that he began to get headaches. (Delle decided the headaches were from bad eyesight and promptly made Charles wear glasses, even though he had twenty-twenty vision.)

Yet Delle couldn't protect Charlie the first time he left home. Right after high school, he enrolled in North Texas State College in Denton—but by the end of his freshman year, he was arrested for being a member of a student burglary ring that broke into three stores and stole several hundred dollars' worth of merchandise. Charlie swore he stole nothing. The other boys, he said, had asked him to keep some things in his dorm room for them. How was he to know the things were stolen?

Delle Albright went to the store owners and tried to reimburse them for what was taken. She tried to persuade the judge to let her act as Charlie's lawyer. She even asked that she take his place in prison. Yet the boy went to prison for a year, spending his eighteenth birthday there. Delle, meanwhile, worked to keep the matter hushed up, so that no one in the neighborhood knew that Charlie Albright had become a convicted felon.

Arkansas State Teacher's College was Charlie's chance for a new start. As he told a probation officer, he was going to mend his ways. He began to date a lovely young English major, Bettye Hester, and made plans to marry her. He did truly brilliant work in science; although he hardly studied, he made an A in his human anatomy course. It was said around school that Charlie Albright was going to go far. He even talked about going to medical school and becoming a surgeon.

But Charlie never stopped playing the role of class clown. Of all his great pranks, no one would forget the one he played on his friend Andrew (not his real name). In a fit of anger, Andrew had broken up with the most beautiful girl on campus, a woman with almond-shaped eyes. After the separation, he tore up several photographs of her and threw them in a trash can in his dorm room. Weeks later, Andrew got a new girlfriend and asked her for a photo. One night, while Andrew was staring at his new girlfriend's picture, he realized that something was wrong. He looked closer. It seemed that her eyeballs had been cut out and replaced with—Good Lord!—the eyeballs of his old girlfriend. In disbelief, Andrew looked up at the ceiling. There, staring down at him, was another pair of his older girlfriend's eyeballs. More eyeballs were above the urinal in the men's bathroom down the hall. No matter where Andrew turned, he was confronted by the sight of his old girlfriend's almond-shaped eyes.

The story soon raced through school. That jokester Charlie Albright had pulled the old photographs out of the trash and saved her eyeballs for just the right moment. Did any of his fellow students, in retrospect, find the stunt a bit strange? Of course not, they said. It was pure Charlie. Who else could have been so inventive?

"Why do you think the eyeballs were missing?" I asked.

"I don't understand either." He sighed. *"Why the eyeballs?"*

"Well, what kind of person would be able to cut out the eyeballs of some hooker?"

"Someone who is sadistic? Just one mean son of a gun? I don't know the purpose behind it, unless that person thought the women wouldn't be able to see without their eyes in the next world—which is sort of ignorant."

December 1990: A Clue

Because the police had not released any information about Mary Pratt's missing eyeballs, her death had only warranted a two-paragraph story in the back sections of the local newspapers. In fact, when patrol officers John Matthews and Regina Smith began their daytime shift on December 13, just a few hours after Pratt's body was found, they had not even heard about the crime.

Only two and a half months before, the two officers had been assigned to a newly created beat on Jefferson Boulevard that included Pratt's streetwalking territory. Once the most popular shopping district in Oak Cliff, Jefferson had deteriorated over the previous 25 years, a victim of urban blight. Some storefronts were shuttered; others were barely profitable. The Texas Theater, infamous for being the site where Lee Harvey Oswald hid out after the Kennedy assassination, was padlocked. Matthews and Smith's assignment was to provide a police presence for the area—to become acquainted with the merchants, shake a lot of hands, and crack down on small-time crime such as burglary, car theft, shoplifting, and prostitution. In police circles, it was far from a glamorous beat. Other officers, used to the action of the streets, considered it more of a public relations position.

Each morning, Matthews and Smith began their day by cruising down Jefferson, herding the prostitutes back toward the Star Motel. On a busy day, about forty women—mostly black, some white, and a few Hispanic—worked the area, charging anywhere from $15 to $50 for a "flatback" (straight sex). The Star was not a high-class call girl operation; Matthews snidely called the forty-room motel "the prostitute condominium." The women there, most of them drug addicts, would have sex in a customer's car in a nearby alley or use a room shared with other prostitutes. Then, money in hand, they would walk down a well-worn dirt path to one of the nearby dope houses and purchase heroin or crack. After a quick hit, they would be out on the street again. Some hookers would work nonstop for two or three days—never changing their clothes, never even taking the time to eat—until they finally crashed back at the motel or in the house of their "sugar daddy" (a regular customer who cared for the woman enough to provide her with food, clothes, and a place to sleep).

Such a dreary scene did not faze Matthews, a stocky, no-nonsense 28-year-old; little on the streets did. The son of a patrol officer in New York State, he had grown up with cops-and-robbers stories. He had been with the Dallas Police Department since he was 21, when he went to work patrolling Harry Hines Boulevard, one of the city's high crime and prostitution areas. On the other hand, when 31-year-old Regina Smith decided to become a police officer, she had never fired a gun, seen a dead person, or even been in a fight. She was a former supermarket cashier, a graduate of a two-year fashion merchandising college, and the single mother of a 6-year-old child. Nonetheless, inspired by a newspaper story about the need for more black female police officers, she entered the Dallas Police Academy in 1988. Her instructors berated her for wearing too much jewelry, mocked the way she shot a gun, and laughed when she couldn't finish her push-ups, but she refused to quit. After graduation she was assigned to one of the rougher night shifts—and still she wouldn't quit.

On the Jefferson beat, Smith discovered she had a knack for talking to prostitutes. She wanted to talk to them; she felt it was her duty as a police officer to try to improve people's lives. "Tell me, girl," she would say to a new prostitute, "what are you doing whoring out here? You know you can make more money working at Burger King than you do here." She even started a "hook book," a kind of photo album that contained the mug shots of the whores on the street. She would wistfully leaf through her hook book the way some people pore over their high school annuals.

On this particular morning, Smith was not surprised to see Veronica Rodriguez, a brazen charcoal-eyed prostitute who would try to flag down tricks even when she knew the cops were watching. Usually, when she spotted Matthews, she would lean forward so he could see her cleavage and say, "How ya doing, Officer?" Rodriguez, barely 26 years old, had lived a miserable life. She had been arrested for prostitution numerous times, once when she was nine months pregnant. Although that baby was stillborn, she was the mother of at least one child—a baby born on a raggedy bed in a whore motel down the road from the Star.

As Matthews pulled the squad car alongside Rodriguez, Smith rolled down her window. She noticed a nasty gash across Rodriguez's forehead and what looked like a thin knife cut across the front of her neck. "Girl, what happened to you?" she asked. "Don't arrest me," Rodriguez gasped. "I almost got killed!"

Rodriguez told the officers that the previous night, she had been picked up by a trick, driven a long way south to a field, and raped. The man—a white man, she said—then tried to kill her, but she escaped and ran toward a house. The man at the house just happened to be someone she knew. He also just happened to know the man who was trying to kill her.

Matthews and Smith gave each other a look. Rodriguez was a notorious liar. No doubt she had been in some kind of fight, but in the middle of nowhere she ran right into the house of someone she knew? This was probably another of Rodriguez's "pity stories," which she often told the cops so they would feel sorry for her and leave her alone.

Yet two days later, on an afternoon drive past the Star, Matthews and Smith saw Rodriguez again. She was sitting with a balding middle-aged white man in the cab of an eighteen-wheeler. While Matthews went to one side of the truck to get Rodriguez and escort her to the squad car, Smith went to the other side to speak to the man. She asked him for his driver's license, which he produced: His name was Axton Schindler, of 1035 Eldorado. When Smith ran Schindler's name through the computer, he came up clean, except for some unpaid traffic tickets. Suddenly, Rodriguez started shouting, "Oh, don't arrest him! That's the man who saved me from the killer! That's him!"

The officers looked at the address again: 1035 Eldorado. It was not out in south Dallas, where Rodriguez's attack allegedly took place. It was in an Oak Cliff neighborhood, just a five minute drive from the Star. The man—a sort of nervous guy who spoke incredibly fast—said he had no idea what Rodriguez was talking about. He said he had known her for years and was just giving her a ride to the motel. He didn't protect her from any killer. He didn't even have sex with her. He was just a long-distance truck driver doing her a favor. Rodriguez, the officers decided, was lying once again. They carted her to jail for prostitution and hauled Schindler in for his unpaid tickets.

Although Matthews and Smith would not know it for months, a clue to the murderer's identity had fallen right in their laps.

September 1969: Con Man

Charles Albright was 36 when he began teaching high school science in Crandall, a small town east of Dallas. The principal at Crandall, who had been looking for a teacher the entire summer, was ecstatic when the astute young man called him up right before the school year was to begin. According to his college records, Charles Albright had a master's degree in biology from East Texas State University and was working on another master's in counseling and guidance. He was also about to enter ETSU's Ph.D. program in biology.

Albright's students found him fascinating. On field trips, he could recite, in flawless Latin, the scientific name for every plant he came across; he could split open a rotted log and talk about each insect he found inside. He drove a green Corvette to school and wore lizard-skin shoes. (A few girls, smitten by his charm and masculine looks, wrote him love letters.) He even helped coach the football team. After a heroic play by one Crandall player won a game for the school, Albright lifted him up and carried him off the field.

How, the principal would later ask, was anyone supposed to know that the promising young teacher had forged all of his transcripts? He was simply flabbergasted when an ETSU official told him that Albright had never even earned a bachelor's degree. Everything—his degrees, his teacher's certificate—had been faked. Apparently, he had slipped into three different offices at East Texas State, grabbed all the necessary forms, copied them, added his name, forged signatures, and then sneaked them back into the files. He had even stolen the registrar's typewriter so the typeface on his records would look the same. Had an ETSU administrator not realized that he had never met the Charles Albright whose name kept popping up on the school's list of graduate students, Albright would have gotten away with the scam.

When Albright was confronted, he grinned ruefully and admitted to the crime. He needed to bend the rules a little, he explained, in order to get a teaching job. After he quit Arkansas State Teacher's College—well, okay, he was kicked out for being caught down at the train station with suitcases full of stolen school property, including his own football coach's golf clubs—he didn't think he was going to get a second chance to prove how smart he was. By then, he had married his college sweetheart, Bettye, and she had given birth to their daughter. Frankly, he didn't have time to begin all over at a university. It was a crying shame, he said. If only he could have finished his degree, there was a professor at Tulane University in New Orleans who would have hired him to do biology research.

Because the forgery was a victimless crime—and because Albright himself, according to one ETSU administrator, was such a nice, repentant fellow—the university decided to keep the transcript scandal out of the newspapers. It was embarrassing, after all, that a school could get bamboozled. Albright pleaded guilty to a fraud charge and received a year's probation.

As the seventies began, Albright was back in his old Dallas neighborhood with his wife and daughter, living in a house not far from his parents' home. Once again, no one had any idea of what he had done. The Charlie Albright the neighbors knew was a happy-go-lucky figure who could master anything but simply didn't care about settling down in a nine-to-five job. He had some money from his parents, and his wife had a job as a high school English teacher. He was free to latch on to one new project after another; he rarely had a job that lasted longer than three months. He worked as a designer for a company that built airplanes. He worked as an illustrator for a patent company. He was a well-regarded carpenter. He collected wine bottles from the famous Il Sorrento restaurant in Dallas, hoping to start his own winery. He bought a lathe and made baseball bats. He collected old movie posters. He regularly went to the Venetian Room at the Fairmont Hotel to get autographs from the stars performing there. On a lark, he went to a Mexican border town and became a bullfighter—"Señor Albright from Dallas," the posters read.

Albright still had a Pied Piper–like ability to captivate people. After visiting a friend who worked at the beauty salon in a Sanger Harris department store, Albright promptly went off to beauty school, got his beautician's license, and then persuaded the salon to hire him, with no experience at all, as a stylist. Albright took to calling himself Mr. Charles. He would spend at least an hour with each woman to get her hair exactly right.

When Albright told his stylist friend that he was also an accomplished artist, the friend paid him $250 to paint a picture of his wife. Albright was indeed a good painter; self-taught, he had won a prize at the Texas State Fair for his portrait of a dark-haired woman in a long green gown. His goal, he said, was to be like Dmitri Vail, the famous portrait artist of Dallas.

Albright worked for weeks on the woman's painting without finishing. He insisted that he needed to keep working on one special feature, the most difficult part of the painting. Tired of waiting, the friend decided to go to Albright's house to look at the work in progress. There, in the living room, was the six- by three-foot portrait. It was richly colored and remarkably realistic. The woman's hair, her mouth, her nose, her ears, her neck—everything was finished. Well, not everything. The stylist stared curiously at his wife's painting. In the center of his wife's face were two round white holes.

After all this time, Albright hadn't even begun working on the eyes. It was as if something held him back, as if he preferred the portrait to remain as it was on his living room easel. "Charles," asked the friend, "when are you going to paint the eyes?"

"When I am ready to," Albright replied.

Months later, Albright finally painted the eyes. He then painted them again, to get them just right. He painted the proper shadows under the eyelashes; he gave the eyelids just the right droop in the corners; he shaded the eyeballs to make them look perfectly round. When Albright was finished, his friend could not believe how well the painting had turned out. It was, he realized, a mesmerizing portrait—especially the eyes. His wife's eyes were so perfectly re-created that they seemed to follow a person across the room.

"There's no question you love eyes," I said.

"Well, I do want to paint fine eyes. That's every other artist's weakness—they can't paint eyes."

"Would you ever love eyes enough to—"

"No, no, I've never taken the eyes out of anything. I've never had the desire to. To me, what matters is what the eyeball looks like in the woman's face, or the guy's face—not what the eyeball itself would look like."

"Could you figure why someone might want to keep the eyeballs? Would they want them as sort of a souvenir?"

"I don't think anybody would want to keep eyeballs. That would be the last thing I would want to keep out of a body. It would be a hand or a whole head, maybe, if you were a sick artist and you thought the woman was fabulous. You might not want to see that beauty go to waste."

February 1991: Susan Peterson

The second victim was found on a Sunday morning, on the same south Dallas road where Mary Pratt was dumped. Like Pratt, she was mostly naked. Like Pratt, she was a prostitute. Her name was Susan Peterson, age 27. She had been shot in the head, chest, and stomach. Her eyelids were closed.

Because her body was discovered on the other end of the road, just outside the city limits, the jurisdiction for the case fell to the Dallas County Sheriff's Department. A detective named Larry Oliver, who had not heard about the Pratt killing, was called to the scene. Eerily, the same scenario unfolded. Oliver accompanied the body to the autopsy room, where a pathologist began the standard external examination. The pathologist opened one eyelid, then the other. He motioned for Oliver to come closer to the table. Oliver couldn't believe what he was seeing: The dead woman's eyes had been expertly cut out.

When the pathologist mentioned that the Dallas Police Department had had a similar case just two months earlier, Oliver did some checking. Within 24 hours he traveled to the police department's homicide offices to see John Westphalen. Soon there were meetings with sergeants and lieutenants and with the chief in charge of homicide. While police officials deliberately avoided the phrase "serial killings" to describe what was happening—Westphalen kept referring to the killer as "a repeater"—everyone in the room knew what they were hunting for: a twisted, brilliant murderer, someone who dropped bodies on quiet residential streets, where they were certain to be found the next morning.

At that point, a contingent of detectives favored keeping a lid on the story. If the press discovered that the killings were linked and turned the spotlight on the Star Motel, the killer might get nervous and start picking up women from other areas. But homicide supervisors decided that the police department had a greater obligation to warn the community that it might be in danger—even if it meant warning low-dollar hookers. Besides, publicizing the case might bring in some leads. Lord knows, there was little else to go on.

As flyers were posted around the Star asking prostitutes to stay off the streets, detectives met with the press to discuss the two killings. Although no information was officially divulged about the missing eyes, word quickly leaked to reporters that the women's faces had been strangely mutilated. "The guy was almost surgical in the way he did it," one detective told a reporter. To the police department's dismay, a media frenzy ensued. The prostitute murders sent the city's imagination into overdrive; calls came in from reporters all over the country.

As John Matthews and Regina Smith sat in their squad car reading the front-page newspaper stories about the prostitute's deaths, they too were shaken. These were women from their beat, women they were supposed to protect. They knew Susan Peterson: She used to be the most beautiful white prostitute in Oak Cliff. Although her five years on the street had taken their toll—her once-alluring smile had turned winterhard and her body had grown plump—she was still able to put on her brown go-go boots and denim miniskirt and pick up ten to twelve tricks a night. And she was a fearless hooker. She threatened other prostitutes who tried to work too close to her corner. She even cursed Matthews and Smith when they tried to move her off Jefferson Boulevard. Like a good pickpocket, she was an expert at clipping a trick—stealing money from his billfold while he was having sex with her. If the killer could get Peterson, Matthews and Smith said, then he could get any of the women. They surmised that the killer knew every corner of the whore district, all the alleys and all the streets. He was able to pick up Peterson and vanish within seconds. He also must have been one of her regular customers. Otherwise, she never would have let her guard down. Certainly she wouldn't have allowed him to shoot her three times. She would have pulled out a razor and fought back.

This time when Matthews and Smith pulled up to the Star, the prostitutes didn't keep their distance. They poured out of their rooms, surrounded the squad car, and began to pass on their own personal lists of suspects. The women talked about their kinkiest tricks, the men who wanted to tie them up or whip them. Smith made her usual impassioned speech, asking the girls to get off the street, but the black prostitutes, at least, were not buying it. "He's after the white girls, honey, not us," they said. Oddly enough, the black prostitutes saw the killings as an opportunity for them to get more business.

And then there was Veronica Rodriguez. Rodriguez had been telling a lot of people—reporters, other prostitutes, and Matthews and Smith, as well as other officers—any number of stories since the killings began. At first, she said she had witnessed Mary Pratt being shot. Then she said she had met a man who had only bragged about having killed Pratt. Then she said she knew nothing at all about Pratt's death. About her own rape in the south Dallas field, she no longer said the killer was white; now he was Hispanic. Then she said he might have been black. Almost everyone who spoke with her thought she was "brain-fried" from drugs.

What bothered Matthews, however, was that Rodriguez had never changed her basic story about being attacked. Usually, she would forget whatever pity story she had told the day before. Did someone really try to kill her in that field? Could the man who supposedly saved her, Axton Schindler of 1035 Eldorado, know the killer too? Or could Schindler have something to do with the killing himself? Could it be that the real reason Rodriguez was changing her story was simply because she was afraid?

Matthews and Smith didn't know what to do next. They had already told the homicide division that Rodriguez claimed to have information about Mary Pratt. They had mentioned the attack and the possible Axton Schindler connection. With that, they figured they had done their job; it would have been way out of line for the two young officers to cross into homicide's territory and conduct a murder investigation on their own. Later, Westphalen would say that he never got the officers' tips. Among all the phone calls, all the messages, all the reports flooding in, the name "Axton Schindler" never crossed his desk, he said.

Whatever the case, a potential break was slipping away—and the killer was preparing to strike again.

March 1985: Dark Secrets

The incident was kept very, very quiet. There would be no trial, no headlines. The district attorney had arranged for him to serve a probated sentence of ten years, which meant no jail time. Probation was fine with him—just as it was in 1971, when he was arrested for forging some cashier's checks, and in 1979, when he was caught shoplifting two bottles of perfume. In 1980, when he was sent to prison for stealing a saw from a Handy Dan, he had to serve six months. But then, at least, his mother could tell everyone that he was leaving Dallas temporarily to take an important job at a nuclear power plant in Florida.

This case, however, was different. If the news got out, it could humiliate him. Not that he was guilty, he kept saying over and over. He had never touched that little girl. The girl's family was just looking for a scapegoat—and they had picked him, Charlie Albright, one of the most dedicated members of St. Bernard's Catholic Church in east Dallas. He had first met the family in 1979, when he began singing in the church choir. People admired his voice, even if it was untrained. In one hushed service, he performed the tenor solo, "Comfort Ye My People," from Handel's *Messiah*. Soon he was acting as a eucharistic minister, standing before the altar in a robe, reading Bible passages, helping with Communion—almost like an assistant priest, for goodness sake. He loved to help people; everyone knew that. The monsignor at St. Bernard's called him Good Old Charlie. Albright was known to slip a $100 bill to someone who was down on his luck. After he met the little girl's family, he brought them a big box of steaks. He dressed up as Santa Claus and gave the girl and her siblings presents. Did anyone seriously believe he would sneak into her bedroom and molest her?

The girl's parents tried to keep the matter quiet—especially at the church—because they did not want to stigmatize their daughter. But they also wanted Good Old Charlie to pay. Albright worried that if he fought them, the story would leak. So on March 25, 1985, in a nearly empty Dallas courtroom, he stood before a judge and confessed to "knowingly and intentionally engaging in deviate sexual intercourse" with a girl under the age of 14. He was 51.

For the first time, Charles Albright's mask seemingly had slipped. Was there, on the other side of his gentlemanly Jekyll-like personality, a kind of sexually perverted Hyde? Women who heard the story couldn't believe it. After Albright dissolved what he called his loveless marriage to Bettye in 1975, he developed a reputation as an old-fashioned ladies' man. He was still getting by with odd jobs and family money, but women saw him as a grand romantic figure, someone who showered them with flowers and music boxes and candy. To one woman, he recited from memory all 42 verses of "The Eve of St. Agnes," by John Keats. To another, he gave a slew of presents, along with a fully decorated Christmas tree. Women found him virile and sexy; one said he could do six hundred push-ups without stopping. Yet Albright never made a sexual advance toward a woman until she asked him to first—at least that's what he proudly told his friends.

In late 1985, Albright fell in love with Dixie Austin, a pretty, shy widow whom he had met on a trip to Arkansas. It was one of the most romantic times of his life. At dinner, he charmed Dixie with stories about nature and art. He showed her the autographs he had collected from Ronald Reagan, Marlene Dietrich, and Bob Hope. He took her hunting in the country for salamanders. His dream, he told her, was to find a new species of salamander that could be named after him. Sex with Albright, Dixie later said, was gentle and satisfying. He never talked dirty to her, and he never wanted her to do anything that might be considered unconventional. He certainly did not sneak off and have affairs.

By the time he met Dixie, however, Charles Albright had already created another life for himself. Although he masterfully hid his secret from everyone who knew him, he was a veteran of red-light districts all over Dallas. To some prostitutes, he was a whoremonger—a regular trick. To others, like Susan Peterson, he was even a sugar daddy. At Ranger Bail Bonds, the company she used to bail her out of jail, Peterson listed Charles Albright as her cosigner on bond applications. On one form, she listed him as her best friend in the event that she skipped town and the bondsmen had to hunt her down.

There is also evidence that Albright was a friend of Mary Pratt's long before she became a prostitute. In the early eighties, Mary lived in a south Dallas neighborhood where Albright's parents had long ago invested in cheap rental property. At the time, Albright was temporarily living in one of the rental homes. According to several sources, Albright had a brief fling with one of Pratt's female friends and brought that woman and Pratt over to his house for parties.

Other prostitutes say that when Pratt started turning tricks at the Star, Albright became one of her customers. Pratt told them that "Old Man Albright" was a good trick, willing to pay a little more than the going rate. Soon Albright was making the rounds. With some of the girls, he had a platonic relationship. He would pick them up, talk to them, take them to get a hamburger, and drop them back off, never even attempting sex. With others, he had standing sexual appointments—always in the afternoons, when Dixie was at work as a sales clerk at a gift shop in Redbird Mall.

Every Friday afternoon, for instance, he had sex with a married woman who hit the streets after her husband had gone to work and her children were at school. Albright, whom she called Pappy, felt sorry for her, she said: "He was a sweet gentleman. If I ever needed extra money, I would call him and he would drop it off." But the married woman said that by late 1987 she had to put an end to her dates with Albright because he began to get more and more aggressive. She said he asked her to beat him—"to spank him like a child." Another prostitute, Edna Russell, remembered meeting Albright when her friend Susan Peterson asked her to do a "double." She said she and Peterson went with Albright into a motel room. There, he handcuffed them to the bed and began hitting them with a belt and an extension cord, all the while shouting, "Scream, bitch! You know you like it!"

Perhaps it was no coincidence that Albright's life began to spin out of control after the death of his parents, Delle and Fred. Without them around to look out for him, a repressed part of Albright may have finally unleashed itself. He and Delle, who died of cancer in 1981, were not close in her last years. Delle was disappointed in the way her son had turned out, while Albright found her to be a pest—especially when she would bang on his door early on Saturday mornings to get him to help her with one of her little fix-up projects. But as his final gesture of devotion to his mother, Albright went out and bought a dress for the undertaker to put on her body—the first new dress he had ever seen her wear. Surprisingly, he wept at her funeral, wracked with grief or maybe guilt over the way he had let her down.

He also cried at Fred's funeral a few years later. Frankly, it had not been until after Delle's death that Albright and his father became close. Albright remembered how Delle constantly nagged at her quiet husband, bickering with him about problems around the house. With her gone, Fred seemed more relaxed. Several nights a week, Albright would take him to dinner at a nearby cafeteria.

After Fred's fatal heart attack in 1986, Albright inherited at least $96,000, along with all of his parents' homes and property in south Dallas. For what friends said were sentimental reasons, he kept the property in his father's name. To bring in some extra money, he rented out one of the tiny ramshackle frame homes, on a street called Cotton Valley, to a truck driver named Axton Schindler. Known as Speedee because he talked so fast, Schindler was a singularly weird individual. He stacked the rooms of his house with trash up to three feet high. He put an automobile engine in the living room. He lived without electricity and running water: He used a Coleman lantern for light and bottled water to wash himself. Albright's friends said he should get another renter, that Speedee was too unusual. But the always agreeable Albright, who had met Schindler through a female friend, said he wasn't that bad of a fellow, so he let him stay.

At this point, Albright had made the decision to move back into the old family home in Oak Cliff, which, like the rental homes, was still listed in the property rolls under Fred's name. Although the neighborhood had grown somewhat shabby over the years and the house was definitely in need of a new paint job, Albright said the place would do nicely. He brought his new love, Dixie Austin, down from Arkansas, and together they settled in for a quiet, romantic life.

The address of their home was 1035 Eldorado.

"You know Irv Stone, the head of the Dallas County forensic science department, which studies physical evidence found at crime scenes."

"Yes," he said. "We played on a softball team together. He was sort of a standoffish person. Everyone would call him 'Dr. Stone.' So finally I said something to him about my supraorbital foramen bothering me. He'd say, 'Huh?' I'd say, 'You know, where the ophthalmic division of the trigeminal nerve comes through and feeds my eyebrow up here. It's really been bothering me.' And Irv, sort of cocky, said, 'I hate to inform you that I am not a medical doctor.' I'm surprised he didn't know his anatomy."

"What were you describing, the area above your eye?" I asked.

"Yes, the little ridge there, right where the nerve comes through."

March 19, 1991: Shirley Williams

John Westphalen had filled up four black spiral notebooks with notes on the prostitute murder case. He had gone back and reexamined the crime scenes. Special undercover units had been sent to stake out the prostitution areas and run computer checks on the license plates of vehicles that cruised by, just to see if the owners might have any unusual criminal records. Everything added up to zip. This was a killer in total control, a man who refused to panic. "We've got to answer three questions," Westphalen said again and again at meetings about the case. "Number one, Why is he after prostitutes? Number two, Why were both bodies dumped on that same street? And number three, Why are those eyes cut out?"

Sitting around Westphalen's battleship-gray metal desk in the heart of the fluorescent-lit homicide office, detectives started throwing out theories. Maybe the killer had gotten AIDS from a prostitute and was out for revenge. Maybe he believed the old superstition that a murderer's image always remains on the eyeballs of the person he kills. Maybe he believed a dead person's eyes would follow him forever. Or maybe the killer took the eyeballs to fuel some sexual fantasy. Maybe he wanted to eat them—or cook them. The only thing Westphalen knew for sure was that the killer came out late at night, was strong enough to drag those girls in and out of a car, and had surgical skills. He also probably needed a well-lit room to do his surgery. Hell, somebody said, maybe this guy is a whacked-out doctor.

Suddenly, in the early morning hours of March 19, the killer changed tactics. On Fort Worth Boulevard, another whore hangout a few miles from the Star, a black prostitute named Shirley Williams emerged from the Avalon Motel, where she worked as a maid during the day and turned tricks at night. According to another prostitute who saw her, Shirley was wearing jeans and a yellow raincoat and appeared to be in a stuporous drug high as she tottered alone on the sidewalk.

She was found at six-twenty the next morning,

dumped on a residential street half a block from an elementary school in the heart of Oak Cliff. As children walked to school, they could see the naked woman crumpled against the curb. An unopened condom was beside her body. "Go look at her eyes and tell me if they're there," Westphalen said to the medical examiner's field agent at the scene. The field agent flipped open the eyelids. "Gone," he said.

Westphalen turned to his partner, Stan McNear. "We've got number three," he said.

The autopsy on Shirley Williams' body would show that the surgery had been hurried. The broken tip of an X-Acto blade was found embedded in the skin near her right eye. But there were still no witnesses, nor murder weapon, no fingerprints. Worse, the killer had now murdered a black woman, and he had moved locations. Just as the detectives had feared, the publicity about the case had sent the killer away from the Star and his south Dallas dumping ground. There was no telling where he would hit again.

October 1990: A Son's Vengeance

In the autumn before the killings began, Charles Albright was the model of domestic propriety. During the day, he put his carpenter's skills to use around the house, installing new cabinets for the kitchen, adding a skylight in the bathroom. If he was preparing to become a modern-day Jack the Ripper, none of his friends or family had any idea.

But on October 1, Albright did something that, even for him, seemed a little peculiar: He took a job delivering newspapers in the middle of the night for the *Dal-*

las Times Herald. Albright told Dixie, who by now was his common-law wife, that he needed more spending money. He had never been good with his finances; in four years he had gone through his inheritance, and he had yet to get a full-time job. Because Dixie got a monthly annuity check and worked daily in the gift shop, she paid most of their bills. Dixie wasn't exactly pleased with Charlie's decision—she said she couldn't get a good night's sleep with him gone. But Albright said it would work out fine. He would wake up around three in the morning, deliver papers on an Oak Cliff route between four and six, and then be back in bed by six-fifteen.

He and Dixie agreed that most of the money he made would go for the trips he took with his softball team. The well-built Albright was one of the better players in the city's senior slow-pitch softball league. He played for both a day team and a night team, and he was chosen as an outfielder for a local all-star team that went to the Senior World Series in Arizona. Albright, of course, was the league's most colorful personality: He wore red shoes while everyone else wore black, and he twisted a coat hanger inside his cap so the cap would sit perfectly upon his head. He brought a cooler of soft drinks to every game for the others players to share. At the end of the game, there was nobody who could regale an audience with a funny story the way he could.

"No one ever saw Charlie upset—I literally mean that," said a man who managed one of Charlie's teams in the fall of 1990. "He went out of his way to try to be liked," said a longtime friend who also played ball with him. "Every now and then there would be some jawboning during a game, maybe a scuffle between two players from opposing teams. But if somebody came after Charlie, he would back down, as if he was scared. He literally could not stand the idea of fighting. He would rather give you a present. Every time he saw one of my daughters, he gave her a gift or a ten-dollar bill."

Because Albright's former teammates were so fond of him, it is difficult even today for them to talk about a certain incident that took place a few months before the murders. Many of them still deny knowing anything about it; others say they have only heard about it secondhand. But at least two men have confirmed that Charlie Albright let his mask slip again.

At the end of one game, some players for the Richardson Greyhounds, Charlie's day team, were sitting around the ballpark, shooting the breeze and eating some candy that Charlie had brought, when two women in a car drove slowly by. After the men joked that the women must be prostitutes, the team's manager shouted, "Hey, Charlie, you're single. Why don't you take after them whores?"

Albright said, "Hell, I'd kill them if I could."

Stunned, the men turned toward their mild-mannered friend. On his face was a dark scowling look. "What do you mean?" the manager said, trying to keep the conversation light. "We've got to have whores. It keeps men from chasing married women."

"The hell it does!" Albright snapped. Then he marched off to his car and left.

It was the first time anyone had ever seen Albright show any kind of anger. When the team assembled again for practice a few days later, the manager tried to apologize. "We were just shooting the bull," he said.

"Well, that's a touchy subject with me," Albright replied. "My mother was a prostitute."

He was not talking about Delle, he said, he was talking about his birth mother. The other men were speechless. Was this just one of Albright's tall tales? In the months to come, a number of people tried to verify the story, including an FBI agent and private investigator working for Albright's defense attorney. They learned that while his biological father could not be traced, his biological mother was a nurse who had lived and died in Wichita Falls. Perhaps she never was the brilliant law student whom Delle Albright had described to her son. But there was no way they could determine if she had ever been a prostitute. Albright's relatives, in fact, insisted that after a lengthy search through court records, Albright had been thrilled to find his biological mother. As an adult, he had visited her several times in Wichita Falls and had brought her gifts. He had even introduced her to Fred Albright and to his own daughter.

Yet somewhere in Albright's mind, the connection between prostitution and motherhood had been made. It is possible that Charles Albright was wrestling with a very twisted version of the madonna-whore complex, unconsciously seeking revenge on the mother figures who disappointed him by associating with prostitutes—the worst possible women he could find. On one hand, he seemingly cared for prostitutes like Susan Peterson and Mary Pratt. He helped them financially, bought them dinner, and gave them presents. On the other hand, he wanted to punish them. Perhaps he hated what they had become. Perhaps he hated what he had become in their presence.

Whatever the reason, if Albright had truly decided the time had come to kill, he had put himself in a perfect position to do it. His paper route gave him an excuse to be out at night. He had prostitutes who trusted him enough to let him take them on a little trip. He had his parents' old property just a ten-minute drive south of the Star, where, unseen, he could carry out the murders and mutilations. And because the property was in his father's name, nothing could be traced back to him.

There was only one flaw in the plan—one Albright didn't even know about. Charlie's truck-driving tenant, Axton Schindler, had decided a few years back not to list his south Dallas address on his driver's license. As he liked to say, he preferred to keep his privacy; he wanted the government to stay out of his business. Instead, he put down 1035 Eldorado, the address for Charles Albright.

"The police told me you had a number of true-crime books in your house," I said.

"Oh, hell, there were other books—books of poetry, several Bibles, cookbooks, all kinds of books on art, watercolors, oils, and some books on science. It was as well-rounded a library as you wanted to find."

"But in any of those murder books you read, did you learn why a serial killer acts the way he does?"

"Well, just for the sheer pleasure of killing a girl, I would imagine."

"A serial killer," I said, *"would not have—"*

"Would not have dumped them on the street where they would be easily found," he quickly said. *"Look, if I made up my mind I wanted to be one, I wouldn't have been caught on the third killing. If I had decided to be*

a serial killer, I sure would have been a good one. You can ask anybody about anything I have ever done. I tried to be the best at what I did."

March 22, 1991: Caught

Once word of Shirley Williams' killing spread, the Star Motel turned into a ghost town. Some prostitutes, black and white, told officers John Matthews and Regina Smith that they were leaving Dallas. Others said they were getting out of the business. A few women, so desperate for drug money that they couldn't leave, moved together to a street corner next to the home of a man who promised to serve as their lookout and bodyguard.

Cruising the area, Matthews and Smith spied a black prostitute, Brenda White, a seventeen-year veteran of the neighborhood. White tended to work alone on a street corner in front of a church, away from the other prostitutes. The officers decided to stop and make sure she knew about the murders. "Girl," Smith said, "don't you know there's a killer loose? He's now killing the black girls too." "Well, I'm going to get my black ass out of here," White replied. "I just had to Mace a man who jumped bad on me the other night."

White told the officers that a few days before, a trick in a dark station wagon had pulled up alongside her and that she had gotten inside the car. He was a husky-looking white man with salt-and-pepper hair, cowboy boots, and blue jeans. "Let's go to a motel," she told him. "No," he said. "I've got a spot we can use." As a way to protect herself, White never allowed a new trick to take her anywhere but a whore motel, so she told him to drop her off immediately. Suddenly, "a change came over his face," she recalled. "It was like anger, rage. He said, 'I hate whores! I'm going to kill all of you motherf—ing whores!' " Before he had a chance to grab her, White shot a stream of Mace into his face, threw open the door, and jumped out, breaking the heel of one of her favorite red leather pumps.

For the rest of the day, Matthews and Smith could not shake White's story from their minds. They flipped through their notebooks. They thought about everything the whores had told them since the killings began. Always, they returned to Veronica Rodriguez's rambling talk about being raped.

The next morning, as they were checking in for work at their police substation, Smith said, "We need to run a computer check on that Axton Schindler." Because county government computers contain more information about citizens than city computers, she and Matthews drove to the Dallas County constable's office near Jefferson Boulevard. There, a deputy constable on duty, Walter Cook, agreed to help them. Seated around the terminal, the officers asked Cook to type in Schindler's address: 1035 Eldorado. The name Fred Albright popped up as the owner of the property.

Fred Albright? Where was Axton Schindler?

Cook punched in another code. It turned out that this Fred Albright also owned property on a street called Cotton Valley. Wasn't Cotton Valley in the very neighborhood in south Dallas where the first two prostitutes were found? Cook kept typing. Fred Albright, the computer reported, was dead.

Matthews and Smith stared at the screen: The only clue in the case led them to a dead man. Then, after a pause, Cook said softly, "Maybe this has something to do with a man named Charles Albright."

Several weeks before, Cook explained, he had come to the office early one morning and had answered a call from a woman who would not identify herself. The woman had been friends with Mary Pratt, she said, and through Pratt had met a man whom she briefly dated. He was a very nice man, she said, but he had an odd love for eyes. She also happened to mention that he kept X-Acto blades in his attic. Cook asked for the man's name. "Charles Albright," she said.

If any other constable's deputy had been helping Matthews and Smith that day, the link to Albright might never have been made. But good fortune prevailed. Cook typed in another code, and personal information for Charles Albright popped up on the screen: "Born—August 10, 1933. Address—1035 Eldorado."

Somehow, they said, Schindler and Albright were connected. Perhaps Albright was Schindler's "friend," the one who had tried to kill Veronica Rodriguez. Their hearts racing, Matthews and Smith rushed to the county's identification division and asked to see Albright's criminal record. The officers discovered a string of thefts, burglaries, and forgeries and the charge of sexual intercourse with a child. The clerk then pulled out a mug shot of Albright, a photo of a rather handsome well-built man with grayish hair, angular features, and deep-set dark eyes—just like the man Brenda White had described. In the picture, Albright was frowning, his face perplexed, as if he was surprised he had been caught.

The clerk wondered why Smith was so excited. "Honey," Smith said, "I think we've got the killer."

On their way to the homicide department, Matthews and Smith rehearsed everything they wanted to say. They could not seem unprepared, Matthews insisted; it was nervy enough for two raw patrol officers to visit the legendary Westphalen and tell him they believed they had found the killer—although they had no solid evidence to prove it.

Westphalen greeted them politely. Matthews started, then Smith interrupted, and soon they were both talking at once. Westphalen sighed. "Calm down," he said. "Let's take it slow." A few minutes later, after they had finished their presentation, Westphalen decided they were on to something. He put together a photo lineup of six mug shots and told Matthews and Smith to show it to Brenda White.

Immediately, Smith and Matthews tracked White down on her usual street corner and asked her if she recognized any of the men in the mug shots. White unhesitatingly pointed to Albright's picture and said he was the man who had attacked her. A little while later, they showed the same lineup to Veronica Rodriguez. According to Matthews, when Rodriguez got to the third picture—Albright's—she started trembling. Suddenly fearful, she refused to identify anyone. Matthews called Westphalen with the bad news. Rodriguez is so afraid of the killer, he said, that she won't pick out his picture. "Bring her down here to see me," Westphalen growled.

Westphalen knew if he could not get Rodriguez to break, he wouldn't have the evidence to go after Charles Albright. Brenda White's story offered only the prospect of a misdemeanor assault charge. But if Rodriguez identified Albright, the Dallas police could file charges for attempted murder, get a search warrant, and look through his house for evidence that might connect him to the three murders.

Smith and Matthews dragged Rodriguez downtown. In a small interrogation room, Westphalen stared with his icy blue eyes at the crack-addicted Rodriguez. Rodriguez began to shake again. Tears poured out of her eyes. She wouldn't look at the pictures laid out before her. Trying to control his anger, Westphalen took a different tack. He told Rodriguez about the three girls, how they were brutally killed, how the police couldn't get the killer off the street without her help. "This is so easy," he said. "Pick out the picture of the guy who assaulted you, and we will get him and put him in jail, where he can't hurt you." Slowly, Rodriguez looked over the mug shots. While Westphalen and another officer watched, she reached for Albright's photo, turned it over, and signed her name.

At two-thirty in the morning on March 22, as a gentle rain fell on Oak Cliff, a team of tactical officers burst through the front door of 1035 Eldorado. Despite the home's shabby exterior, the treasures of Charlie Albright's eclectic life decorated room after room. One cabinet was filled with exotic champagne glasses; another held delicate expensive Lladro figurines of pretty young women. On one wall were *Life* magazine covers and valuable Marilyn Monroe movie posters.

As Charles Albright was handcuffed and led away, he never said a word. Stumbling out of bed in her nightgown, Dixie Austin looked incredulously at Albright and then back at the police. Unable to imagine what the man she loved could have done, she began to scream.

December 1991: Convicted

For a long time after Charles Albright's arrest, most everyone involved in his case wondered whether the police had enough evidence to convict him of murder. Despite a withering all-night interrogation by Westphalen, Albright refused to confess to anything. He acted as if he had never heard the names of the murdered prostitutes. Police searched through every square inch of the south Dallas properties. They searched his Oak Cliff house six times. The FBI even brought in a high-tech machine that could see through walls. Although the searches produced an array of interesting items—carpenters' woodworking blades, X-Acto blades, a copy of *Gray's Anatomy*, at least a dozen true-crime books—they never came up with the eyeballs. Behind Charlie's hand-built fireplace mantel, police discovered a hidden compartment filled with pistols and rifles. None, however, turned out to be the murder weapon.

Nor could police find anyone who would admit to seeing Charlie with the three prostitutes on the nights they were killed. Dixie claimed that on the nights in question, Charlie did not leave the house early for his paper route and that he always came home on time. As the trial date arrived, Veronica Rodriguez decided to testify as a witness for the defense. She claimed that she and Albright had never been together and that Westphalen had coerced her into picking Albright's photograph from the lineup. Axton Schindler continued to deny that he had saved Rodriguez from Albright. He said a Hispanic man named Joe had brought her to his door.

But Toby Shook, a low-key 33-year-old prosecutor working for the Dallas County district attorney's office, had a trump card. For the first time in its history, the DA's office was going for a murder conviction based solely on controversial hair evidence. Days after Albright's arrest, the city's forensic lab reported that hairs found on the bodies of the dead prostitutes were similar to hair samples taken from Albright's head and pubic area. As evidence goes, hairs are not as conclusive as fingerprints—it's impossible to tell how many other gray-haired men's hairs might look similar to Albright's hairs under a microscope—yet in this case, the lab kept running tests. Lab technicians said that hairs found on the blankets in the back of Albright's pickup truck were similar to hair samples from the first two prostitutes killed, Mary Pratt and Susan Peterson. Hairs found in Albright's vacuum cleaner matched the hair from the third prostitute killed, Shirley Williams.

An additional piece of the puzzle came from John Matthews and Regina Smith. The officers found a prostitute, Tina Connolly, who claimed that Albright was one of her regular afternoon customers on Fort Worth Boulevard. She never saw him cruise after dark, she said, except for one time—the night Shirley Williams disappeared. Connolly took Matthews and Smith to a secluded field near Fort Worth Boulevard where Albright used to take her for sex. There, they spotted a yellow raincoat, just like the one Williams was last seen wearing, and a blanket. Hairs on the coat and blanket matched Albright's hair.

Albright's defense attorney, Brad Lollar, tried to convince the jury that the case against Albright depended on the flimsiest circumstantial evidence. The killer, he said, was probably Axton Schindler, who just happened to skip town the week of the trial. Admittedly, the police had many unanswered questions about Schindler. Westphalen had spent hours interrogating him, trying to determine if he assisted Albright in the killings or was at least aware that Albright was murdering women on the rental property. But there was nothing to tie him to the case except for an empty .44-caliber bullet box found behind the house, which Albright might have dropped there himself. When Schindler's and Albright's photos were shown to dozens of prostitutes, none recognized Schindler, but many recognized Albright. Nor were there any hairs found on the dead prostitutes that could be linked to Schindler. Most important, no one who had ever met Axton Schindler could imagine he would have the slightest skill required to perfectly remove a set of human eyes.

Albright never testified. Throughout the trial, he sat quietly in his chair, his shoulders slumped, like a weak, humbled figure. Shook, in his closing argument, derisively called Albright "this former biology teacher, bullfighter, college ace, smart man who just can't seem to have a job." But Shook warned the jury not to underestimate Albright—that he had grown much smarter during this trial, that if he ever got out of jail, he wouldn't make the same mistakes again.

On December 19, when the jury returned with a guilty verdict and a life sentence, Dixie collapsed in the courtroom. Albright's friends avoided the reporters in the courthouse hallway; it was as if they did not want to be blamed for having lived with a vicious killer without recognizing him for what he was. But a stunned Brad Lollar, who genuinely thought he was going to get his client acquitted, strode tight-lipped out of the courtroom. "It's always a miscarriage of justice," he told the press, "when an innocent man is convicted."

He was confident, he told me, that he would win his case on appeal. Another judge, he said, would see through the lies told at the first trial. He leaned forward in his chair and grinned optimistically. He couldn't complain about prison life, he said. He was reading two books a week on the Civil War; he was taking notes for a book he wanted to write on the wives of Civil War generals. He was busy working as a carpenter in the prison woodworking shop, coaching the prison softball team, and writing letters to Dixie. He had just sent a request to Omni magazine for a back copy of its first issue because there was a painting on the cover that he liked. He grinned again and told terrifically funny stories about how crazy the other inmates acted. For a moment, it was hard for me to remember exactly what Charles Albright had been accused of doing.

But then I'd lock on the image of an eyeless young woman lying faceup on a neighborhood street. Why would such a kindly, lighthearted man want to cut out a prostitute's eyes? Why was he so plagued by eyes, that potent and universal symbol, the windows to the soul? In the ancient myth, Oedipus tore out his own eyes after committing the transgression of sleeping

*with his mother. Did Charles Albright, a perverted Oe-
dipus, tear out the eyes of women for committing the
transgression of sleeping with men? Perhaps he removed their eyes out of some sudden need to show the
world he could have been a great surgeon. Maybe he
dumped that third body in front of the school to show
his frustration over never having become a biology
teacher. Or maybe a private demon had been lurking
since his childhood, when the eyes were left off his little
stuffed birds. Just as he long ago wanted to have a
bagful of taxidermist's eyes, maybe he decided to collect human eyes for himself.*

*"Oh, really, I have never touched an eyeball," Al-
bright declared again, for the first time becoming indignant with me. "I truly think—and this may sound
farfetched—that the boys in the forensics lab cut out
those eyes. I think the police said, 'We want some sort
of mutilation.' " Almost cheered by his reasoning, he
returned to his psychologically impenetrable self.
Whatever secrets he had would remain with him forever.*

*Weeks after that conversation, I remembered Al-
bright's comment about wanting the first issue of Omni
magazine. Intrigued, I went to look for it at the library.
I opened a bound volume to the cover of the first issue,
which was published in October 1978. There, staring
out from the center of a dark page, was a solitary
human eye, unmoored, as if floating in space. The eyelid slid down just to the top of the eyeball; the eyeball
was lightly shaded; the eyelashes were curved like
half-moons.*

*It was, I thought, exactly the kind of eye Charles Al-
bright would wish he had painted.*

(May 1993)

Charles Albright's appeal of his life sentence failed, and he continues to serve out his time in a state prison in Amarillo, where he is still considered a model prisoner. About once a year, he writes me a letter, furious over my portrayal of him. Still proclaiming his innocence, Albright continues to ask me if I could arrange for him to take a lie-detector test.

Breaking the Bank

ALEX HECHT

My brothers at the Zeta Beta Tau fraternity at the University of Texas did not typically spend their summers in Austin. Some interned at prestigious law firms in Houston or hospitals in Dallas; others were floor runners on the Chicago commodities exchange. Many finagled trips abroad from their parents. But in the late summer of 1993, Joshua Alan Levine wasn't interested in such pursuits. The philosophy major and honor student had a problem: He had thousands of dollars of debts—many of them from gambling—but he didn't have the cash to pay them off. He found himself near the Drag, heading for the First State Bank. Wearing blue jeans and a Chicago Bulls cap that covered his sandy brown curls, he looked like any frat rat ready to make a withdrawal. Only this transaction would be made not with a pen but with a gun.

Josh had been casing the bank for a month. He would go there as often as three times a day, each time asking for his balance. Then he would ask to use a phone and—pretending to make a call—observe the bank in action. The tellers knew Josh on sight. One had even memorized the name of the person to whom he regularly sent large money orders. What the teller didn't know was that the person was a Houston-area bookie and that several months earlier he had threatened to castrate Josh if he didn't pay up. Josh had lost $11,000 to the bookie during that year's National Football League playoffs.

Many UT fraternities have become clubs for the sons of millionaires; belonging to one is in many ways a game of survival of the richest. Throughout his four years at UT, Josh always had to struggle to afford the Zeta Beta Tau (ZBT) lifestyle. But his financial circumstances were of little importance to his fraternity brothers. I knew many students at UT with serious personal problems, but I'd never have figured Josh as a candidate for collapse. I pledged ZBT in the fall of 1988, a year ahead of Josh. We were more than casual acquaintances—he was the "little brother" of one of my pledge brothers, and we shared bong hits and pickup basketball games. Josh had every reason to be successful: He worked two jobs to help pay his tuition and ZBT's $1,350-per-semester tab. After his first semester, his grade-point average never fell below 3.0. He was exceedingly handsome and fit—the kind of guy who never lost his tan. Josh was an aspiring writer, and he could talk about deep philosophical questions with ease. He had been president of ZBT and was a member of UT's elite Silver Spurs, the service organization that watches over UT's Longhorn mascot, Bevo, at home football games.

Along with the drinking, drugging, and partying that have been facts of frat life for decades, now there is widespread gambling. When Josh was a member of ZBT, the stiffest competition at the fraternity house, with the exception of the basketball court, was at the card table. Before dinner every night there was a poker game, with eight to twelve regulars playing at a round table in a dimly lit corner of the dining room. It was a tight crowd, not very friendly to strangers. Complicated wild-card games were the norm. Most players usually won or lost $50 in an afternoon, though it was not unheard of for someone to win $250. A pledge brother of mine who now works in Los Angeles quit his job waiting tables at a pizza joint because he was winning so much. No one really got into the hole too deep, except for one brother who had constant problems accessing his trust fund.

Poker and blackjack aren't the only forms of gambling in the UT fraternity system. The most prevalent form of illegal gambling is sports betting. "I don't think it's ever been a problem for a UT frat student to find someone who'll take a bet," explains Austin Police Department (APD) vice officer William H. Horn, who handles most of the city's gambling cases. For rich kids, who do most of the betting, there's little risk: They can always get their parents to cut them another check. After the Austin police busted a $600,000 bookmaking ring, one fraternity man told Horn that he planned to pay off a $12,000 debt by "cashing in some stock." Fraternity gambling is so ubiquitous that the cops tend to look the other way—or use the kids to get to bigger bookies. Of course, the police can't look the other way when a compulsive gambler turns to bank robbery.

In his journal entry for July 25, 1993, Josh wrote: "I am seriously considering robbing a bank. Is it possible?" The solution had come to him on one of those lazy summer afternoons when he had nothing better to do than smoke some pot, ingest some psychedelic mushrooms, and dangle his feet in the swimming pool of the apartment complex he lived in. "What day is a good day?" he wrote. "What time?"

On August 17, the time had come. As Josh turned down the alley behind the bank, he felt euphoric, just as he had the summer before, when he had won $25,000 betting on baseball. It was 9:47 a.m. The bank's morning rush was over, and as Josh knew, the security officer was taking his scheduled five-minute break. Josh unzipped a black book bag and pulled out a pair of rose-tinted goggles, black neoprene driving gloves, and a camouflage hunting mask. He hesitated—wondering for a moment if he would be able to live with himself afterward. Then he pulled out a 9mm semiautomatic Astra and stormed the bank.

"This is a f——ing robbery!" he screamed, pointing the gun at two tellers. "Put the money in the bag! In the f——ing bag!" One terrified teller tried to hand him the money. "Not to me," Josh yelled, gesturing with the blue-steel Astra. "In my f——ing bag!"

Then Joshua Alan Levine ran away from the First State Bank with $12,097. He didn't know whether he would be able to live with himself, but for now, at least, he knew he would be able to live.

"Every night of the week, you could find a game to bet on," Josh said. "When I was broke, I could make money for dinner and lunch. It's real easy to win only twenty dollars. Real easy. I was totally in the mania." Josh and I were sitting in the Twin Sisters cafe, a casual lunch spot in San Antonio's Alamo Heights neighborhood, last July, nearly a year after he had robbed the bank. Josh offered an easy smile as he reminisced about the gambling habit he had picked up from his ZBT brothers. In his striped blue shirt and khaki shorts, he still looked like a Zebe, not a criminal out on bail and awaiting sentencing. Beside his barely touched bowl of gazpacho sat the latest issue of the *Paris Review*. It was difficult to believe that just a week before, my friend had been convicted in U.S. district judge Sam Sparks's court on two felony counts: bank robbery and the use of a firearm in a crime of violence.

After the tellers had stuffed the money into his black bag, Josh ran out of the bank, but he forgot to zip up the bag. More than half of the $12,097—in packets of tens, twenties, and fifties—fell on the ground just inside the bank's back door. He kept running. Not a hundred yards farther, he slammed into a man loading a U-Haul truck. Even more money went flying. Josh made it to his car, which was parked a couple of blocks away, and drove to his apartment. He changed out of his robber's gear, made a few phone calls, and brushed his teeth. His plan was to drive to his grandparents' home in Memphis, Tennessee.

He never made it to the city limits. The two tellers had slipped packets of "tracer money" into his bag. Tracer money emits radio waves, and the APD's robbery detail has four vehicles equipped with a device that can track them. Officer Rolando G. Fuertes homed in on Josh's car near Interstate 35 and the UT campus and caught up with Josh when he stopped outside a Planet K off the Rundberg Lane exit. The police recovered the camouflage mask, the neoprene gloves, and the Astra under a white quilt in the trunk of his red

1991 Toyota Corolla. They found his journal, complete with a diagram of the robbery, in a backpack on his front passenger seat. And they recovered all but $4 of the stolen money.

In interviews with the police and FBI agents after his arrest, Josh said he wouldn't be able to afford his own lawyer and repeatedly asked when the court would assign him one. "Son," said FBI special agent James Echols, "this is what we call an open-and-shut case." To save time and money, the government offered to plea-bargain: a four-year prison sentence in return for a guilty plea. After all, he had been caught red-handed. But Josh refused the government's deal. He was still gambling. With financial support from family and friends, the Levines hired Jack Zimmermann, a high-profile defense attorney from Houston, to defend Josh. Zimmermann believed he could best defend Josh with a plea of not guilty due to insanity, and he urged Josh to risk a possible seven-to-ten-year prison sentence. Zimmermann would base his defense on Josh's mental state at the time of the robbery. Psychologists said Josh suffered from bipolar disorder, sometimes called manic depressive illness, a condition that was diagnosed after the robbery. It was a long shot.

In court Zimmermann portrayed Josh as an unstable young writer who didn't believe he could describe a bank robbery until he had committed one. Zimmermann told the jury that Josh had turned himself into the protagonist of his future novel—a "pretentious yet wonderful" character named Reynaldo Zak, who was, in fact, a character in Josh's fiction writing. The jurors were unsympathetic. They saw Josh not as a disturbed young talent but as a spoiled frat boy.

J osh Levine was born on July 19, 1971, in Memphis. When he was five his parents moved to a middle-class neighborhood in San Antonio. His father, Michael, had a master's degree in education with a specialty in counseling from Memphis State University but would later switch to retail sales, becoming part-owner of two Polo shops. Josh's mother, Nancy, is a longtime public-school administrator.

"I was considered rich, upper class," Josh told me at Twin Sisters. "I was wearing the best clothes money could buy. It was an image thing. It confused me a lot." In the public high schools during the mid-eighties, a preppy wardrobe established one's social standing. At MacArthur High School, Josh blended perfectly with the popular, rich crowd. As a senior he was voted vice president of the student council. He was an A and B student, just below the top 10 percent of his senior class. He belonged to the honor society and the creative-writing club and was active in Jewish youth groups.

While Josh was in high school, the Levine family fell on hard times. In 1986 his father's faltering Polo shop was bought out. Michael then opened a women's clothing store, but in 1989—the year Josh went to UT—it went out of business. During his senior year in high school Josh worked evenings, often well past midnight, as a line cook at the Alamo Cafe. After graduation he also worked as a lifeguard. His academic record and financial need helped him win a scholarship and qualified him for financial aid—together worth more than $11,000 over two years.

But Josh was hooked on an upper-class lifestyle. When the kids he hung out with headed for UT, they shunned the on-campus dormitory, Jester, in favor of the private, off-campus dorms—Dobie, the Castilian, and Contessa West—which were almost twice as expensive. Josh and his parents agreed that rooming at Dobie was imperative: It was smaller and more personal than the massive Jester. It was also where all the Jewish women were, and they thought it was important that he be surrounded by his own kind. When it came to fraternities, though, it was harder to convince Nancy Levine that the social advantages outweighed the additional expense.

But ZBT, then the most prestigious Jewish fraternity on campus, was rushing Josh. And for someone as plugged in to the Jewish social scene as Josh was, ZBT was a necessity. Boasting more than 160 members, it was the largest of UT's three Jewish frats. It was also the wealthiest: Two members' fathers owned companies on the NASDAQ. The frat was dubbed Zillions, Billions, and Trillions. ZBT threw parties and mingled with UT's biggest and richest fraternities: Sig Ep, Delta Tau Delta, Fiji, and Kappa Alpha. (In November 1993 ZBT's national organization revoked the UT chapter's charter because of a violation of its "no pledging" policy. Despite several warnings, ZBT had continued to treat its new members as pledges. But in January 1994 ZBT reopened as Pi Lambda Phi.)

In 1989 Josh joined the frat with typical pre-freshman logic—UT was a big school, and to make it at a big school one had to be a part of something. And ZBT wanted Josh. He was articulate and muscular, a natural leader. He could brag about his hometown Spurs or how much he enjoyed the writing of Jorge Luis Borges. He could hold his liquor, and he was good with the girls—in ZBT lingo, he cut butt. The fraternity went out of its way to make itself affordable for guys like Josh. As a freshman, Josh waited tables at the ZBT house during dinner and was the house's lunchtime busboy. During my three years in ZBT, I too was a waiter. Josh and I quickly became close. Our paths had been so similar: We were in the small minority of liberal arts majors. While our pledge brothers discussed their stock options, Josh and I talked about the books we had read recently. Neither of us had a family business to fall back on after graduation, a fact that bothered Josh more than me. Josh was more real to me than the other Zebes were; we shared our doubts and concerns. But I never knew about his gambling.

I was awestruck by what Josh put himself through just to be a Zebe. While his fellow freshman pledge brothers spent as little time as possible at the ZBT house, Josh worked there all day, absorbing nonstop abuse. If the pledge trainers feared that a pledge had spit in their dinner, as was often the case, they would holler for the pledge and order him to take a bite. Then they would throw their food at him. Josh was elected rush captain his sophomore year and—on the promise that he would get new pool cues—president his junior year. "He was the guy who everyone respected," says Elliott Finebloom, one of Josh's pledge brothers. "He was the man." He had a serious girlfriend, a redheaded Jewish beauty from California. Josh also worked outside the fraternity. In his four years at UT he waited tables at the Cadillac Bar, shoveled manure at an equestrian center, and was a salesman for a software company and a page at the state capitol.

By outward appearances, Josh seemed to be in control of his life. But he could never shake the feeling that he didn't belong—that because his parents could afford to send him only $850 a month to cover his living expenses, he was inferior to his pledge brothers. While they went on about how they couldn't get full access to their trust funds until they were 25, Josh dreamed of being a writer. He told his frat brothers that though life would be rough for a few years, someday he would be an established Hollywood screenwriter. "I wanted to be known as the guy who was the Silver Spur," he told me, "but who was also like Michener." But Levine's writings were anything but Michener. His prose was dark and intense, more personal than narrative. "Waking to the sound of running water and far matriculations," reads one of his novellas, "the beamy sun prodded my eyes. . . . The wondrous light rushed me into its searing touch, a nuance of heat that made me secure. Secure to lay beneath it, finally thinking of something else other than her."

In his drive to be accepted, Josh became addicted to some ZBT vices. His problems started with the clique he hung out with. "Team Dobie" consisted of about ten guys, all of whom smoked marijuana at least once a day and—except for Josh—were rich. "I was smoking so much," Josh told me, "that even when I wasn't smoking I was still high." While Josh and a frat brother were driving back to Austin from a spring break in California, a policeman pulled them over just outside of Palm Springs. Levine, in the passenger seat, was too stoned to realize why the car had stopped. When the officer asked for a driver's license and insurance, he noticed Levine, reading the liner notes to a compact disc, with a joint still burning in his mouth, but he was not charged.

Many ZBTs were heavy gamblers, and to maintain respect among his clique, Josh made his first football wagers in the fall of 1990, his sophomore year. He started small, with a few $25 bets. Soon he was betting on up to nine games a weekend, often risking more than $200 a game. Although Josh told me he was "unbelievably successful" from the start, he was asking his pledge brothers for loans as early as that first semester of his sophomore year. On several occasions one of his roommates, a friend from elementary school, loaned him $100.

In the beginning Josh was very businesslike when he needed money and was punctual with repayment. But as his gambling grew more serious, so did his debts. "Most of the big gamblers in the house were rich kids," explained Josh Hanft, who was treasurer of ZBT when Josh was president. "They could afford to lose the money. But Levine didn't have money to pay. It would hurt Levine more. He would bet way too much money trying to get back to even." Hanft loaned Josh $1,000, which Hanft said he paid back on time.

Every UT fraternity had a bookie. Most were strictly small time, refusing to accept bets of more than $300. They never offered official Vegas odds; instead they tweaked the betting lines in their favor. Fraternity bookies also had a bad habit of not paying out winnings on time, if at all. They operated on a credit system in which bettors were free to wager their way out of debt. Since no frat bookmaker would violate the spirit of brotherhood and threaten a fellow fraternity man with bodily harm, there was no effective method of debt collection.

By the spring of his sophomore year, Josh had tired of the fraternity bookmakers. He wanted the thousand-dollar action and better odds. A fraternity brother who was regarded as the biggest gambler in ZBT hooked Josh up with a new bookie, a former ZBT who had become a professional bookmaker. Almost immediately, Josh fell into large debt to the bookie. "I didn't have the money," Josh recalled at the cafe. "I told him I'd pay when I could. It set a bad precedent."

In spring 1992, the second semester of his junior year, Josh was elected president of the fraternity and inducted into the Silver Spurs. By then, Josh had paid back the bookie and persuaded him to take his bets again. But after Josh had a hot couple of weeks, the bookie took his revenge and refused to pay Josh his winnings. And there was nothing Josh could do about it, except get a new bookie. So several Zebes put him in touch with another big-time bookie, this one based in Houston.

During the summer of 1992, gambling became more for Josh than a way of getting enough money to keep up with the fraternity's millionaires. It became a compulsion, an all-consuming emotional commitment. So much so that Josh made the gambler's fatal error: He began to look for a way to beat the system. Employing his background in philosophy, Josh came up with an approach that he believed weighted the odds in his favor. "My thing was that you separate the money from the emotions and desire," he told me. "You make everything completely sober. It's like the powers of chance, the powers of the universe. I tried to do everything in my power to even those out." His idea was to find someone who wasn't a gambler to make his picks, because Josh believed that that person would not be affected by winning or losing.

He found a fraternity brother who was a self-proclaimed baseball expert with a knack for picking winners. That summer, Josh's friend would phone him every morning and rattle off four or five picks of the day; Josh would decide how much money to bet on each game and call his Houston bookie. The only condition was that Josh was never, ever to bet on the Texas Rangers, his friend's favorite team. The friend rarely picked overwhelming favorites; instead, he stuck by the streak theory: Bet on teams on two- and three-game winning streaks, but never on a team that has won more than four. Somehow, it worked. "Every night was super huge," said a smiling Josh. "I was winning nine hundred dollars a night. We couldn't believe it. Every week we'd go eight and one. It was beautiful."

In exchange for his picks, Josh said, he paid his expert 15 percent of the profits—as much as $150 a week. The only rule Josh imposed on his friend was that he could never bet on the same games he gave Josh. That was a karmic violation of Josh's philosophy, the dreaded mixture of emotions and money. But the friend couldn't help himself. Josh said his friend eventually wanted to get in on the action too. He picked a bad night to cross Josh's only rule: Josh lost big, the friend more modestly. The system was ruined, and Josh turned to other frat brothers for picks.

Josh said he won $25,000 that summer. He had finally achieved the financial level of his fraternity brothers. He didn't have to work a real job. He played the stock market. He could afford to buy his girlfriend presents and take his friends out for dinner and buy thick bags of skunky-smelling pot. He and a roommate went on a shopping spree. They bought a big-screen television, a beveled-glass coffee table, and a leather couch. They spent $8,500. "It was," Josh recalled wistfully, "a great summer."

Word of Josh's amazing season quickly spread through ZBT. A sophomore fraternity brother started hanging out with him. After watching Josh's ludicrous system, the sophomore decided to become a bookmaker. "He thought it would be so easy," Josh told me at lunch last July. "He started saying, 'I gotta book. I gotta book.' "

It took Josh and the ZBTs only two weeks to put the rookie bookie out of business. "Well, he was not very smart," said Josh. "A bookie needs to have some savvy." For example, he said, when the underdog Chicago Cubs jumped out to a 3–0 lead against the St. Louis Cardinals in one afternoon game, he phoned the upstart bookie and placed $300 on the Cubs. Unaware that the game had already started, he took the bet.

"He never turned down a bet—it was candy from a baby," added another ZBT. "Everyone was winning money off the dude." After the frat bookie was unable to pay more than a thousand dollars in losses, he abandoned his bookmaking dream for the summer.

Josh was living a gambler's lifestyle. Gone was any vestige of his hard-work ethic. He was more interested in turning a quick buck. Still under the influence of his summer of luck, Josh concocted a scheme: If a frat brother gave him some investment capital, he would guarantee that after one month he'd return the entire amount, plus 50 percent interest. His plan was to bet half of the investment on his pick of the week. A friend of Josh's couldn't believe he was serious. Why would he guarantee so high a return when plenty of ZBTs would jump at a mere 10 percent yield?

"He honestly didn't think they would lose," said the friend, who eventually talked Josh out of the plan. "It blinded him that this was someone else's money he could lose. It just blinded him."

Just before his senior year, Josh moved into a house with seven other Zebes. Thanks to his winning streak, Josh had plenty of cash on hand. Partly because his roommates were lazy but mostly because he wanted to impress them, Josh paid the bills out of his own pocket. He was not always reimbursed.

Josh's gambling addiction impaired his judgment as ZBT president. In what was probably his most popular decree, he reinstated blackjack night, which had been discontinued in 1988, during my freshman year. His reasoning: "The frat needed the money." Blackjack night was usually held on Sunday in the house's library. Josh found three friends who were willing backers, and each night the bank was at least $3,500. The tables were run on Colorado rules—only $5 or $10 bets allowed. The house provided a keg of beer and raked a percentage off the tables each hour. Players from any fraternity could attend, as long as they knew a Zebe.

The blackjack scheme didn't yield much in the way of profits. "The dealers were always too stoned, and they made mistakes," Josh explained. "It was too lax. People were drinking beer, joking. It was more of a social atmosphere." About blackjack night, Josh told me: "I'm not saying that as a good president I should have done that, but as a president with a gambling problem, that's what happened."

In the fall of 1992, the extent and complexity of gambling in the UT frat system seemed to have reached epidemic proportions. A loose group of six ZBT bookmakers had centralized their operations. Their system was simple. They set up a phone number in Austin, which bettors called to hear the latest lines and place bets. The maximum bet was $300, except for the "frat daddies," as the especially wealthy bettors were known. By the NFL playoffs, the bookies were sitting on a $600,000 operation. But in late November 1992, the APD vice squad received an anonymous call from a Zebe in serious debt who had decided to rat on his frat-brother bookies rather than pay up.

Late in the afternoon of January 20, 1993, as a burgers-and-beer party raged at the ZBT house and the daily pickup basketball games were in full swing, the APD vice squad raided the apartments of the ZBT bookies. One complex overlooked the frat house. When the vice cops stormed the apartment, with one officer breaking a window and another knocking down the door, the incident was in full view of the basketball court. "We were in awe," remembers Josh Hanft, who was playing ball at the time.

By the fall of 1992, Josh's gambling had grown out of control. He got a job as a salesman for a software company, working on commission. But his gambling would interfere with that job. "I made no sales," he recalled. "I didn't get a single paycheck." Nevertheless, that fall the company sent Josh to a computer convention in Las Vegas. It was the kiss of death for a compulsive gambler. "The whole time I was supposed to be meeting people and pitching software, I was at the tables," he said.

By the time he got to Las Vegas, the money he had made during his summer hot streak was gone. He left Austin owing his bookie $2,000. At eight o'clock on his final night in Vegas, down to his last $50, Josh started playing craps "for the first time in my life." Twelve hours later he was ahead $6,500. But he couldn't stop. He would finish four hours later— sixteen hours after he had started—with $4,000. "People were cheering my name," he told me. "That isn't good for someone who has a gambling problem. It was like the greatest time of my life."

Josh's hot streak wouldn't last. Three weeks before Super Bowl XXVII, with all of his friends on winter break, Josh sat alone in his apartment, snorting some cocaine he had bought for the weekend. He smoked some marijuana. He stayed up all night formulating a go-for-broke strategy. The drugs gave him the nerve to wager some $30,000 that he didn't have on a series of bets.

While the Houston Oilers were racking up a 32-point lead against the Buffalo Bills in the NFL playoffs, Josh Levine stood to lose the entire $30,000. Sitting in his apartment, which was now a disaster area, he worried first about his own safety, then about his family's. He snorted some more cocaine. He calculated how much he could make selling all of his expensive things—the beveled-glass coffee table, the television, the leather couch, his compact-disc collection. He wondered which of his rich frat buddies could possibly front him some dough. But when the Oilers pulled the biggest

choke in NFL playoff history, Josh was saved—sort of.
At the end of the day he owed his bookie only $11,000.

For several weeks, Josh used his answering machine
to screen his calls, refusing to speak to or call back
the bookie. But one Sunday, while several of Josh's
roommates were watching a game, the bookie had had
enough. "Pay me or I'll cut your f——ing balls off!"
he screamed into the answering machine.

Josh was able to sell his things for $5,500. His
bookie worked out a payment plan for the rest of the
debt: Josh would direct all of his gambling buddies to
him. But Josh balked at what he perceived as a devil's
compact. Painfully aware of gambling's eternal truth—
the bookmaker always wins—Josh didn't want his
friends to suffer his fate. He and the bookie came up
with a new arrangement, in which Josh would direct
his friends to the bookie and make 10 percent of their
losses during the upcoming baseball season. He would
receive the payoff, which he had estimated at $1,500,
after the World Series. Josh planned to take his friends
out for a raucous night of drinking on Sixth Street.
"But," Josh told me later, "my summer ended in the
middle of the baseball season."

After his bloody playoff Sunday, Josh said, he
stopped gambling. Reeling from his losses, he told his
mother that he needed counseling for depression. A
psychologist informed Josh that his condition was no
different from that of any confused undergrad and prescribed a copy of Douglass Coupland's *Generation X*.
The literary prescription didn't work. Josh fell further
into a funk, embarking on a lifestyle that would lend
credence to attorney Zimmermann's insanity defense.

Josh said he lost the taste for gambling that February,

but his debts were a constant reminder. He had sold most of his possessions and borrowed $3,000 from a frat brother. He ignored his bills—the $829.47 he owed for utilities and the $1,058 he owed Southwestern Bell—and had racked up $1,158.05 on his Visa card. In May his longtime girlfriend broke up with him. When his apartment lease expired that month, he lost his place to live. By day he would float from friend's house to friend's house, where he would sit and smoke pot and "talk about many things, namely our existence," he recalled. Some nights he would leave Austin at four in the morning and ride his bike to his parents' home in San Antonio. For two weeks he slept under the stars in Austin's Pease Park. He shaved his head. Josh's journal writings reveal his depression. "Do I truly want to be a writer?" he asked in his journal on July 21. "Do I truly want to be? I f—— things up all the time and do not seem to have a habit, except for scheming and hustling. I believed I had more in me than that, but perhaps I am no better than the everyman." Another entry, from July 19, 1993, says: "Today is my birthday. So much for that. What am I looking for? I have the problem of either being too good-looking or not good-looking enough. Twenty two and still dreaming. Hang on, Josh, hang on." Three days later Josh wrote: "When did I change? Was it when I smoked more dope than my neurons could handle? Or when I realized I was a failure of unimportant circumstances?"

Josh should have graduated by the summer of 1993, but he was a few hours short of the required credits. His parents began to send him less money. He found a job as a midnight baker at the Kitchen Door but lasted only two weeks—the hours were too cruel.

He struggled to make the $330 monthly payment on the loan from his frat brother.

Then, once again, ZBT came to the rescue. A pledge brother agreed to let Josh live in his apartment for the entire summer in exchange for Josh's taking a computer science class for him. Josh continued to worry about how he would support himself after the summer. And in late July, after watching the movies *Reservoir Dogs,* in which a heist fails miserably, and *Point Break,* about a bank-robbing ring of surfers, he made a fateful decision: He would save himself by robbing a bank. Nothing else in life made sense.

Josh began a workout regimen to prepare for his crime. Every day he swam at UT's main pool, rode his bike around Austin, or played basketball—and cased the First State Bank. He jotted notes about his plan on a yellow legal pad. "I am about to write down some ideas," he wrote, "and by doing so I could be making mistake number one." He noted that there were two cameras, one security guard, three tellers, and one manager at the bank.

He figured he needed two partners, one to drive the car and the other to disarm the security guard. He approached his close pledge brother Elliott Finebloom about the idea while the two were on a leisurely drive through the hills of Austin. Finebloom didn't think Josh was serious and told him that the only reason he would even consider participating in a robbery was if he needed the money. Like most ZBTs, Finebloom didn't need the money.

"[Finebloom] truly is worthless," Josh wrote in his journal. Josh next approached another pledge brother, who had a gun, but he too refused.

After they had eaten lunch at Mad Dog and Beans near the UT campus, Josh dropped his idea on a third fraternity brother. "You don't need to gamble," Josh told him as he pointed toward First State. "You need something more exciting. Something more productive. You need to rob a bank." The friend told Josh to take him home.

Even though his friends refused to go along with the plan—none of them thought he was serious—Josh included them with code letters in his written outlines. In the journal version, Josh and "T," equipped with ropes and grappling hooks for a surprise entrance, would meet in front of First State. Afterward, the two would flee two blocks south to Twenty-fourth Street, where another fraternity mate, "L," would wait. They would throw the bag of money into L's open car trunk and split off in three directions.

On August 1 Josh wrote down a list of last-minute things he needed: "what to wear, what to say, what to do." On August 16 he bought the camouflage mask and neoprene gloves at an Academy store in Austin. He got the Astra pistol through a classified advertisement in the *Austin American-Statesman,* telling the gun dealer he was a computer salesman from El Paso who had recently been carjacked. When he went to Red's shooting range to try out his new purchase—he had never fired a gun before—he discovered that he had bought the wrong size bullets.

On July 25 he had written, "This project and K——— [his ex-girlfriend] are the only things on my mind. If I do it and write K——— a letter then there will be nothing on my mind."

I was the only ZBT who showed up for Josh's sentencing on the morning of July 22, 1994, a month after his conviction. He wore a charcoal-gray suit and a gray print tie. He needed a haircut, and his eyes were bloodshot. As he waited for his sentencing, he stared straight ahead, sometimes appearing angry, sometimes listless. Barring a minor judicial miracle, he would soon start a long prison sentence. He fumbled nervously with a copy of *Anna Karenina*.

His lawyer, Jack Zimmermann, had argued that it was not Joshua Alan Levine who had committed the robbery but Josh's fictional alter ego, Reynaldo Zak. The defense had a two-pronged burden of proof. Zimmermann had to prove that Josh was not only mentally ill, but also morally and rationally incapacitated during the robbery. Zimmermann relied on scientific evidence—namely, diagnoses after Josh's arrest indicating that he suffers from bipolar disorder. Since his stay at Laurel Ridge Psychiatric Hospital in San Antonio, Josh has taken several antidepressants, including Prozac and Lithomate. Josh's uncle and father have taken Prozac, and his grandfather had electroshock treatments.

Judge Sam Sparks said during Josh's sentencing, "That ship didn't sail. I agree with the jury. Mr. Levine robbed the bank probably for gambling debts or maybe to see if he could get away with it. . . . I sense not a hint of remorse from Mr. Levine."

"I don't know how to convince you how sorry I am," Josh told the judge. "I'll suffer for my sins every day of my life. I'm an internal person." All that really mattered, he continued, was that his bipolar condition had been discovered. He would accept his sentence

without bitterness, "because I'm a good person again."
His mother cried.

Josh's final gamble—and perhaps his biggest—
didn't pay off. Despite having no criminal record, Josh
was given a 106-month prison term followed by five
years of probation. As two U.S. marshals handcuffed
him, there were no tears from Josh, only a request that
he be allowed to take *Anna Karenina* with him. Today
Josh is out on a $100,000 bond, pending an appeal.

"When I get out of jail, I want to be a skilled writer,
a well-read writer," Josh had told me at the Twin Sisters cafe. He had sounded resigned to prison. A little
hard time might not be so bad. It would free him up to
write Reynaldo's story, which might make a literary
classic, or at least a television movie. He had said he
was looking for an agent. "Who knows? Maybe I'll
meet one in my ninth year in prison.

"I'm high on the career track I've chosen," he had
joked. "I'm high on life." As he explained how he seemed
predestined for prison—his grandfather was a Holocaust
survivor, his father had once worked as a prison social
worker—his voice rose excitedly, his eyes lit up. Just as
they had when he explained the gambling philosophy that
had won him $25,000 two summers before.

(January 1995)

Josh Levine is currently serving his 106-month sentence at the
Federal Correctional Institute in Three Rivers, Texas. His sched-
uled release date is July 28, 2003. After numerous hazing- and
alcohol-related incidents, Zeta Beta Tau lost its charter in 1994.
However, in the spring of 1995, the chapter reopened as Pi
Lambda Phi, ostensibly carrying on the Zeta Beta Tau tradition.
Rumor has it that blackjack night is still on Sunday.

The Horse Killers

ROBERT DRAPER

The horse was a fourteen-year-old sorrel gelding with a blaze face. As it lay there in the blood-stained meadow, with its right eye gone milky and its rear covered with gashes, the softness of its coat remained unmarred, its hindquarters still rippled, and above its sturdy back, its long mane hung in an insouciant tease. Its legs still suggested power and grace, war and play. Even beaten to death, the horse looked strangely indomitable.

Its registered name was Mister Wilson Boy, and in earlier years it had been a prizewinning cutting horse. Of late its knees had become arthritic, and so the horse had passed its final days in a ten-acre pasture just west of the East Texas town of Silsbee. Both the pasture and the horse were owned by Silsbee High School football coach Charlie Woodard, an even-tempered 53-year-old man who taught Sunday school at the First Methodist Church. Woodard was that rare Texas football coach who was more interested in the lives of the boys who played the game than in the game's outcome. He loved children, and one way he showed this was by frequently letting them ride Mister Wilson Boy around his pasture. Woodard trusted his horse around children, and children around his horse—until the morning of Monday, September 18, 1995, when he was informed that the brutes who had clubbed his horse to death four days earlier were seven boys and one girl, ranging in age from eight to fourteen.

The revelation shocked and disturbed Coach Woodard—"It ruins my faith in humanity," he told a friend. The owner's reaction turned out to be the tamest on record. From all over America, letters seething with revulsion and vindictiveness poured in to the Hardin County courthouse: "What horrible children we are raising in this country." "They are our future Mansons, Gacys, and other perverts. Do not allow them back into society." "I believe any punishment you can give these monsters cannot be severe enough!" "I would suggest a public, bare-butt caning of them." "Perhaps we should wrap them in barbed wire and beat them with sticks." "Hang them and get it over with." So hostile was the public sentiment, says Hardin County prosecutor David Sheffield, that "it put me, the prosecutor of the kids, in a position of wanting to defend them. We had to put up metal detectors in the courthouse halls. After reading all these letters about how the kids should be hanged or mutilated, we were worried that some nut was going to come down to Hardin County and take care of the horse problem himself."

Improbably, the Silsbee horse-killing case became one of the most talked-about crime stories of 1995. Readers of the *New York Times,* the *Washington Post,* and newspapers in England and Australia were alerted to the macabre drama; *Time* magazine sent a reporter and a photographer to Silsbee; and Ann Landers waxed indignant in her column. In an age that finds us immunized from any horror we may inflict upon each other, the eight Silsbee youths may have committed one of the last outrages left to commit.

Why they did so was a matter lost in the stampede to punish them. What clues there are suggest a conclusion at odds with the prevailing belief that the horse killing was simply the grisly handiwork of eight Jeffrey Dahmers in the making. The perpetrators shared three elements: their town, which was Silsbee; their attitude toward authority, which (with one notable exception) was disrespectful; and their skin color, which was black. The Hardin County authorities never revealed that last fact to the press, perhaps fearing that the disclosure would only further inflame the public's passions. Since then, however, two mothers whose four children have been sent to correctional facilities insist that the sentences were racially motivated. Few Silsbee residents want to believe that this is true, just as few wish to believe that the experience of being black in East Texas somehow set the stage for the children's violent outburst in Coach Woodard's pasture. Regardless, it is hard to deny that this peculiarly rural crime story harbors more than a few distinctly (and depressingly) urban elements. It is as if William Golding retold *The Lord of the Flies* using the characters from *Boyz N the Hood* and then set his hostile mob loose on Silsbee.

"When we heard about what happened to Charlie Woodard's horse, I said, 'I'll bet I can tell you exactly who did it,'" a faculty member of Silsbee

Middle School tells me. "Sure enough, I was right. They were the worst kids we had."

Then she catches herself and says, "I take that back. Oliver was a big surprise. That one blew us all away."

Oliver (whose name, as with the rest of the juveniles in this story, has been changed) grew up in Silsbee, a quiet East Texas town of lumber mills and churches less than twenty miles north of Beaumont. He grew up on the predominantly black west side, an area abutting the railroad tracks that no one would confuse with suburbia. Of the eight juveniles accused of killing Coach Woodard's horse, none had it worse than Oliver. His mother had died in childbirth, and his father was addicted to crack. Oliver lived with his father and three siblings in a house that seems to be standing only as a monument to decay. Its roof is tattered, its front door is pocked with holes, and the walls appear to be on the verge of collapse. When Oliver's father was sent to county jail on a drug possession charge a few years ago, the children moved in with their maternal grandmother a couple of miles away, in a one-room rural shack that appeared to lack running water, judging by the condition of the house and the smell of urine that accompanied the children to school.

If any of the accused had a right to hate the world, it was Oliver, who wore soiled clothes and shoes that seemed to be rotting off of his feet and was teased even by the other black kids for being poor and malodorous. Yet Oliver won the hearts of the Silsbee teachers. He was shy and unfailingly polite—"You could tell he was raised by his grandma," one of them says—and though he seldom had adequate school supplies, he was, as one teacher puts it, "a wonderful student. Half the time he never had socks, much less pencils and paper, but he still made A's and B's." To avoid being teased by the others in the bus line, Oliver and his younger brother would sit in an art teacher's classroom after school and draw pictures until the bus arrived.

One day in December, when Oliver's father was in jail, a teacher asked Oliver what he hoped to get for Christmas. "Well," the boy said with a rueful grin, "I'd like to get a bicycle. But I don't think Santa will be bringing me anything." The teacher was touched and contacted other faculty members. Pooling their money, the Silsbee faculty bought bicycles, underwear, and socks for Oliver and each of his three siblings.

Oliver did nothing to make the teachers regret their charity. But by the spring of 1995, it was becoming clear that the fourteen-year-old boy was having trouble keeping up with his schoolwork. Perhaps there was turmoil at home with the return of Oliver's father; perhaps the relentless teasing, combined with the onset of adolescent hormones, had gotten the better of him. In any event, the Silsbee Middle School authorities believed they had no choice but to flunk Oliver and have him repeat the eighth grade. Thus stigmatized, Oliver returned to school in August 1995 and found himself in the company of new classmates—including Mason, Willie, and Sam, who along with Sam's younger brother Doyle and Willie's younger sister Charisse were the faculty's consensus choice as some of the worst troublemakers at Silsbee Middle School.

The five had much in common. Like Oliver, they lacked reliable father figures, and their mothers worked for low wages—though each child was far better off than Oliver. All five of them had been given after-school tutoring; all five, wrote one administrator to the Hardin County authorities, "were hand-scheduled to make sure they had the teachers who we felt could give them the opportunities they needed." Yet they were often disruptive in class, given to defying teachers' orders, and consistently involved in hallway skirmishes with classmates. They bullied, stole change from other kids. Four of them had been placed on probation in the spring of 1995 for breaking into the school on one or two occasions, vandalizing the classrooms, and stealing money out of the vending machines.

Sam, the only one who didn't participate in the burglaries, was a college scholarship–quality football player and the smartest of the group—"But also the meanest," says one of the teachers. He was heard to address one black lawman with "Hey, boy" and once lunged at a teacher and had to be restrained in a headlock by the principal. Though county authorities couldn't prove it, they believed that Sam had been involved in a drive-by shooting in 1994 and a related aggravated assault the following year—"The two most violent juvenile crimes we'd had till the horse incident," says one official. Sam was more astute at covering his tracks than his twelve-year-old brother, Doyle, who in addition to the burglary had twice been shipped off to the authorities for disorderly conduct at school. Mason, a frequent runaway whose mother had long ago told probation officers, "I can't control him, and I wish you'd send him somewhere," was perhaps the most openly rebellious of the lot, while Willie saw more sport in bullying his smaller classmates. Willie and his twelve-year-old sister Charisse were inseparable, and the latter was every bit as hard-edged as the former.

Charisse took her schoolwork more seriously than the rest until her wayward attention span or hot temper would inevitably do her in. "They were all scared of her—white kids, black kids, even the teachers," says one faculty member.

The company that Oliver fell into was, by all accounts, unsupervised—"a pack of kids running around like a pack of dogs," as one local law enforcement official puts it. They roamed the streets of Silsbee day and night. School sports would have been available to them had they not been thrown off the teams or kept from trying out because "their stubborn behavior and poor attitude made them impossible to work with," according to one coach. When disciplined, several of them would claim that they were being singled out because of the color of their skin. In fact, most of the Silsbee teachers were white; then again, about 30 percent of the students were black and seemed to get along fine with the faculty. It dismayed faculty members to hear children so readily playing the race card.

Then again, a few of the veteran teachers had an insight into the matter. After all, they had taught the children's mothers too.

"It was a racist thing, that's what it was," Joyce says as she disperses her cigarette smoke and stares furiously at the ground. "They've done 'em so wrong. Shackled down and all. Locked up like animals. The good Lord ain't sleepin', I'll tell you that."

"They come from good homes," chimes in Darlene, her voice louder but less bitter than Joyce's. "Good homes! Sometimes I pull double shifts trying to make

ends meet. I don't have no record. They try to make it
sound like they was runnin' wild."

"Like we was drug addicts," spits out Joyce. "Street
women. You can't watch any child seven and twenty-
four. It ain't like that. I felt like telling 'em, 'Okay, just
take *me* to jail, 'cause I was wrong. I wasn't paying
more attention.' But we was working. Every last one of
us was working. Working hard."

There is a pridefulness about the woman that must
be terrifying to some, including the waitress at the local
Golden Corral who tiptoes up and asks if Joyce would
like her glass refilled, a question Joyce sullenly an-
swers in the affirmative only after it is asked three
times. Her attractiveness is the hard kind, while Darlene is rounder and more genial. In the restaurant,
everyone is staring at us. The two women are conspicuous in every way, and they are not apologizing, not for
anything. Darlene and Joyce work together at a retirement home. They have known each other since childhood, during which time they cultivated fearsome
reputations. ("Darlene would meet you at the candy
machine, and if you didn't give her your change, she'd
whup you," remembers one former classmate. "And
Joyce was just as mean as a snake.") Though they have
little good to say in return about their birthplace—
"Hardin County: Hard on Blacks" is their summa-
tion—they have remained in Silsbee, as if daring the
city to make the first move. In the meantime, they have
raised their children to wear chips on their shoulders as
they have, to grow up in a posture of resentment, and
to obey a singular commandment: "Thou shalt not respect any white authority figure." Today, each woman
has two children in state correctional facilities, all four

having been punished for their role in the killing of Coach Woodard's horse.

"When they sent Sam off, they made him get down on his knees and they shackled him," Joyce remembers in her low, venomous voice.

"And my Charisse—when I go visit her in that reform school, they bring her out in shackles," moans Darlene. "They got her in a place where they don't let her see sunlight or nothin'. And if they get bad, they get strapped down to a chair. I told her, 'Girl, behave, you do what you have to do. But don't you let them strap you down to no chair.'"

"Jesus ain't sleepin'," murmurs Joyce.

"Now, my boy Willie owned up to what he did," Darlene says. "He said that he hit that horse one or two times."

"They were chunking sticks at it," nods Joyce. "But the horse was still alive when they left. Those children did *not* beat that horse to death."

One of the more embarrassing elements of the mothers' shared sense of victimization is that they promote this classic child's lie—namely, that a *second* group of children actually arrived on the scene and killed the horse after their own children had vacated the premises. Repeatedly the two women undercut their own credibility: criticizing the media for sensationalizing the horse-killing case and then asking me if I intend to pay for this interview; extolling their sense of parental responsibility and then falsely claiming that they are meeting the court-ordered restitution payments for the horse's death; and generally refusing to acknowledge that their children are somewhat less than angelic.

All the same, there is something inherently sympathetic about their predicament. It has been all too easy to criticize the mothers, all too easy to forget the fathers who long ago abandoned the household. No thanks to the fathers, the women are not welfare mothers; they do not have arrest records. There is little doubt that they truly believe they are doing the best job possible of raising their children. In fact, Joyce offers me a challenge: "You come to our houses, and you tell me if we live like street trash." And after we hop into the car and drive to her apartment, I find that she is right: It is neat and modestly fashionable—and Darlene's house, though forbidding in appearance from the outside, is warmly cluttered with pictures of her two incarcerated children.

The public response to their children's crime has staggered the two mothers. Men and women they grew up with have written to the *Silsbee Bee,* suggested that the children be neutered or beaten to death. People they have never met, from all over the world, have labeled their children monsters. After Joyce, in the heat of indignation upon her children's arrest, made the unfortunate remark to a reporter that "if they're gonna make me pay restitution for that horse, I better get some of that meat in my freezer," one student told her that a schoolteacher had remarked to her class, "They ought to give her the meat with maggots in it." A schoolteacher! "People get shot every day," Darlene says with a sigh. "A baby got killed around here recently, and the next day everyone forgets about it. But every day we hear it: *horse killing, horse killing.*" It wasn't teenage white kids in nearby Lumberton selling crack on schoolyards, it wasn't a drive-by-shooting in Kountze—it wasn't those less-publicized crimes, it was an animal, only an animal, and after all, it was still alive when their children left . . .

And besides, there is the pool. Among whites and blacks alike, it is acknowledged that the Silsbee Swim Club, located on the northeast edge of town, continues to discourage black children from using the only "public" pool in town. Compared with most small East Texas towns, Silsbee has always struck me as a harmonious and inviting place; no one could put it in the same league as its Klan-friendly neighbor, Vidor. But it is easy to see how blacks in Silsbee have viewed the pool as an ugly reminder that there will always be two distinct classes, one with privileges withheld from the other.

"I'm gonna show you where *our* children swim," Joyce says as we drive. She directs me toward a battered old mulecart dirt road that zigzags its way until it dead-ends in the middle of a pine thicket. Directly below us is a fast-moving, malt-colored slough. It is of indeterminable depth, and one can only imagine what lurks beneath the surface. We glumly stare at the creek in silence for a while. Then Joyce says, "A little girl came and told us our children was swimming in here. We come over here and we yell at 'em. 'Y'all get out of that ol' nasty water right now!' "

"We whupped 'em right there on the spot," remembers Darlene.

A friend of the women who has accompanied us begins to shiver. "They never should've been out here," she murmurs.

"That's right," Joyce says. "They never should've. But they got nowhere else to go."

Apparently it all began with the children swimming in Coach Woodard's stock tank. They had discovered the tank while following a trail that led from the projects into the Piney Woods. After a mile or so, the trail emptied out to a pasture surrounded by barbed wire. A mile and a fence were nothing for bored kids looking to stay cool on summer afternoons. There was too much heat, and too much time to kill—beginning in May, when Willie, Charisse, Doyle, and Mason were all suspended through the end of the semester following the second burglary of Silsbee Middle School.

Now it was a new semester, though it was starting pretty much as the last one had ended. On Wednesday, September 13, Doyle was hauled into the principal's office. Someone had spray-painted the word "Doyle" on the kindergarten walls. There was only one Doyle in the school system. "Why did you do it?" an administrator asked him.

He shrugged. "I thought it would be fun," he said. Then he added, "I just didn't have nothing to do."

It had been that kind of day, and not just for Doyle. His big brother Sam, along with the chronic runaway Mason, had been disruptive in school and were now spending their daytime hours in detention cubicles at the Student Alternative Center, adjacent to the high school. Getting lectured at, hunched in a little space all day long like a dog at a kennel—on days like this one, they had to get out. They had to hit the trail.

When they got to the pasture, two cows and a calf were standing by the tank. Suddenly no one was thinking about swimming. They advanced on the cattle. The dumb animals skittered away. The kids began to chase them, around and around the pasture, laughing at the cattle, throwing sticks at them. In a panic, the cattle rammed through a rickety wooden gate and fled to another area of the property. The kids agreed that the whole episode was rather thrilling. They resolved to come back the next day.

Eight of them did. Accompanying Willie, Charisse, Sam, Doyle, Mason, and their new classmate Oliver were two brothers, Tory and Horace, who were eight and nine respectively but already well on their way to establishing themselves as classroom scourges. A ninth boy, Maurice, had chased the cattle with them the previous day but was grounded by his parents that day after his progress report arrived in the mail. He would miss out on the fun.

Along the trail they happened upon two other boys, who were walking their dogs. "We're going to the pasture to chase some cattle around," someone explained. Why not, said the two boys. And so a throng consisting of nine boys, one girl, and two dogs followed the trail, crawled under the barbed wire, and roamed around the pasture, searching for the cattle until they saw, instead, the horse.

It stood alone, grazing in the meadow, about 150 yards away from the barn where it spent its nights. Only an hour or so earlier, at five in the afternoon, Coach Woodard had paid it his daily after-school visit. Now it stared at ten young strangers. They were not here to feed it, or to ride it. Still, they were coming its way. Mister Wilson Boy began to run.

They gave chase. The horse galloped around the pasture several times with Willie, Sam, Doyle, Mason, Oliver, Tory, and Horace on its heels. The meadow was littered with oak limbs ranging from one to two feet long and one to two inches wide. The boys began to pick up the sticks and hurl them at the horse. Tory, the eight-year-old, found a glass bottle and flung it, but the horse was too fast. The others, however, were hitting their mark. Charisse tossed one stick, missed, and then began scrambling around the meadow, gathering sticks for the boys.

Suddenly they had the horse backed up against the fence. The boys closed in. The horse tried to pivot away, and one of its hind legs became entangled in the barbed wire. Sam, Doyle, Willie, Mason, and the nine-year-old boy, Horace, began to flail away at the horse, hitting it repeatedly in the backside, ribs, belly, and neck. Then, from shock or a well-aimed throw, the animal fell hard to the ground.

The boys descended upon it and went to work on its head while the horse lay defenseless. The two boys with the dogs had seen enough. They retreated to the woods as the others jeered at them.

When the horse was no longer moving, one of the boys took a stick and rammed it hard up the animal's nostril. Their blood-stained weapons were strewn around the horse. The children looked around. It was still daylight. To round off the afternoon, they broke into Coach Woodard's toolshed, stole a few ropes, a machete, and a few cans of spray paint, threw a Weed Eater into the stock tank, and started the tractor engine—which was still running at seven o'clock Friday morning, when Coach Woodard visited the pasture to pay his ritual morning visit to Mister Wilson Boy.

On Monday, September 18, one of the two boys who had retreated from the pasture showed up at school crying. He wouldn't say why he was upset. But across town, in the Student Alternative Center, Mason put the finishing touches on a sketch he had been making of a demon figure, scrawled "Lord of Pain" above it, and then leaned over to the boy in the adjacent detention cubicle. "Me and Sam and Doyle was the ones that killed the horse," he whispered.

The horse killing had been the talk of Silsbee all weekend long, but the perpetrators were thought to be gang members from Kountze or perhaps some satanic cult—until Mason opened his mouth. The listener told what he had heard to Hardin County deputy sheriff Thomas Tyler, a hefty and amiable black man who had lived in west Silsbee his entire life. Tyler plucked Doyle from class that morning. The twelve-year-old boy gave the deputy the names of all the children who had been out at the pasture.

That Monday evening, the mothers of the perpetrators took their children to Tyler's house and conferred in the deputy's garage. He knew all of them—was kin; in fact, to more than one. The mothers were upset, the children less so as they recounted the episode. They didn't know it was Coach Woodard's farm. They hadn't tried to kill the horse. They were just playing around, and one thing led to another. The horse, they insisted, still looked alive when they last saw it.

The parents offered to pool what money they had to give Coach Woodard. Several pledged to give their kids a whipping. When they had run out of things to say, the deputy weighed the situation. "Well," he said, "I'll do all I can to help. We've got to bring 'em all in to the juvenile office tomorrow—there's no way around that.

At the very least, I'll try to see to it that they don't punish the girl since she didn't hit the horse."

On Tuesday morning, the ten children who had been out at the pasture were taken by their mothers to the Hardin County courthouse. With their mothers present, deputy sheriff Darrell Werner questioned the children individually. By Werner's questions, the ten suspects could apparently tell that the crimes, in increasing order of severity, seemed to be: chasing the horse, throwing things at the horse, hitting the horse while it was standing, hitting the horse while it was on the ground, and, worst of all, causing the horse to fall to the ground. Several of the children adjusted their stories accordingly. When asked, "Who knocked the horse to the ground?" four of them replied, "Oliver."

Deputy Werner also wanted to know who the leader of the mob was. Several of them said, "Oliver."

Oliver told Werner that none of this was true. All he did, according to his written confession, "was just chase the horse. I did not hit the horse or take anything from the property." Werner didn't believe him. Too many of the others had fingered him as the ringleader.

While each suspect was being questioned, the other children sat outside in the courthouse hallway with their parents. One building employee stepped out of her office and saw two children on their knees in front of a vending machine, reaching up into its guts, and pulling out bars of candy, the mothers sitting obliviously nearby.

The children were released to their parents. But angry callers had already begun telephoning the courthouse. At the same time, Silsbee faculty members and administrators confronted the Hardin County authorities. Why were these brutes being allowed to go back to school, and back to the streets of Silsbee? What kind of message did this send to the other students? Kill a horse, and see you at school tomorrow!

Less than 24 hours after their release, state district judge Bill Beggs ordered Willie, Charisse, Sam, Doyle, Mason, and Oliver held without bail until the conclusion of their hearings (the eight- and nine-year-old boys were too young to be removed from their parents, and the two boys with the dogs were exonerated). Beggs would later explain, "I considered a number of factors, including the safety of the community and the safety of the children involved." But Beggs, who had been appointed to fill the vacated 88th District post, was doubtlessly considering politics too. An unelected Republican judge who ignored the outcries of angry white community leaders and let black hoodlums roam the streets of Silsbee would feel the voters' wrath in the 1996 election.

And so the horse killers were again rounded up, driven away from school in marked vehicles, and imprisoned on the third floor of the Hardin County courthouse, in the cramped juvenile detention center. Extra mattresses were dragged in and tossed on the floor of the three-bedroom cell to accommodate the overflow—which was eased somewhat when Oliver and Mason were caught brawling in the cell and were subsequently shipped off to a juvenile center in Conroe.

The severity of their predicament took a while to sink in. Three or four days into their detention, the children were carrying on so loudly that a probation officer was moved to strip the center of all of its televisions, games, and furniture. The atmosphere became less fes-

tive after that, but it still did not exactly resemble a
prayer-group meeting. Juvenile probation officer Ed
Dickens, who had seen more than his share of miscre-
ants during his five years of service at the Hardin
County office, became disgusted with the seeming non-
chalance of the horse killers. "Don't any of you have
so much as an ounce of remorse for what you did?" he
demanded during a visit. Not one of them volunteered
a show of contrition. Later, however, they penned notes
of apology to Coach Woodard. Through visitors, they
learned what was being said about them outside the
courthouse. They began to ask Dickens questions
about what reform school was like.

On October 5, after two weeks in custody, Willie and
Mason were brought before Judge Beggs. Both of the
fourteen-year-old boys were already on probation for
breaking into Silsbee Middle School, which qualified
them for a minimum three-year sentence at a Texas
Youth Commission (TYC) correctional facility for juveniles. But because the TYC accepts only so many
juveniles from each county, Beggs gave Willie a lighter
sentence: six months at a private boot camp facility in
Cotulla. With a rap of the gavel, two men in fatigues
stepped forward and fitted the boy with shackles.

Mason, whose record included several runaway incidents as well as a citation for "making terrorist threats"
and whose confession of the horse killing seemed far
less believable than the others', was sent off to a TYC
facility along with Doyle. Doyle's big brother Sam was
sentenced to the Cotulla boot camp. Despite his repeated denial of wrongdoing, Oliver was sentenced to
Cotulla as well.

On October 13, Charisse stood before Judge Beggs

in the quiet courtroom, while just outside, a throng of TV cameramen and reporters angled for position. The twelve-year-old girl had not been implicated by the others in the actual beating of the horse. On the other hand, no boot camp facilities existed for girls, and Beggs did not wish to consider a lighter alternative, such as a wilderness camp. The judge ordered her to be sent to a TYC correctional institution two hundred miles away. For the first time since the horse killing a month earlier, Charisse broke down into loud, almost terrifying sobs.

Before the children were led away, investigating deputy Darrell Werner made a point of shaking each one's hand. "Best of luck to you," he told them.

They will need plenty of it. All six will return home this year, as the TYC needs the bed space for incoming juveniles and Hardin County cannot afford more than five months' worth of the $237 daily fee charged by the Cotulla boot camp to house Willie, Sam, and Oliver. They will return to a world that considers them sick and twisted, and to a community that deeply resents the negative attention that the juveniles have drawn to Silsbee. It is an open question whether the six children will have learned anything—or, for that matter, whether learning anything will do them any good. For although the boot camps in particular are designed to teach respect for authority and to rehabilitate self-esteem, the lessons do not wear well in the precarious environment that helped spawn the crime to begin with. "It's hard to come home and say no to your peers," says Ed Dickens, the probation officer for the six. "And if the parent doesn't grasp the seriousness of the matter, how can we expect the kid to?"

He manages a rueful smile from behind his desk at the county juvenile probation office and adds, "No, if experience holds true, we'll see them back here again."

But for what it is worth, the six are doing well— particularly Oliver, who is a squad leader at the Cotulla boot camp and has been chosen to march with the honor guard at a Texas A&M function. We can hope that the children will somehow beat the odds and somehow give this story a happy ending. For now, the following will have to do:

Throughout the shrill ordeal, Coach Woodard maintained a low profile. Unlike the Silsbee school officials, he made a point of not attending the trials or giving interviews. ("It's best for the community that I not say anything," he politely told me.) Letters of sympathy poured in from all over. Some of the envelopes contained checks to help buy the coach a replacement for Mister Wilson Boy, whose monetary value had been set by authorities at $10,000—though Woodard could easily have pressed for more, had he so chosen. The checks totaled somewhere in the neighborhood of $20,000; one check was written for $7,000. Coach Woodard sent each check back with a thank-you note. He wasn't looking for charity—even though only one of the four families had made any of the $49.41-per-child monthly restitution payments. Besides, things had a way of working out. A friend named Jane Hill phoned the coach one day and said she had a four-year-old gelding that wasn't getting much attention. How about if the coach kept the horse out at his pasture?

Coach Woodard looked embarrassed, but a little

eager as well. "Well, Jane," he stammered, "how long do you want me to keep him?"

"Just as long as you want," she assured him.

A more troubling question came to mind. "But what if something were to happen to him out at my place?" he asked.

Take the horse, she urged him. And he did. The coach called the horse Jane, after its original owner. It was a sorrel with a blaze face.

(March 1996)

All the children involved in the killing of Mister Wilson Boy returned to Silsbee within the year, except one, who had to stay in custody longer due to disciplinary problems. According to Hardin County prosecutor David Sheffield, about half have been in trouble with the law since their release. One was even involved in an armed robbery but testified as a witness for the prosecution in January 1998. "The others have made an attempt to stay on the right track," Sheffield says. "This crime was a real awakening for them."

The Killer Cadets

SKIP HOLLANDSWORTH

They probably first saw each other at a cross-country meet in the early autumn of 1995—two high school girls from neighboring small towns, competing in the two-mile run. There is no evidence that they said hello. Nor did they shake hands, as athletes sometimes do before the start of a race. Why should they have? It is doubtful the two girls even knew one another's names. Adrianne Jones was a clear-complexioned, sun-kissed blonde, the kind of girl one boy described as "not just good looking, but I mean, *good lookin'*." Diane Zamora, thinner and not as tall, was mesmerizing in a different way—her hair a dark circle around her face, her eyes dark as well, her eyebrows like slim shadows against her skin. "When she looked at you," another boy would later say, "it was hard for you to stop staring back."

There was no reason for the two to imagine that they had anything in common beyond cross-country. They were just pretty young teenagers in the full bloom of youth. What Adrianne and Diane did not know about each other, however, was that they were both drawn to the same boy—a lean, muscular high school senior named David Graham, who was described as "the perfect guy" by one classmate and "a brilliant student" by another. David was the kind of young man any parent would admire. He made straight A's. He said "yes, sir" and "yes, ma'am" when talking to adults. "His life was so unblemished," said one woman who knew him, "that he didn't so much as throw a spitwad in school."

At the time, David had chosen to be with Diane, who was called "the disciplined one" of the family by her mother because she would start studying for school before six o'clock each weekday morning. But David could not deny that there was something intriguing, and somewhat seductive, about Adrianne, who was called "bubble butt" by her mother because her bottom moved in sexy little circles when she walked. He found himself spending more time with her, talking to her, staring at her hazel eyes.

The two girls lined up for the cross-country race, waiting for the starter's gun. It would not be long before they would meet again.

I thought long and hard about how to carry out the crime. I was stupid, but I was in love.

—From the killer's confession

In the early morning hours of December 4, 1995, a farmer driving along a desolate country road saw the body of a teenage girl on the ground behind a barbed-wire fence. At first, he thought he was looking at road kill. The girl's face was nearly unrecognizable. One bullet hole was in her left cheek, another in her forehead. She had been hit so hard on the left side of her head that the part of the skull above her ear was caved in like a pumpkin. She was wearing flannel shorts and a gray T-shirt that read, "UIL Region I Cross Country Regionals 1995." Within hours, police officers identified her as Adrianne Jones, a sixteen-year-old high school sophomore from the town of Mansfield, southeast of Fort Worth.

A former farming community built around a grain elevator, home to an old indoor rodeo arena and some cheery antique stores along Main Street, Mansfield was one of the last places in the Dallas–Fort Worth corridor that still felt like a small town. In 1984, looking for a safe place to raise his family, Bill Jones moved his wife, Linda, and his three children—Adrianne and two younger brothers—to Mansfield from the Dallas area. He found a modest neighborhood where the homes were clustered together, the yards were like little green squares, and the echoey sound of children at play drifted down the streets. Jones, who made his living repairing heavy construction equipment, was a no-nonsense, bearded man who kept his heavy brown work boots on when he arrived home at the end of the day, wearing them even when he sat in his easy chair. He also was determined to keep a tight rein on his children—especially Adrianne, who was known as A.J. "I truly felt that if we had some rules that kept her away from teenage temptations," Jones said, "we'd be okay." It was only that autumn that he had allowed Adrianne to stay out past nine o'clock on weekends. If she told him she was going to a movie or to Six Flags Over Texas in nearby Arlington with friends, he would often make her produce a ticket stub when she came home to prove where she had been. He had nailed her bedroom windows shut so she couldn't sneak out of the house at night.

It could hardly be said that Adrianne was a rebel. She took advanced honors courses, studied at least two hours a night, and was a good athlete. After she hurt her knee playing for the girls soccer team, she decided to join the girls' cross-country team to get in better shape, and she became so good in the two-mile run that she helped the team qualify for the November regional meet in Lubbock. "Her school spirit was just so awesome," said Carla Hays, an editor for the school newspaper, the *Mansfield Uproar,* bestowing upon Adrianne one of the greatest compliments a high school girl could receive. "I could see her becoming a cheerleader someday." She also managed to work twenty hours a week at Golden Fried Chicken, a local fast-food restaurant. "She was my superstar employee," said the restaurant's manager, Tina Dollar. "I made her the cashier at the drive-through window because she knew how to put a smile on everyone's face. She wore a hat with a smiley face drawn on the visor, and after taking an order, she'd say funny things to the customers like, 'Okay, drive forward to the ninety-ninth window to get your food!' "

Adrianne thrived on attention, especially when it came from the teenage boys around town. One of Adrianne's closest friends, Tracy Bumpass, called her "a big flirt." Linda Jones, a chatty blonde who worked during the day as a massage therapist in a Mansfield hair salon, said her daughter would spend two hours putting on makeup just to make it look like she wasn't wearing any: "When I asked her why she went to such trouble to put her makeup on before she went out of the house, she said, 'Mom, you never know who you might meet.' "

And there were plenty of high school guys who wanted to meet her. They'd slowly cruise by the Joneses' house. A few of the courageous ones would pull into the driveway to talk to Adrianne, who would be waiting for them in the front yard, casting quick glances toward the front door to see if her father was watching them. "I'm sure lots of guys really liked Adrianne," said Sydney Jones, a friend and former soccer teammate. "She was the kind of girl who would say hi to you in the hallway at school even if you didn't know her."

It was precisely Adrianne's popularity that was going to make the investigation into her murder so difficult. (Because Adrianne's body had been found in the outskirts of the Dallas suburb Grand Prairie, detectives from that city's police department—Dennis Clay and Dennis Meyer—and their boss, deputy police chief Brad Geary, were put in charge of the case.) Adults who are murdered rarely have more than a couple of dozen people close to them. But a high school student crosses paths with hundreds of other students every day. And it quickly became clear to the detectives that Adrianne knew her killer, or killers. There was no sign at the crime scene that she had struggled. There were no marks that her hands or legs had been restrained. Nor was there any indication that someone had broken into her house or had gone through her window to abduct her. Furthermore, an autopsy found no evidence that Adrianne had been sexually assaulted, which meant that this was not the act of a rapist. Adrianne's death, the cops realized, was more like an execution, the result of some colossal fury. As one investigator would later say, "It takes a cold-blooded person to shoot a pretty young girl in the face from two to four feet away. That girl was mangled, and it was sickening to look at."

Never did I imagine the heartache it would cause my school, my friends, Adrianne's family, or even my community.

It was a story that would eventually send shock waves across the entire country: a terrifying, macabre tale that would have people everywhere asking what had happened to the best and brightest of America's youth. At the start, however, Adrianne Jones's murder was just another killing in a small town. Because so much local media attention was then focused on the kidnapping and brutal murder of a little girl named Amber Hagerman in Arlington, Adrianne's death barely made the front pages of the Dallas and Fort Worth newspapers. In a society long accustomed to drive-by shootings and metal detectors at school entrances, dead teenagers didn't warrant the press that they once did.

But within Mansfield itself, the news had residents reeling. High school administrators set up special rooms for students to meet with counselors. A tree was planted in memory of Adrianne next to the junior varsity soccer field, and more than 150 of her classmates joined hands around the tree and shouted, "Unity! Strength! Courage!" Some residents wore ribbons in her memory, and a small cross made from two branches wrapped with red electrical wire was placed where her body had been discovered. After the family held a private funeral for Adrianne at the Methodist church, Linda Jones agreed to allow the cross-country and soccer teams to come to the church for a second memorial service. On the altar was a glamorous color photo of Adrianne, taken a few weeks earlier, that Linda had planned to give her for Christmas. "Try to remember the good things about Adrianne," she said in a spontaneous eulogy, trying to bolster the spirits of the students. "Do you remember the way she walked with that bubble butt of hers?"

Nearly crazed with grief, Linda consulted psychics to try to find out what had happened to Adrianne. She made sure to wear some item of her daughter's almost every day—either a piece of clothing or her shoes or her makeup. At night, she and Bill left the light on in Adrianne's bedroom, as if hoping their daughter would find her way back home. Kids drove past the house, staring through the open curtains, able to see Adrianne's vanity, where she had put on her makeup, her stereo, and her bookcase, which still held a couple of her Stephen King novels.

Among the nearly 2,500 students at Mansfield High, it didn't take long for the rumors to start flying. "A lot of us had this weird feeling that the killer was walking the halls with us," said April Grossman, a friend of Adrianne's who also ran cross-country and played on the soccer team. "Those of us who were really close to Adrianne were scared because we thought she might have been killed because of something she knew. And we thought, 'Well, will the killer come after us thinking that Adrianne had told us the secret?' "

Some kids said they had heard that Adrianne used to slip out of the house to attend all-night "rave" parties as far away as Denton (an hour's drive north of Mansfield). Maybe, they whispered, someone she met at a rave had wanted to kill her. Others said they had heard that she knew drug dealers. There was so much gossip about the boys Adrianne had been with that Linda went so far as to tell one reporter that her daughter was no "sleep-around." There was even a preposterous story that a close girlfriend of Adrianne's had wanted to kill her because Adrianne had told that girl's mother about her getting drunk at a party. "About the only thing we didn't hear," Bill said, "was that Adrianne had been abducted by aliens."

Still, for the investigators in the case—who had come to include the Mansfield police, a Texas Ranger, and extra Grand Prairie detectives—Adrianne's murder had all the makings of a high school whodunit. Although the Texas Education Agency had named Mansfield High a mentor school (a distinction given only to the best high schools in the state), the teenagers there were like teenagers anywhere, their lives often driven by insecurities, inchoate yearnings, and a provincial restlessness. Wavering in that territory that lies between childhood and adulthood, the students tried on and discarded different selves as quickly as they went through blue jeans, always searching for the perfect fit. It was here that they confronted raw new emotions, like their own budding sexuality, and here that they first attempted to make their way through such moral dilemmas as whether to "do it" or not.

Sitting outside the high school in their unmarked cars, watching students troop in and out, the detectives prepared themselves to enter the humid realm of adolescence. They talked to school officials about the students who had a knack for minor trouble. They asked other kids if they knew anyone who was jealous of or angry at Adrianne. Within days, they had compiled a long list of kids they wanted to talk to.

Bill and Linda Jones had told the police that on the night of Adrianne's death, they had reluctantly allowed her to talk on the phone past her usual ten o'clock cut-off time. Her new boyfriend, Tracy Smith, had been out of town that weekend with his parents, and he didn't call until ten-thirty. Bill and Linda didn't know Tracy that well. He was a large kid who was built like a lineman on a college football team, and he went to high school in the nearby town of Venus. Apparently, he and Adrianne had met just a couple of months earlier at the Golden Fried Chicken. Bill told Adrianne she could talk to Tracy but only for a few minutes.

During that call, Linda heard her daughter say, "Hold on, there's someone on the other line." Adrianne punched the call-waiting button and spoke quietly for a minute, then clicked back over and finished her conversation with Tracy.

"Who was that who called in?" Linda later asked.

According to Linda, Adrianne replied, "Oh, that was David from cross-country, and he's upset about something."

After talking with Tracy, Adrianne went to her room. At ten forty-five, Linda Jones saw that Adrianne was still awake, ironing her pants for school the next day. She seemed "sort of antsy," Linda said. Linda told her to turn off the lights and go to bed.

Sometime after midnight, one of Adrianne's younger brothers heard the constrained rumble of a slow-moving engine outside the house. When he looked out the window, he saw what he thought was a pickup truck driving away.

The next morning, Adrianne was nowhere to be found, and Linda and Bill thought she might have risen early to go running. But when they discovered her running shoes in her bedroom, they got anxious. Linda called Lee Ann Burke, the cross-country coach at Mansfield High, and asked, "Who is someone named David on the cross-country team?"

"Well, there's David Graham," Burke replied.

"Adrianne's missing," Linda said, "and I think he called her last night."

Burke was baffled. She didn't even know David and Adrianne were friends. David, a senior, was a decent cross-country athlete, but he was best known around the school for his position as battalion commander of the school's Junior ROTC program. Burke sent April Grossman to David's second-period math class to ask him if he had called Adrianne the previous night. David stared at April as if she were not making sense. "Did I talk to Adrianne? No. Why would I?"

As their investigation began, the detectives did conduct a perfunctory interview with David Graham, but they were so certain he was not involved that they didn't even try to give him a polygraph test. For one thing, David's name was not among the thirty or so listed in Adrianne's personal phone book. Nor did the detectives hear his name mentioned by any of Adrianne's friends when they asked who might have had a close relationship with her. In fact, Tracy Bumpass said that Adrianne told her all of her "deepest, darkest secrets," but not once did she ever talk about David.

Besides, David had supposedly been seen with tears

in his eyes at the memorial service, seemingly stunned like everyone else that Adrianne was gone. Few students considered themselves good friends with David—"We all knew him, but we really didn't know him, you know?" said Kenny Grant, whose locker was next to David's throughout high school—and he certainly was not part of the school's most popular crowd. Still, he intrigued other kids. With his military burr haircut and ramrod posture, he seemed to be a throwback to a different era. The youngest of four children, David lived with his father, Jerry Graham, a retired Mansfield elementary school principal. He was divorced from David's mother, Janice, a former teacher who lived in Houston. At the age of seven, after seeing his first air show, David told his father he wanted to become an Air Force pilot, and he never wavered from his dream. Although ROTC students at Mansfield High were usually the subjects of jokes—"We thought of all of them in their green uniforms as sort of geeky," one girl said—it was clear that David was going places. He was a National Merit commended student (just below the rank of National Merit semifinalist), and Congressman Martin Frost had agreed to support his application to enroll the next fall in the U.S. Air Force Academy in Colorado Springs. "Some of the more sarcastic guys in school would address him as Colonel Graham," said Jennifer Skinner, who sat near David in a government class his senior year. "But you could tell they sort of said it out of respect." Added another classmate, David Brennan, "He could fall asleep during class and then wake up and still answer the teacher's questions."

David Graham might have seemed tailor-made for the military—when he and others in the ROTC squad-ron presented the colors before the football games, he stood so perfectly still that people tended to watch him instead of the flag—but he never came across as one of those overly aggressive GI Joe types. He quit the football team after his freshman year because, it was said, he didn't have the necessary ferocity to make it in Texas high school football. What's more, girls liked him for his courtly manners. Angel Lockhardt, who was on the girls' cross-country team, said David gave her rides home a few times after cross-country practice, "and he always acted like a gentleman."

Plenty of girls would have dated David—"He was one of the last cool guys on earth," a girl who served with David in the Mansfield High ROTC would later tell a reporter—but what few of them knew was that he already had a girlfriend. Her name was Diane Zamora, and she was a high school senior in the nearby town of Crowley. She was just as smart as David, and she was equally determined to get into one of the U.S. military academies. She was a member of the student council, the Key Club, the National Honor Society, and the Masters of the Universe, a science organization. She played flute in the marching band, and like David, she ran on her high school's cross-country team. "When you looked at the two of them together," one of Diane's relatives said, "you just knew that a great future lay before them."

The plan was to (and this is not easy for me to confess) break her young neck and sink her to the bottom of the lake . . .

The first major suspect to emerge in Adrianne's murder was a Mansfield teenager, Tara (not her real name), who lived in a trailer park and already had something of a reputation around town. A year before, she thought her boyfriend had had a sexual encounter with one of Adrianne's closest girlfriends. According to police records, Tara attacked the girl with a baseball bat, hitting her over the head, breaking her cheekbone, and leaving her with a concussion. Tara also shot and wounded her boyfriend. A restraining order was filed against Tara to keep her out of school and away from the girl she had attacked. At the hearing, Adrianne testified for her friend. Tara, in turn, allegedly told Adrianne, "I'll get you for this." Some students were convinced Tara was the killer. She fit their picture of what a killer would be: a surly, aimless individual far removed from the mainstream of suburban teenage life who had already shown her willingness to use a gun and a bat.

But the police discovered that Tara had a solid alibi, and she passed a polygraph test. Although Bill and Linda told the police they were suspicious of Adrianne's boyfriend, Tracy Smith—Linda said he had never tried to contact the family after Adrianne's killing—he too passed a polygraph.

Tracy did, however, give the police another clue. He said that Adrianne had told him that it was someone named Bryan who had clicked through on the phone that night. She had never mentioned David. She had said that "Bryan" was depressed and wanted to meet her that night to talk.

The detectives then learned that a Mansfield teenager named Bryan McMillen worked at an Eckerd's near a Subway sandwich shop where Adrianne once worked. According to Adrianne's friends and family, Bryan had become infatuated with Adrianne and often dropped by the Subway to see her. "He began to bother her so much that when she saw him coming, she started ducking her head behind the counter," Linda Jones said.

The investigators' suspicions were heightened when they discovered that the seventeen-year-old Bryan took four kinds of medication to battle symptoms of clinical depression. They asked him to come to the police station for an interview. According to an affidavit, Bryan first said he didn't know an Adrianne Jones. Then he admitted that he did. A detective asked him if he had talked to Adrianne the night she was murdered. Bryan said he could have talked to her, but he didn't remember. He had been drinking that night for the first time in six months, he said, and had become intoxicated. When asked why he had been drinking, Bryan said he had gotten upset because all of his friends had found girlfriends, but he hadn't. He told detectives he felt like the "odd man out."

It wasn't hard for the police to put this scenario together: a lonely boy, unable to get the beautiful blonde from the high school to pay attention to him, devising a way to meet her late at night, then losing control. The detectives bored in, asking Bryan if he had gone to Adrianne's house that night. Bryan said he might have. He said it was also possible he could have taken her somewhere. He just didn't remember, he said.

A week later, in the pre-dawn hours of December 15, 1995, police officers armed with guns and a search warrant arrived at Bryan's house. He was arrested for murder, and his pickup truck was impounded. This time, the story made the front pages of the newspapers, but several of Bryan's friends defended him, saying that he was a gentle, slightly baffled kid who would never resort to violence. Bryan's father insisted that the night of the murder, Bryan came home and never left the house.

Finally, after Bryan had spent Christmas and New Year's Eve in jail, a lead prosecutor in the district attorney's office arranged for a polygraph. "He not only passed," the prosecutor said, "he passed with flying colors."

Bryan's release triggered more rumors, but no other suspects emerged. Because Adrianne's brother had said that he had seen a pickup truck, the police ran computer checks to find any student who owned one. It never occurred to anyone that the vehicle her brother had seen might not have been involved in the murder. Nor, apparently, did anyone guess that Adrianne had told Tracy about a "Bryan" to keep him from learning about her relationship with someone else. Only months later would Tina Dollar, the manager at the Golden Fried Chicken, remember that Adrianne had once pulled a small photo of a boy out of her wallet and showed it to her.

"His name is David," Adrianne had said.

. . . [Her] beautiful eyes have always played the strings of my heart effortlessly. I couldn't imagine life without her; not for a second did I want to lose her.

Davi Graham and Diane Zamora first met about four years before Adrianne Jones's murder, when their parents began dropping them off at a small airfield south of Fort Worth. They went there for weekly meetings of the Civil Air Patrol, an Air Force auxiliary organization that teaches the basics of the military life and leads search-and-rescue missions for downed aircraft. But there was no romance between them in their younger years. Despite her good looks, Diane was careful around guys. She did have a boyfriend during her sophomore year in high school, but the relationship was not particularly heated. When the two went out for dinner on Valentine's Day, Diane asked to be taken home at eight-thirty because she needed to study. "She kept telling us she wanted to focus on her studies and her goals instead of on guys," said her aunt Sylvia Gonzalez. "And she always made it a point to tell us she was never going to lose her virginity unless she got married. When two of her cousins got pregnant in high school, she said she couldn't believe how stupid they were. She swore that nothing like that would happen to her."

In the world of high school sexual skirmishing, Diane firmly put herself into the camp of "good girls." A girl who goes too far, she would often say to her family, gets called a slut. When she realized during her sophomore year that her boyfriend was bent on having sex with her, she dumped him.

Diane's father, Carlos, a kind, soft-spoken man, was an electrician; her mother, Gloria, was a registered nurse. The family was deeply religious. Gloria was the daughter of a minister who led a nondenominational Spanish-speaking church on the south side of Fort Worth. Gloria, her five sisters, and their families never missed Sunday services, and after church, the entire Zamora clan would gather for lunch at a cafeteria. Diane was the eldest of the Zamoras' four children, and the most driven. When she was nine years old, she announced to her family that she wanted to become an astronaut. She sent off for NASA brochures, and by high school she was keeping a spiral notebook containing a list of achievements she had to accomplish to get a college scholarship. She knew exactly what her grade point average and SAT scores needed to be. She carried a knapsack full of schoolbooks everywhere in case she got stranded and had some time to fill.

At Crowley High School, Diane was not one of the social girls who gathered between periods in the school's chalky-smelling hallways to swap gossip. While she was not considered unfriendly, she was known around school as someone who kept to herself. "She didn't have a whole lot to say," one student said. She preferred associating with the smart kids at school—"homework buddies," she called them—and she was determined to become an academic star. Late in her junior year, when she posed for her high school graduation picture, she asked that she be allowed to wear the special tassel for being in the top 10 percent of her senior class—even though she had no idea at that time whether she would achieve that honor. Diane said she wanted to have the photograph as a way to keep her motivated.

Diane did end up in the top 10 percent of her senior class. Gloria Zamora told her friends that the reason Diane worked so diligently was because she knew her parents could not afford to send her to a good college. When her father got laid off from work, Diane watched Gloria take on two nursing jobs a day and then sell Mary Kay cosmetics on the side to help pay the family's bills. At one point, the electricity was cut off in their small house for more than a week. Diane studied by candlelight. But even with her ambition, Diane was still a teenager, filled with the same impulses and longings as any other girl her age. While she kept Civil Air Patrol military fatigues in her closet, she also had a collection of teddy bears on her bed. She took an after-school job at Fast Forward, a store oriented to teenage girls, because she liked the discount she could get on hip clothes. She listened to both contemporary Christian music and popular groups like Pearl Jam. "Diane was a really sweet girl," said one former neighbor, Dale Rogers. "But I thought she was a little naive and sheltered from the outside world. She was really a virgin in life, you know? She hadn't really experienced anything. She didn't know all the things that could happen between people."

And then, in August 1995, just before the start of her senior year, her life changed. She told her parents that she had fallen for a boy: David Graham. He was just like her, she said breathlessly. It was not only that they had known as children what they wanted to do with their lives. They both loved calculus, physics, and government, and they talked on the phone late into the night about their homework. Their feelings, well known to any adolescent, were a mixture of adoration and total possessiveness. When they were together, they never stopped touching. Diane would put her arm around his waist, sliding one finger into a belt loop, and David would encircle her with his arms. "He always had both arms around her, like he was afraid she was going somewhere," said Diane's aunt Sylvia. "The two of them looked like they were wrapped up in one another."

It was not difficult for David and Diane to be swept away by the romantic grandeur of their relationship. By then, they were the stars of the Civil Air Patrol—David was a cadet-colonel in the CAP's youth division, the highest accolade given, and Diane was the wing secretary—and they saw themselves as the top guns of the twenty-first century. David saw himself becoming a great fighter pilot, Diane a famous astronaut. Abandoning her plans to study physics at an academically elite major university, Diane applied to the Air Force Academy, where David was set on going. After she learned that the deadline had passed for applications, she applied to the U.S. Naval Academy with the intention of transferring her commission after graduation from the Navy to the Air Force so she could be stationed with David.

Diane's family knew that David's personality was a little different. He had a collection of hunting rifles, which he once brought over to their house. When he came to church with Diane, he wore his combat boots, pants, and a T-shirt, and he kept his arms closely around her through the service. He once showed up at the Zamoras' house with a couple of his ROTC buddies from Mansfield. For entertainment, David took them out to the front yard and ordered them to march back and forth. "Diane was laughing, thinking it was funny," said Sylvia, "but I think the rest of us wondered a little when David said, 'I can get these guys to do whatever I want.' "

Still, no one could say that David was ever impolite around Diane or her family. On weeknights he drove the eighteen miles from Mansfield to Crowley and quietly sat in the Zamoras' living room to do homework with her. When her parents couldn't afford a pair of $100 combat boots for Diane, David bought them.

After Diane had a serious wreck driving David's pickup truck, requiring pins to be put into her left hand, David spent entire nights at the hospital with her. "Unlike that other boyfriend of hers who just wanted to go all the way," said a relative, "David genuinely cared for Diane. I don't think Diane had ever had that kind of attention."

That September, about a month after they started dating, they told Diane's parents that they were engaged. David had sold a couple of his hunting rifles to make a down payment for an engagement ring. They were going to get married, they said, on August 13, 2000, after they graduated from their military academies. They already had the wedding planned. They were going to charter a bus to carry their relatives in Texas to the famous Cadet Chapel on the Air Force Academy's campus. There, David would wear his uniform, Diane a white wedding dress, and at the end of the ceremony, they would walk under crossed swords held by other cadets.

Not long after they announced their engagement, her family confirmed, Diane lost her virginity to David—an act that had a dramatic impact on her life. "After it was over, she was real confused by what had happened," one relative said. "I know she felt guilty because she had wanted to wait. But once she went through with it, she became more committed than ever to David. I remember her saying, 'If I can't be Mrs. David Graham, then I will die as Miss Diane Zamora.' "

Indeed, they were hopelessly in love, focused as laser beams on each other. In that classic teenage way, they developed their own secret love code. She called him Tiger (the Mansfield High School mascot was a tiger), and he called her Kittens. And they ended many of their telephone conversations with the words, "Greenish brown female sheep."

Greenish brown is the color olive. A female sheep is a ewe. Olive ewe. I love you.

When this precious relationship we had was damaged by my thoughtless actions, the only thing that could satisfy her womanly vengeance was the life of the one that had, for an instant, taken her place.

On the first weekend in November, David traveled to Lubbock with other members of the Mansfield High cross-country team for the regional meet. Both the boys' and girls' squads had qualified, and the school provided them a large van for the trip. One of the students who went on that trip was Adrianne Jones.

In many ways, Adrianne was Diane Zamora's polar opposite, an ebullient girl who knew how to charm guys and get them to look twice at her. When she posed for one studio portrait, she made sure to show some cleavage. Although she wasn't overtly promiscuous in a way that would make her an outcast among the more popular girls, she was far from sexually naive. Diane, on the other hand, rarely put on makeup for school, and except for David, she thought most high school guys were immature.

It is not known if anything happened between Adrianne and David in Lubbock. No one can remember whether they sat next to one another on the van or stayed up late talking at the motel. Some of Adrianne's friends think she would have kept her distance from

David. As one friend pointed out, Adrianne had her standards: She would never sleep with another girl's boyfriend.

But something did happen when they returned to Mansfield. For whatever reason—perhaps Adrianne looked at David on that van and saw the kind of guy that even her father would like—she asked him to give her a ride home. They didn't go straight to her house. Adrianne surprised him by asking him to take some turns that he knew were out of the way. They ended up behind an elementary school, where David parked the car, and he and Adrianne had sex—a brief but truly fatal entanglement.

Apparently they told no one. Their encounter seemed to have been an impulsive, one-night fling. But a month later, late in the evening, a friend of David's who lived in the nearby town of Burleson heard a tapping at his window. David and Diane, their clothes bloodied, came through the window. According to the friend, David begged him to ask no questions. But the friend noticed that both David and Diane were upset. They lay on the floor and held each other. It was the same night Adrianne Jones disappeared from her home and was murdered.

But the friend never reported the incident to the police, and soon David and Diane were back to their old ways. Using his father's credit card, David bought Diane and Gloria leather coats as Christmas presents. He got Diane's engagement ring out of layaway so she could begin to wear it. On Valentine's Day, he gave her a teddy bear and flowers.

Diane's family could not help but wonder about the relationship as it progressed. David and Diane seemed so absorbed in one another's lives . . . so *obsessed.* "No matter what we were talking about, Diane brought up David's name. She was always talking about David this or David that," said Diane's cousin Ronnie Gonzalez. One night when they were apart and David didn't call, Diane tearfully begged her mother to call his house to see if anything terrible had happened to him. David was no different. He came over every afternoon to run with Diane, and some nights he would stay so late that he would fall asleep on the couch. His father would call, demanding that he come home, but David would dawdle for hours before leaving. Whenever Diane would go to a school function at night, David would phone every hour from his home until she got back.

That spring, they learned within days of each other that they had been accepted to their academies—David to the Air Force, Diane to the Navy. At special ceremonies at their high schools, they were presented with their academy acceptance letters. The Mansfield students gave a long ovation to David, who had Diane at his side. "I know this sounds strange to say now," recalled Becki Strosnider, the former editor of the *Mansfield Uproar,* "but we thought it was so cool that he had followed his dream." For her part, Gloria was so proud of what her daughter had done that she called the Hispanic-oriented La Estrella section of the *Fort Worth Star-Telegram* and suggested a story. When the reporter, Rosanna Ruiz, spoke with David and Diane, she asked them if they were being realistic about being married in the year 2000, considering they would be so far apart. But the two insisted that they would stay in touch daily through e-mail. "I was surprised at how adamant they were," Ruiz recalled. "They said they were certain the marriage was going to happen and that there were not going to be any outs. Then they stopped and looked at one another."

In the summer of 1996, after nearly three hundred interviews, detectives put the case on what they called slow-down mode. Bill and Linda Jones sank deeper into despair. Bill had to restrain himself to keep from interrogating every teenager he saw in town. Linda would get into her car at night and drive to the site where Adrianne was found, hoping she might come across the killer. Some students continued to see counselors about Adrianne's death. April Grossman painted a portrait of Adrianne in art class to honor her. She showed it to David, who sat behind April in government. He looked at it, paused, and then said, "You did a good job, April."

We realized it was either her or us . . . I just pointed and shot.

Only 1,239 young people were accepted out of the 8,736 who applied to enter the Air Force Academy for the fall 1996 semester. Of the nearly 10,000 who applied to the U.S. Naval Academy in Annapolis, Maryland, only 1,212 were accepted, 200 of those being women. Just by getting into their academies, David Graham and Diane Zamora had become part of a select group of American teenagers. To stay there, however, they had to survive grueling summer boot camps designed to eradicate their civilian habits and teach them the exacting discipline of military life. For the freshmen at the academies—known as plebes at the Naval Academy and Doolies at the Air Force Academy—the six-week summer sessions were humid days of nonstop marching, push-ups, running, and taking orders. Upperclassmen belittled them every time they made a mistake. At meals, the freshmen were required to keep their eyes focused on their plates at all times except when questioned by a superior. They had to be prepared to answer a barrage of questions and recite long passages about academy rules from memory. The system was unnerving and often demoralizing, and it was not unusual to see a cadet or midshipman resign his or her commission before the summer was over.

By all indications, David successfully completed his Basic Cadet Training in Colorado Springs. According to relatives who read them, Diane's letters home indicated that she was capably enduring "plebe summer" in Annapolis. She wrote in detail about her daily schedule, from the ninety-minute calisthenic sessions at six in the morning to the evening drill period in which they marched with M16 rifles. She wrote that she was going to church again at the Naval Chapel and that she had joined the glee club.

But her squad leader, Jay Guild, a good-looking plebe from suburban Chicago, said Diane was not physically keeping up with the other plebes and seemed emotionally distracted. "She liked to talk about David," Jay said. "She missed him a lot. She often talked about him very strangely, as if she didn't trust him but she still wanted to be with him. It was very odd."

Jay said Diane went on "crying fits" when David wouldn't answer her e-mail. She told him she suspected David was cheating on her with a female cadet at the Air Force Academy. Apart from David for the first time since they had begun dating, Diane became plagued with jealousy, and she decided, in turn, to make David jealous. According to one source, Diane stopped sending David e-mail for several days, telling him that her computer had broken. A few weeks into the plebe summer, Jay added, Diane told him that she was considering breaking up with David, and she suggested that the two of them become boyfriend and girlfriend. She then sent David an e-mail telling him that Jay had kissed her.

David and Diane, who once had found such security in their all-consuming devotion, seemed to be whirling out of control. When David heard about Diane and Jay, he attempted to contact Navy officials to inform them that Jay was sexually harassing Diane. He sent threatening e-mail to Jay, demanding that he have nothing more to do with Diane. One person close to the investigation said that David wrote Diane letters begging her not to deceive him. In the letters, David would write such lines as, "Remember what binds us together."

It was clear that Jay was captivated by Diane. When Diane's parents and Jay's mother arrived in Annapolis for Parents' Weekend on August 9, they were told that Jay and Diane had been reprimanded by upperclassmen for fraternizing. He had been seen sitting on the edge of her bed at night at Bancroft Hall, the coed dormitory where all the midshipmen lived. The truth was that Gloria was relieved to hear the news about Jay and Diane. "I got the very strong feeling that Diane's parents felt the relationship between Diane and David had become an unhealthy one," said Jay's mother, Cheryl Guild. At one point in the weekend, Diane and her parents went to lunch with Jay and his mother. During that lunch, Diane got up to call David. Cheryl could see

Diane across the room, talking on the phone, and she noticed the girl was physically shaking. Gloria leaned toward Cheryl and said, "I wish Diane had met Jay first."

Jay said that at one point in the summer, Diane told him that she and David had a secret "that we'll take to the grave." He asked Diane if David had ever cheated on her before. "She said yes, and I said, 'What did you do about it?' She told me that she had asked David to kill the other girl."

Stunned, Jay listened as Diane told him that she had watched David kill a girl named Adrianne. She never said she had participated. "All she said is that she told him to do it and she saw him do it," Jay said.

Although the Academy's strict honor code, known as the Brigade of Midshipmen Honor Concept, states that a midshipman must immediately report another midshipman who lies, cheats, or breaks the law in any way, Jay told no one—and would eventually be asked to resign from the Academy because of his silence. "I didn't want to believe it," he said. "I thought maybe she was trying to get attention."

But in late August, Diane told the story again, this time to her two roommates, Mandy Gotch and Jennifer McKearney. They were having a late-night conversation, and one of the girls mentioned how Diane and David seemed so in love. According to sources at the Naval Academy, one roommate said to Diane, "You two sound like you would do anything for each other."

Diane replied, "Yes."

"Even kill for one another?" the roommate asked.

Diane paused. "We have," she said. Then she told them the story about Adrianne—whether out of guilt or pride, no one is sure. Initially, the two roommates were skeptical about what they had heard, but the next day, they nervously told a Navy chaplain about the conversation. The chaplain contacted a Navy attorney at the Academy, who then began calling police departments in the Dallas–Fort Worth area to ask if they had an unsolved murder of a teenage girl. On August 29 he contacted the Grand Prairie Police Department. The next morning, detectives were on a flight to Annapolis.

I just wanted it to be a dream. . . . I wanted to be able to drive Adrianne back home, to go to sleep, and to wake up back on December 3, free to make my decisions all over again.

They pulled her out of the first pep rally of the season for Navy's football team, the first night when the plebes were allowed to mingle with upperclassmen and feel a part of the Academy. Across the Yard came the sound of pounding drums and cheering midshipmen as Diane was escorted down a long hallway in the administration building and then was led into a room where several detectives and Navy officials waited.

She admitted to nothing. She said only that she had been insecure throughout plebe summer, and she thought such a tale about murder would make her look tougher in the eyes of other plebes.

The cops weren't buying it, but what could they do? They had no evidence against her. Navy officials told her they were temporarily suspending her and sending her home until the matter was straightened out. They gave her an airplane ticket that took her from Baltimore to Atlanta and then on to Dallas. When Diane reached

Atlanta, however, she changed planes and flew to Colorado Springs, where she went to see David.

No one knows what was said between them. But the two did have their photographs taken by a friend of David's. David was wearing his Air Force uniform, Diane her all-white Naval outfit. In that one moment, they looked at the camera with a nearly desperate look, as if they knew that this was their last time together—that the fairy tale was over.

When the detectives arrived in Colorado Springs, David insisted that he couldn't imagine why Diane would tell such a blatantly false story. But the cops told him they had found his friend in Burleson and had heard the story of the bloody clothing. Then the Air Force officers told the young cadet that he had a duty to reveal the truth. Finally, David broke. He sat down at a word processor and typed a four-and-a-half-page confession (reprinted in part in the *Dallas Morning News*) that one forensic psychologist would later equate with a Danielle Steel novel. David wrote that for a month after his evening with Adrianne, he was tormented by "guilt and shame." The "perfect and pure" relationship between him and Diane, he added, had been defiled by "the one girl [who] had stolen from us our purity." Eventually, he told Diane about his tryst. "For at least an hour she screamed sobs that I wouldn't have thought possible. It wasn't just jealousy. For Diane, she had been betrayed, deceived and forgotten." He then said Diane gave him an ultimatum: kill Adrianne. David agreed. "I didn't have any harsh feelings for Adrianne," he wrote, "but no one could stand between me and Diane."

And so, David admitted, he called Adrianne on the

night of December 3, 1995, and said he wanted to see her. He picked her up in a Mazda Protegé owned by Diane's parents. Diane was hiding in the hatchback. They drove out to a secluded country road, and Adrianne reclined the passenger's seat, no doubt hoping for another romantic interlude. According to David's confession, while he held Adrianne, Diane raised up from her hiding place and hit her in the head with a dumbbell that belonged to David. Adrianne, however, did not die. "I realized too late that all those quick, painless snaps seen in the movies were just your usual Hollywood stunts," David wrote. "Adrianne somehow crawled through the window and, to our horror, ran off. I was panicky, and just grabbed the Makarov 9mm to follow. To our relief (at the time) she was too injured from the head wounds to go far. She ran into a nearby field and collapsed. . . . In that short instant, I knew I couldn't leave the key witness to our crime alive. I just pointed and shot. . . . I fired again and ran to the car. Diane and I drove off. The first things out of our mouths were, 'I love you.' " And then Diane said, her thirst for revenge suddenly slaked, "We shouldn't have done that, David."

The police recovered the handgun along with several dumbbells from the attic of the Grahams' home. They also confronted Diane, who by then was back in Texas. She stared at the officers. Then she quietly went to the station to give her own confession. She was put in a solitary cell on a separate floor from David—she looked like a harmless teenage girl in a sleeveless shirt and blue jeans. Every day, she did push-ups and sit-ups in her cell. She asked her mother for history and government textbooks so she could continue her studies. She said little to the guards or to her fellow female inmates, except for one prisoner who regularly cried because she missed her children. Diane sang her a contemporary Christian song she had memorized back in high school titled "Faith."

In Mansfield, as everywhere else, the question on everyone's mind was, Why? It was one thing, residents said, to read about urban gang kids shooting it out over a rivalry, but how did the culture of the streets—where loyalty and vengeance are values above life and law—infect upstanding small-town kids? There were the usual discussions about teenagers' values being shaped more by shabby movie violence and the angry lyrics of their favorite singers than they were by moral lessons from their parents. Other citizens were shocked to learn that more than one of David's friends had suspected that David was involved in Adrianne's murder, yet never said anything to the police. It was as if the most important thing among these teenagers was not "narcing" on a friend.

After the initial wave of national publicity over the arrests, Anna Barrett, a reporter for the *Mansfield News-Mirror*, began looking for positive stories to write about the high school to help the community's morale. "But something has changed in this town," she said. "You can feel it." Indeed, within a month after the arrests, a junior at Mansfield High was shot in the face with a shotgun and killed. A girl who had been on the cross-country team hanged herself because of personal problems. As for Bill and Linda Jones, they changed their phone number to avoid the calls from reporters, television shows, and movie producers. One producer, explaining why David and Diane's story would be a great miniseries, said in an interview, "It's a modern-day *Romeo and Juliet*—only they kill someone else instead of each other."

What remained unfathomable was how David and Diane could convince themselves that only death could eliminate the one blot on their perfect teenage love affair. How could they imagine that sexual betrayal was a far worse crime than murder? It seems clear that David convinced Diane that Adrianne was a seductress who lured him behind the elementary school. According to one police source, Diane told her roommates at the Naval Academy that just before she hit Adrianne in the head, she looked at her and said, "I know who you are! I know what you've done!"

Perhaps a trial will provide the definitive answer to why they did it. The district attorney's office has not determined whether it will seek the death penalty for the two eighteen-year-olds. There is an outside chance that David's attorney, Dan Cogdell of Houston, will get David's confession thrown out of court because he had allegedly been confined to his quarters at the Air Force Academy for more than thirty hours before the police took the confession. If a judge rules that the confession is admissible, however, then it is possible that Cogdell and John Linebarger, a prominent Fort Worth defense attorney who has been hired by Diane's family, will try to position their clients to point fingers at each other. "If I think attacking the Zamora girl is the appropriate line of defense, I will do it," said Cogdell, who added that he believed David wrote his confession to cover for Diane. A couple of investigators agreeing with him, believing that Diane had a Lady Macbeth–like control over David's life, coaxing and taunting him into letting his impulses and desires overcome his scruples. But others suggest that David, who brought guns and violence, sex and betrayal into Diane's sweet and studious life, exercised his spell over her by enlisting her as a partner in murder—using death to bind them together for life. There is even a third theory that David, wanting to prove that he cared nothing for Adrianne, took one shot, and Diane, consumed with fury, took the other.

Still, it is difficult to imagine that David and Diane will someday turn into adversaries in court. When David was being escorted to the county jail in Fort Worth, a television reporter asked if he had anything to say to Diane. David looked at the camera and said, "I love you." As for Diane, one afternoon she motioned toward a guard and asked if she would pass on a message to David.

"What is it?" the guard asked.

Diane paused. "Tell him, 'Greenish brown female sheep.' "

(December 1996)

The national attention was so great about the Graham–Zamora story that NBC-TV made a highly controversial decision to broadcast a movie about the case, based on the *Texas Monthly* article, before David's and Diane's trials. By the time of their separate trials—each trial was carried on Court TV—their devotion to each other had come to an end. In her trial Zamora testified that she had no idea Graham, whom she said was an intimidating bully, was plotting to murder Adrianne, and that she was an innocent bystander on the night Adrianne was shot.

In his trial Graham said that he never had a romantic relationship with Adrianne, that he said that to Diane only to make her jealous, and that Diane went into such a rage that she did the shooting. Graham said that he was not even present when Adrianne was killed. Both were convicted and are now serving life terms in prison.

The Last Ride of the Polo Shirt Bandit

HELEN THORPE

On November 27, 1996, William Guess sat in a rented maroon Nissan Maxima surrounded by Harris County sheriff's deputies, holding a blue steel semiautomatic to his head. Guess was 46 years old, and he was a big man—more than six feet tall, around 240 pounds. He had graying blond hair and a square face. At that moment he was wearing a windbreaker, blue jeans, low-heeled boots, and glasses, bearing little resemblance to the person who had just robbed Guaranty Federal, a small bank north of Houston. About fifteen minutes earlier, however, Guess had been wearing a fake beard and mustache, sunglasses, a baseball hat, and the shirt that had come to be the signature of his alter ego, a serial bank robber known as the Polo Shirt Bandit. Once he had driven away, he had hurriedly pulled off the disguise, and a heady surge of relief probably had flooded through him—he thought he was going to escape once more, back to the part of his life that was ordinary and respectable. On the floor of the car on the passenger side was $12,460. The money had been in Guess's briefcase when he had walked out of the bank. He could have dumped it out shortly after getting into the car to see how much was there, or it could have tumbled out during the fast turns he had taken in his unsuccessful attempt to shake the deputies who had cornered him. Either way, all those crisp-as-if-starched bills were now spilled out over the carpet: all that easy money, obtained at such immense risk.

Guess had just wrecked the Nissan on FM 1960, a busy four-lane stretch bordered by strip malls, Chinese restaurants, and auto body shops that intersects Interstate 45 and U.S. 290, the Northwest Freeway. The banks that stand along the road's length are quintessentially modern; they are small outfits, staffed by three or four people, that sit next to day care centers and Hunan Palaces and Repp Big and Tall clothing stores. The branches are as homey and cheerful as a Hallmark greeting card, and you wouldn't think a robbery would ever happen inside one of them. But to Guess, they must have once looked like a row of cherries, his personal jackpot. This was where he had started robbing banks. Over the span of his career, he is suspected of pulling off at least 38 robberies—making him the most prolific bank robber in the history of the state—and stealing in the vicinity of $600,000. He robbed more banks than Jesse James, John Dillinger, Willie Sutton, or Bonnie and Clyde, although he never hurt anyone. Guess committed one robbery in a town called Salado, two in Austin, and nine within the limits of Houston, but he always came back to FM 1960 or Texas Highway 6 (as the road is known south of 290): Of the 26 additional bank robberies that he is believed to have committed in parts of Harris or Fort Bend counties, 21 occurred somewhere along the road where he now sat. There were never many witnesses around, never that many bank employees to control, and afterward he would slip into the speeding stream of traffic on U.S. 290 or I-45 and vanish.

Not this time. The front of Guess's Nissan was stuck under the bed of a red pickup truck, and the back of it had been rear-ended by a Harris County Sheriff's Department patrol car. Two other squad cars had swerved to stop beside the Nissan. What kind of desperation filled Guess, knowing that he was trapped? It would not have been the kind that a crime victim feels—the sudden shock of an entirely unexpected threat. It would have been the sort of dread that steals over a person when he finally confronts a scenario that he has been courting yet running away from for a long time. Four uniformed deputies hurried out of the patrol cars with their guns drawn and took aim at the Polo Shirt Bandit. But Guess had already taken aim at himself.

As detectives learned after they discovered his identity from his driver's license, William Guess lived in Oenaville, an unincorporated town six miles northeast of Temple, in a redbrick ranch house. He shared it with his wife, Geneva, and the youngest of their three sons. Oenaville is far removed from the urban sprawl of roads like FM 1960; the town consists of a main crossroads, one convenience store, half a dozen ranches, and some houses, surrounded by a vast expanse of rolling prairie. The revelation of the Polo Shirt Bandit's identity was greeted by the residents of Oenaville with total disbelief. "This is a farming community," said a neighbor who lives two houses down from the Guess family. "This is the least likely place in the world for something like this to happen."

William Guess grew up in Temple, where his father worked as the director of the city's utilities. His family life was unremarkable. He was known to be friendly but reserved—he rarely initiated conversations, although he was happy to stop and talk if you did. "He was quiet, confident, calm, self-assured, intelligent, and a natural athlete," remembered one friend. As a student at Temple High School, he had achieved nearly perfect grades without having to study hard, and he was an all-around athlete who served as the captain of both the basketball and the golf teams in his senior year (class of 1969). He dated one of the school's homecoming princesses, Geneva Sanderson. "When I saw him for the first time, it was, like, wow, love at first sight," Geneva told me over the phone. "We got engaged right after high school."

Guess' single quirk was his apparent lack of drive. Classmates had assumed that because things came to him easily, he would go on to become something of importance, but he didn't. While friends like Brad Dusek won a football scholarship, left for Texas A&M and went on to play professionally for the Washington Redskins, Guess attended local colleges but never obtained a degree. As his athletic and academic successes faded, his relationship with Geneva must have taken on an even greater significance. They were married on August 7, 1971. In the mid-seventies, after floundering for a while, Guess found work in Houston as a deliveryman, driving all over the city and its outlying suburbs. On the weekends he would return to Temple, three hours away. Within a few years he gave that up to work as a cleaning-supplies salesman in Temple, and then he started a used-car business with a friend; they called it Two Guys Car Lot. "Many of us felt he was badly underutilized," said one friend. "He just never seemed to have much ambition."

After he started Two Guys Car Lot, Guess began spending a lot of time with Cliff Lambert, who worked as a mechanic in an auto shop at a local salvage yard. At the same time, he maintained ties to many Temple residents who were, in the conventional sense, far more successful, such as Brad Dusek and Joel Garrison, who had become homebuilders. He played golf regularly at the Wildflower or Mill Creek country clubs with some of the most prominent people in town, including one of the city's former mayors, John Sammons. If the disparity between the public images of these people and his own bothered him, he didn't let on. But he had a big ego, and he liked to prove himself; he played golf to win, and he liked to bet on the outcome. He started off betting $40 or $50 on a round, but in recent years he sometimes wagered ten times that amount.

After friends learned about his secret life as a bank robber, they came to see Guess as an enigma, as if his name proved to be prophetic. They found it impossible to reconcile the character of the man they knew with the activities of the bank robber who wrecked his Nissan on FM 1960. "He was a good friend and a good guy," said Joel Garrison. "I guess he was just a different person than we all knew." But in truth Guess's public life and his hidden one were linked, and the frustrations Guess felt with his daily routine fed the growth of his alternate persona. Those frustrations piled up over time, particularly after he sold his interest in his car business and his marriage began to founder. "There were days, and I mean days, when I wouldn't hear from him," said Geneva. "I would stand at the window wondering if he was dead or alive. Then he would show up again thinking everything was hunky-dory." In 1989 William made an attempt at a permanent break, leaving a note that said, "I can't go on like this," but he returned in several days, and the couple decided to stay together for the sake of their children. He was drinking too much—he was twice charged with driving while intoxicated and once checked into an alcohol-abuse treatment clinic. And he started to gamble more.

While people who live in Temple like to think of their city as the last place that would spawn a bank robber, it is a place where a person can easily develop a serious gambling problem, if he has the inclination. The city has always catered to Fort Hood soldiers looking for action, and several used-car businesses in the area (though not Guess's) have been investigated by the police for serving as fronts for local bookmaking operations. Temple is also home to two weekly high-stakes poker games; the first is strictly private and includes a number of prominent businessmen, while the second is run by local bookies and hard-core gamblers and is more open. Guess played in both. On a routine night, he might win or lose anywhere from $500 to $5,000. If he had been looking for a warning of how far afield the cards might lead him, he had only to look across the poker table: Another regular at one of the games was a man from Temple who had once served time in federal prison. As a young man, he had forced his way into the home of a wealthy widow and held her hostage until she wrote a check for $11,500, which he supposedly needed because of gambling debts.

But if Temple provided the temptation, Guess was willing to be tempted. Besides betting on golf and poker, he started wagering as much as $15,000 on professional football games with two bookies in the Temple area known to their clients (and later to police investigators as well) as Shorty and Champ. Guess started making regular trips to the horse track at Manor Downs, east of Austin, where he would drop as much as $1,500 on a horse, and then he started going to the Isle of Capri casino in Bossier City, Louisiana. He even played the lottery heavily. Nobody seems to have been aware of the extent of his gambling habit. "When I cleaned out his office, I found all these tickets," said Geneva. "I said, 'What are these?' " They were from the race track. But people who saw Guess bet could see that he liked to take risks. "William lived on the edge," said one person who used to bet with him. "He would play blackjack for any amount you wanted. He kept wanting to play for more and more." So much did Guess come to define himself in terms of his risk taking that when his children were asked what he did for a living, they sometimes replied that he was a professional gambler.

Nobody knows precisely what went through Guess's mind as he decided to slide into criminal behavior, but the broad outlines of the situation are plain: He was gambling too much, he probably needed money to pay off a debt, perhaps he felt intrigued by images of himself usurping control of something as solid and as reputable as a bank. Did the idea of robbing banks hold some gritty, Western romance for him? Was it his way of getting even with all the people who had grown up to lead ordinary, dull, successful lives? Or maybe he studied the idea with a cold pragmatism, concluding that sticking up banks was a sure way to make easy money.

Several years before he started robbing banks on a regular basis, he apparently committed one isolated robbery in Harris County. That stickup wasn't linked to others committed by the Polo Shirt Bandit until recently (when a woman who had worked at the bank called the Houston Police Department after seeing Guess on TV and said, "That's the asshole that robbed me back in 1985"). Four years later, however, Guess started robbing on a systematic basis. On September 29, 1989, he was in Houston—probably to attend an automobile auction—and had checked into a Holiday Inn on 290 where he often stayed. It's likely that he went somewhere else to change clothes. The branch of San Jacinto Savings that he had decided to raid was in a strip mall on Texas Highway 6, next to a Montessori Children's Cottage, a Kids Kuts barbershop, and Copperfield Family Dental Care. It was a small bank, only women worked there, and Guess knew he could keep an eye on all of the employees at once. When he walked into the place at around noon, Guess looked like any nine-to-five businessman: He was wearing a dress shirt, a light blue vest, a tie, dress slacks, a driving cap, and dark sunglasses. He had painstakingly applied a realistic-looking false beard and mustache (a crepe beard, as the disguise is known, involves brushing spirit gum on the face, then attaching fake facial hair clump by clump), and he was carrying a large zippered daily-planner case, but the only thing inside was a small blue revolver, probably a .38. Guess took out the gun and told the tellers to dump the cash from their tills into the daily planner. From behind his pitch-dark sunglass lenses, he might not have been able to make out the tellers' features, but he must have sensed the fear and vulnerability that he aroused. One minute the employees had been in charge of the bank, and the next minute he was. After warning the tellers that he had an accomplice outside who was also armed, which wasn't true, Guess drove away in a brown Mercedes that he had probably bought at the auction.

Guess lifted a total of $1,000 from San Jacinto—not that much money. None of his early robberies was particularly lucrative; he knew tellers usually trigger a silent alarm, and he had only minutes before the police would arrive. Typically he got away with between $4,000 and $15,000. Only much later did he get larger hauls. But he must have found that first job rewarding enough, but it wasn't long before he struck again. One month after robbing San Jacinto Savings, he held up tellers at an NCNB (as NationsBank used to be known) on Highway 6, in Fort Bend County. Two weeks later, he returned to Harris County to rob First Federal Savings and Loan on FM 1960. Witnesses saw him flee in another Mercedes, this time dark blue, license plate number 437 HFT. In December he hit the same NCNB again, and in January 1990 he returned to rob the branch for the third time. Then there was a lull.

S omebody had just pulled off five bank robberies in less than four months, which was galling to the detectives assigned to solve the cases. Among the law enforcement agents who converged on San Jacinto Savings after the first robbery in 1989 were Lieutenant Grace Hefner, who was in charge of the Harris County Sheriff's Department robbery division, and Detective Tom Keen, who reported to her. Hefner is a reserved, soft-spoken, tenacious woman who is known for her ability to crack tough cases by carefully cataloguing large amounts of data. Keen, by contrast, is a gung ho, right-off-the-streets detective. Keen and Hefner would spend the next seven years trying to solve the San Jacinto robbery, but at the time it looked like a run-of-the-mill crime, and there was no reason to suspect that the investigation would prove inordinately long. Later they came to realize that the robbery was unusual in one respect: "That was the first time we saw such an elaborate disguise," said Hefner recently. "Usually they just wear a hat and sunglasses. We don't usually see fake beards." But back then, nobody knew that the bank robber's beard was false. They did notice the luxury automobile that he had driven off in, which was how Guess acquired his first nickname—originally the police referred to him as the Mercedes Bandit.

Most bank robberies are solved within a matter of weeks, but the robberies attributed to the Mercedes Bandit continued to mount, while Keen and Hefner made no progress. At least in his secret life, Guess must have felt charmed. Once he was almost caught when a police officer arrived in the middle of a robbery, but the officer mistakenly accosted another bearded man as Guess drove away from the scene. Another time Guess robbed a bank while an armed security guard was in the back of the institution fixing a cup of coffee. "This man was just fortunate," said Keen. "He had lots of breaks."

Guess was also smart; when Keen checked his computer system, the license plate number that the tellers at First Federal had written down popped up as belonging on a Hyundai. The owner of that car had reported its plates stolen from the parking lot of a medical office building on FM 1960. Guess was taking off the stolen plates and removing his false beard as soon as possible after each robbery (he had abandoned the crepe beard in favor of a prefabricated one that he could rip off all at once) to confuse any law enforcement officers he encountered. He also coated his fingertips so that they left no prints. About the only clue Keen and Hefner had to the bank robber's identity was his peculiar ability to get his hands on different cars, none of which were being reported stolen; this seemed to indicate that he was in the used-car business. The detectives also believed the bank robber had to be from Houston, because he knew his way around. In the spring of 1990 the theory that the Mercedes Bandit was a local car dealer led the sheriff's office to charge an innocent man with some of the robberies that Guess is now suspected of having committed. Frustrated by the lack of progress, the sheriff's office distributed a surveillance photograph of the Mercedes Bandit to television stations and newspapers in the Houston area. Somebody called in and said the person looked a lot like Aubry Lee Kelley, who was in the vehicle-repossession business. Several witnesses picked him out of a lineup. Although Kelley immediately protested that he was innocent, he spent the next two months in jail—until Guess returned to San Jacinto Savings, the first bank he had held up and one of the two that Kelley was charged with robbing. This time he fled in a black Mazda, but the tellers were certain he was the same man who had robbed them before. The charges against the unfortunate Kelley were dropped. "Nobody listens to you in that jail," Kelley told the *Houston Chronicle* shortly after his release. "They don't care if you're guilty or innocent. They're just pushing people through court." If he sounded bitter, he had good cause; while Kelley was in jail, he lost his repo business, was kicked out of his apartment in the Woodlands, and his wife suffered a miscarriage.

Soon after Guess resurfaced, inadvertently springing Kelley from jail, he decided to move into new territory and alter his disguise, as if he felt he had to vary his routine to keep ahead of the police. On May 21 he ventured into Houston and hit Mason Road Bank (now called Comerica), a small adobe-style building much like the institutions he had been robbing up and down FM 1960. On July 3 he robbed the same bank again. Despite its name, the bank lies on Blalock Road, which runs directly into I-10, and after both robberies Guess simply disappeared into traffic. By now he had abandoned his Mercedes for cars that were less noticeable. In the second robbery of Mason Road Bank he also abandoned the Mercedes Bandit's business attire for a more casual look: He was still using a fake beard and mustache and sunglasses, but now he wore a white polo shirt with blue stripes, blue jeans, low-heeled boots, and a baseball hat. From that point on, he wore a polo shirt in every robbery he committed.

Why Guess reconfigured himself as the Polo Shirt

Bandit remains an unanswered question; maybe he adopted the look to make the police think they were dealing with a different bank robber. Whatever the reason, the new disguise was an improvement: While the Mercedes Bandit had posed as a typical businessman, the Polo Shirt Bandit was even more ordinary, and therefore more invisible. The new apparel seemed to transform Guess into a generic Bubba, a Texan Everyman, just another big guy in a gimme cap.

The two Houston robberies brought Guess's heists to eight and the number of law enforcement agencies hunting for him to five, as the Houston Police Department joined the Harris County Sheriff's Department, the Fort Bend Sheriff's Department, the Sugar Land Police Department, and the FBI. Guess must have spent some time conjecturing about his pursuers, but he must have felt secure enough once he made it back to Oenaville; the town was surely too tiny, too rustic, and too remote to be the scene of his unmasking. And if his occasional trips to Houston began to acquire an element of serious risk, well, Guess had long had an appetite for risk. Before he had chanced his livelihood; now he was gambling with his freedom.

During his next jobs, Guess displayed an unusual ability to think fast under pressure. On September 18, 1990, he visited a branch of Guaranty Federal Savings that sits in a shopping center on Jones Road, near FM 1960. He was wearing his disguise, and he issued the same set of instructions, but before he left the bank, a dye pack that he had scooped into his briefcase along with the money exploded, shooting a fine red powder that looked like smoke into the air, staining his skin and clothing, and spraying a chemical agent that made his eyes burn and water. If he had taken the time to look for clean money, Guess might have been caught, but he immediately threw the briefcase down and ran off, leaving the cash behind. Apparently he had a pressing debt to pay, however, because only three weeks after the dye pack went off, Guess returned to rob a bank called Commerce Savings. The following year, he robbed Guaranty Federal for the second time. "Okay, girls," he said to the tellers with characteristic aplomb. "Let's do it right this time: No dye packs."

Several months later, the same audacity helped Guess brazen his way through the most harrowing moment of his criminal career. In the summer of 1991, perhaps because he was concerned about hitting too many banks near Houston or the target was too tempting, Guess decided to rob a branch of Taylor Banc in Austin. The one-story, redbrick building stands on the crest of a hill at the intersection of Braker Lane and I-35. It is clearly visible from the highway, and Guess probably spotted it on a trip to Manor Downs. As soon as he saw the building, he must have imagined how easily he could rob it: The bank was just the right size, and a getaway looked simple—although as it turned out, it wasn't.

At eleven-fifteen in the morning on July 18 Guess drove up to Taylor Banc in a two-tone Chevy pickup. He walked into the lobby wearing a fake beard and a polo shirt and carrying a Titan chrome .32-caliber semiautomatic in his briefcase. The robbery went off without a hitch, but the Austin police responded within minutes, and when Guess tried to disappear into the northbound traffic on I-35, he kept running into patrol cars. A police helicopter soon appeared overhead.

Spooked, Guess finally drove down a dead-end street and got rid of every piece of evidence that could tie him to the crime. He shucked off his shirt, jeans, belt, boots, hat, and beard—everything he had worn into the bank—shoved them into a plastic trash bag and heaved it out the window of the truck. He also dumped the money, the stolen plates on the truck, and the Titan semiautomatic. "He got naked," said one detective. Then he pulled on different clothing and drove away. The police didn't have a vehicle description, and they were looking for a bearded man in a baseball cap and a polo shirt; if any officers encountered Guess, they didn't recognize him as their suspect. Shortly after Guess left, a patrol car turned onto the street. A woman who had seen Guess change his clothes pointed out the pile of belongings in the trash bag, but by then Guess was gone.

On that occasion the debts that Guess had amassed must have been particularly onerous. One day after leaving Austin empty-handed he showed up in Harris County and robbed a Bank of America, and the day after that, as if he still hadn't gotten the amount he required, he robbed a branch of San Jacinto Savings. Before the end of 1991, he robbed four more banks, all in Harris County, boosting the number he had hit to nineteen.

Keen, Hefner, and the other detectives looking for the Polo Shirt Bandit obtained the first and only items of physical evidence they ever got during their investigation from the pile of stuff Guess left in Austin. From the fake beard, they learned that their suspect had been using a disguise. The investigators had already decided that the bank robber probably had a steady source of income, since his robberies took place in an irregular sequence; considering his actions after the botched Austin robbery, Keen and Hefner felt certain that their suspect had a gambling problem. "Who else would be going through that kind of money other than somebody with a drug problem?" asked Keen. "And he didn't look like somebody who was into drugs. He stayed the same weight."

But the evidence and the suppositions led nowhere. Keen and Hefner contacted casino officials around the country, but their quest turned up no useful tips; partial fingerprints recovered from the license plate Guess left behind in Austin didn't match any on file. The Harris County Sheriff's Department turned to the media for new leads. On December 17, 1991, the *Houston Chronicle* published a surveillance photograph obtained the week before, and after the picture ran, the sheriff's office got a tip that the bandit resembled another man who owned a car-repossession business. The suspect's partner also looked like the Polo Shirt Bandit, however, and detectives decided the two had been taking turns at wearing the same disguise. Early in 1992 the sheriff's office arrested both men and charged them with some of the Polo Shirt Bandit's robberies. "In each case they would wear sunglasses, a baseball hat, and a beard," someone from the sheriff's department told reporters at the time. "If you look at the surveillance photos, it's hard to tell the difference."

Both men were released, but they soon would have been cleared anyway: On February 19, 1992, the Polo Shirt Bandit returned to Harris County to rob a branch of Cypress National Bank on Jones Road that he had robbed once before. "This is the last time I'm going to rob a bank," Guess told the tellers at Cypress National. "I need this money for my son." And then the robberies stopped, as abruptly as they had begun.

William Guess did not have a sick son. Detectives now believe he was just trying to justify his actions to the people he was holding up. However, it is possible that the strain of leading a double life had begun to affect him; Geneva recalls that William had constant stomach problems and was always eating Tums. (Three years later Guess would suffer a heart attack.) If he was ever to interrupt the cycle of compulsive gambling and criminal activity he had fallen into, this would have been the occasion. However, whatever qualms he may have felt were no match for the pull of his addictions: On February 23, 1993, a year after saying he was through with crime, Guess packed up his gun, his fake beard, one of his polo shirts, and resumed his bank-robbing spree. He stole the license plates off a car that belonged to an employee of a fast-food restaurant on U.S. 290 and put them onto the white Ford Thunderbird he was driving. Like many of the cars he used from then on, it looked new; apparently Guess started using rental cars instead of used ones. Guess then headed for the Bank of America on FM 1960 and held it up for the second time.

Three months later Guess committed a robbery that was the one most likely to have led to his capture—it was like a beacon announcing his approximate home base, although none of the detectives searching for him understood this at the time. On May 20, 1993, Guess held up Peoples National Bank in the scenic town of

Salado. It was the only robbery that he ever committed in Bell County, where Oenaville is located—Salado is only about twenty miles from Guess's home. While his success in evading capture thus far was largely because he had avoided robbing banks in places where he might be recognized, Guess must have found Peoples National irresistible: The old stone building sits so close to I-35 that the highway entrance ramp is visible from the bank's parking lot, and Salado has no police department of its own. Law enforcement agents had to come from Belton, ten minutes away. Breaking from the routine he had used in the past, Guess stayed inside the bank long enough to force the employees to open its vault, and while the police have never disclosed how much money he got, it was far more than his usual plunder.

One week later the *Temple Daily Telegram* linked the Salado robbery to "a professional bandit" who was described as being from around Houston. The article outlined the Polo Shirt Bandit's methods and appearance, and it included a photograph of Guess in disguise. "Authorities do not believe the robber remained in the Central Texas area," reported the paper. "However, anyone able to confirm the true identity of the man pictured in the photograph is urged to call the sheriff's department." Half of Temple must have read the story—Guess probably saw it himself. In the meantime, FBI agents showed photographs of the Polo Shirt Bandit at work in other banks to Jerry Kopriva, who was in charge of security for Peoples National in the area at that time. Kopriva had known Guess in high school, and they had become reacquainted when their children started attending the same schools. Kopriva studied the photographs and never realized he was looking at William Guess. "I had no earthly idea," he said recently.

In retrospect it seems weird that a beard, a gimme cap, and a pair of sunglasses were enough to render Guess unrecognizable, but apparently people who knew him were incapable of seeing through his disguise because the idea that he might be a bank robber was unthinkable. And Guess never revealed any sign of his illicit career to his friends or neighbors; he never changed his lifestyle in any obvious fashion, and he was never suddenly and inexplicably rich. "He never flashed a hundred dollar bill," said a neighbor in Oenaville. "He's lived here for ten years, and he's always driven around in an old vehicle." Geneva and William had separate bank accounts, and his family was never aware of any change in William's finances. "He was a penny-pincher," said Geneva. "It was a big joke with the kids: 'Daddy's cheap, cheap, cheap.' When we went on vacations, he would want to stay in some dumpy old motel. He was happy buying clothes at WalMart." He never boasted of his illegal exploits, not even when he was drunk.

Perhaps he never slipped because nobody knew him that well anymore. After selling the car business, Guess had drifted into buying old cars at auctions, fixing them up, and selling them to other car dealers, and he was spending almost all his time at the garage owned by Cliff Lambert. The property sits on a bluff, and it is strewn with every model of vehicle imaginable, including two-doors, four-doors, old pickups, a few Winnebagos, and even an old powerboat. When friends asked if he was going to get back into the used-car business

on a more formal basis, Guess replied no, not unless
he had to. "Gradually he built a shell around himself,"
said an old friend. "In the last five or six years, it was
like he had a chip on his shoulder. He was more aloof."

As if Guess was alarmed by the publicity the Salado
bank robbery attracted, he committed no more robberies that year. He started up again in 1994, however, and
from that point on he became more and more effective
as a criminal. Guess had been learning on the job, and
in the last phase of his career, he figured out how to
avoid security measures like dye packs and how to co-
erce employees into letting him into the vaults. While
the life went out of William Guess, who was sitting in
a junkyard for hours at a time, the Polo Shirt Bandit
grew more potent; it was as if one waxed and the other
waned.

Early in 1994 Robert Davenport, a detective newly
assigned to the Houston Police Department's robbery division, was handed material on the serial bank
robber. The police department's interest in the Polo
Shirt Bandit had been reignited on January 4, when the
bank robber hit his third institution within the city limits. A subsequent Houston robbery—at Pinemont
Bank, on Memorial, on May 19, 1994—provided Davenport with what he thought was a big break. "We got
an excellent video," he said. "It showed his every
movement. It showed him pointing, holding his
weapon, walking. There was a strong front-on facial
shot, a good profile, even a shot of the back of his head.
It was perfect." The videotape of the Polo Shirt Bandit
robbing Pinemont first ran on the TV show *City Under
Siege*, then appeared on local news, and eventually

aired again on *America's Most Wanted.* Davenport re-
searched every name that turned up and found many
people who bore a striking resemblance to the Polo
Shirt Bandit, but nobody who had committed his
crimes. "One woman was so upset she went into convulsions because she thought it was her ex-husband,"
he remembered. Investigators began to feel certain that
the bank robber didn't live in the Houston area, since
the publicity would have unearthed him if he did. Davenport distributed wanted posters at police roll calls
around the city and held seminars for bank employees
to teach them about the bandit's habits. He worked
until he had the sense that he knew the Polo Shirt Bandit, even though he didn't know his name, and still the
bank robber wasn't caught. He robbed eight more
banks in the next year and a half. Then he started using
a semiautomatic that carried more firepower than any
he had used before.

On April 11, 1996, Guess showed up at a Compass
Bank on Bissonnet in Houston. The wedge-shaped
bank building looked small from the outside, but once
Guess was inside, he discovered that it was much bigger; Guess was forced to spend far longer in the bank
than he wanted to, as he had to round up employees
from various offices before he could get his money,
and he grew visibly jittery in the process. During his
next robberies, his manner became increasingly omi-
nous. Guess started getting more aggressive, more nervous, and more demanding; he began pointing the gun
directly at bank employees, whereas before he had only
displayed a weapon to show them that he was armed.
How had the years of assuming the role of the Polo
Shirt Bandit changed William Guess? What actions

was he now capable of? On July 24 Guess got into the vault of a Savings of America on Post Oak and walked off with $31,823—a vast difference from the $1,000 he had taken from San Jacinto Savings almost seven years before.

As Guess's behavior became more threatening, law enforcement officers began to put more and more effort into his capture. The Harris County Sheriff's Department formed a task force to catch the man that everyone in the robbery division had come to think of as their nemesis and put Grace Hefner in charge. In the middle of 1995 a bank association had offered a $10,000 reward for information leading to the capture of the Polo Shirt Bandit. By last summer, when Guess showed up with a bigger gun, the reward being offered was up to $26,000. Davenport said, "We didn't know whether he was making a statement: 'I've got more bullets. I'm ready for a shoot-out.'"

And then Hefner noticed a pattern. Beginning in February 1996, as if he had been lulled into complacency or was getting sloppy, Guess had started robbing a bank every 50 to 56 days. He had robbed on February 15, April 11, May 31, and July 24. By September 11, the Harris County Sheriff's Department, the FBI, the Houston Police Department (HPD), and the Texas Rangers convened to figure out how to respond. One week later Guess cleaned out the vault at a branch of Coastal Banc, scoring more than $60,000, and that caused law enforcement agencies to disagree about what he was going to do next: The FBI and the HPD argued that the robber had just gotten so much money that he wouldn't rob again for some time, while Hefner thought his gambling had become so compulsive that he would strike again within the 56-day time frame. The sheriff's department and the Texas Rangers decided to set up a surveillance operation over a three-week period in November, when they thought the Polo Shirt Bandit was going to hit, but the FBI and the HPD decided not to participate.

After juggling schedules and rearranging long-planned vacations, a team of eighty uniformed and nonuniformed officers was assembled. Hefner briefed them about the bandit's habits. She also told them to anticipate that the bank robber would try to kill himself or shoot his way out of a corner if faced with the prospect of arrest—the Polo Shirt Bandit was relatively young and had committed dozens of serious crimes, meaning that he was facing an extremely long prison term. Beginning on November 5, the officers sat in parked cars outside of banks that looked like the kind of places that the Polo Shirt Bandit liked to stick up, and waited. He never showed.

By November 25 the three weeks were up, and the sheriff's department was about to call off the surveillance. Then bank executives requested that the extra protection remain in place through the Thanksgiving holidays. The sheriff's office decided that it couldn't afford to keep all 80 officers on the lookout for a bank robber who might not show up, but it did keep about 25 officers on the alert.

On Sunday, November 24, William Guess got a phone call from a friend in the car salvage business in Houston. The friend told Guess that there was going to be a big automobile auction on the following day. On Monday, Guess drove to Houston, checked into the Holiday Inn he often stayed in, and went to the car auction. On Wednesday morning, he put on his bank-robbing attire and drove a rented Nissan over to Guaranty Federal, at 3902 FM 1960. Apparently he sat in the car for some time (police officers later found a cooler and a lot of empty beer cans in the car). At ten-thirteen Guess went into the bank, where he displayed his gun and ordered the tellers to fill his briefcase with cash. But then, as if a fickle wind turned the weather vane of his fortune around, everything started to go wrong.

A woman who worked at another branch of Guaranty Federal had stopped by the location on FM 1960 that morning, and as she was leaving, she noticed Guess enter the bank. As it happened, the woman had attended one of Davenport's briefings, and she recognized Guess as the Polo Shirt Bandit. Recalling what Davenport had said to do during such a situation—"If you ever see this man, call 911"—she dialed the emergency number on her cellular phone. The dispatcher kept her on the phone until Guess emerged, and the woman was able to report that he left the bank in a maroon Nissan Maxima, license plate STS 05X, heading west on FM 1960.

Ron Fleming and Mitch Hatcher, who were normally assigned to a narcotics unit, were among the only Harris County deputies still out looking for the Polo Shirt Bandit that morning. After patrolling up and down Jones Road for a while, Fleming, who was driving, had said, "There's nothing going on here, let's cruise over to 1960." Right after they turned onto FM 1960, the dispatcher announced that the Polo Shirt Bandit had struck again and gave them a vehicle description and location. "He was heading right to us," Fleming recalled afterward. As the dispatcher was repeating the bank robber's vehicle and license plate number, Hatcher and Fleming spotted the maroon Nissan in oncoming traffic. Thirty seconds later, and they would have missed him. Fleming made a U-turn. "We got him! This is him!" he started yelling to his partner.

When the patrol car pulled up behind him, Guess waved as if to show that he would pull over momentarily. His mind must have raced to consider whether he had committed a traffic violation or whether this was the confrontation that some part of himself must always have been anticipating. The patrol car moved up behind him, close enough for him to study the faces of the two deputies in his rearview mirror. Apparently something told him that they knew exactly who he was. As soon as he saw a break in traffic, Guess took off, running a red light. The patrol car turned on its siren and followed. Guess led Hatcher and Fleming on a chase through a Builders Square parking lot, several other red lights, and up and down streets that intersected with FM 1960. Two other Harris County Sheriff's Department patrol cars joined the caravan along the way. Guess kept leaving the main thoroughfare in a vain attempt to shake the cars on his tail, but he always came back to his primary getaway route.

About ten minutes after the chase began, Guess and the three patrol cars came tearing down FM 1960 toward the intersection at Perry Road. Sitting in a red pickup in the far left lane was Steve Sharum, a Deer Park plumber. Sharum had been just a few cars ahead of Guess when Hatcher and Fleming had first spotted the Nissan, and he had watched as the patrol car turned around, and the maroon car had zipped out to run the red light. Sharum's younger brother had been killed in a car accident, and the reckless driving of the man in the Nissan had ticked him off. "That guy's driving ignorant," Sharum had thought. "He must have stolen that car." Now when Sharum looked up and saw the same Nissan Maxima in his rearview mirror, bearing down fast, he thought, "Well, if I stop, he'll either have to stop too or go around me." Sharum closed his eyes, held on to his steering wheel, and punched the brakes. He felt two jolts—Guess smashing into his pickup, and the third patrol car slamming into Guess. Then Sharum heard someone yell, "He's got a gun!" so he lay down on the front seat of his truck and didn't move.

Once he rear-ended Sharum's pickup, Guess knew his long charade was finished. He had planned what he would do in such a moment. Perhaps he knew the moment was inevitable, because he robbed banks like he gambled—he didn't stop until he was completely out of luck. Guess put the blue steel semiautomatic to his temple. When the deputies jumped out of their cars and surrounded him, he fluttered his other hand at them, as if he could shoo them away. "It's over," he said. "I haven't hurt anybody. I don't want to hurt you. It's over." Guess let the gun slip down a little bit, then lifted it back up and fired. His head slumped forward on his chest.

Tom Keen was the first detective to arrive at the crime scene. He took one look and knew that he wasn't going to learn much about the hidden life of the man in the car. All the essential facts were bleeding out of him. "Fellah, I've been looking for you for a long time," Keen said to the slumped-over man. "Now I finally get to see you, and look how it's ending." Robert Davenport had learned that a chase was in progress from an HPD dispatcher; once it ended, he started to head over there, but he changed destinations once he learned that Guess was being flown to Hermann Hospital. Davenport was waiting at the emergency entrance when Guess arrived. "I was hoping that I could look at him and just know, but a self-inflicted gunshot wound to the head is a pretty ugly thing," said Davenport. While doctors hurried to stabilize Guess's condition, Davenport snapped photographs of his immobile figure. The hospital staff also allowed the police to take fingerprints of the still-unconscious man. Davenport immediately contacted the police department's lab and had them compare Guess's prints with those left by the Polo Shirt Bandit in Austin. "Lo and behold," said Davenport. "Bing. They were his."

Geneva was at home preparing for Thanksgiving when she learned from a reporter that her husband was the Polo Shirt Bandit. She never went to Houston to visit him. "I didn't want to," she said. "I was just so angry that he could do such a thing. What really upset me was the statement he made to the police about how he had never hurt anyone. I thought, 'Well, who are we?' "

William Guess died without regaining consciousness on January 4. Since his secret life was unmasked, Geneva has discovered bills for credit cards that she didn't even know he had. William had been taking out large cash advances on the cards and Geneva has been left with the bills. "I just cannot figure out what happened to the money," she said. "There is no money. His savings account, everything, it's all wiped out. I think he left me with $184."

To his surprise, Davenport felt none of the elation he had expected to feel, no sense of satisfaction, at the conclusion of his investigation. Even though Guess had been found, it was as though he had eluded capture after all. "I was just so disappointed," the detective said. "I was mad, I guess, mad at him, more than anything. I was crushed to see him and know that he would never answer the biggest questions I had. I knew the what, where, when, and how. But why? What made this man turn to a life of crime?"

(March 1997)

In the spring of 1999 police officers held a press conference to announce several new arrests in the Polo Shirt Bandit's hometown of Temple. As we reported, William Guess had developed his gambling habit by playing high-stakes poker games and placing bets with bookies on football games. Local law enforcement authorities were perturbed by the idea that Guess's bank robberies had grown out of these other illegal activities and decided to crack down on several of the bookies who were mentioned in the story. At the press conference announcing their arrests, police officers in charge of the investigation held up a copy of the issue of *Texas Monthly* containing this story and said the article had led to the prosecutions.

Midnight in the Garden of East Texas

SKIP HOLLANDSWORTH

Marjorie Nugent was the richest widow in an eccentric town full of rich widows. Bernie Tiede was an assistant funeral home director who became her companion. When she disappeared, nobody seemed alarmed. When he confessed to killing her, nobody seemed outraged.

Sitting at his regular table at Daddy Sam's BBQ and Catfish ("You Kill It, I'll Cook It") in the East Texas town of Carthage, district attorney Danny Buck Davidson began to realize that he might have some problems prosecuting Bernie Tiede for murder.

"Bernie's a sweet man, Danny Buck," a waitress said. "He's done a lot of good things for this town. He's given poor kids money to go to college and everything."

"You got to admit nobody could sing 'Amazing Grace' like Bernie could," someone else said.

The bulldog-faced Danny Buck took a bite of slaw and sipped his iced tea. "Now y'all know that Bernie confessed, don't you?" he said, trying to keep his voice calm. "He came right out and told a Texas Ranger that he shot Mrs. Nugent four times in the back and then stuffed her in her own deep freeze in her kitchen."

There was a long silence. "Danny Buck," one man finally said, "it's just hard for me to believe that old Bernie could fire a gun straight. He acts . . . well, you know . . . effeminate! You can tell he's never been deer hunting in his entire life."

"And you know what?" a woman told Danny Buck later at a convenience store. "I don't care if Mrs. Nugent was the richest lady in town. She was so mean that even if Bernie did kill her, you won't be able to find anyone in town who's going to convict him for murder."

Danny Buck Davidson had spent almost all of his fifty years in Carthage, the past three as district attorney, and neither he nor the town of 6,500 was accustomed to high-profile killings. Every couple of years or so a murder case would come across the DA's desk, usually involving a resident from one of the poorer neighborhoods. But nobody from the respectable side of town ever seemed to get in trouble, as long as you didn't count the recent conviction of Carthage state senator Drew Nixon, who was caught soliciting an undercover cop posing as a prostitute in Austin. Even then, Carthage's civic leaders were able to put a good spin on Nixon's arrest, saying that Nixon never would have had any problems if he had just stayed in Carthage. Carthage has no prostitutes.

This past August, however, Carthage captured the attention of the entire country when the news broke that the town's richest and snootiest widow, 81-year-old Mrs. Marjorie Nugent, had been found in the bottom of a large freezer in her home. What made the story peculiar was that Mrs. Nugent had been dead for almost nine months before people began searching for her. What made the story truly bizarre was the way many of the townspeople rallied around the 39-year-old man who had admitted to killing her and stealing her money—the soft-spoken, chubby-cheeked Bernie Tiede, the former assistant funeral director at Hawthorn Funeral Home who had gotten close to Mrs. Nugent when he supervised her husband's funeral.

For out-of-town reporters, the story of Bernie Tiede and Mrs. Nugent was like an East Texas version of *Midnight in the Garden of Good and Evil,* featuring a down-home gallery of characters entangled in an off-beat, tragic mystery. Wearing his flaming red chamber of commerce blazer, the town's mayor, Carson Joines, posed for a *People* magazine photograph and then announced that Bernie might be acquitted. When *Hard Copy* arrived, Bernie's former funeral home boss agreed to be interviewed sitting out by his backyard pool. Carthage's congenial Methodist minister, the Reverend E. B. Beasley, gave reporters copies of a sermon he had preached the Sunday after Bernie's arrest titled "When Life Doesn't Make Sense." "No matter what the truth is," Beasley proclaimed, "Bernie will need our prayers. He needs to be with God, and he needs to know that we are with him." The town refused to abandon Bernie even after Sheriff Jack Ellett announced during his Friday morning talk show on the local radio station, KGAS ("The Heartbeat of East Texas"), that deputies had confiscated nearly fifty videotapes from Bernie's house, some showing men involved in illicit acts. "From the day that deep freeze was opened, you haven't been able to find anyone in town saying, 'Poor Mrs. Nugent,' " said city council-man Olin Joffrion, a respected Carthage insurance agent. "People here are saying, 'Poor Bernie.' "

In fact, throughout last fall, a stream of mostly fe-male well-wishers visited Bernie in jail, bringing him cakes and pies. "If I made a list of people I knew were going to heaven," one woman told the *Houston Chronicle,* "Bernie would be the first on that list." At the grocery store and at Daddy Sam's, other women came up to the district attorney and said they were praying for him to do the right thing. A disgusted Danny Buck told me, "It's almost as if everyone has already forgotten that an elderly lady was shot to death."

Tucked away in east Texas' Piney Woods, about twenty miles from the Louisiana border, Carthage sits on what used to be one of the largest natural-gas fields in the world. In the forties and fifties the town was known as the gas capital of the U.S., and its citizens believe it is so rich in history that they've built dueling historical museums on opposite sides of the town square: the Panola County Historical Jail Museum and the Panola County Heritage Museum and Texas Tea Room. These days chamber of commerce representatives are promoting Carthage as Texas' country music capital, the birthplace of such sensations as Tex Ritter, Jim Reeves, and budding solo star Linda Davis, a backup singer for Reba McEntire and a former Miss Panola County, who, according to one of her high school classmates, "would surely have won Miss Texas if she had gotten a boob job before the state pageant." To improve tourist traffic, the chamber is planning to open a new museum this year devoted solely to Texas-born country music stars—the Texas Country Music Hall of Fame.

All in all, Carthage, which made it into the 1995 edition of *The Best 100 Small Towns in America,* is an immensely likable place—"The kind of town," says KGAS owner Jerry Hanszen, "where people get out of their cars to see which neighbors they can help whenever there's a traffic jam around the town square." Carthaginians are also conservative, politically and socially, which makes it hard to imagine that Bernhardt Tiede II, who moved here in 1985, would end up becoming one of the most popular people in town. Compared with the men who passed their afternoons at Leon Choate's barbershop just off the square, the portly, mustachioed Bernie was, in the words of one person who knew him, "peachy and sweet." When he wasn't in his dark funeral suit, he wore colorful Tommy Hilfiger clothes and drove around town in his Lincoln Continental, smiling broadly at whomever he saw. "He wasn't bad-looking, and there were numerous girls in the community who would have dated him," says Don Lipsey, the former owner of Hawthorn, who had hired Bernie. "But he showed no romantic interest in women his age at all. I think some of the men during their coffee shop talks would insinuate that Bernie was a little light in the loafers."

Despite the questions about Bernie's personal life, Carthage's citizens couldn't help but take a shine to him. Bernie clearly loved the small-town life of East Texas. At First United Methodist he was the tenor soloist in the choir, he taught Sunday school, and sometimes, when the minister was sick or on vacation, he gave the sermon. ("Let me tell you, he was doggone better than the paid preacher," one elderly member says.) Bernie got involved with the drama and music departments at Panola College, and he became so renowned for his knowledge of Broadway musicals that he was asked to conduct the drama department's performances of *Showboat* and *Guys and Dolls*. He sang with the Shreveport Chamber Singers, a professional singing group just across the state line, and he served on the chamber of commerce's Christmas decorating committee, giving advice about where the lights and wreaths should be placed around the town square.

"He brought a lot of compassion to Carthage," says Paula Carter, a fellow church member and a counselor at the high school. "He was very quick to shake your hand and ask how you were doing, and if you told him you weren't doing too well, he would drop everything to talk to you and see what he could do." He sewed curtains for people who needed them, he helped others with their tax returns, and he began buying so many gifts for his new Carthage friends that, according to Lipsey, "the UPS truck started arriving in Carthage every day with something that Bernie had ordered from a catalog."

Born in Tyler, Bernie spent his earliest years in Kilgore, a 45-minute drive from Carthage, where his father was the chairman of the fine arts department at Kilgore Junior College. His mother died in a car wreck when he was only three, and his father, after remarrying and moving Bernie and his younger sister to Abilene, died after a long illness when Bernie was fifteen. To help support himself and his sister, Bernie took an after-school job at an Abilene funeral home, first doing yard work and then helping out at the funerals. "I really think that because of the loneliness he went through in his childhood, Bernie made it his calling to serve people in times of their own need," says his sister, a Central Texas social worker who asked not to be identified. "He wasn't a dour boy. He was popular at high school, and for kicks he'd sneak the hearse on Fridays out of the funeral home and drive a bunch of us around Abilene. But he said a long time ago that he was meant to take care of others—and I think that's why the funeral business appealed to him."

He received an associate's degree in mortuary science from McNeese State University in Lake Charles, Louisiana, worked at a funeral home in town, and in 1985 came to work in Carthage, living in a small apartment just behind the Hawthorn Funeral Home. "He was probably the most qualified young man I have ever seen," says Lipsey. "He waited well on the families, he would sing solos behind the screen during the funeral, and he was a darned good embalmer. He had a talent of making the hair of the deceased look really natural."

He was especially empathetic with older ladies who had just lost their husbands. He led them weeping to a sofa in the parlor, handed them handkerchiefs, quoted comforting Scripture, and stood close to them at the interment, always prepared to catch them in case they fainted as their husbands' caskets were lowered into the earth. In the weeks after the funeral, he would call the widows, offering to pick up their medicines at the drugstore. Some of them loved him so much that they told their children that Bernie had to sing at their funeral when they passed on. "With that nice tenor voice of his, I just knew Bernie could sing me right into heaven," one Carthage widow says.

Carthage is full of well-to-do widows who have inherited small fortunes from their rich husbands. Some of them can be seen driving their huge Cadillacs up and down the town's streets, occasionally bumping into trees or stop signs when their tiny feet miss the brake pedal. They are a spirited bunch, even if they are somewhat behind the times. Speaking to me on the phone, one widow said that a man who had just delivered lunch to her house knew Bernie. "Chris," she said to him, "why don't you tell this reporter what you know. Shall I introduce you as Negro, black, or colored?"

Bernie was not partial outright to the wealthier widows. One of the first women he took a special interest in was Gracie Duke, the widow of a mechanic. When she complained about an ache in her bones, Bernie felt so sorry for her that he took her to Hot Springs, Arkansas, so she could sit in the baths. But he would eventually give the most attention to the richest widow in Carthage—Mrs. Marjorie Nugent, who arrived at Hawthorn in March 1990 for the funeral of her husband, who was worth between $5 million and $10 million.

Born in 1915 just outside Carthage—her father ran a grocery—Marjorie Midyette attended Louisiana Tech, where she met R. L. "Rod" Nugent, who had recently graduated from the school with an electrical engineering degree. After their marriage, Nugent took a job with Magnolia Oil (which later became Mobil), and the two of them lived throughout Louisiana, New Mexico, and Texas, spending more than a dozen years in Midland, where their only child, Rod Junior, was raised.

In 1989, at the end of his career, the elder Nugent decided to bring his wife back to her hometown. He bought controlling interest in the First National Bank of Carthage, and the couple built a sprawling, six-thousand-square-foot stone home at the edge of town, surrounded by a stone wall and electronic gates. Although Mrs. Nugent rarely left the estate, it wasn't long before she became the talk of the town. Curious neighbors learned that she refused to speak to her own sister, who was also a Carthage resident (another sister lived in Ohio), because of an argument the two had back in the eighties over their dead mother's estate. Mrs. Nugent had so many disagreements with her son, who had become a prominent Amarillo pathologist, that she would only occasionally speak to him. According to most locals, she acted as if she was too good for Carthage. "If she had held her nose any higher," one man once said of her, "she would have drowned in a rainstorm." It was said that when she made an appearance at the bank, she sat in a chair in the lobby and barely nodded to people. She didn't participate in any civic activities or contribute to worthy Carthage causes, and she seemed to hate spending money around town. When a local veterinarian told her that he would charge $45 for treating her dog, she argued with him until he lowered his price.

Even those close to her admit that she was imperious and critical, lashing out at whoever disappointed her. "If she liked you, she sent lovely birthday cards and thank-you notes," says Lloyd Tiller, one of her stockbrokers. "But you had to cater to Margie and constantly flatter her. She could throw a temper tantrum if everything didn't go her way." A close relative, who wishes to remain anonymous, says that there were times when Mrs. Nugent seemed to lapse into a low-level clinical depression: "It was like these blue periods came on, and when they did, she could be very biting in her comments to people. Margie was a very difficult woman to love."

Much of the gossip about Mrs. Nugent was, no doubt, exaggerated. "She wasn't all that unfriendly, but she didn't go out of her way to be friendly, which can mean a lot in a small town," says a teacher at the high school. Nevertheless, when Mr. Nugent died unexpectedly of heart failure, only a handful of people came to the funeral to offer her their condolences. Bernie Tiede would later tell others that he could see the loneliness etched in Mrs. Nugent's stern face as she stood by the casket. When Mrs. Nugent started shivering, Bernie gave her his coat. At the funeral service, held in the chapel, he sang a hymn, then he helped Mrs. Nugent to her car for the trip to the cemetery.

In the months after the funeral, the only person who took an active interest in Mrs. Nugent's well-being was Bernie Tiede. "I don't know if Mrs. Nugent had a single friend in town other than him," admits Danny Buck. Bernie would arrive at her estate for lunch, leave little notes of endearment for her around the house, and take her to see theatricals at the local college. Says Tiller: "Bernie made her smile, he gave her plenty of attention, he was an excellent conversationalist. It was like he made her feel young again."

And Mrs. Nugent was apparently willing to do what it took to keep him around. Soon after the funeral, she gave Bernie Mr. Nugent's Rolex watch, worth

$12,000—a startling act of generosity from a woman known as the town Grinch. In 1991 she ordered officials at First National Bank to accept checks from her account signed by Bernie so that he could handle some of her bills. When Tiller asked if she was certain she could trust Bernie, Mrs. Nugent grew livid and threatened to move all her stocks out of Tiller's brokerage.

Bernie began spending his days off with Mrs. Nugent, which reportedly upset some of the town's other widows, with whom he'd spent so much time over the years. One afternoon Don Lipsey called Mrs. Nugent looking for Bernie. She told him that Bernie was in one of her bedrooms taking a nap. Then word spread that Mrs. Nugent had gone on a cruise—something her husband had never wanted to do—and that she had paid Bernie to go with her. The two even slept in the same cabin.

Rumors flew through Carthage. Was the cherubic Bernhardt Tiede II trying to seduce the haughty Marjorie Nugent? Or was it the other way around? Some people were shocked when Bernie was seen holding Mrs. Nugent's hand in town, but Bernie was quick to explain that Mrs. Nugent wobbled when she walked. "I think Margie truly enjoyed the companionship with Bernie, and I think Bernie truly enjoyed Margie's money," says a close relative of hers. For Bernie, who was making a reported annual salary of about $18,000 at the funeral home, Mrs. Nugent's money must have been tempting. She was making between $200,000 and $300,000 a year in oil and gas royalty payments alone. He was constantly behind in his American Express payments, and he owed the IRS $4,000 in back taxes. "Bernie was a buyaholic," says his sister. "He not only wanted to experience the finer things in life, he loved buying as much as he could for others. He'd order the same items over and over—like three of the same chairs or boxes of Cross pens—just so he could give them away."

In late 1993 Bernie told Don Lipsey that Mrs. Nugent had asked him to work for her—at a much higher salary—as her business manager and escort on trips around the world. A barrel-chested, plain-talking East Texas, Lipsey had grown fond of Bernie, despite his discomfort with what he described as Bernie's "tutti-frutti speaking voice." "Bernie," he warned, "you know what kind of woman Mrs. Nugent is. Whatever you think you're going to get out of her, you're going to have to earn every penny of it."

"Mrs. Nugent is already so possessive of you," added Sally, Don's wife. "She's already making you drive out there every morning just to fix her coffee! Is that really what you want for yourself?"

"Now, Don and Sally," Bernie replied, "Deep down inside she's a sweet woman. We will get along just fine."

What few in town knew—and what Bernie was not saying—was that Mrs. Nugent had already changed her will, making Bernie the sole heir to her multimillion-dollar estate. (Mrs. Nugent later told a cousin that she didn't want to leave a cent to her son or her immediate family because they didn't "appreciate" her.) How could Bernie risk Mrs. Nugent's wrath, and thus risk losing her money, by turning down her job offer?

With money Mrs. Nugent advanced him, Bernie bought a two-bedroom home about a mile from the Nugent estate. He set out his collection of black-and-white plastic penguins in the front yard. (He liked penguins, he told others, because they looked so well-dressed.) He hung white curtains on the living room window and displayed his collection of more than seventy wristwatches in the hallway. He threw a Christmas open house, inviting members of the chamber of commerce, professors at the college, and other Carthage VIPs. One widow who was there took a look at the polished furniture and the porcelain penguins on the side tables and said, "Bernie, you've created a doll house!"

"Bernie found himself living a dream," says his sister. "For the first time in his life, he got to be *somebody*." Bernie earned his pilot's license and bought a couple of small airplanes. He took Mrs. Nugent's seat on the board of the First National Bank, and he regularly placed calls to Lloyd Tiller, irritating the stockbroker to no end with recommendations of stocks that he thought should be bought for Mrs. Nugent. "What do you know about the stock market?" Tiller once shouted at Bernie. "You're nothing but an undertaker!" A few minutes later Mrs. Nugent called Tiller and told him in an icy voice that if he spoke that way to Bernie again, she would be changing stockbrokers.

On their vacations together, Bernie and Mrs. Nugent traveled all over the world, visiting the Orient, Egypt, and Russia. They flew to New York to see new Broadway musicals, and they sailed for Europe, returning on the Concorde.

It was a glamorous life, but as Lipsey warned, Bernie paid a price. According to Bernie's friends, he had to have Mrs. Nugent's medicines laid out every day. If he wasn't at her house by eleven forty-five for lunch, she would become extremely frustrated—"Almost panicky," says one man—and call his pager incessantly until he arrived. When visiting someone else, Bernie would have to interrupt the conversation at regular intervals and use the phone to check in with Mrs. Nugent. "If I don't call her, she will give me living hell," Bernie would say.

Perhaps Bernie decided he deserved extra pay for his service to Mrs. Nugent. Or perhaps he thought he could do whatever he wanted with her money since he knew it would be coming to him anyway after her death. Or, as his sister suggests, maybe Bernie genuinely believed in the good of giving. For whatever reason, Bernie became the town's Robin Hood. Unbeknownst to Mrs. Nugent, he started slipping money out of her hefty bank accounts and giving it to anyone he thought could use help. He bought at least ten cars for people who couldn't afford one, telling them to pay him back when they could. He bought a home for a struggling young couple. He provided scholarships to students at Panola College, he pledged $100,000 to the new building campaign at First United Methodist, and he led the fundraising drive for the Boy Scouts. When a woman who owned a local trophy shop told him that her business was failing, Bernie stepped in and bought it so that Carthage High School and youth sports teams could get their trophies for another year. Bernie was on a one-man campaign to improve culture in Carthage, giving away tickets to the college theater productions and paying for the expenses of choir concerts. When a man who once worked with him at the funeral home told him that he wanted to open a clothing store, Bernie agreed to fund it, saying that Carthage needed its own Neiman Marcus. The man's idea of what Carthage needed was a little different. He proudly opened Boot Scootin' Western Wear.

Some townspeople thought Bernie's presence did have a positive effect on Mrs. Nugent. At his urging she joined the Methodist church, and she once had the women's Sunday school class over to her house for brunch. But sometime in 1995, Bernie told his sister that he thought Mrs. Nugent was developing a mild dementia. Mrs. Nugent had fired the gardeners, he said, because the flowers hadn't bloomed on time. She also made Bernie buy a .22 rifle to shoot the armadillos that were rooting up her front yard. Bernie found himself stalking the armored pests while Mrs. Nugent supervised from the front porch. "Bernie said to me, 'She's so controlling, it just wears me down,' " his sister recalls. "I asked him why he didn't quit, and he gave me this tortured look and said, 'Because I'm her only friend. I have to stay because I'm the only one she has.' "

At Thanksgiving, 1996, Bernie went alone to see his sister, telling her that Mrs. Nugent had decided to spend the holiday in Ohio with the one sister she was still talking to. At Christmas, Bernie decorated Mrs. Nugent's home, but he again told those who asked that Mrs. Nugent was in Ohio. Early that spring, he began telling people that Mrs. Nugent was in bed because of an illness and not accepting visitors. By late spring, he said she was in a nursing home outside Carthage, recuperating from a stroke. He told Lloyd Tiller, who was concerned that Mrs. Nugent had not answered any of the messages he had left on her home phone, that she was losing her mind and perhaps had Alzheimer's.

Tiller says he didn't entirely believe Bernie's explanations, but it never occurred to him that Bernie might have harmed her. Ruth Cockrell, a Carthage widow who was Mrs. Nugent's first cousin, was also dubious: "I was worried something had happened to her, but I didn't know who to talk to about it. Bernie was so beloved in Carthage that if I suggested he had done anything wrong, I would have been laughed out of town."

Meanwhile, the maid continued coming to the empty estate to clean the house, and the yardmen kept cutting the yard. And Bernie kept giving: money for jet skis and pickup trucks, and to every student who performed in Panola College's production of *Guys and Dolls* a $200 gift certificate to Boot Scootin' Western Wear. In April Bernie performed with the Shreveport Chamber Singers. His solo rendition of Stephen Foster's "Beautiful Dreamer" was so heartfelt the audience gave him a prolonged ovation. In June he went on a Carthage Chamber of Commerce trip to Nashville to view a new Opryland exhibit honoring Tex Ritter. When he made sure to pay extra attention to one of the Carthage widows who had come along on the trip, pushing her through Opryland in her wheelchair, people patted him on the back and said, "Good old Bernie."

Then, in early July 1997, an unidentified Carthage woman called the sheriff's department and said she was worried about Mrs. Nugent—had anyone there seen her lately? Because of more pressing matters around town, sheriff's deputies didn't look into the matter for nearly a month. Bernie, whom they found in Las Vegas singing at a Panola College student's wedding, explained that Mrs. Nugent was staying in a hospital in Temple under an assumed name and did not wish to be contacted. But deputies couldn't find anyone at the hospital who matched her description. They called Mrs. Nugent's son in Amarillo, and he came to Carthage with his eldest daughter to search the house. When she told a deputy how odd it was that the deep freeze had been taped shut, he took a look inside. At the bottom, wrapped in a white sheet underneath some frozen food, was Mrs. Nugent.

Not wanting to destroy evidence, the sheriff ordered his deputies to lift the entire deep freeze, with Mrs. Nugent still inside, onto a pickup truck and drive it to Dallas for an autopsy. (The deputies connected a gasoline-powered generator to the freezer to keep it working.) Other deputies spread through town looking for Bernie. They found him preparing to take a team of Little League baseball players and their parents to dinner. He seemed surprised that deputies wanted to ask him some questions. With officers looming over him in a small room at the sheriff's department, Bernie tried to keep his composure. But he grew increasingly nervous, and he finally, calmly admitted to shooting Mrs. Nugent the previous November 19. He said he had used the same gun she made him buy to shoot armadillos. When asked why he killed her, Bernie looked at the officers in bewilderment, as if the answer were obvious. At last, he said that Mrs. Nugent had become "very hateful and very possessive."

The uproar in Carthage over Bernie's arrest was, in the words of Danny Buck, "like a bunch of fireworks going off." After a group of women tried to raise the money to meet Bernie's $1.5 million bond, the DA went to the justice of the peace and filed additional theft charges against him (for stealing money from Mrs. Nugent's account after she was dead) and got the bond raised to $2.7 million. He got so mad at the Reverend E. B. Beasley for publicly praying every Sunday for Bernie that, for a time, he stopped going to church. "Bernie is a con man and an accomplished actor," Danny Buck kept telling anyone who would listen. "He duped a really nice, trusting town. He's evil."

IRS agents arrived in Carthage to charge Bernie with money laundering—it is estimated that he took more than $1 million from Mrs. Nugent—and Sheriff Ellett set off another round of fireworks when he said that certain Carthage men were seen on the videotapes confiscated from Bernie's house. Soon there were rumors that everyone from elected city leaders to a DPS trooper to a sheriff's deputy was seen on the tapes, engaged in what the local newspaper, the *Panola Watchman,* described as "misconduct." One man showed up at a Carthage High School football game wearing a T-shirt that read "I'm the only one in Carthage NOT on the videotapes."

Some of Bernie's friends hired famous East Texas criminal defense attorney Clifton "Scrappy" Holmes to defend him. "Let's face it, Bernie's ox is in a ditch," Holmes told me. He is reportedly trying to discuss a plea bargain for Bernie, which would be just fine with Danny Buck, who's worried about finding an impartial jury in Panola County. "A couple of people have said to me that Bernie deserves to fry for what he's done," he says, "but I know there are a lot more who just want the whole thing to go away. They keep asking me if there aren't some extenuating circumstances that would help his defense. And I think, 'Good God-al-mighty, do people really think Mrs. Nugent was so mean to him that he had to shoot her in the back in self-defense?' "

What drove Bernie Tiede, the gentlest and most compassionate man in Panola County, to kill Mrs. Nugent? Many townspeople wonder if Bernie suddenly snapped and had a psychotic breakdown. They think he should plead temporary insanity. Danny Buck assumes that Mrs. Nugent finally discovered Bernie was looting her bank account and that Bernie panicked and shot her when she said she was going to expose him. But Bernie's sister says that when she phoned him at the jail, he told her that there had been no particular problems that November day between him and Mrs. Nugent. They were about to go to Longview to run errands and have lunch when suddenly Bernie picked up the .22 rifle in the garage and started firing. He dragged Mrs. Nugent into the kitchen, put her in the freezer, and washed the blood off the garage floor with a garden hose. "He said, 'I started thinking about having to live with her for the rest of her life, and I just couldn't take it,' " recalls the sister. "He said, 'I realized I couldn't stand it another day.' "

But why on earth did Bernie leave Mrs. Nugent in the freezer for nine months? Sure, Bernie was used to being around dead bodies from his funeral home days. But Danny Buck admits that he probably never would have been able to file murder charges against Bernie if he had simply dumped her somewhere where she would never be found. "I don't understand why Bernie didn't put her in one of his little airplanes and fly her over the Gulf of Mexico and kick her out," one of the town's widows told me matter-of-factly.

According to Bernie's sister, Bernie said that he couldn't be so cruel as to abandon Mrs. Nugent.

"You couldn't be so cruel?" the astonished sister asked. "Bernie, what were you going to do?"

In a very soft voice, Bernie said, "I wanted to give Mrs. Nugent a proper burial. You know, everyone needs a proper burial."

Mrs. Nugent did get her proper burial, in a small rural cemetery outside Carthage. Some of her relatives, who hadn't spoken to her in years (including her sister in Carthage) came for the service, hoping in some way to say goodbye to a woman they never really understood. A granddaughter stood and sang "Amazing Grace."

One Carthage widow, who didn't make it to the funeral, later asked if Mrs. Nugent's granddaughter had sung well. She said she was looking for a soloist for her own funeral now that she knew Bernie was going to be unavailable.

(January 1998)

In the spring of 1999 Bernie Tiede was tried in the tiny town of San Augustine, about an hour's drive south of Carthage, after the judge decided that most of Carthage's citizens already knew too much about the case or were too close to Bernie Tiede to listen to the proceedings impartially. The twelve jurors in San Augustine, many of whom sipped on large Big Gulp–size soft drinks during the testimony, convicted Tiede despite his tearful testimony toward the end of the trial. At that time he said he deeply loved Marjorie Nugent and killed her only because "she had made my life a prison to some degree," and that she had even gone so far as to lock the front gates of her home with a remote-control device just as he was trying to escape from her in his car. He is now serving a life sentence in a Texas prison.